The Adam Smith Review
Volume 8

Adam Smith's contribution to economics is well-recognised but in recent years scholars have been exploring anew the multidisciplinary nature of his works. *The Adam Smith Review* is a refereed annual review that provides a unique forum for interdisciplinary debate on all aspects of Adam Smith's works, his place in history, and the significance of his writings to the modern world. It is aimed at facilitating debate between scholars working across the humanities and social sciences, thus emulating the reach of the Enlightenment world which Smith helped to shape.

The eighth volume of the series contains contributions from a multidisciplinary range of specialists, including Fonna Forman, Ryan Patrick Hanley, Dionysis Drosos, Matti Norri, Adelino Zanini, Cesare Cozzo, Estrella Trincado, Michaël Biziou, Carsten Herrmann-Pillath, Heinrique Schnieder, The Right Honorable Gordon Brown, Gavin Kennedy, Iain McLean, Vernon Smith, Alan Lopez, John Thrasher, Tom Martin, Brian Glenney, Şule Özler, Paul A. Gabrinetti, Craig Smith, Michelle A. Schwarze, Edwin van de Haar, Farhad Rassekh, Lauren Brubaker, Gordon Graham and Eric Schliesser.

Themes of the volume include:

- Translating Smith's *Theory of Moral Sentiments*
- Smith and China
- Adam Smith in Kirkcaldy

Fonna Forman is Associate Professor of Political Science and Founding Co-Director of the Center on Global Justice and the Blum Cross-Border Initiative at the University of California, San Diego, USA. She is Editor of *The Adam Smith Review* on behalf of the Adam Smith Society.

The Adam Smith Review

Published in association with the International Adam Smith Society
Editor
Fonna Forman
Department of Political Science, University of California, San Diego

Book Review Editor
Craig Smith
Department of Moral Philosophy, University of St Andrews

Editorial Assistant
Aaron Cotkin
Department of Political Science, University of California, San Diego

The Adam Smith Review is a multidisciplinary annual review sponsored by the International Adam Smith Society. It aims to provide a unique forum for vigorous debate and the highest standards of scholarship on all aspects of Adam Smith's works, his place in history and the significance of his writings for the modern world. The Adam Smith Review aims to facilitate interchange between scholars working within different disciplinary and theoretical perspectives and, to this end, it is open to all areas of research relating to Adam Smith. The Review also hopes to broaden the field of English-language debate on Smith by occasionally including translations of scholarly works at present available only in languages other than English.

The Adam Smith Review is intended as a resource for Adam Smith scholarship in the widest sense. The Editor welcomes comments and suggestions, including proposals for symposia or themed sections in the Review. Future issues are open to comments and debate relating to previously published papers.

The website of The Adam Smith Review is: www.adamsmithreview.org/

For details of membership of the International Adam Smith Society and reduced rates for purchasing the Review, please contact the Membership Secretary, Chris Martin (internationaladamsmithsociety@gmail.com).

Books available in this series

The Adam Smith Review (Volume 1)
Edited By Vivienne Brown
Published in 2004. Please note: *available in paperback*

The Adam Smith Review (Volume 2)
Edited By Vivienne Brown
Published in 2006. Please note: *available in paperback*

The Adam Smith Review (Volume 3)
Edited By Vivienne Brown
Published in 2007. Please note: *available in paperback*

The Adam Smith Review (Volume 4)
Edited By Vivienne Brown
Published in 2008. Please note: *available in paperback*

The Philosophy of Adam Smith
The Adam Smith Review, Volume 5: Essays commemorating the 250th Anniversary of *The Theory of Moral Sentiments*
Edited by Vivienne Brown and Samuel Fleischacker
Published in 2010. Please note: *available in paperback*

The Adam Smith Review (Volume 6)
Edited by Fonna Forman-Barzilai
Published in 2011

The Adam Smith Review (Volume 7)
Edited by Fonna Forman
Published in 2013

The Adam Smith Review (Volume 8)
Edited by Fonna Forman
Published 2015

The Adam Smith Review
Volume 8

Edited by
Fonna Forman

Routledge
Taylor & Francis Group

LONDON AND NEW YORK

IASS

First published 2015 by Routledge

2 Park Square, Milton Park, Abingdon, Oxfordshire OX14 4RN
52 Vanderbilt Avenue, New York, NY 10017

Routledge is an imprint of the Taylor & Francis Group, an informa business

First issued in paperback 2019

British Library Cataloguing in Publication Data
A catalogue record for this book is available from the British Library

Library of Congress Cataloging in Publication Data
A catalog record has been requested for this book

ISBN: 978-1-138-83060-8 (hbk)
ISBN: 978-0-367-87176-5 (pbk)

Typeset in Times New Roman
by FiSH Books, London

Contents

Book reviews   291
Guest editor: CRAIG SMITH

Contributors

Michaël Biziou is Professor of Philosophy at the University of Nice, France. He works on eighteenth-century British and French philosophy and has a special interest in Adam Smith and classical liberalism. He has translated into French Smith's *Theory of Moral Sentiments* (Presse Universitaire de France, 1999) and his essay on *The Imitative Arts* (Vrin, 1997). He has published three books: *Le Concept de Système dans la Tradition Anglo-Écossaise des Sentiments Moraux. De la Métaphysique à l'Économie Politique (Shaftesbury, Hutcheson, Hume et Smith)* (ANRT, 2000), *Adam Smith et l'Origine du Libéralisme* (Presse Universitaire de France, 2003) and *Shaftesbury. Le Sens Moral* (Presse Universitaire de France, 2005). He has also edited *Adam Smith et la Théorie des Sentiments Moraux*, special issue of *Revue Philosophique de la France et de l'Étranger* (2000, no. 4) and *Adam Smith Philosophe. De la Morale à l'Économie, ou Philosophie du Libéralisme*, co-edited with Magali Bessone (Presse Universitaire de Rennes, 2009).

Gordon Brown served as Prime Minister of the United Kingdom and Leader of the Labour Party from 2007 to 2010. His tenure as Prime Minister coincided with the start of the global financial crisis. He was one of the first to initiate calls for global financial action, while introducing a range of rescue measures in the UK.

Previously, Brown served as Chancellor of the Exchequer from 1997 to 2007, making him the longest-serving Chancellor in modern history. His time as Chancellor was marked by major reform of Britain's monetary and fiscal policy and sustained investment in health, education and overseas aid.

His time in government shaped his views on the importance of education as a fundamental right of every child in the world, and an engine of future global economic growth. In July 2012, he was made UN Special Envoy for Global Education and he is a passionate advocate for global action to ensure education for all. He has advised the World Economic Forum and chairs their Global Strategic Infrastructure Initiative. He also serves as New York University's inaugural Distinguished Global Leader in Residence.

Brown, who has been a Member of Parliament since 1983, is the author of several books and the founder, with his wife, of Their World, a charity which engages young people, business leaders, health and education professionals and civil society to create a brighter future for every child. He is married to Sarah Brown, a charity campaigner, and the couple have two young sons.

Lauren Brubaker has taught at the University of Notre Dame (political science), the United States Air Force Academy (philosophy) and St. John's College Santa Fe. His articles on Smith have appeared in several edited volumes, including *New Voices on Adam Smith* (edited by L. Montes and E. Schliesser) and *Enlightening Revolutions* (edited by S. Minkov).

Cesare Cozzo studied at Rome, Florence and Stockholm. He is Associate Professor of Logic at the Department of Philosophy of the University of Rome 'La Sapienza'. His main research has been in theory of meaning and philosophy of logic. He is author of three books: *Teoria del Significato e Filosofia della Logica* (1994), *Meaning and Argument* (1994), *Introduzione a Dummett* (2008) and of several articles. A significant part of his work has been focused on the idea that the sense of a linguistic expression is given by some rules for its use in arguments: he has developed a fallibilist and non-holistic version of this idea.

Dionysios Drosos is Professor of Moral Philosophy, Department of Philosophy, University of Ioannina and Tutor of European Philosophy at the Hellenic Open University. He is author of *Market and State in Adam Smith. A Critique of the Foundations of Neoliberalism* (1994); *Virtues and Interests. The British Moral Philosophy Debate on the Threshold of Modernity* (2008); *The Gentle Commerce of Sympathy. Civilized Society and Moral Community in the Scottish Enlightenment* (Forthcoming); and Adam Smith, *Theory of Moral Sentiments* (1st critical edition of *TMS* in Greek, 2011). Since 2011, he has run, with the help of a intermediterranean group of colleagues, the *Mediterranean Society for the Study of Scottish Enlightenment*, organizing a workshop every summer.

Paul A. Gabrinetti, Ph.D. completed his doctoral work at the University of Southern California. He is a psychologist and a Jungian psychoanalyst. Paul is a member of and teaches at the C. G. Jung Institute in Los Angeles, and also teaches at Pacifica Graduate Institute in Carpinteria, California. In addition, he maintains a private practice in the Los Angeles area.

Brian Glenney is an Assistant Professor of Philosophy at Gordon College. He received his Ph.D. from the University of Southern California. In addition to his work on Adam Smith, he has published a diversity of articles on perception: from ancient descriptions of blindness in journals, such as the *Journal for the Study of the New Testament*, to contemporary empirical research in journals such as *Biology and Philosophy*.

Gordon Graham is Henry Luce III Professor of Philosophy and the Arts at Princeton Theological Seminary, where he also directs the Center for the Study of Scottish Philosophy. He is editor of the *Journal of Scottish Philosophy*.

Ryan Patrick Hanley is Associate Professor of Political Science at Marquette University. He is the author of *Adam Smith and the Character of Virtue* (Cambridge University Press, 2009), editor of the Penguin Classics edition of *The Theory of Moral Sentiments* (Penguin, 2010), editor of *Adam Smith: A Princeton Guide* (Princeton University Press, forthcoming) and past president of the International Adam Smith Society. His most recent book is *Love's Enlightenment: Rethinking Charity in Modernity* (Cambridge University Press, forthcoming).

Carsten Herrmann-Pillath is Professor of Business Economics at the Frankfurt School of Finance and Management and founder and Academic Director of the East-West Center for Business Studies and Cultural Science at the Frankfurt School. His research interests include evolutionary economics, Chinese studies, international trade and the philosophy of science. He has published in numerous journals and, recently, has published *Hegel, Institutions and Economics: Preforming the Social* (Rutledge, 2013), with Ivan Boldyrev, and *Foundations of Economic Evolution: A Treatise on the Natural Philosophy of Economics* (Edward Elgar, 2013).

Gavin Kennedy is Professor Emeritus, Edinburgh Business School, Heriot-Watt University. He is the author of *Adam Smith: A Moral Philosopher and his Political Economy* (2nd ed., Palgrave, 2010) and *Adam Smith's Lost Legacy* (Palgrave, 2005) and has contributed the chapter 'Adam Smith on Religion' to the *Oxford Handbook of Adam Smith* (Oxford University Press, 2013). He Blogs at: www.adamsmithslostlegacy.blogspot.co.uk and is presently active in Edinburgh Business School's efforts to restore Adam Smith's Panmure House, his home from 1778–90, as an international education centre for Adam Smith studies and general economics education for 2015.

Daniel B. Klein is Professor of Economics and JIN Chair at the Mercatus Center at George Mason University, where he leads a program in Adam Smith. He is the author of *Knowledge and Coordination: A Liberal Interpretation* (OUP, 2012) and chief editor of *Econ Journal Watch*.

Alan Lopez works in early modern literature and drama, with specialization in Shakespeare. He is presently at work on a book project, *Shakespeare's Jurisprudence*.

Thomas R. Martin is Jeremiah O'Connor Professor in Classics at Holy Cross, Worcester, MA. He is the author of books, articles and reviews on ancient Greek and Roman history, including *Ancient Greece: From Prehistoric to Hellenistic*

Times. 2nd. ed. (2013), *Ancient Rome: From Romulus to Justinian* (2012) and, with Christopher W. Blackwell, *Alexander the Great: The Story of an Ancient Life* (2012).

Iain McLean is Professor of Politics, Oxford University and a fellow of Nuffield College. He was recently a visiting fellow at the International Center for Jefferson Studies, Monticello, VA. Relevant publications include *Adam Smith: Radical and Egalitarian* (Edinburgh University Press, 2006) and I. McLean and S. M. Peterson, 'Adam Smith at the Constitutional Convention' in the *Loyola Law Review* 2010. He is a vice-president of the British Academy and a Fellow of the Royal Society of Edinburgh.

Paul D. Mueller is a Ph.D. candidate in economics at George Mason University and intends to finish the degree in May of 2015. He received his M.A. in economics from GMU in 2013 and his B.Sc. in economics and political philosophy from Hillsdale College in 2009. His academic interests include monetary policy, financial markets, Austrian economics, business cycle theory and economic history (particularly regarding the works of Adam Smith).

Matti Norri is lawyer based in Helsinki, Finland, whose research interests include the nature of law, contracts and ownership. He is the author of *Summa Ius* and numerous legal handbooks. Additionally, he has translated works into Finnish and including the Gospel of John from the original Greek and Adam Smith's *Theory of Moral Sentiments* from English.

James R. Otteson is Executive Director of the BB&T Center for the Study of Capitalism, and Teaching Professor of Political Economy, at Wake Forest University in North Carolina, USA. He has taught previously at Yeshiva University, New York University, Georgetown University, and the University of Alabama. His most recent book, *The End of Socialism*, was published by Cambridge University Press in 2014.

Şule Özler has received her Ph.D. in economics from Stanford University and her Psy.D. from the New Center for Psychoanalysis. Professor Özler currently works at the Economics Department of UCLA and has also taught at the Kennedy School, Harvard University and Stanford University, as well as winning national awards, such as the Hoover Institute National Fellowship and a fellowship at the National Bureau of Economics. Prior to obtaining her doctorate in psychoanalysis, Professor Özler published a wide range of articles on international trade, finance and women in economics, in major journals. She has written a psychoanalytically oriented paper on John Stuart Mill's life and his essay *The Subjection of Women*. In addition, she is currently working on a book that psychoanalytically analyses the works of Adam Smith and a psychoanalytical analysis of alienation in Marx. Dr Özler has a psychoanalytical/psychotherapy practice in Santa Monica.

Salim Rashid is Professor Emeritus at the University of Illinois and Visiting Professor at the University of the South Pacific. He is the author of *The Myth of Adam Smith*. His main interest is in economic development.

Farhad Rassekh is Professor of Economics at the University of Hartford. He has published numerous articles in several areas in economics including on the relevance of Adam Smith to modern field of business ethics. He has also published on the historical and intellectual affinity between Smith's concept of the invisible hand and the emerging science of complexity.

Eric Schliesser is BOF Research Professor, Philosophy and Moral Sciences, Ghent University; he has published widely on early modern philosophy and the sciences and also in philosophy of economics.

Henrique Schneider is Professor of the Philosophy of Economics at the University of Graz, Austria. His other areas of research include Chinese philosophy (especially legalism), globalization and theory of actions.

Michelle A. Schwarze is the Benjamin Franklin Initiative postdoctoral fellow in the Political Science department at the University of Wisconsin, Madison. Her research centres on moral motivation in Scottish Enlightenment political thought and its subsequent practical and theoretical impact. She is currently working on a manuscript that addresses how violent passions become beneficial motives in the moral and political thought of Smith and Hume, as well as the rich account of incentive given by Kant.

Vernon L. Smith is George L. Argyros Chair in Finance and Economics, Chapman University, and President, International Foundation for Research in Experimental economics. He was awarded the Nobel Prize in Economics, 2002, 'for having established laboratory experiments as a tool in empirical economic analysis, especially in the study of alternative market mechanisms'. He has held appointments at Purdue University, Stanford University, Brown University, University of Massachusetts, USC, California Institute of Technology, University of Arizona, University of Alaska-Anchorage, George Mason University and Chapman University. Professor Smith received his bachelor's degree in electrical engineering from California Institute of Technology (1949), his Masters in economics from the University of Kansas (1951) and his Ph.D. in economics from Harvard (1955). He has authored or co-authored over 290 articles and books on capital theory, finance, natural resource economics, experimental economics and the housing origins of economic instability, 1920–2014. Professor Smith is a Fellow of the Econometric Society and the American Association for the Advancement of Science. Purdue University awarded him an Honorary Doctor of Management degree in 1989. Dr Smith was elected a member of the National Academy of Science in 1995. In 1996, he received Cal Tech's Distinguished Alumni Award. He became Kansan of the year (Topeka

Gazette) in 2002, received a Distinguished Alumni award from the University of Kansas in 2011 and, in 2014, an Honorary Doctor of Science degree. He has served on numerous editorial and editorial advisory boards and as president of several national economic associations. He has served as a consultant on the liberalization of electric power in Australia and New Zealand and has participated in numerous private and public discussions of energy privatization and liberalization in the United States and around the world. In 1997, he served as a Blue Ribbon Panel Member, North American Electric Reliability Council.

John Thrasher is a lecturer in philosophy at Monash University. He specializes in political philosophy and normative ethics. His research focuses on the relation of individual practical rationality to social rules. His work has been published in *Philosophical Studies*, the *Journal of Moral Philosophy, Ethical Theory and Moral Practice*, the *European Journal of Philosophy*, *Rationality, Morals, and Markets* and in several edited volumes.

Estrella Trincado is Lecturer in History of Economic Thought at the Complutense University of Madrid. She is a specialist in utilitarianism and anti-utilitarianism. She has a degree in economics and a degree in philosophy and obtained a Ph.D. in economics in 2003. Her doctoral dissertation dealt with David Hume, Adam Smith and Jeremy Bentham's theories. Visiting post-doctoral Fellow at the Departament of Economics in Harvard University, she was awarded the History of Economic Analysis Award in 2005 by the ESHET and the ESHET Young Scholar of the Year Prize for 2011. She can be reached at: estrinaz@ccee.ucm.es.

Edwin van de Haar is an independent international relations scholar who specializes in the liberal tradition in international political theory. He is the author of *Classical Liberalism and International Relations Theory: Hume, Smith, Mises and Hayek* (2009) and *Beloved Yet Unknown: The Political Philosophy of Liberalism* (2010, in Dutch). Recently, he contributed to the *Oxford Handbook of Adam Smith* (2013) and wrote a chapter entitled 'David Hume and Adam Smith on International Ethics and Humanitarian Intervention' for *Just and Unjust Military Intervention. European Thinkers from Vitoria to Mill*, edited by Stefano Recchia and Jennifer Welsh (Cambridge University Press, 2013).

Adelino Zanini teaches political philosophy and history of economic thought at the Department of Economic and Social Sciences of the Università Politecnica delle Marche, Ancona. His main interests are in the philosophy of economics, with particular regard to authors such as A. Smith, K. Marx, J. A. Schumpeter and J. M. Keynes. He is the author of several books and articles, including *Joseph A. Schumpeter* (2000), *Economic Philosophy: Economic Foundations and Political Categories* (2008) and *Adam Smith: Morale, Jurisprudence, Economia Politica* (2014).

From the editor

I would like to thank the Editorial Board, our editorial team at Routledge and especially my Editorial Assistant, Aaron Cotkin, for their help bringing Volume 8 into print. My thanks as well to the International Adam Smith Society and to its outgoing President, Ryan Hanley, for many years of friendship and collegiality, and for his great service to the Society.

Finally, a note of gratitude to Gordon Brown for his contribution to this volume. I would like to acknowledge not only his support of the journal and for his participation in the Kirkcaldy symposium that produced the fine collection of papers that he introduces here but mostly for inspiring generations of global actors and scholars with his uniquely Smithian vantage on the world – for demonstrating through his work: 1) that ethics and economics need not be at odds – that indeed the ethical path very often coincides with the path economically most efficient and advantageous for all; and 2) that our ethical duties must expand beyond our own narrow spaces and particular interests in an age of information, capacity and interdependence. This way of thinking is exemplified by Gordon's most recent initiatives to advance the Millennium Development Goal of universal primary education. Not only is this the right thing for us to do as a global community – to educate the world's poorest children, 57 million of whom are presently not in school, likelier thus to become victim to child labour, child marriage, trafficking, disease and early death – but it is also estimated that universal primary education will stimulate per capita growth in the world's poorest countries by as much as two per cent per year.

With much gratitude, I would like to dedicate this volume to the memory of our colleague, teacher and friend, István Hont (1947–2013).

Fonna Forman
Editor

Symposium

Translating Smith's *Theory of Moral Sentiments*

Guest editor: Ryan Patrick Hanley

Moral sentiments in translation

Introduction

Ryan Patrick Hanley

As readers of this *Review* and members of this Society know all too well, *The Theory of Moral Sentiments* (*TMS*) long lived in the shadow of its author's other book. But that, happily, has changed in recent years. The publication of the Glasgow Edition of Smith's works in hardback by Oxford University Press in 1976 and their subsequent republication in paperback by the Liberty Fund of Indianapolis soon after made high-quality editions of all of Smith's works, including *TMS*, widely available. This was an event that had important implications for Smith's legacy. Where earlier generations of readers often knew Smith's work only through abridged or excerpted versions of his writings, the publication of the Glasgow Edition made possible direct access to complete versions of Smith's texts. And this, in turn, had important implications for scholarship. As Jonathan Wight demonstrated in his excellent quantitative analysis of scholarly citations to Smith's works between 1970 and 1997, in the wake of the release of the Glasgow Edition, the ratio of citations of *TMS* to *WN* shifted from 1:10 to 1:3 – leading Wight to suggest that 'these numbers support the hypothesis that citation interest in Smith's moral philosophy is growing faster than interest in his political economy' (Wight 2002: 68).

Whether one regards this shift as a matter of correlation or of causation, it remains the case that English-language scholarship on *TMS* – which was essentially moribund prior to the publication of the Glasgow edition, with only a few important exceptions – has flourished since. But, for present purposes, what bears mentioning is that there is some evidence that would seem to suggest that the same shift that English-language Smith scholarship experienced after publication of the Glasgow Edition is now occurring worldwide. In particular, the past few years have seen a remarkable proliferation of new translations of *TMS* into a range of languages, from French and Spanish and Italian to Greek and Finnish and Chinese. In some cases, the new translations offer improvements and refinements on earlier translations, often including new apparatus making them especially useful to scholars. In other cases the translations are firsts in that language, making it possible not only for scholars but also for students and popular audiences to access *TMS*. But in all cases it seems reasonable to expect that these new translations will continue to stimulate interest in *TMS* worldwide and will contribute to an increasingly global reassessment of Smith's contributions as a moral philosopher.

In an effort to call attention to these exciting developments, the International Adam Smith Society hosted a roundtable at the Annual Meeting of the Eighteenth-Century Scottish Studies Society held in 2011 in Aberdeen. The symposium sought to bring together translators of several recent and forthcoming editions of *TMS* and afford them an opportunity to reflect on the challenges of translating Smith, and also to report on the state of Smith scholarship in their respective national communities. Our hope is that the publication of their essays here will contribute to a growing appreciation in the English-speaking scholarly world of some of the excellent work on *TMS* now being done around the world.

Reference

Wight, J.B. (2002) "The rise of Adam Smith: Articles and citations, 1970–1997." *History of Political Economy* 34: 55–82

On the reception of Adam Smith's *Moral Theory in modern Greece* and the Greek edition of *Theory of Moral Sentiments*

Facing the roots of misunderstanding moral sentiments

Dionysios Drosos

Samuel Fleischacker has introduced a distinction between a "minimalist" and a "maximalist" perception of Enlightenment.[1] This distinction is very useful for understanding why the ideas and the attitudes of Scottish Enlightenment failed to find fertile soil in Modern Greece.

Scottish Enlightenment, and Smith's moral theory in particular, endeavors to foster a common language fully conversant with an individual's inherited common sense, as the condition for the moral development of the individuals forming a moral community within a perspective of openess. This pursuit for a common moral language can be traced to Smith's treatment of sympathy as the *par excellence* mechanism of triggering and communicating moral sentiments. The classical loci of moral theory, such as assessment of motives and consequences of actions, merit or demerit, moral duty, customs and manners, virtue and vice and rules of justice are treated in terms of sympathy. Sympathy is not meant as a kind of innate moral sense (in Hutcheson's way), but as a common human capacity to put oneself in the place of the other and to enter through imagination into the other's sentiments. Moreover, to evaluate and judge such sentiments by means of conjecturing in what measure an imagined impartial spectator would approve or disapprove of them. The impartial spectator procedure provides a kind of moral standard, which is tantamount neither to a commitment to certain views nor a to an abstract *a priori* moral imperative. What is really enlightening is the public and open process of evaluation and judgment, resulting in common standards, by correcting and refining moral sentiments. For humans to be adequately engaged in such a process, allegiance to a common good or cause is not a prerequisite. What is needed is cultivation of the natural human capacity for sympathy, imagination and independent judgment. Seen in this light, sympathy binds together in moral community, individuals who are independent and equal. This communicating through sympathy can be understood in terms of an ongoing cultivation, refinement, and scrutinizing of spontaneous and habitual sentimental reactions; in other words, as a process of becoming mature in one's moral sentiments through enlightened self-scrutiny and perception of others. This focus on a morality rooted in sentiments, aspired, and in a considerable measure, resulted in transforming the inherited structure and norms by which people came by their moral sentiments. Far from endorsing a specific moral doctrine or maximalist vision of "enlightened" man, the Scottish Enlightenment asserted a fundamental trust in an individual's capacity to arrive independently at moral maturity by means of cultivating and refining their moral sentiments

Thus, eighteenth century Scotland bequeaths a perhaps "over-particular", and "parochial" even, rather than universal, but nevertheless an fundamental early contribution to a "minimalist" view of Enlightenment.

Against this background, we cannot stress enough how much the so-called Neo-Hellenic Enlightenment[2] failed to achieve something analogous. The influx of new ideas, coming mainly from France, clashed with existing mentalities, resulting in the bitter and forthright confrontation between profane "rationalism" and religious "sentimentalism". The long-standing imperatives of common moral conscience endured in great measure, barely leaving any space for anything other than a superficial acceptance the new ideas, and thereby making the transition, from traditional communal to modern manners and ethics, partial and problematic. Sentiments as a basic component of morality remained entrapped in mystical, quasi-communal sentimental forms, which prevented the modern deployment of individual moral responsibility. In the absence of the latter, "modern manners" were reduced to an unbridled individualism, tending to assume asocial, nihilistic, and anomic forms. In such a context, the moral foundations of economic liberalism where either bypassed or proved too difficult to apprehend, by both its proponents and its enemies, making it hardly possible to understand economic liberalism as anything other than a licentious system of unrestrained selfishness and acquisitiveness. This *état d'esprit* has shaped the poor reception of Adam Smith's ideas in Greece until recently.

The ideas of European Enlightenment were an important influence in the development of the modern cultural movement known as "Neo-Hellenic Enlightenment", which dates from the last century of the Ottoman period (eighteenth to nineteenth century) and comprised intellectuals, members of the Greek diaspora (merchants and officers of the Ottoman administration) nurtured for the most part in the higher education establishments of continental Europe. Owing to the historical context of the Ottoman rule, the movement was faced with the following conditions and challenges.

It was inexorably interwoven with the ideal of national renaissance and independence.

The social structure of the lands under Ottoman rule bore no resemblance to the corresponding class systems of Western Europe and the movement's educated elites, serving as a kind of "importer" of new ideas, were the product of social and cultural developments never experienced in the homeland.

This intelligentsia wished to reconcile nostalgic aspirations to reinstate the lost classical tradition and restore the historic continuity of the nation, with forward-looking aspirations advocating new ideas and the modernization of society.

This two-faceted aspiration combining the nostalgic and the progressive came up against fairly new cultural and ideological traditions (cultivated during the later centuries of Ottoman rule) which were firmly rooted in pre-modern community mores. The church nurtured and protected these traditions and the official construal of the Greek Orthodox religious confession formed the stronghold of the resistance to the new ideas, despite the noteworthy fact that not a few important Neo-Hellenic thinkers of the Enlightenment belonged to the clergy.[3]

The encounter of such thoroughly contrasting trains of thoughts resulted in eclectic and inconsistent ideological forms, which prevailed in both the constitution and the government of the newborn state for a long period. A characteristic, and even emblematic, paradox of this sort, was the choice made by the first constitutional assembly (1822) to establish a full, modern constitution, inspired directly by the ideals of French Revolution, as the appropriate constitutional charter for a society so fundamentally different from that where those ideas were born in the first place.

Modern scientific ideas, contemporary methods and philosophical approaches were uncomfortable marriage partners with traditional creeds and superstitions. The initial radical momentum of the movement soon capitulated and gave way before the vehement reaction of the Church, and the political agenda of the revolution and the ideological formation of the independent state.[4] In this context, a good number of Enlightenment ideas resulted in mere lip service, under which pre-modern ideological structures survived in a renewed form, assuming a new role. At the same time, more radical strands of the Enlightenment remained marginal, and without deep roots in society.

Not surprisingly, 'maximalist' versions of Enlightenment were trapped in a sterile imitation of occidental patterns (both liberal and marxist). A highly abstract formalism, poorly connected with or even cut off from inherited structures of thought, left the realm of sentiments, feelings, affections, and passions to be predominated by a joint mixture of secular and religious nostalgic and romanticizing discourses, converging in an extravagantly ambitious nationalistic narrative.[5] This resulted in a characteristic peculiar "sentimentalist thinking",[6] radically different from Scottish enlightened sentimentalism.

Many scholars have thrown light upon the peculiarities of Neo-Hellenic Enlightenment in the last decades.[7] Worthy of further exploration, however, are the patterns of the traditional pre-modern modes of thought and belief which prevented the reformation of the old ideas and manners and excluded a fruitful synthesis of the two, and which in fact to this day are a persisting hindrance for constructive social development. This predicament offers, in my view, a background against which one could best investigate why the moral sentimentalism of the Scottish Enlighteners has had such negligible influence on modern Greek philosophy, and why Adam Smith has been almost ignored as a moral philosopher and read exclusively as the founding father of laissez-faire economics.

What seems distinctive in Scottish Enlightenment is the endeavor to face the moral crisis of Early Modernity, through reforming and "opening" the *process* of other and self-understanding and recognition among peers, engaged in a social conversation and mutual checks and balances of moral sentiments. In this respect, the inherited practices and beliefs were not sweepingly dismissed but were fairly assessed for value in a public, critical discussion between independent individuals in search of a common language and a reawakened common sense as a result of enlightened education. This discursive process, in which a vast community of scientists, philosophers, theologians, and men of arts and letters (the *literati* of Scotland) participated was extremely fruitful. For Scottish society in transition, this manifold process of communal exchange between disciplines, broadening of knowledge and cultivation of manners was a transforming force vastly increasing the potential for moral sentiment. This dynamic molded a new form of civil life and civilization. And, as the goods of civilization are indivisible and cannot be made the object of any kind of contract, but are shared in common, in this sense, the Scottish Enlightenment provided a *modern* conception of a moral community within society.

It is *par excellence* in Adam Smith that we can trace this concern wherein the modernization of society should not be established at the expense of a common civilization, but should give rise to modern forms of moral community. The concept of moral community is built on the double premise of the workings of sympathy and the *impartial spectator*. Through sympathy, we not only perceive (by a switch of roles in imagination) the sentiments of other real persons, but we also anticipate an ideal impartial spectator conforming our conduct so that we can gain his approval before whose unbiased arbitration we submit our conduct for approval.

The catalyst enabling this process is the crucial virtue of *self-command*. In the sixth edition of the *Theory of Moral Sentiments* (*TMS*), *self-command* is described as the most important of virtues; it is the virtue from which every other virtue derives its dignity and merit. The more one aspires to moral excellence, the more his/her conduct has self-command, and the more his/her moral conscience approximates the standards of the ideal spectator. This ideal, although never to be accomplished in this less than perfect world, constitutes, nevertheless, the moving force furthering moral development and betterment. We have here a modern conception of conscience, neither divine gift not innate sense, but as continuous, historical process of intercourse and mutual information between the "man within", observation and common sense.

What makes this scheme so original is the self-regulating role it ascribes to moral sentiments, avoiding the road of a direct confrontation between passions and reason. While in agreement with Hume's analysis of the passions as motives of the will, Adam Smith understands self-command, not as a domination of pure reason over irrational passions, but as a process of enlightenment each individual is enriching, educating, refining the sentimental "capital" of the moral community. This results in an *internalization* of the ideal moral community into the "man within". The moving force of this internalization is the ideal spectator function, a means of comparing one's inner man with the wise and virtuous, and assuming a higher standard as a result, which in fact engages one in a process of broadening and enriching moral consciousness. This engagement is not limited to the individual's own self-satisfied and self-sufficient or self-congratulating excellence. This is not to say that a moral community engaged in a process of refinement and modernisation is not exempt from the common traits of human nature, which are both to distinguish oneself and to communicate one's sentiments and views, and to earn the approbation of others. In fact, the latter is, as Smith insists, the most prominent of all human characteristics, which is why the possibility of communication between the educated moral elites and the greater part of mankind was kept open.

Smith's vision of Enlightenment as a process for acquiring a deeper sentiment-rooted morality gives Enlightenment a transforming role and relevance for a civilized, commercial society. Focusing on a deeper sentiment-rooted morality, Scottish Enlightenment, and Smith's approach in particular, endeavors to build a common language with inherited common sense, in an open perspective of moral development. His enterprise was greatly facilitated by a series of social and ideological transformations in eighteenth-century Scotland: 1) The decline of religious intolerance after the Union and the demise of the ideological and political dominance of the Church; 2) The rise within the Church of Scotland of the party of the Moderates, who allied themselves with the Enlightenment; 3) The introduction of the English language in the universities, which, combined with the literacy of the people (inheritance of the Reformation), paved the way for the formation of a common language between the *literati* and the common people; 4) Sacrificing the dream of national independence allowed the channeling of the patriotic spirit towards a common national course of modernization and improvement of both economy and manners.

It is interesting to contrast the socio-political context of Scottish Enlightenment to that of the short-lived period of the Neo-Hellenic Enlightenment. The Orthodox Church (an integral part of the Ottoman administration), was the sovereign ideological and political power ruling the orthodox *milliyet*.[8] Except for a short interval at the beginning of the seventeenth century, under the Patriarch Cyril Loucaris, the Church as an institution and in its role as moral educator, was utterly inimical to any effort towards either religious reformation or political change.

In a substantially illiterate population, religious superstition and bigotry played a dominant part in the formation of common moral ideas. The deeply reactionary and true enemy of the Enlightenment was never the authority flowing from the theological or philosophical assertions of a doctrine, but that of the confessor – the authority of the confessor has proved to be far more dangerous than the authority of sacred scripts and, moreover, directly hostile to Enlightenment: the very effort to rely in one's own rational capacity is traditionally stigmatized as a sin of arrogance.

The majority of the Enlighteners used a sophisticated form of Greek, an idiom modeled upon Ancient Greek, in which to speak and write. This idiom differed from the spoken language of the common people and also from the language they were accustomed to hearing in the Bible and in the hymnology of the Church; the adoption of this idiom raised an additional barrier against any effort to engage a dialogue with received ideas, beliefs, and forms of conscience and made the formation of a common language between the *literati* and the common people very problematic.

Ideas of the French Enlightenment were introduced – "imported", one dare say – in a culture with no experience of the historical conditions of those leading to the Reformation and Enlightenment in Western Europe; these revolutionary ideals were good enough to ideologically inspire the war of national independence, but never resulted in a thorough moral reformation, leaving common sense dominated by an eclectic amalgam of deep rooted traditional values, on the one hand, and isolated modern attitudes, on the other.

The conclusions that one is tempted to formulate by way of a working hypothesis with regard to the Greek Enlightenment go like this: The long-standing trends along which common moral conscience evolved remained for the most part in place, becoming only superficially affected by the ideas of Enlightenment. More specifically, the transition from traditional community to modern societal ethics happened only partially, was problematic, and resulted in a confrontation between profane "rationalism" and religious "sentimentalism" with an unrewarding focus on the contrast between "profane" and "religious" rather than creatively looking at the faculties of reason and sentiment. The dynamics of moral sentiment remained entrapped in mystical, quasi-communal forms of sentiment, which prevented the modern deployment of individual moral responsibility. As a counterpart to this, individualism tended and tends still to assume asocial, nihilistic, and anomic forms. In such a context, the moral foundations of economic liberalism proved difficult to embrace, and its founders' tenets on the whole, have been misunderstood by proponents and enemies alike, and are seen as a doctrine advocating a licentious system of unrestrained selfishness. This has been the common view of Adam Smith's ideas until the 1990s, when the interest in his moral theory began to flourish, albeit in short and modest steps. These steps are the focus of the subsequent discussion.

On the Greek translation of *Theory of Moral Sentiments*

The first step towards a critical reassessment of Adam Smith was made by Kosmas Psychopedis in 1990.[9] He was also the first scholar who introduced the teaching of *TMS* in the curriculum of the University of Athens.[10] He also have encouraged and edited the translation of fragments of the *TMS*.[11] My first contribution in the translation of Adam Smith's opus into the Greek language was an extended fragment of the Part VII of *TMS* included in a critical anthology of texts by British Moralists.[12] No sooner than 252 years after the first Edinburgh edition, the first translated edition of the integral text of *TMS* in the Greek language is now in bookstores.[13] This translation is based on the the *Glasgow Edition of the Works and Correspondence of Adam Smith I: The Theory of Moral Sentiments*, edited by D. D. Raphael and A. L. Macfie (1976).[14] The Greek edition includes the comments of the editors of the Glasgow Edition, and it is preceded by an original introduction of 52 pages. I have divided the introduction into five parts as follows:

- A presentation of the character and the claims of Smith's moral theory, with a brief summary of the argumentation in each of the seven Parts of *TMS*.

- A statement on the importance of *TMS* in the context of Scottish Enlightenment and an assessment of its contribution to the "science of human nature". Emphasis is given to the differences of Smith's conception of sympathy in contrast to Hume's, and what consequences these differences had in Smith's treatment of self-command, moral conscience and the theory of justice.
- A critical assessment on the reception of *TMS* before the renaissance of Adam Smith studies in the 1970s. This part is further divided in two sections:
  - The reactions of Smith's contemporaries are broadly presented and include those of Lord Kames,[15] Adam Ferguson,[16] Thomas Reid,[17] and those of the subsequent generation: Dugald Stewart,[18] James Macintosh,[19] Thomas Brown,[20] Theodore Jouffroy.[21] Objections stemming from the common-sense philosophy point of view are emphasized.
  - A brief account is given of the difficulties nineteenth-century thinkers had in reconciling *TMS* with the *Wealth of Nations*, after the momentous success of the latter and the prevalence of Manchester Liberalism. In this context, reference is made to the *Unschlangstheorie*[22] and the first formulation of the so called *Adam Smith Problem*.[23] In addition, there is a note on Max Scheler's critique on Smith's conception of sympathy.[24]
- A review of the main tendencies in recent Adam Smith scholarship serves as a guide for further reading and is also divided into two sections:
  - "Ethics and Political Economy: the myth of *laissez-faire* revisited". Emphasis is given to the shift in perspective and approach in assessing the relation between the moral and economic theories in Smith's thought, and different arguments from a selection of representative contributors are briefly summarized.[25]
  - "The moral theory of Adam Smith: a re-appreciation". This section also gives an account of a series of influential modern contributions to Adam Smith scholarship, with a brief summary of each.[26] It ends with a brief account of the recent debate between Amartya Sen and Fonna Forman-Barzilai on the relevance of Smith's conception of justice for today's world.
- A post-scriptum on the broader importance of the sentimentalist approach for understanding morality beyond the interests of strict Adam Smith scholarship closes the introduction. This part sketches out affiliations, worthy of exploration, with usages of Smith's language of emotions, such as sympathy, empathy, and so on, which depart from Smith's own usage. In this respect, references are made to different fields of research such as neuroscience,[27] critical psychology,[28] cultural studies,[29] anthropology,[30] and ethology.[31] This last section was included in the introduction, because, as stated in the first part of the present paper, scientific interest in throwing light on the function of sentiments does not have deep roots in modern Greek philosophical tradition.

The above-mentioned reason imposed the need for elaborating a relevant vocabulary to adequately express Smith's conceptualization of sentiments. For example:

Feeling is translated as αίσθημα [esthima].

Sentiment corresponds to συναίσθημα [synesthima], which means "feeling with" and has a slight connotation of communication with other's feelings.

Sympathy is a word of Greek origin – συμπάθεια [sympatheia] – and is commonly used in everyday Greek language in the same manner as in English. So the difference in its technical use in Smith's theory is exactly the same.

Empathy has no place in Smith's vocabulary, yet it is widely used in modern Adam Smith scholarship. Empathy is of Greek origin, too – εμπάθεια [empatheia] – but in Greek language it has a totally different meaning. It means the passionate disposition to act in a malevolent way. So it is absolutely necessary to stress the difference in the technical use of the term or use another word: ενσυναίσθηση [ensynesthisi], which means the ability to enter in someone else's feelings.

Emotion is translated as συγκίνηση [synkinisi], which commonly means to be moved or touched by something, and it is barely used in the plural. So it is necessary to point out the difference of the meaning in its technical use.

Affections is very difficult to translate. Literally it means αγάπη [agapi] (love) or στοργή [storgi] (tenderness, mainly towards a child or a pet or a lover or someone in need of protection). These meanings are not relevant. So I had to forge a more inclusive expression: αισθηματικές επενδύσεις [esthimatikes ependyseis], which means feelings or emotions investment.

Propriety is a problem. I've chosen the word ευπρέπεια [euprepeia]. Etymologically, ευπρέπεια is the combination of the prefix ευ [eu], which means "good", "well", "easily" and the verb πρέπει [prepei] which means "ought". The opposite is απρέπεια [aprepeia]; the prefix α [a] meaning "not","lack of", "without", "absence". The word ευπρέπεια in everyday modern Greek means something like "correct manners". But its usage in ancient Greek and in Hellenistic Koine (common) of the Septuagint has the connotation of moral *and* aesthetic beauty; it means a quality that evokes admiration, approbation and respect. I find this usage interesting.

Resentment is usually translated as μνησικακία [mnisikakia]. But this word is a little too strong, meaning an insatiable craving for revenge followed by malevolence: etymologically, μνησικακία is a combination of μνήμη [mnimi] (memory, remembrance) and κακία [kakia] (malevolence). It describes a permanently impoisoned heart, unable to forget or to be satisfied with proper retribution. This is more appropriate for Nietsche's usage of *resentment*. Mnisikakia is frequently used in cases of unprovoked (or scarcely provoked) pathological resentment. I preferred to this, the word παροργισμός [parorgismos], drawing again from Septuagint. This word means the 'righteous wrath (or anger)'. This expression, when used to denote human emotional reaction to injury, has the merit to bring out the tension between one's right to react against injury and the failure of such reaction to be righteous in its own right. Misguided by self-preference, everybody tends to give expression to his/her wrath in a Godlike manner. This is checked and balanced by the sympathy of the real spectators and the conjectured sympathy of an impartial spectator.

Merit is translated as αξιομισθία [axiomisthia], meaning "re-compensatory worthiness". This word is a theological term. In everyday language it is barely used, although its components are very common: άξιο [axio] means "worthy", "of value", "competent", and μισθός [misthos] means "re-compensation", "wage". By using the prefix α, we have the opposite: αναξιομισθία (demerit).

Things are much easier when it comes to the vocabulary of ancient philosophy. The rich language of Platonic, Aristotelian, and Stoical philosophy is in full use in modern Greek philosophical thought. Sometimes the problem is rather in the translation from Greek into English. For example, Smith in some places seems to use "prudence" [which commonly translates *phronesis*] as an equivalent for σοφία [wisdom].[32]

Summarizing, the translation of *TMS* in Greek had to deal with two classes of problems. First, the general problems of translating modern philosophy into a language which disposes of a priceless treasure of resources, but whose rich philosophical tradition stops abruptly well before the advent of modern philosophical thought, which has been articulated in foreign languages. In this respect, between Classical and Hellenistic ages and Modernity, a gap is to be bridged in terms of philosophical language. The second consideration bears a relation with the first and concerns the particular issue of introducing the vocabulary of feelings, sentiments, emotions, and so on, into the language of modern Greek philosophical thought.

I am inclined to trust the Greek language's capacity to assimilate new terms or to recollect ancient usages, and I am hopeful such an enterprise can bring forth a new turn in Greek philosophical thought, a challenge well worth taking.

Notes

1   While on the "maximalist" view, "people will be enlightened only if they come to certain views", on the "minimalist" view, "enlightenment is an open-ended *process*, which mandates certain norms of reasoning or conversation but no particular conclusions or attitudes". Sam Fleischacker, "Why we still need (Kantian) Enlightenment", Lecture, University of Ioannina, May 2011. pp. 2–3.

2   Neo-Hellenic Enlightenment (for others, "Neo-Hellenic Renaissance"), is the name usually given to an intellectual revival movement, inspired by both the ideas of French Revolution and the renaissance of ancient Greek literacy. This movement took place during the period from late eighteenth to early nineteenth centuries in the main commercial centers of Ottoman Empire, in South Russia and central Europe, and it was supported materially by the rising merchant class of Greek Orthodox diaspora, who encouraged the education of young people in Italian and German universities. For an English language introduction to the character of Neo-Hellenic Enlightenment, see L. S. Stavrianos, "Antecedents to the Balkan Revolutions of the 19th Century", *Journal of Modern History*, vol. 29, 1957, pp. 333–48; Paschalis Kitromilides, *Tradition, Enlightenment, and Revolution: Ideological Change in Eighteenth and*

Nineteenth Century Greece (unpublished Harvard Ph.D. thesis, Sept. 1978); and, for a brief introduction, Raphael Demos, "The Neo-Helleninc Enlightenment (1750–1821)", *Journal of the History of Ideas*, vol. 19, 1958, pp. 523–541. See also, Jonathan I. Israel, *Enlightenment Contested: Philosophy, Modernity, and the Emancipation of Man, 1670–1752*, New York: Oxford University Press, 2006, chapter "Locke, Newton, and Leibniz in the Greek cultural diaspora", pp. 317–25. For an account of the socioeconomic background of this movement, see Traian Stoianovich, "The Conquering Balkan Orthodox Merchant", *Journal of Economic History*, vol. 20, no. 2, 1960, pp. 234–313. And for a survey of the most prominent intellectual figures of Neo-Hellenic Enlightenment, see G. P. Henderson, *The Revival of Greek Thought* (Albany: SUNY Press, 1970).

3   Among them, the most notable intellectual and scholar of the Neo-Hellenic Enlightenment, Eugenios Voulgaris (1716–1806), a disciple of Leibniz and Wolf, influenced by Newton, Locke, Gassendi, and Descartes. Other also important enlightened priests were: Theophilos Kaïris (1784–1853), Benjamin Lesbian (1759–1824). Both were accused of atheism by the Church. The second one, together with the very important precursors of Enlightenment, Methodios Anthrakitis (1660–1736), also a cleric and a mathematician and theologian, and Iosipos Moisiodax (1730–1800), a follower of Locke and supporter of Voltaire, have been excommunicated.

4   After the dual acts of national independence and autocephaly of the Church of Greece (1833–1850), the latter was "transformed into an official arm of the civil state". See P. Kitromilides, "Imagined Communities and the Origins of the National Question in the Balkans", *European History Quarterly*, vol. 19, 1989, pp. 149–94. This entailed a dramatic change (not without tensions) in the values and priorities of the Church. Departing from Orthodox Christianity's twin traditions of ecumenism and inner spirituality, the official religious teaching of the Church degenerated into doctrinal support of secular nationalist values, the Church thus becoming an ideological mechanism of the state. In the religious imaginary, nationhood as community took the place of the ecumenic community of the faithful. In this way, a pre-modern – *par excellence* – institution became modern and an "integral part of the same symbolic universe" as the national state (ibid.). The Church thus became a stronghold of conservatism: fiercely hostile to social reforms, and immune to any call for inner reformation. This development jeopardized *both* the potential for independence of spiritual life from secular power, and the modern character of the nation's civil and political life.

5   Adamantios Koraes (1748–1833), one of the most influential intellectuals of late Neo-Hellenic Enlightenment was born in Smyrna [Izmir] and died in Paris. He was a merchant, and also a physician, a philologer and a commentator of classic ancient philosophy, influenced by Hobbes, Locke, and Jean-Jacques Rousseau, a friend of the French encyclopedists, and correspondent with Thomas Jefferson. He is considered as one of the emblematic figures of the newborn Greek Nationalism. See Benedict Anderson, *Imagined Communities: Reflections on the Origin and Spread of Nationalism* (London: Verso, 1991) pp. 72, 79, 195. This spirit of Hellenic *risorgimento* is quite characteristic for almost all the intellectuals of the period. A different and quite original political figure was Rigas Ferraios (1757–1798), a schoolteacher, poet and polymath, and a political activist, ardent supporter of French Revolution. He was exceptional and alone in his revolutionary, not nationalist vision of emancipating all Balkans (Muslim and Turks included) from the yoke of Ottoman despotism, in the perspective of building a liberal multinational Balkan Confederation. He was, arrested and eventually executed in the prison of Belgrade, while he was condemned by the Patriarch.

6   I borrow this concept from Stelios Ramphos, *The Unthinkable Nothingness. The Philocalic Rhizomes of Hellenic Nihilism. An Essay on Philosophical Anthropology* (Athens: Armos Publishers, 2010) [in Greek]. In a different perspective, the author explores the reception of the Patristic texts of *Philocalia*, in the nineteenth century, as a reaction to the ideas of Enlightenment, and as the spiritual touchstone of modern Greek sentimental understanding and self-understanding.

7   Among the most important contributions [in the Greek language] are: A. Aggelou, *Facets of Neo-Hellenic Enlightenment* (Athens: MIET, 1999); K. Dimaras, *Neo-Hellenic Enlightenment* (Athens: Hermes, 1997); P. Kitromilides, *Neo-Hellenic Enlightenment* (Athens: MIET, 1996); P. Kondylis, *Neo-Hellenic Enlightenment: The Philosophical Ideas* (Athens: Themelio, 1988); P. Noutsos, *Neo-Hellenic Enlightenment* (Athens: Ellinika Grammata, 2005); Roxani Argyropoulou, *Neo-Hellenic Moral and Political Thought: From Enlightenment to Romanticism* (Thessaloniki: Vanias, 2003); G. Karafyllis, *Neo-Hellenic Enlightenment. Philosophical Approaches* (Athens: Gutenmberg, 2008); K. Petsios, *The Discussion "On Nature" in Modern Greek Thought: Aspects of the Philosophical Investigation from the 15th to the 19th Century A.D.* (Ioannina 2002); N. Psemmenos, *Greek Philosophy from 1453 to 1821. An Anthology* (Athens: Gnwsi, 1989). A rich collection of manuscripts (32,500), printed books, archives, and digital data on Neo-Hellenic Enlightenment is to be found in the Modern Greek Philosophy Research Centre (under the direction of prof. K. Petsios), University of Ioannina. Available online at: www.kenef.phil.uoi.gr/en/index.php?text_id=203 (last accessed 12 July 2014).

   For English-speaking readers, Richard Clogg's, "Elite and Popular Culture in Greece under Turkish Rule", *Indiana Social Studies Quarterly* vol. 32, 1979, pp. 107–43; Raphael Demos, "The Neo-Hellenic Enlightenment (1750–1821)", *Journal of the History of Ideas* vol. 19 no. 4, 1958, pp. 523–41; M. Kitromilides Paschalis, "The Enlightenment and the Greek cultural tradition", University of Athens, Athens, Greece, Institute for Neo-Hellenic Research/National Hellenic Research Foundation, Athens, July 2009; Athanasia Glycofrydi-Leontsini, "Enlightened Intellectuals in Modern Greek Society" *The European Legacy. The Official Journal of the International Society for the Study of European Ideas*, vol. 2 no. 3, 1997; P. M. Kitromilides, *Enlightenment, Nationalism, Orthodoxy: Studies in the Culture and Political Thought of South-eastern Europe*, Variorum Collected Studies Series, CS453 (Farnham: Ashgate, 1994); P. Kitromilides (ed.), *Adamantios Korais and the European Enlightenment*, Studies on Voltaire and the Eighteenth Century, vol. 10 (Oxford: Voltaire Foundation, 2010); Roderick Beaton and David Ricks (eds), *The Making of Modern Greece: Nationalism, Romanticism, and the Uses of the Past (1797–1896)* (Farnhgam: Ashgate, 2009); Stathis Gourgouris, *Dream Nation: Enlightenment, Colonization, and the Institution of Modern Greece* (Redwood City, CA: Stanford University Press, 1996); Athanasia Glycofrydi-Leontsini, "The Rhetoric of Nation Building during the Neo-Hellenic Enlightenment and the Evolution of the Notion of Greekness in the 20th Century" Macquarie University, MGSAANZ Biennial Conference, Sydney, 2010; Athanasia Glycofrydi-Leontsini, "Teaching Princes: A Vehicle of Moral and Political Education during the Neo-Hellenic Enlightenment" in *Classical Russia 1700–1825*, vol. 3–5, 2008–2010, pp. 71–90.

8   For the *milliyet* system and the transition to national state, see Victor Roudometof, "From *Rum Millet* to Greek Nation: Enlightenment, Secularization, and National Identity in Ottoman Balkan Society, 1453–1821", *Journal of Modern Greek Studies,* vol. 16, 1998; Murat Önsoy, "From Millet to Nation: Modern Greek Enlightenment

and 19th Century Greek Nationalism", International Conference on Mediterranean Studies, Athens, 20–23 April 2011.

9   Kosmas Psychopedis, "Adam Smith and the Critical Method of Political Economy", *Axiologica*, no. 1, 1990 [in Greek]. Kosmas Psychopedis (1944–2004) was a most eminent figure in modern Greek political philosophical thought, and a never to be forgotten teacher for my generation. He was certainly not an Adam Smith scholar. His interests lay mainly in critical theory, Marxism, and Kantian philosophy. His main contributions are: *Untersuchungen zur Politischen Theorie von Immanuel Kant* (O. Schwartz, 1980); *Geschichte und Methode: Begrundungstypen und Interpretationskriterien der Gesellschaftstheorie Kant, Hegel, Marx und Webe*. (Campus, 1984); Werner Bonefeld, Richard Gunn and Kosmas Psychopedis (eds), *Open Marxism* vols. 1, 2, 3 (Pluto Press, 1992–1995); Werner Bonefeld and Kosmas Psychopedis (eds), *The Politics of Change: Globalization, Ideology and Critique* (Palgrave Macmillan, December 2000); Werner Bonefeld and Kosmas Psychopedis (eds), *Human Dignity: Social Autonomy and the Critique of Capitalism* (Ashgate, 2005).

10 Before K. Psychopedis, a publication worth mentioning is Athanasia Glykofrydi-Leontsini's contribution to Scottish Enlightenment studies, *The Epistemological Foundations of Thomas Reid's Aesthetics* (Athens: University of Athens, 1988) [in Greek]. In the 1990s, the debate on Adam Smith began to grow. The first book on Adam Smith was published in 1994 (D. G. Drosos, *The Market and the State in Adam Smith*, Athens: Sakis Karageorgas Foundation, 1994 [in Greek]. Since then, a series of contributions were made in Greek and English languages, and Adam Smith and the Scottish Enlightenment studies were systematically introduced in the curriculum and the postgraduate programs of the University of Ioannina and the University of Crete, and a new generation of scholars with growing interests in Smith's moral theory made its appearance: Spiros Tegos, Fotini Vaki, Ioannis Tassopoulos, et.al. [see *Adam Smith Review* 7 ("Adam Smith in Athens")].

11 An anthology of fragments from *TMS* [50 selected pages from: 1) Part I, section I, chap. I: *Of Sympathy*; 2) Part I, section I, chap. V: *Of the Amiable and Respectable Virtues*; 3) Part I, section III, chap. II: *Of the Origin of Ambition, and of the Distinction of Ranks*; 4) Part IV, chap. I: *Of the Beauty which the Appearance of Utility Bestows upon all the Productions of Art, and of the Extensive Influence of this Species of Beauty*; 5) Part II, section II: *Of Justice and Beneficence*, chap. I: *Comparison of those two virtues*; 6) Part II, section II, chap. II: *Of the Sense of Justice, of Remorse, and of the Consciousness of Merit*; 7) Part III, chap. VI: *In What Cases the Sense of Duty Ought to be the Sole Principle of our Conduct; And in What Cases it Ought to Concur with Other Motives*; 8) Part VII, section IV: *Of the Manner in which different Authors have Treated the Practical Rules of Morality*; 9) part VI, section II: *Introduction*: 10) Part II, section II, chap. III: *Of the Utility of this Constitution of Nature*; 11) Part V, chap. I: *Of the Influence of Custom and Fashion Upon our Notions of Beauty and Deformity*: 12) Part VI, section II, chap. II: *Of the Order in which Societies are by Nature Recommended to our Beneficence*. Translated from the Glasgow Edition, *op.cit.*, by Diogenis Pylarinos, in Kosmas Psychopedis, Manolis Aggelidis (eds), *Texts on Political Economy and Political Theory* (Athens, Exantas, 1996 [in Greek].

12 Dionysis G. Drosos (ed.), *Virtues and Interests. Moral Philosophy at the Threshold of Modernity: The British Debate*. (Athens: Savvalas Publishers and Sakis Karageorgas Foundation, 2008) [in Greek].

13 Adam Smith, *H Theoria twn Ethikwn Synaisthimatwn* [*The Theory of Moral Sentiments*], edition, introduction, translation by D. G. Drosos, (Athens: Papazisis, 2011).

14   R. H. Campbell, D. D. Raphael, and A. S. Skinner, General editors (Oxford: Oxford University Press, 1976). I have also consulted the following editions: Adam Smith, *Théorie des Sentiments Moraux*, texte traduit, introduit et annoté par Michaël Biziou, Claude Gautier and Jean-François Pradeau Presses Universitaires de France, 2007; Adam Smith, *Theorie der ethischen Gefühle* (Auf der Grundlage der Übersetzung von Walther Eckstein neu herausgegeben von Horst D. Brandt) (Hamburg: Felix Meiner Verlag, 2010); Adam Smith, *Teoria dei Sentimenti Morali*, Introduzione et note di Eugenio Lecaldano, traduzione di Stefania Di Pietro (Milan: BUR Rizzioli, 2009).

15   Henry Home, Lord Kames, *Essays on the Principles of Morality and Natural Religion*, 3rd ed. (Edinburgh, 1779) pp. 109–13. Re-edited in *On Moral Sentiments. Contemporary Responses to Adam Smith*, edited and introduced by John Reeden (Bristol: Thoemes Press, 1997), 61–63.

16   Adam Ferguson, "On the Principle of Moral Estimation" [1761?], *Journal of the History of Ideas*, vol. 21 (1960), 226–32.

17   MS 2131/2II/6 and MS 2131/3/I/28, University of Aberdeen. Re-edited by J. C. Stewart-Robertson and David Fate Norton, "Thomas Reid on Adam Smith's Theory of Morals", *Journal of the History of Idea*s, vol. 41 (1980), 381–98 and vol. 45 (1984), 309–21.

18   "Account of the Life and Writings of Adam Smith" (1794), in Adam Smith, *Essays on Philosophical Subjects* [Oxford, 1980]; and "Of Sympathy" *Contemporary Responses*, o.π., 121. *Collective Works of Dugald Stewart* (Edinburgh, 1854–60), vol. 6, 328–33.

19   James Macintosh, *Dissertation on the Progress of Ethical Philosophy*, 2nd ed. (Edinburgh, 1836).

20   Thomas Brown, *Lectures on the Philosophy of Human Mind* (Edinburgh, 1820).

21   Theodore Jouffroy, *Cours de Droit Naturel* (Paris: Prévost-Crocius, 1834) [Adamant Media Corporation, 2002] *Introduction to Ethics, Including a Critical Survey of Moral Systems*, English translation by William H,Channing (Boston, 1840), vol. 2.

22   Witold von Skarżyński, *Adam Smith als Moralphilosoph un Schoepfer der Nationalökonomie* (Berlin, 1878).

23   August Oncken, "Das Adam Smith Problem", *Zeitschrift fur Sozialwissenschaft*, 1899.

24   Max Scheler, *The Nature of Sympathy* (Piscataway, NJ: Transaction, 2008).

25   Jacob Viner, "Adam Smith and Laissez Faire", *Journal of Political Economy*, vol. 35, no. 2, Apr. 1927, pp. 198–232; Joseph Cropsey, *Polity and Economy: With Further Thoughts on the Principles of Adam Smith* (South Bend, IN: St. Augustine's Press, 2001 [1957]); Spencer J. Pack, *Capitalism as a Moral System: Adam Smith's Critique of the Free Market Economy* (Cheltenham: Edward Elgar, 1991); and Spencer J. Pack, *Aristotle, Adam Smith, and Karl Marx: On Some Fundamental Issues in 21th Century Political Economy* (Cheltenham: Edward Elgar, 2010); Donald Winch, *Adam Smith's Politics: An Essay in Historiographic Revision* (Cambridge: Cambridge University Press, 1978); Samuel Fleischacker, *On Adam Smith's "Wealth of Nations": A Philosophical Companion* (Princeton, NJ: Princeton University Press, 2004); Gavin Kennedy, *Adam Smith's Lost Legacy* (London: Palgrave Macmillan, 2005); and Gavin Kennedy, *Adam Smith: A Moral Philosopher and His Political Economy* (London: Palgrave Macmillan, 2008); James Alvey, *Adam Smith: Optimist or Pessimist? A New Problem Concerning the Teleological Basis of Commercial Society* (Farnham: Ashgate, 2003); Dennis Rasmussen, *The Problems of Promise of Commercial Society: Adam Smith's Response to Rousseau* (University Park, PA: Penn State University Press, 2008); Craig Smith, *Adam Smith's Political Philosophy: The Invisible Hand and Spontaneous Order* (Abingdon: Routledge, 2006); Emma Rothchild, *Economic Sentiments*

(Cambridge, MA: Harvard University Press, 2001); Iain McLean, *Adam Smith. Radical and Egalitarian: An Interpretation for the 21st Century* (Edinburgh: Edinburgh University Press, 2006); Michaël Biziou, *Adam Smith et l'Origine du Libéralisme* (Paris: Presses Universitaires de France, 2003); and Magali Bessone, Michaël Biziou, *Adam Smith Philosophe: De la Morale à l'Économie ou Philosophie du Libéralisme* (Rennes: Presses Universitaires de Rennes, 2009); François Dermagne, *Le Dieu du Marché: Éthique, Économie et Théologie dans l'oeuvre d'Adam Smith* (Geneva: Labor et Fides, 2003); Jean Claude Michéa, *Impasse Adam Smith: Brèves Remarques sur l'Impossibilité de Dépasser le Capitalisme sur sa Gauche* (Castelnau-le-Nez: Climats, Coll. Sysyphe, 2002).

26   A. L. Macfie, *The Individual in Society: Papers on Adam Smith* (London: Allen and Unwin, 1967); Tom D. Campbell, *Adam Smith's Science of Morals* (London: Allen and Unwin, 1971); D. D. Raphael, *The Impartial Spectator: Adam Smith's Moral Philosophy* (Oxford: Oxford University Press, 2007); Knud Haakonssen, *The Science of a Legislator: The Natural Jurisprudence of David Hume and Adam Smith* (Cambridge: Cambridge University Press, 1989); Vivienne Brown, *Adam Smith's Discourse: Canonicity, Commerce and Conscience* (Abingdon: Routledge 1994); Charles Griswold, *Adam Smith and the Virtues of Enlightenment* (Cambridge: Cambridge University Press, 1999); Samuel Fleischacker, *A Third Concept of Liberty: Judgement and Freedom in Kant and Adam Smit* (Princeton, NJ: Princeton University Press, 1999); James Otteson, *Adam Smith's Marketplace of Life* (Cambridge: Cambridge University Press, 2002); Stephen J. McKenna, *Adam Smith: The Rhetoric of Propriety* (Albany, NY: SUNY Press, 2006); Leonidas Montes, *Adam Smith in Context* (London: Palgrave Macmillan, 2004); Nicholas Phillipson, *Adam Smith: An Enlightened Life* (London: Allan Lane, 2010); Ryan Patrick Hanley, *Adam Smith and the Character of Virtue* (Cambridge: Cambridge University Press, 2009); Gloria Vivenza, *Adam Smith and the Classics* (Oxford: Oxford University Press, 2001); Jerry Evensky, *Adam Smith's Moral Philosophy* (Cambridge: Cambridge University Press, 2005); Amartya Sen, *The Idea of Justice* (London: Allen Lane, 2009); Fonna Forman-Barzilai, *Adam Smith and the Circles of Sympathy: Cosmopolitanism and Moral Theory* (Cambridge: Cambridge University Press, 2010).

27   Antonio R. Damasio, *Descartes' Error: Emotion, Reason, and the Human Brain* (Mahopac, NY: Putnam, 1994); Antonio R. Damasio, *Self Comes to Mind: Constructing the Conscious Brain* (New York: Pantheon, 2010); Dr. Lee D. Carlson (ed.), *Moral Psychology, Volume 3: The Neuroscience of Morality: Emotion, Brain Disorders, and Development* (Cambridge, MA: Bradford Books, 2008); Andrea Polonioli, "Recent Trends in Neuroethics: A Selected Bibliography", *Etica & Politica/Ethics & Politics*, vol. 9, no. 2, 2009, pp. 68–87.

28   Michael Billing, *The Hidden Roots of Critical Psychology* (London: SAGE, 2008).

29   Martha C. Nussbaum, *Upheavals of Thought: The Intelligence of Emotions* (Cambridge: Cambridge University Press, 2001).

30   Jean-Pierre Dupuy, "Invidious Sympathy in *The Theory of Moral Sentiments*", *Adam Smith Review* vol. 2, 2006, pp. 81–112.

31   Frans de Waal, *Primates and Philosophers: How Morality Evolved* (Princeton, NJ: Princeton University Press 2006); Frans de Waal, *The Age of Empathy: Nature's Lessons for a Kinder Society* (New York: Three Rivers Press 2010).

32   The Glasgow Edition of *TMS*, p. 268.

Some reflections on translating Adam Smith

Matti Norri

A translation is impossible, because of the different structures of different languages, because almost all words have many meanings with different allusions in different languages and, for other reasons, a fact that Martin Luther explained in his *Sendbrief vom Dolmetschen*.

How I translate?

- **First**: I get acquainted with the writer, or dictator, his character; e.g., when translating the Gospel of John I wrote sentence after sentence, three-quarters of the text, and after that I learned to know the old man. He was not the man I had known earlier from other translations or theological literature.
- **Second**: I sit in the environs he sits; e.g., when an eighteenth-century person writes to a friend that he will come to visit him single-handed, one must know that teamster and servant will follow.
- **Third**: I try to understand *what the writer tries to say*. To do that, I try to acquaint myself what was said before him and what he knew of it.

After this, the Finnish text creates itself. I cannot explain how. However, to illustrate this I use Smith's concept of shame.

Shame

Adam Smith spoke on jurisprudence on Friday, January 21st 1763. He said, of gratuitous promises, which at that time could not be legally enforced, 'It is without question a very improper and blameable piece of conduct for one to break thro his engagement, and such as he would be justly condemned for'.[1] In 1766, he said:

> The canon law, which judged from principles of honour and virtue, obliged men to perform even the promises that were made gratuitously. This was imitated by the civil law, and by our law if a promise be clearly proven he who promises must perform it.'[2]

So, *Smith means that morality is binding and any attempt at retreat will be scorned by others*. It is learned that Smith knew canon law (third). And the text tells of a world developing from a tribe community into an open society (second).

He had earlier written in the *Theory of Moral Sentiments* of the guilty feeling arising from a broken promise:

> The violator of the more sacred law of justice can never reflect on the sentiments which mankind must entertain with regard to him, without feeling all the agonies of shame, and horror, and consternation…By sympathizing with the hatred and abhorrence which other men must entertain for him, he becomes in some measure the object of his own hatred and abhorrence. The situation of the person, who suffered by his injustice, now calls upon his own conduct, and feels at the same time that they have rendered him the proper object of the resentment and indignation of mankind, and of what is the natural consequence of resentment, vengeance and punishment. The thought of this perpetually haunts him, and fills him with terror and amazement.[3]

I have been told that the style used by Smith is described by the Scottish as 'pawky', which could be called as 'drily humorous'. The word 'pawky' does not exist in the Finnish tongue. One must express that by means of the Finnish language.

Smith ponders the question and reverses it, when the promise is not given voluntarily but is forced:

> A highwayman, by the fear of death, obliges a traveler to promise him a certain sum of money. …It is to be observed…that whenever such promises are violated, though for the most necessary reasons, it is always with some degree of dishonour to the person who made them. After they are made, we may be convinced of the impropriety of observing them. But still there is some fault in having made them. It is at least a departure from the highest and noblest maxims of magnanimity and honour. …He appears to have been guilty of an action with which, in the imaginations of men, some degree of shame is inseparably connected.[4]

So, *Smith means: he who goes back on an obligation, installs a feeling of shame and guilt on himself.* The text tells of a world where highwaymen still existed (second). And we learn a lot about the man who dictated these words, a gentleman of a kind that scarcely exist today (first). That gives some hint what he means with shame. And this should be kept in mind when translating such words as propriety. If the text be translated unto modern English, would propriety translate propriety?

The subject matter of Smith's treatise are sentiments, feelings, passions, emotions. They are caused by impulses. The circumstances one lives in and the general and individual attitudes of a person have an effect on which sentiments are caused by certain impulses. Most certainly they are not the same today that they were for Smith, because of changed circumstances and attitudes. Thus, I had to peruse these three questions.

Terms

Answering the question 'What', relating and describing the facts, is no science. One must also seek an answer to 'Why'. Adam Smith answers the question: 'Why promises are kept?' Shame, that is, the fear of losing face, make us to keep our promises. If we do not do that, we dare no longer look society in the face but imagine ourselves as rejected and thrown out from the affections of all mankind.[5]

Adam Smith projected the theory of jurisprudence but he did not live to finish that work. I have tried to do it in some detail.[6] The following may seem to be far away from the theme of our discussion but I think it is not.

Influence of society's rules or custom

In Section V of the *Theory of Moral Sentiments*, Smith deliberated on the effects of custom and fashion on feelings of approval and rejection, finding that they generally do not have a particularly big effect, the effect is more devastating 'in the case of specific practices'.

Georg Simmel describes the 'mechanism' through which customs and fashion work in his *Die Mode*: 'The feeling of shame is in vogue, as it is mass action, smothered in the same way as the sense of responsibility in those participating in collective crimes, who in many cases would shudder at the act as individuals'.[7]

Custom may reduce the feeling of the shame that upholds the law. In this way, a custom may 'justify' violating another person's ownership and avoiding responsibility. The feeling of shame can be compared to 'brake' or 'retarder'. The latter expression is more correct, as the brake is not fully efficient.

On ownership

The brake fails with ownership and exchange for different reasons. It does not prevent stealing modest properties. A pharmacist steals medicines for himself and his family from the chemist with little remorse. Few people abstain from this sort of stealing, even if they might feel a little ashamed at first. People know that others steal in the same way and thus are not afraid of being exposed personally. Custom tones down the feeling of shame. But experience suggest that shame keeps four out of five people from stealing something bigger; the fifth is kept back only by the fear of punishment.

On promise

The retarder does not in all cases prevent the breaking of a major promise. Experience suggests that about one-fifth of people can, in this situation, smother their shame and invent a justification for rejecting to fulfil their commitments. In this case, custom has little bearing. On the contrary, the person breaking his engagement justifies his action, both to himself and others, by believing that it is justice which led him to contradict custom. Hardly anyone breaks a minor engagement. Shame prevents him from that.

By breaking a promise, 'every thing seems hostile, and he would be glad to fly to some inhospitable desert, where he might never more behold the face of a human creature, nor read in the countenance of mankind the condemnation of his crimes'.[8]

Trust is the point at issue. We trust that others will respect our property and that others will keep their promises. Trust is a feeling. In defining the foundation of morality, Kant describes a feeling that is unlike all the feelings and emotions connected with tendency or desire (that is affection) or fear (that is antipathy). It is a respect for moral law not simply for a person but following a moral law (*Grundlegung zur Metaphysik der Sitten*). Its motive is 'the very equity and merit of observing the laws of equity' (David Hume). The shame of having broken the law would have made it impossible to look straight into the eyes of another person. Losing one's face engenders the fear of shame.

Conclusion

Foundations of justice and law are enforced by shame, a concept of psychology. Custom, belonging to sociology, weakens the effect of shame.

Smith often uses the word 'justice' alone. I had to make this intellectual exercise to know when he means *lex*, when *ius* and when *iustitia*, and which of the meanings of *iustitia*, so that I can express the correct meaning in Finnish. As science advances, terms usually divide into subterms.

Notes

1   *Adam Smith, Lectures on Jurisprudence*, edited by R.L. Meek, D.D. Raphael and P.G. Stein, Oxford 1978, p. 95.
2   Ibid. p. 474.
3   *Adam Smith, The Theory of Moral Sentiments*, edited by K. Haakonssen, Cambridge 2002, pp. 98–9.
4   Ibid. pp. 392–3.
5   Ibid. p. 99.
6   Matti Norri; *Summa ius, Philosophical Treatise on the Foundations and Elements of Law*, Jyväskylä 2010.
7   Originally published as an essay, *Philosophie der Mode*, 1905, subsequently in *Philosophische Kultur*, 1923.
8   *Moral Sentiments*, p. 99.

The first Italian edition of Adam Smith's *Theory of Moral Sentiments*

The Italian philosophical milieu

Adelino Zanini

I

The first Italian edition of Adam Smith's *Theory of Moral Sentiments* (*TMS*) was published in 1991, by Istituto della Enciclopedia Italiana Treccani, one of the main Italian cultural institutions. In the following years, the new edition has been deemed as a point of reference and a stimulus for a new and more updated research on Smith's philosophical and economic thought in Italy. The translation has been considered as accurate and the interpretation advanced by the editor in his Introduction[1] has been widely discussed by scholars with different interests. Eugenio Garin stated that the publication represented an 'event' in the Italian philosophical landscape (Garin, 1991). Nevertheless, such an 'event' was made easier and viable because, in the period spanning the end of 1980s and the early 1990s, the Italian philosophical scene showed an increasing acceptance of empirical philosophy and ethics (Lecaldano 1991), which led also to the rediscovery of Adam Smith's philosophical work. In the same period of time, the seminal works by John A. Pocock and Quentin Skinner were translated, making it possible to extend the diffusion of a very 'different' interpretation of the Western political historiographical canon to a wider educated audience.

Until that moment, however, although Smith's economic work was well known among Italian scholars, *TMS* did not enjoy any significant fortune, nor was it regarded as worthy of notice by the large majority of Italian philosophers. This depended, first of all, on the particular climate of the Italian cultural scene during the nineteenth and the first half of the twentieth century – a scene very sceptical with respect to any form of philosophical empiricism, in particular, if applied to moral theory. Thus, in Italy, for almost two centuries, the foundations of an empiricist (and thus also the Smithian) ethical theory was considered as if it were based on unacceptable theoretical terrain, when not devoid of any interest whatsoever. It is true that the 'dialectics of distincts' advanced by Benedetto Croce (1900) entailed an interesting argumentation addressed to evaluate – rather than to set against – the differences between economy (matter of fact) and ethics (matter of value). In this way, however, the formal character of moral theory, its relationship with transcendental conditions, was simply reasserted, whereas the comprehension of the Smithian perspective, in particular, would have required a very different approach.

At that time, the specificity of the Italian situation was underlined by Ludovico Limentani, one of the few Italian philosophers who discussed in a noteworthy way Smithian ethics. In his *La Morale della Simpatia* (1914, p. viii), he noted that, notwithstanding the high number of Smith's Italian economic disciples, *TMS* was never considered as an object of research by any of them: 'It would be impossible to quote even a Smith's disciple alone in the ambit of morals'. Undoubtedly, this was the situation at the beginning of the twentieth century. Nevertheless, it did not change during the following decades, apart from a few but significant exceptions, represented, in particular, by the contributions of Eugenio Garin (1941), Luigi Bagolini (1952; 2nd ed., revised and extended, 1966) and Giulio Preti (1957). Their works remained isolated examples[2] until the beginning of the 1980s, when, also in Italy, a renaissance of interest in Adam Smith's philosophical thought took place.[3]

In the first part of this critical note, after a short review of the older but seminal contributions mentioned above, the essential outlines of current philosophical research on Smith's thought in Italy will be discussed. Then, in the second part, the main problems concerning the translation into Italian of *TMS* will be analysed by the translator.

II

Limentani's approach to *TMS* is based on the assumption that Smith's ethics are understandable from their 'syncretistic character', which is not, however, a negative connotation. More simply, it represents an 'happy synthesis' of the results reached by the past generations of philosophers. Undoubtedly, in Limentani's approach an explicit heritage of the late nineteenth century philosophical historio-graphy emerges[4] but that inheritance does not compromise the exact understanding of Smith's work. A 'syncretistic character' means that, also in *TMS*, the principle of the uniformity of human nature is a postulate 'tacitly admitted'. Consequently, if the tradition represented by the Scottish ethical thought is a pilaster of the architecture of *TMS*, nevertheless, the way in which Smith reformulates that tradition entails relevant differences, which have been adequately underlined by Limentani. As he correctly points out, the theory of passions (the distinction between social, selfish and unsocial passions) and the role played by sympathy pave the way for an original manner of intending moral approval or disapproval. This is particularly relevant if compared with the most mature results of the Scottish tradition of thought: Humean moral philosophy (Limentani, 1914, p. 44). Thus, although Limentani disputes the originality of Smith's ethics, he identifies the same topics defined by the most recent historiography as crucial: namely, sympathy as a criterion of moral approval or disapproval, the sense of duty and the relationships between benevolence, prudence and justice. Facing an historio-graphical tradition that was still discussing the so-called 'Adam Smith's Problem', Limentani's contribution would appear to be worthy of attention.

Following Limentani's argument, Eugenio Garin provides an articulate analysis concerning the 'moral of sympathy' in the English and Scottish Enlightenment. He clearly explains the evolution of the relationship between 'reason', 'sentiment' and 'human nature' by observing that, if in the first part of the eighteenth century nature was usually associated with reason, in the second half of the century it was associated with sentiment. Such a shift called for the primacy of social affections, which could be understood in the establishment of the pre-eminence of sensibility. In this context, Garin points out, in particular, the relationship between morality and natural religion from Cambridge Platonists to the end of the eighteenth century. In doing so, he asserts the originality of Smith's contribution to the ethical doctrine: a mundane ethics, which pays attention, first of all, to human relationships. As Smith affirms at the beginning of *TMS*, moral life has its fulcrum in the possibility of surpassing the mere interest of singular individuals.

> How selfish soever man may be supposed, there are evidently some principles in his nature, which interest him in the fortune of others, and render their happiness necessary to him, though he derives nothing from it except the pleasure of seeing it.
>
> (*TMS* I.i.i.1)

Therefore, even when the action reaches its accomplishment in a individual scope, what represents the good for us should be put in relation to the good of mankind as a whole (Garin, 1942, p. 226). As a consequence, hetero-evaluation and self-evaluation make possible a moral judgement which is related to the social dimension of human life. Nevertheless, as Garin affirms, judgement is not a mere 'image' produced by a sort of 'social mirror'. Exactly for this reason, mundane ethics requires a morality freed from factual contingency. Put differently, according to Bagolini (1966, p. 54), the relationship between 'the man within' and 'the man without' implies, at the same time, a more marked social character of the first in comparison with the second, and the impossibility of ignoring the latter. In fact, the 'abstractness' of the former requires the 'immediacy' of the latter. Briefly, the 'abstraction' made possible by the man within the breast needs the concrete existence of the real spectator.

> The man within the breast, the abstract and ideal spectator of our sentiments and conduct, requires often to be awakened and put in mind of his duty, by the presence of the real spectator: and it is always from that spectator, from whom we can expect the least sympathy and indulgence, that we are likely to learn the most complete lesson of self-command.
>
> (*TMS* III.3.38)

Hence, by following his own line of reasoning, Bagolini takes into consideration the relationship existing among the general rules of morality and justice. He underlines, first of all, Smith's insistency upon the 'social necessity' of the juridical rule: the main pillar that upholds 'the immense fabric of human society' (*TMS* II.ii.3.4). However, given that this social necessity is at the same time related by Smith to the absolute, unconditioned and cosmic necessity expressed by the will of deity, Bagolini notes also that a sort of contradiction could be found here. How can one compare what is related to a 'social dimension' with 'a superior instance' of justice, which is, *ex definitione*, absolute? (Bagolini, 1966, pp, 72–73).

Regarding this, after having identified the weakness of *TMS* both in the absence of a transcendental horizon and in the affirmation of an ethicism as established social ethos, Giulio Preti, moving from the phenomenological tradition of thought, notes that in Smith, the ethics of sentiments – as it is a social disposition, *lex naturae*, distinct, if not opposed to juridical norm – is doomed to generate a contradiction as soon as 'the harmonic circle of sentiment' is under check, being unable to resolve itself in positive justice, and being forced to appeal to an infallible judge as a last resort. Here the 'theological hat' becomes inevitable. After the attempt to establish an ethics without theology, Preti concludes, Smith should surrender to the fact of 'being unable to achieve his aim' (Preti, 1957, pp.149–65).

III

This was the Italian philosophical scene within which Smith's *TMS* had been read until that moment. A scene that showed how difficult it was to comprehend the way in which Smith transposes the *micro* ethical dimension – where moral judgements are formed – into the *macro* one: namely, how difficult it was to understand the mechanisms of transforming the individual ethical dimension 'into rules of behaviour which are perceived and obeyed by society at large' (Skinner, 1979, p. 63). We are here in the presence of a transposition that is implicit in what David D. Raphael (1985, p. 5) defines as 'morality as a social phenomenon'.

From the very outset, it is clear that this is a seminal issue, posited at the centre of a critical discussion that, although not recent, is nevertheless still essential. As is well known, at the beginning of the 1920s, it was Max Scheler (1973, vol. 7, pp. 17–18) who noted, for example, that because Smith's *moral value* can only be deduced by the judgement of impartial spectator who reacts emotively to the experience and behaviour of others – the ethics of sympathy always seems to assume what it wants to infer. Consequently – Scheler concluded we are faced with a presupposed ethical deduction, with a social ethics without foundations. Deprived of its moral dynamism, however, ethics loses its universal connotation. Similarly, Preti would argue that Smith's analyses are confined to the sphere of ethical taste, that is, to the *ethos* itself, to the custom of an epoch and of a social class (Preti, 1957, p. 100). As a result, this means that mundane ethics would coincide with a kind of unproblematic 'ethicism'.

In introducing *TMS*, I have attempted to confute a similar conclusion, which finds its roots in Scheler's phenomenology. Smith's ethics – 'morality as a social phenomenon' – certainly requires a universal system of values, but not a transcendental one. Exactly for this reason, that system represents the philosophical background without which it would be hard to grasp Smith's relevance in the Scottish and European intellectual landscapes. Only a mundane, ethical approach can indeed outline the relationship between virtue and commerce and its synthetic representation *par excellence*: the market. This latter is an anthropological correlation, which reveals the inefficacy of the moral sense, as well as the aberration of the selfish system. Therefore, the difference between 'self-interest' and 'selfishness' plays a fundamental role (Roncaglia, 1995, p. 7). And along this path – already delineated by Enzo Pesciarelli, by introducing the Italian edition of the *Lectures on Jurisprudence* (1989) – one may say that the prudent man reveals in what the 'mundane value' of Smith's 'ethicism' consists. As Pesciarelli (1989, p. xxvii) points out, 'the multiplication of the number of prudent men within a social system would represent the best guarantee of the spreading of impartial and, exactly for this reason, concretely propaedeutic mechanisms, able to establish a system of natural liberty.'

Surely, within this 'system', taking into account the differences between positive, inferior, and negative virtues, the rules of justice embody the *extrema ratio* of 'the immense fabric of human society'. Hence, as Andrea Villani notes (1994, p. 220), the crucial role of justice and the related concept of injury can be considered in relation to both natural jurisprudence and a system of positive justice. But, if this is true, it cannot be denied that the absence of a (possible) distinction entails some relevant theoretical problems (Zanini, 2008, pp. 82–94).

As Gloria Vivenza, whose research on Adam Smith's debt with classic culture is well known (1984; 2001), correctly points out, Smith seems to have had in mind 'not only the "negative character" of justice, but also the search for general principles upon which all systems of law should be grounded'. Thus, apart from any phenomenological and 'anachronistic' reasoning, the typical aporias characterizing the nexus nature/society in the Age of Enlightenment affect Smith's very theory of justice.

Nevertheless, what is more relevant in Smith's work is that justice and politics proceed together. In fact, as Donald Winch's and Knud Haakonssen's seminal contributions have shown, their synthesis is represented by 'the science of a legislator', which is the fulcrum of Smith's political and economic thought. The explicit cognizance of the significance of this synthesis also characterizes current research on Smith's thought in Italy.

Vivenza observes, for instance, that, albeit the promised treatise on natural jurisprudence did not see the light of day, the distinction between utilitarian and more strictly jurisprudential aspects (defined by Smith with regard to 'police, revenue and arms') does not rest on a utilitarian foundation; 'rather it originates from disapproval at seeing an evil deed committed and satisfaction at seeing injustice punished'. According to Sergio Cremaschi (2005), far from being a utilitarian, Smith was a semi-sceptical philosopher, upholder of a pluralistic normative ethics, based on the virtues of prudence, justice, and benevolence. Briefly, far from being the putative 'father' of capitalism, Smith could be considered as the 'father' of liberal left and the 'grandfather' of the opponents to globalization. Further, the reference to Adam Smith's theory of justice appears to be fundamental also in those Italian authors who, moving from the necessity of going beyond the Adam Smith's paradigm, in which, they say, the *alter* is never considered as if he were one of the two terms of a 'friendly relationship', assert the primacy of a relational economy (*economia civile*), in which the sentiment of 'gratuity' cannot be disjoined from 'market' (Zamagni and Bruni, 2003; Bruni, 2010).

In conclusion, it is possible to note that the crescent attention devoted in Italian philosophical and economic scene to Adam Smith's *TMS* has been confirmed by the interest shown with regard to the relationship between ethics, economics, and justice by the academic research in recent years – even along with the ever more widespread diffusion of the works by Amartya Sen on the same topics. Certainly, Italian scholars did not need the publication of the Italian translation of *TMS* to be cognisant of the relevance of Adam Smith's philosophical thought. In a sense, however, one may say that the Italian edition, by making a neglected book available to a larger educated audience, worked as a stimulus (first of all, for economists) to reconsider the articulated thought of the (erroneously) supposed 'father' of political economy.

Some remarks concerning the Italian translation

Cesare Cozzo

I

A translator should take reader interests into account. Intelligibility is the reader interest which takes priority when translating a philosophical text. If a text is systematic and the translation blurs its systematicity, its intelligibility is also compromised. The systematic nature of *TMS* seemed to me manifest (as it still does today). Essential to a systematic work is a consistent terminology. I therefore considered it important to preserve this terminological rigour. To this end, I made an effort to keep my translation as uniform as possible.

It often happens that a translator, to avoid repetitions or for other stylistic reasons, fails to translate a word uniformly. If the word in question is theoretically irrelevant and a deviation from uniformity makes the translation more elegant, this choice may be laudable. If a word plays a theoretical role in the text to be translated, however, translating that word with two or more different words or phrases makes the translation less intelligible and obviously misleading.

The ideal uniformity is a one-to-one correspondence between the theoretically relevant translated words and the correspondent translating words: if the translation is from English into Italian, *the same* Italian word Y in the translation should always correspond to each occurrence of the relevant English word W in the original text and *every* occurrence of Y in the translation should correspond to an occurrence of W in the original text. Of course, the policy of ideal uniformity is limited by certain contextual constraints imposed by the target language. For example, the English word *feeling* should in many contexts be translated by the word *sensazione*. Were this true in all contexts, uniformity could be fully respected: the Italian *sensazione* would translate *feeling* and the Italian *sentimento* would translate the English *sentiment*. But *sensazione* can have physical, bodily overtones that *sentimento* lacks. As a consequence, there are contexts where we cannot use *sensazione* without undesired effects, and where *sentimento* is clearly a far better translation of *feeling*. These contexts necessitate a deviation from uniformity.

II

In the Appendix at the end of this chapter, the reader can find a list of all the terms I deemed to be theoretically relevant and the corresponding Italian translations.

Three of these, *affect*, *fellow-feeling*, and *propriety* are, in my opinion, particularly problematic for an Italian translator. Therefore my choice requires some explanatory comments.

A non-uniform translation of *to affect* would conceal the theoretical role of this notion, which is not negligible. In order to appreciate the sense of this Smithian term it is worth citing some passages of *TMS*.

> As we have no immediate experience of what other men feel, we can form no idea of the manner in which they are affected...It is the impressions of our senses only...which our imaginations copy
>
> (*TMS* I.i.i.2)

> ...we are chiefly affected by those circumstances which strike our senses
>
> (*TMS* I.i.i.13).

> ...as soon as he comes from considering the object, to observe how I am affected by it, according as there is more or less disproportion between his sentiments and mine
>
> (*TMS* I.i.3.1).

> ...the painfulness of that sorrow with which the view of his situation affects us
>
> (*TMS* I.i.2.6)

> ...proportion or disproportion which the affection seems to bear to the cause or object which excites it
>
> (*TMS* I.i.3.6).

> ...analogous to the external senses. As the bodies around us, by affecting these in a certain manner
>
> (*TMS* VII.iii.3.5).

From these passages, we can conclude that, for Smith, the verb *to affect* denotes a relation obtaining between external perceptible non-mental objects or circumstances and a human being in whose mind a sensible impression, sentiment or feeling is aroused, which Smith sometimes calls *affection* (cf. e.g. *TMS* I.i.3.5 and I.i.3.6). The external object or circumstance is a cause of the corresponding affection.

It is clear that the verb *to affect* plays a significant role in Smith's moral theory. To highlight this role a uniform translation is necessary, but the choice of a suitable Italian word is not obvious. One might translate *to affect*, like the Kantian *affizieren*, with the Italian *affettare* or with *modificare*. The former is sometimes used by Giacomo Leopardi in a sense similar to that of *to affect* in Smith's *Theory*. But this choice has at least two flaws. The first is that, in today's spoken Italian, *affettare* in this sense has very old-fashioned literary overtones. The second flaw is an embarrassing ambiguity: *affettare* has many meanings in Italian, even more than *to affect* in English. It can be translated *to affect, to feign, to pretend*, but it also has the meaning *to slice*, which can give rise to odd associations of ideas. *Modificare*, the usual Italian translation of *to modify*, on the other hand, is overly generic and vague. It blurs the specific character of Smith's notion which, as the above passages show, is rather clear-cut. I thus considered and discarded *affettare* and *modificare* and decided to translate *to affect* with the Italian verb *impressionare*. This choice was not without hesitation: the verb *impressionare* can well express the causal relation that intervenes when an external circumstance arouses a feeling in a person, but translating *to affect* with *impressionare* loses the kinship with *affection* (translated *affezione*) and creates a new connection between *impressionare* and *impressione* (which translates *impression*). In the end, I came to the conclusion that this change was harmless. The Italian reader, however, should not forget that the mental correlate of the relation denoted by *impressionare* is not necessarily a sensory feeling: it can be a sentiment, like sorrow.

The crucial term *fellow-feeling* appears already in the first pages of *The Theory of Moral Sentiments*, in a passage where Smith connects it with *pity, compassion* and *sympathy*.

> Pity and compassion are words appropriated to signify our fellow-feeling with the sorrow of others. Sympathy, though its meaning was, perhaps, originally the same, may now, however, without much impropriety, be made use of to denote our fellow-feeling with any passion whatever.
>
> (*TMS* I.i.i.5)

In a note to this passage, the editors D. D. Raphael and A. L. Macfie, call it 'Smith's unusually wide definition of "sympathy"'. If this is a definition, the translator should be careful to preserve the distinction between *definiens* and *definiendum*. Therefore *fellow-feeling* cannot be translated with the Italian *simpatia*, which translates *sympathy*. Nor should it be translated *comprensione*, as Ida Cappiello sometimes did.[5] *Comprensione* is the translation of *understanding*, a much broader concept. Therefore translating *fellow-feeling* with *comprensione* would have been likely to engender confusion. The translation chosen, *sentimento di partecipazione*, which literally means *feeling of participation*, seems a good choice because it captures the concept with sufficient precision without losing the connection with *feeling*, translated by the Italian *sentimento*.

The third term, *propriety*, expresses a key-notion applied to both actions and feelings. I tried to apply the methodological principle of translating English words belonging to a certain lexical family with words belonging to a corresponding family of Italian words that can be considered analogous. *Propriety* belongs to the same family as *proper, improper*, and *impropriety*. So, I translated *propriety* with *appropriatezza* and the other words with *appropriato, inappropriato*, and *inappro-*

priatezza, respectively. The fact that Smith often associates *proper* with *suitable* (translated *adeguato*) confirms that *appropriatezza* is an apt choice. Other possible translations of *propriety* might be *convenienza* or *proprietà*. The Italian word *convenienza* is misleadingly suggestive of pragmatic or utilitarian qualities (besides being more remote than *appropriatezza* from the English *propriety*). The other word, *proprietà*, might give rise to misunderstandings because it is already the obvious translation of *property* and because the corresponding adjective *proprio* is the translation of *own* (as in 'one's own'). Where the propriety of actions, feelings or sentiments is concerned, my translation is thus *appropriatezza*. This is the most common sense of *propriety* and related words in *TMS*. Less frequently, however, *propriety*, *proper*, *improper*, and *impropriety* refer to the correctness or incorrectness of linguistic usage. For example, in the passage quoted above, Smith writes that sympathy (and he means the word 'sympathy') may be used 'without much impropriety' to denote fellow feeling. In this different sense it seemed to me preferable (and in agreement with current Italian usage) to translate this family of words with *proprietà*, *proprio*, *improprio*, and *improprietà*, respectively.

III

This short note is not a thorough inquiry but only an illustration of some problems arising in an Italian translation of *TMS*. By way of a conclusion, I shall add a few remarks concerning the interest of a possible more detailed study. In my opinion, the interest of an inquiry into a translation lies not so much in the translation itself as in the many issues disclosed by analysing the choices facing the translator. Some of these issues are very general and transcend even the content of the translated text. One cannot deny, for example, that, since translation aims at preserving meaning, the general question concerning the very nature of meaning sometimes emerges. But there are also many specific issues concerning the original text which would have been passed over, if the task of translating or the critical assessment of a translation had not drawn attention to them. The above-described problems posed by the translation of *to affect* raise interesting questions regarding Smith's philosophy of mind. I believe that many other facets of Smith's work can be highlighted by an inquiry into translation problems. Italo Calvino wrote: 'authors are only read properly when they are translated, or one can compare the original text with its translations, or compare different versions in more than one language'.[6] Calvino's words, paradoxical as they may seem, contain much truth. He was dealing with a literary translation of Edward M. Forster's novel, *A Passage to India*, but the same may be said about Adam Smith's philosophical work.

Notes

1   Cf. also Zanini 1995, 1997.
2   But see also P. Salvucci 1966.
3   See, among others, Cremaschi 1984, Pesciarelli 1988, Lecaldano 1995, Fiori 2001, and Zanini 1995; 1997; 2008.
4   Cf. Leslie 1876, II, p. 70.

5   A partial Italian translation of *TMS* appeared in the anthology *Morale dei sentimenti e ricchezza delle nazioni*, Ital. Transl. by I. Cappiello, Guida, Naples 1974.
6   I. Calvino, *Letters 1941–1985*, intr. by M. Wood, English transl. by M. MacLaughlin, Princeton University Press, Princeton 2013, p. 248.

Bibliography

Bagolini, L. (1952) *La Simpatia nella Morale e nel Diritto*, Giappichelli, Turin (2nd ed., revised and extended, 1966).

Bruni, L. (2010) *L'Ethos del Mercato*, B. Mondadori, Milan.

Calvino, I. (2013) *Letters 1941–1985*, intr. by M. Wood, Eng. transl. by M. MacLaughlin, Princeton, NJ: Princeton University Press.

Croce, B. (1900) *Filosofia della Pratica*, Laterza, Bari.

Cremaschi, S. (1984) *Il Sistema della Ricchezza*, F. Angeli, Milan.

Cremaschi, S. (2005) 'Adam Smith antiutilitarista,' *La Società degli Individui*, 24: 17–32.

Fiori, S. (2001) *Ordine, Mano Invisibile, Mercato: Una Rilettura di Adam Smith*, Utet, Turin.

Garin, E. (1942) *L'illuminismo Inglese. I Moralisti*, Bocca, Milan.

Garin, E. (1991) 'La morale della simpatia,' *L'Indice*, p. 5.

Haakonssen, K. (1981) *The Science of a Legislator: The Natural Jurisprudence of David Hume and Adam Smith*, Cambridge University Press, Cambridge.

Lecaldano, E. (1991) *Hume e la Nascita dell'Etica Contemporanea*, Rome-Bari, Laterza.

Lecaldano, E. (1995) *Introduzione*, in A. Smith, *Teoria dei Sentimenti Morali*, Ital. transl. by S. Di Pietro, Rizzoli, Milan.

Leslie, S. (1876) *The History of English Thought in the Eighteenth Century*, Smith, Elder, London.

Limentani, L. (1914) *La Morale della Simpatia: Saggio sopra l'Etica di Adamo Smith nella Storia del Pensiero Inglese*, Formiggini, Genoa.

Pesciarelli, E. (1988) *La Jurisprudence Economica di Adam Smith*, Giappichelli, Turin.

Pesciarelli, E. (1989) *Introduzione*, in A. Smith, *Lezioni di Glasgow*, Ital. transl. by V. Zompanti Oriani, E. Pesciarelli, Giuffrè (ed.), Milan.

Preti, L. (1957) *Alle Origini dell'Etica Contemporanea: Adamo Smith*, La Nuova Italia, Florence.

Raphael, D.D. (1985) *Adam Smith*, Oxford University Press, Oxford.

Roncaglia, A. (1995) 'Introduzione' in A. Smith, *La Ricchezza delle Nazioni*, Ital. transl. by F. Bartoli, C. Camporesi, S. Caruso, Newton, Rome.

Salvucci, P. (1966) *La Filosofia Politica di Adam Smith*, Argalia, Urbino.

Scheler, M. (1973) *Wesen und Formen der Sympathie* (1923), *Gesammelte Werke*, hrsg. von M. S. Frings, Francke, Bern und München, Bd. 7.

Skinner, A.S. (1979) *A System of Social Science*, Clarendon Press, Oxford.

Smith, A. (1976) *The Theory of Moral Sentiments*, D.D. Raphael and A.L. Macfie (eds), Clarendon Press, Oxford.

Smith, A. (1991) *Teoria dei Sentimenti Morali*, Ital. transl. by C. Cozzo by A. Zanini (ed.), Istituto della Enciclopedia Italiana Treccani, Rome.

Smith, A. (1974) *Morale dei Sentimenti e Ricchezza delle Nazioni*, Ital. transl. by I. Cappiello, Guida, Naples.

Villani, A. (1994) *Gli Economisti, la Distribuzione, la Giustizia*. Adam Smith e John Stuart Mill, F. Angeli, Milan.

Vivenza, G. (1984) *Adam Smith e la Cultura Classica*, Ipem, Pisa.

Vivenza, G. (2001) *Adam Smith and the Classics: The Classical Heritage in Adam Smith's Thought*, Oxford University Press, Oxford.

Vivenza, G. (2010) 'Justice as a virtue, justice as a principle in Adam Smith's thought,' *Revista Empresa y Humanismo*, 13 (1): 297–332.

Winch, D. (1978) *Adam Smith's Politics: An Essay In Historiographic Revision*, Cambridge University Press, Cambridge.

Zamagni, S. (2003) Bruni, L., *Lezioni di Economia Civile*, Editoriale Vita, Milan.

Zanini, A. (1995) *Genesi Imperfetta. Il Governo delle Passioni in Adam Smith*, Giappichelli, Turin.

Zanini, A. (1997) *Adam Smith: Economia, Morale, Diritto*, B. Mondadori, Milan.

Zanini, A. (2008) *Economic Philosophy. Economic Foundations and Political Categories*, Peter Lang, Oxford.

Appendix: a list of theoretically relevant terms and their translations

to affect = *impressionare*
affection = *affezione, affetto, sentimento*
agent = *colui che compie l'azione*
agreeable = *gradevole*
agreement = *accordo*
amiable = amabile
approbation = *approvazione*
to approve = *approvare*
atonement = *espiazione*
attachment = *attaccamento, affetto*
becoming = *conveniente, acconcio*
beneficence = *beneficenza*
beneficient = *benefico*
benefit = *beneficio*
benevolent = *benevolo*
care = *cura*
concern = *preoccupazione, interesse, cura*
concord = *concordanza*
compassion = *compassione*
correspondence = *corrispondenza*
demerit = *demerito*
desert, good desert = *encomiabilità*
ill dessert = *colpevolezza*
desire = *desiderio*
disagreement = *disaccordo*
disgrace = *vergogna, disonore*
dissonance = *dissonanza*
distress = *angustia, angoscia, disperazione*
emotion = *emozione*
to enter into = *prender parte a, immedesimarsi in*
to excite = *suscitare*

esteem = *stima*
to feel = *sentire, provare*
feeling = *sentimento, sensazione*
fellow-feeling = *sentimento di partecipazione*
fit = *adeguato*
fitness = *adeguatezza*
generosity = *generosità*
to go along with = *seguire, condividere*
graceful = *leggiadro, garbato*
grief = *angoscia, tristezza*
hatred = *odio*
humanity = *umanità*
impartial spectator = *spettatore imparziale*
impression = *impressione*
improper = *inappropriato*
impropriety = *inappropriatezza*
injury = *offesa, danno, torto*
inmate = *compagno interno*
joy = *gioia*
justice = *giustizia*
kindness = *gentilezza*
malevolent = *malevolo*
manhood = *atteggiamento virile, virilità*
man within the breast = *uomo interno*
mediocrity = *medietà*
merit = *merito*
mind = *mente*
mischief = *danno, male*
misery = *infelicità, sofferenza, miseria*
offence = *offesa, delitto*
offender = *offensore*
order = *categoria, ordine*
pain = *dolore, pena*
passion = *passione*
perception = *percezione*
person principally concerned = *persona direttamente interessata*
pity = *pietà*
pride = *orgoglio*
proper = *appropriato*
propriety = *appropriatezza*
proportion = *proporzione*
regret = *rammarico*
resentment = *risentimento*
respectable = *rispettabile*
revenue = *reddito*

right (substantive) = *diritto*
right (adjective) = *giusto*
romance = *racconto sentimentale, romanzo*
romantic = *romantico*
self-approbation = *autoapprovazione*
self-denial = *abnegazione*
self-command = *autocontrollo*
self-estimation = *autostima*
self-government = *autonomia*
self-interest = *interesse egoistico*
selfish = *egoistico*
selfishness = *egoismo*
self-love = *amor di sé*
sentiment = *sentimento*
sensation = *sensazione*
societies (plural) = *comunità*
society (singular) = *società*
sorrow = *dispiacere, dolore*
suitable = i
suitableness = *adeguatezza*
supposed impartial spectator = *ipotetico spettatore imparziale*
sympathy = *simpatia*
vain = *vanitoso*
vanity = *vanità*
wish = *desiderio*
wrong (substantive) = *torto*
wrong (adjective) = *erroneo, sbagliato*

The translation into Spanish of the *Theory of Moral Sentiments* by Adam Smith

Estrella Trincado

Introduction

This chapter examines the influence of the Spanish translation of the book by Adam Smith, *The Theory of Moral Sentiments* (*TMS*), through the demand–supply model for the transfer of ideas. With regard to Adam Smith's moral ideas, there has been a double impulse, in terms of both supply and demand, as a result of some specific features of the translation itself. So, first I look at the background in terms of the translation into Spanish of Adam Smith's books. I then go on to develop the supply and demand model for the transfer of ideas, using as an example the translation of the *TMS* and examine the influence that this "supply" has had on Spanish-speaking countries. Finally, we will focus on the long-running debate about the translation and use of the word *sympathy* in the Smithian context and the misleading translation of the word *propriety* in the Spanish version.

The Spanish translation of *The Theory of Moral Sentiments*

Spanish translations of *The Wealth of Nations* date back to late eighteenth-century Spain (Schwartz, 1990, 2001, Calderón 2000).[1] This is due to the early arrival and reception of the book in Spain (Perdices 1999, Schwartz 2000, Smith 1957).[2] On the contrary, the *TMS* was fully translated into Spanish for the first time in 1997. This translation, *La Teoría de los Sentimientos Morales* (*TSM*), by Carlos Rodríguez Braun published as *el libro de bolsillo* (paperback) in Madrid by the publishing house Alianza Editorial, had its second edition in 2004 (in 596 pages).

As Rodríguez Braun (Smith 1997, 7) says, this asymmetry reflects the mistaken perception among Spaniards – and among other people – that Smith was an unrestricted free-market champion defending the invisible hand; or even an extreme liberal championing ruthless capitalism and the individual selfish interest.[3] Actually, this interpretation has been the cause and the consequence of errors in the translation of Adam Smith's *The Wealth of Nations* into Spanish, with Gabriel Franco in Smith (1992, 17) translating self-love as *egoísmo* (selfishness) instead of *amor propio*, which is the correct translation.[4] This confusion still continues in some discussions about Adam Smith.[5]

There was another incomplete translation of the *TMS* in 1934, with a second edition in 1941, by *El Colegio de México* in the collection *Textos Clásicos de*

Filosofía of the *Fondo de Cultura Económica* (166 pages).[6] This translation by Edmundo O'Gorman contained an introduction by the philosopher Eduardo Nicol.[7] The publishing house issued this translation again in 1979 and in 2004.[8] The foreword in the 1934 translation considers Smith's theory as part of the English moralist movement and as a minor genre of the French Enlightenment, comparing Smith's theory to Pascal's moral theory and according it a minor role (Smith 1934, 14).

However, the translation by Carlos Rodríguez Braun is much more accurate, being accompanied by a foreword that rightly classifies Smith's work as being part of the Scottish Enlightenment movement. Rodríguez Braun defends the falseness of *Das Adam Smith Problem* and the more questionable idea that Smith was a 'contemplative utilitarian', as argued by I. S. Ross, and that he was a conservative (Smith 1997, 24). So, Rodríguez Braun is assuming that Adam Smith's theory is part of the conservative utilitarianism credo.

Then, all of Adam Smith's published works are now available in Spanish – *La Riqueza and Teoría de los Sentimientos Morales* from Alianza Editorial and *Essays in Philosophical Subjects (Ensayos Filosóficos)* translated in 1998 in Ediciones Pirámide, all these three by Carlos Rodríguez Braun. There is also a Spanish translation of *Lectures on Jurisprudence (Lecciones sobre Jurisprudencia)* in 1995 from the publishing house Comares.[9] Still, the *Lectures on Rethoric* have yet to be translated. For the Spanish bibliography on Adam Smith, see Reeder and Cardoso (2002).

Demand and supply of ideas

Two and a half centuries went by, after *TMS* was first published in London and Edinburgh in 1759, before demand arose in Spain for a translation of the book. This book on ethics by Adam Smith was translated in a decade when liberal policies were being introduced into Spain and into Europe in general, precisely after the fall of the Berlin wall in 1989. Before the 1990s, Smith, in the eyes of the Spanish, was a champion of capitalism. During the 1990s, many sectors that had traditionally been monopolies, such as energy, telecommunications, post and air transport, were liberalized in Spain (Bel, Calzada and Fageda 2006). It is tempting to draw the conclusion that something of a moral justification for capitalism was added to the translation.[10] According to this argument, the translation ought to make the Spaniards learn that the liberal Adam Smith saw sympathy and benevolence as sentiments that moved human beings.

Prior to this, demand for the translation was scarce. Smith was only a familiar figure to economists and economists did not have much interest in classical liberal ethics.[11] Furthermore, the role of capitalism was very limited in Spain during the nineteenth century, when there was still an *ancien regime* (Álvarez Junco 1996, 90). The Franco dictatorship after the Civil War (1936–1975) meant the absolute triumph of the corporatist regime and "Catholic Spain" at the expense of more modern elements (Casanova 1994, 81). Changes in its society and its entry into the European Union in 1986 reinforced the position of Spain as part of a democratic

Europe, but a socialist government then came into power. It was not until the centre-right People's Party, led by José María Aznar, won the Spanish elections of 1996 and 2000 that liberal capitalism was seen in Spain as an acceptable system of government. Latin American countries have seen a similar evolution, with the acceptance of liberalism being even more recent.

Religious and philosophical beliefs are part of the issue here. As in other Mediterranean countries, in Spain, educated people were sceptical about any form of philosophical empiricism, especially if applied to moral theory (see Trincado and Ramos 2011). It is noteworthy that the foreword in the 1941 edition of the *TSM* reads "Undoubtedly, truth is absolute and it can only be absolute; but it is not so clear if, being absolute, it must be universal and timeless" (Smith 1941). As mentioned above, Nicol places Smith among the "English moralists" and says that possibly "none of them possess the brilliant insight and the deep human sense of a Pascal" (Smith 1934, 14). He points out that Englishmen pay attention to the actual man and that "in that attention they never reach very remote depths of the human heart, but they move in a general, very British, way involving seriousness and good sense".

However, the publishing house Alianza sold 500 copies a year of the *TSM* translated in 1997; 70 per cent of these were sold in Spain, with the remaining 30 per cent sold in Latin America. Sales were concentrated in cities with universities, particularly Madrid and Barcelona, probably because it was recommended reading on the syllabus of some courses at some universities. The volume of sales has been erratic but sales have increased modestly over the last five years.

This may be in contradiction with the above-mentioned hypothesis that the translation of the *TMS* has been set in Spain as a justification of capitalism: anti-liberals have made a big impact on politics with the president Zapatero's socialist government and especially after the 2007 crisis. So, looking at the more recent sales records of the *TSM*, we may think that, perhaps, Rodriguez Braun's excellent translation was simply a spontaneous phenomenon. But the truth is that the publication of the *TSM* implied a significant break with tradition in Spain. The enormous influence of Kantian philosophy, in particular via the ethics of the German idealist philosopher Krause, in some cases considered a counter-paradigm to utilitarianism, made it really hard for the alleged utilitarian ideas to be spread in Spain. Actually, the general rejection of utilitarianism significantly predated Krausist ideas, owing to Thomist influences and the idealism championed by the Spanish "national hero" Don Quixote.[12] The situation did not change much through most of the twentieth century, as the Franco regime made confined philosophy to those creeds sanctioned by the political power. However, something changed in 1989, when the right-wing Spanish party, Alianza Popular, which was initially headed by a former minister of the Franco regime, was renamed "Partido Popular" (People's Party). Then, the People's Party, under the sway of liberal conservatism ideas, backed different conservative organizations, such as the *Fundación para el Análisis y los Estudios Sociales*, nurturing the population with a liberal creed. In 1996, José María Aznar gained control of government. The translation of the *TMS* was published in 1997.

Influence

While it is certain that there was demand for the Spanish translation of the *TSM*, it is also true that the translation has influenced Spanish-speaking societies. Over the first decade of the twenty-first century, three different centres of Smithian thinking have been created in Spanish speaking countries.

The first is Madrid, where there has been a long tradition of liberal economic historians with utilitarian and liberal ideas. This tradition revolves around the teachings of Pedro Schwartz from Madrid Complutense University, who, after having studied at the London School of Economics, wrote a doctoral dissertation, tutored by Lionel Robbins, called "Aspects of the Theory of Economic and Social Policy in the Works of John Stuart Mill". Schwartz has published articles on Adam Smith's morality and influence in Spain (see Schwartz 1978, 1990, 1992, 2000, 2001). He has founded three "think tanks" in Spain, the Instituto de Economía de Mercado, the Centro de Economía Liberal-Conservador and the Instituto de Estudios de Libre Comercio. He is also President of Honour of the Sociedad Ibéroamericana de Estudios Utilitaristas. This society studies utilitarian ethics and carries out research in A Coruña (northwest of Spain), where there are scholars of Smith's moral theory (see Pena and Sánchez Santos 2006, 2007). Madrid is also home to Carlos Rodríguez Braun, an economist born in Argentina and the aforementioned translator of Smith's books, who has had a long career as a proponent of liberal economic and moral theory. He has run a course on Adam Smith ethics at the Complutense University of Madrid and at the Universidad Católica Argentina in Buenos Aires. He has also published on Smithian theory and influence (see Rodríguez Braun 1984, 1989, 1992, 1997, 2006). John Reeder, the editor of *Contemporary Responses to TMS* (Reeder 1997) also lectures at this university, as does Luis Perdices, who has studied the influence of classical economists on Spanish economists (see Perdices and Fuentes 1997, Perdices 2000a, 2000b, Perdices and Reeder 2003, 2010). In this context, Estrella Trincado presented a doctoral dissertation on Adam Smith which constituted a criticism of the extended idea that Smith was a utilitarian (see Trincado 2003a and 2011); that dissertation was the basis for an article which led to her being awarded the History of Economic Analysis Award 2005 by the European Society for the History of Economic Thought (Trincado 2004). She has also published about Adam Smith ethics and economics (Trincado 2001, 2003b, 2005, 2006, 2007, 2008, 2009). Also in Madrid, Rey Juan Carlos University has an active group of people spreading the word about liberalism. There, the Instituto Juan de Mariana, founded in 2005, disseminates classical economics and has Gabriel Calzada as its president. It also publishes a journal, *Procesos de Mercado. Revista Europea de Economía Política,* edited by the liberal publishing house *Unión Editorial* (created in 1973 and with Promoción Exportación y Márketing Editorial as a wholesaler in Argentina) and directed by the Austrian school economist Jesús Huerta de Soto.

The second centre of Smithian thinking is the University of Navarre, a privately owned university in the north of Spain, linked to the Catholic Church, which has a research group based around Miguel Alfonso Martínez-Echevarría (see Martínez-Echevarría 2004). There, the Instituto Empresa y Humanismo, founded in 1986, publishes a series of journals, such as *Revista Empresa y Humanismo* and *Cuadernos de Empresa y Humanismo,* with contributions from scholars such as Lázaro Cantero (2001), Scalzo (2009) or Carrión (2008).

Finally, a third centre of Smithian thinking exists in Latin America, particularly in Guatemala, Chile and Argentina. In Argentina, the Centro Adam Smith de Estudios y Actividades para la Libertad, which belongs to the Fundación Libertad, was founded and they now publish the electronic journal *Orden Espontáneo.* The Francisco Marroquín University in Guatemala actively promotes debate on Adam Smith and liberalism; there, Leonidas Montes, and even Gabriel Calzada and Carlos Rodríguez Braun themselves, have disseminated Smithian economics and morals. Leon Montes is dean of the Adolfo Ibáñez University in Chile and has published an important body of work relating to Smith; he published the influential *Adam Smith in Context* (Montes 2004a) and edited *New Voices of Adam Smith* (Montes and Schliesser 2006a) and also published widely (Montes 2003a, 2003b, 2004b,c, 2006a,b,c,d 2008a,b,c, 2009). He is an advisor for the journal *Estudios Públicos*, to which three more Spanish-speaking academics have contributed articles on Adam Smith: Jimena Hurtado-Prieto, lecturer at the University of the Andes, Bogotá, Colombia (see also Hurtado-Prieto 2003a,b, 2004, 2005, 2006a,b,c); María Alejandra Carrasco and María Elton, lecturers in Chile and with PhDs from the University of Navarre (see Carrasco 2004, 2006, 2009 and Elton 1989, 2006, 2009).

As we see, most of Smithian works in Spain have been published after the publication of the *TSM* translation in 1997; since then, not only has the book been demanded but it has also created a supply of Smithian ideas.

The translation problem of the word "sympathy"

Finally, we are going to solve a translation problem over two words in the 1997 version of *TSM*: the translation of the words "sympathy" and "propriety".

The first word, "sympathy", was translated into Spanish by Rodríguez Braun as *simpatía*. Many readers argue that this term should not have been translated as *simpatía* but instead should have been translated as *empatía*.[13] We should mention that there is also debate in the English language about the need to replace the word "sympathy" with "empathy" in Smith's work (see Montes 2004: 45–55). Today, the word "sympathy" is defined in English firstly as "feelings of pity and sorrow for someone else's misfortune" and secondly as "understanding between people; common feeling" or "the state or fact of responding in a way corresponding to an action elsewhere". Smith develops the nature of the mechanism of sympathy in different ways throughout *TMS* (see Raphael 2007, 120, or Griswold 1999);[14] however, Smith wanted to use sympathy in a way that was different to its traditional use: "Sympathy, though its meaning was, perhaps, originally the same, may now, however, without much impropriety, be made use of to denote our fellow-feeling with any passion whatever" (Smith 1982, I.i.1.5, 10).[15] This implies a linguistic challenge. Like Hume, Smith understood social unions in terms of "sympatheia", a stoic word used in the Scottish Enlightenment (Dwyer 1987, 1998) implying links based on citizenship and self-command and on the theories of Marco Aurelio, Epicteto or Cicero. However, Smith's description of sympathy is different from the somewhat aphatic stoic sympatheia (see Smith 1982: VII: II: I, 488) and it is also different from that of Hume – for Hume, and contrary to Smith's views, even animals can feel sympathy (Hume 1964, III, II, I, 256).[16]

Fontaine (2001) argues that Smith is talking about empathy. The term "empathy" was coined not long ago, in the late nineteenth century, although the general idea was undoubtedly present in Adam Smith and David Hume's "sympathy". It was not until the end of the nineteenth century that the term "empathy" acquired its current meaning. Empathy is "the ability to understand and share the feelings of another" (from the Greek *empatheia: em-* "in" and *pathos* "feeling"). Someone who empathises is not necessarily worried about the other person and can have either good or bad intentions. The distinction is based on the origin of the terms. Sympathy is a concern for others that directly affects our individual wellbeing (to feel for another). Empathy is linked to the imaginative process of placing yourself in the other person's shoes (to put yourself in the place of another).[17] Subjects are supposed to be able to put themselves in the other person's place or consider their circumstances and predict their reactions, meaning that they are aware of their wellbeing. So, on the one hand we have a cognitive identification or empathic ability and, on the other, an identification with circumstances or sympathy ability (*TSM* VII, 3).[18]

However, when we consider how the Spanish word *simpatía* is translated into English, we find: "friendliness, come to like someone, affection, liking, charm". There is only a medical use of the word *simpatía* (also from physics and biology), which is translated as sympathy, and the plural, *simpatías*, which can be translated as sympathies. Actually, the definition of *simpatía* in Spanish is "affective and friendly inclination between persons, generally spontaneous and mutual" or "a person's character that makes him attractive or agreeable to others".

On the other hand, sympathy can be translated into Spanish as "*compasión, lástima, condolencias, pésame, acompañar en el sentimiento, acuerdo, solidaridad, comprensión*" and the plural voice could be translated as "*simpatías, tendencias*". So, in reality, although it is usual to associate the word sympathy in English with feelings of pity and sorrow for someone else's misfortune, it maintains its original Greek sense of *sumpathēs* (*sun* "with"; *pathos* "feeling"), having a general sense of common feeling and understanding between people. Conversely, in Spanish, the word always relates to a certain passive subject and you feel "*simpatía*" for a person, not for his or her feelings. This is why Nicol says in the foreword to the 1934 translation of the *TMS* "The reader must not overlook a certain disagreement or lack of systematic rigor in Adam's Smith ideas…in general the whole terminology related to the affective phenomena is confused…we do not sympathize with the feelings of other people, but with the people themselves" (Smith 1934, 25–27).

Solutions for the translation of the word "sympathy"

The confusion of translation of the word "sympathy" should have been resolved in the 1997 translation. This translation choice may be interestingly connected with the idea presented in the previous section over the supply and demand of the Spanish edition of the *TMS*. In particular, there are three possible combinations of supply and demand of the *TMS* translation: 1) accurate but specialist translations; 2) less accurate but more accessible translations; 3) less accurate but tied to the broader moral philosophical literature translations.

Accurate but specialist translations

In the first case, for an accurate but specialist translation of the word "sympathy", it may have been enough to simply add a clarifying footnote or to put the English word in brackets the first time it was translated in the book. This has, in fact, been done at times; for instance, Edmundo O'Gorman does not find a translation in 1934 of "fellow-feeling for the misery of others" and he puts the English words in brackets giving a tentative translation into Spanish: "*condolencia* (fellow-feeling) *por la desventura ajena*". Carlos Rodríguez Braun gives a single translation for this word, "*conmiseración*", a word that in Spanish has the same connotation of "pity and sorrow for someone else's misfortune" as the word "sympathy".

We may provide an alternative translation into Spanish of the word "sympathy" in Adam Smith's context. In current ethics, "*el co-sentir*" or "*sentir con otros*" is used for this purpose. This word has been created *ad hoc* for this circumstance and could be a good alternative to "*simpatía*". However, this would be a translation for experts rather than for the general public. Other options include "*identificación, adhesión, inclinación, solidaridad, apoyo, respaldo, filia, armonía, acuerdo, avenencia, concordancia, coincidencia, cambio de posiciones*", which are better than "*simpatía*" but still not perfect. In Trincado (2011), the best translation is shown to be "*simpatía empatizadora*".[19]

Less accurate but more accessible translations

We may have less accurate but more accessible translations, however. As mentioned above, one possibility would have been to use the word "*empatía*". However, there are advantages and disadvantages involved in switching to that word. The disadvantage is that traditionally the word sympathy, as used by Hume, has been translated by scholars into Spanish as "*simpatía*", and Smith was actually referring to the previous sense of this word. Rodríguez Braun, presenting Smith's work as part of the Scottish Enlightenment movement, may have simply wanted to maintain the same terminology used by previous authors.[20]

Besides, in the *Diccionario de la Real Academia de la Lengua Española*, the following definitions are given for the word, *empatía*: "affective, and generally emotional participation, of a subject in a foreign reality". The word *empatía* implies a mental and emotional identification with feelings; it is the ability to identify with other people and share their feelings. In contrast, Smithian sympathy is a cognitive transfer rather than an emotional one, and it is the basis for moral approval or disapproval; so, it implies being able to criticise (see *TSM* I, 1, 3 and I, 1, 4; see the discussion in Pena and Sánchez 2007, 70). Smithian sympathy does not consist only in knowing how others are feeling. The spectator combines sympathy and gratitude; pleasure from sympathy arises as a result of the comfort we find in sharing feelings, be these of pleasure or pain, and this is why it is always agreeable. Gratefulness, in contrast to pleasure, may be felt by both the agent and the spectator. In addition, the moral approval requires the feelings of the spectator to coincide with the motives of the agent.[21]

Less accurate translations tied to the broader moral philosophical literature

Then, finally, we come to the less accurate translations tied to the broader moral philosophical literature. Tradition would suggest that the right word to use is "*simpatía*". This means that the translation is aimed at experts, instead of at the general public, and that fact limits its influence on the real economy and morality – this may explain why the demand for the *TSM* has not decreased with the extension of socialist ideas in Spain. Besides, proof that there is a translation problem is that many authors, Rodríguez Braun included (Rodríguez Braun 2006), have put the word "*simpatía*" in inverted commas when referring to Smith's *TSM*. The word creates some strange meanings and contradictions in Spanish that do not reflect the original.[22] Thus, Hurtado says,

> In contemporary terms…Smith's "*simpatía*" corresponds to the term "*empatía*", that is to say, a mental and emotional identification with other people. To avoid confusion, I shall use the term "*simpatético*" instead of "*simpático*", except for quotes from the texts of Rawls or Smith.
>
> (Hurtado 2006b, 5)

"*Simpatético*" is a newly forged word – it only existed as a specialist medical grammatical term – but the alternative of using "*simpático*" is not an option because this word means nice and amusing in Spanish.[23]

The translation of "propriety"

Another word that poses a problem in Carlos Rodríguez Braun's Spanish version of the *TMS* is his translation of the word "propriety" as "*corrección*". Using "*corrección*", Rodríguez Braun gives to this concept a Kantian load that is not what Smith really aimed at with propriety. "*Corrección*" in Spanish is linked to the correctness of an action in the sense that it follows a certain law. There are two senses implied in this word: first, acting with *corrección* implies a well-mannered behaviour, an action in accordance with the social ways of education. This is related to the amiable virtues more than to the virtues that, according to Adam Smith, our dignity and honor and the propriety of our own conduct, require. The other sense of the word *corrección* is related to the sense of duty, be it with a religious stance or with regard to some established rules of behavior. But, according to Adam Smith:

Many men behave very decently, and through the whole of their lives avoid any considerable degree of blame, who yet, perhaps, never felt the sentiment upon the propriety of which we found our approbation of their conduct, but acted merely from a regard to what they saw were the established rules of behaviour.

(Smith 1759, part III, chapter V, II.I.100)

Probably, the word propriety should have simply been translated as "*propiedad*". In Spanish, this concept has a moral sense, as has the word propriety in English. "*Propiedad*" also means "*atributo o cualidad esencial de alguien o algo*" but both words have in both languages a material and moral sense, in Smith's theory being even the grounds for sympathy (Montes 2004, 101–10). As we have said, the moral implication of "*corrección*" has to do with the following of laws but the moral implications of "*propiedad*" do not have that implication but is related to the quintessence of somebody, a person who acts according to his innermost sense of what is due to the reality of the things. So, using *corrección* as the translation of propriety is at least misleading, if not mistaken.

Conclusion

As we have seen, demand for the Spanish translation of the *Theory of Moral Sentiments* arose during a period of economic liberalization in Spain. At that time some political advisers needed to find a justification for capitalism and liberalism. However, once being demanded and published, although the influence of anti-liberals increased after 2007, the volume of sales of the translation did not decrease. It seems that the demand of the *TSM* translation in Spanish-speaking countries is quite inelastic and limited to the academic environment, where there has been an influence of the book, particularly through the three centres of Smithian thinking mentioned above. In fact, the translation seems to be aimed at experts, as can be seen from its use of "*simpatía*" as the translation for sympathy. The advantages and disadvantages of alternative translations for the word sympathy, as discussed in this chapter, show that there are three possible combinations of supply and demand of the *TMS* translation of the word sympathy: accurate but specialist translations; less accurate but more accessible translations; 3. and translations that are less accurate but are tied to the broader moral philosophical literature. There is no clear or ideal solution and the word used by Rodríguez Braun may be seen as a happy medium. However, the translation of the word propriety in the Spanish version is actually misleading and should have been avoided. Further possibilities have been set out here.

Notes

1   When we talk about a Spanish translation, it should be noted that we are talking about a very large potential audience, as there are approximately 400 million native Spanish speakers and a total of 500 million Spanish speakers worldwide. Spanish is the second most widely spoken native language in the world, after Mandarin Chinese.

2   However, the influence in Spain of authors, such as Say or Bastiat, was greater in the nineteenth century and there was no complete translation of *The Wealth of Nations* until 1956 (Perdices 2003, 762).

3   Here, we are talking about being "liberal" in the European sense, meaning advocating the free market and usually supporting right wing and even conservative policies; we are not referring to the American liberalism sense of advocating progressivism and reform, and left-leaning movements.

4   See Schwartz 1992; Rodríguez Braun 1997, 14–15; Martín 1998; or Chaves 2002, 12–13.

5   See, for instance, Lazzari and Simonetta 2006, 26 or Ramos Torre 2001, 29.

6   This translation is missing chapters 1, 2, 3 and 5 from section II and all section III of part I; it is also missing sections II and III of part II; chapters II, II, V, VI of part III, and all of part V and part VI. Actually, there is a handwritten but complete translation into Spanish of the TMS dated 1801, which may also be an example of the supply and demand thesis defended in this article. The translation was published during a liberal period that resulted in the Spanish Constitution of 1812 passed by the Cortes de Cádiz. The complete record is: Smith, Adam: "Teoría de los Sentimientos Morales. Obra escrita en inglés por Smith. Traducida por José Deza y Goyri", 1801, 2 vols., Manuscrito: AHN, Consejos, leg. 50831/546-7.

7   Eduardo Nicol I Franciscá (1907 Barcelona–1990 México) was a psychologist philosopher prominent in the Hispanic contemporary arena. He created a new epistemology beyond the subjective–objective distinction and had many followers.

8   It is a translation of the sixth edition from 1790. The text selected reproduces the anthology reedited by L. A. Selby-Bigge in British Moralists, Oxford, Clarendon Press, 1987, 2 vols.

9   In the *Lecciones*, the title itself poses a translation problem, as the term "jurisprudence" should have been translated as "*teoría general del derecho*" or "*filosofía del derecho*". Actually, the Spanish word "*jurisprudencia*" means "law of precedent" or "case law".

10 In the *TSM* foreword, Rodríguez Braun takes the opportunity for an extreme liberalism interpretation of Smith's theory, saying that "you cannot remove from the rich people even what they have in excess" (Rodríguez Braun in Smith 2004, 17). So, he does not take into account Smith's defence of the progressive principle in tax collection. However, Rodríguez Braun recognizes that Smith was a tinged liberal.

11 It is interesting to note that, in 2011, when I took out the 1941 edition of *TSM* from the Economics and Business School library at the Universidad Complutense de Madrid, the most important University in Spain during the entire twentieth century, the book was still not separated or sealed: nobody before me had tried to open it.

12 The influence of Krause implied that positivism in general would never achieve the success in Spain that it had in other sister countries such as Brazil, Mexico, or Argentina (Trincado and Ramos 2011).

13 See, for instance, Alonso-Cortés 2008 16; Argemí, Béjar 2001, 99; Calero 2003; Fernández Tresguerres 2007; Guisán 1994; Hurtado Prieto 2006a and 2006b; Pfefferkorn 2008, 232; Trincado 2000–2001; or the discussion by Pena and Sánchez 2006, 2007.

14 See also Darwall 1998, 1999; Sugden 2002; Levy and Peart 2004.

15 The translation by Rodríguez Braun of this is: "*La palabra simpatía, en su sentido más propio y original, denota la compañía de sentimientos con el padecer, y no con el placer, de los demás*" (Smith 2004, 113).

16 It appears that Hume replaced the word sympathy with the word empathy in the revision of Book III of the *Treatise* while writing the *Enquiry* because Smith had begun to use the

term with connotations that were unacceptable to him (Holthoon 1993). See Mossner and Campbell (1987, 43) Letter 36 from David Hume to Adam Smith, 28 July, 1759.

17 Fontaine (1997) proposes to differentiate between the connection that makes us contribute to the wellbeing of relatives or friends (sympathy) and the one established when we know those with whom we interact frequently (empathy).

18 Then, Smith is talking about complete empathetic identification, which is the imagined change of circumstances together with subjective features (see Smith 1982, VII, III, I, 554), rather than partial empathetic identification, which refers to an imagined change of circumstances with someone else. See the discussion by Fontaine (1997), Holthoon (1993) or Binmore (1994, 56). On the other hand, Nieli (1986), Heilbroner (1982) and Pack (1991) do not make that distinction. See also Kirman and Teschl (2010).

19 The Spanish word "*simpatía*" has taken on a utilitarian connotation – it implies that the company of a certain person produces a differentiated pleasure. The word empathy involves a projection of the ego; it is a mental condition independent of filiations, not an inclination towards a particular person. Therefore, sympathy implies a double relationship between ideas and the ego; empathy implies the removal of the ego and the need to feel the things themselves (Eisenberg and Strayer 1987).

20 In ethics, there is a whole semantic debate about the word "simpatía", from the Greek συμπάθεια or *sumpathēs* to the Latin or stoic *simpathĭa* or *sympatheia*, and from Hutcheson or Joseph Butler's sympathy to Max Scheler's sympathy.

21 Holthoon (1993, 45) says that the pleasure due to people having the same feelings is the pleasure of understanding human nature, related to the Smithian theory of admiration and curiosity for scientific systems.

22 For instance, when reading "*La gota o el dolor de muelas, aunque extraordinariamente dolorosos, suscitan muy poca simpatía; las enfermedades más peligrosas, aunque las acompañe un dolor muy pequeño, provocan la máxima simpatía*" (Smith 2004, I.ii.I, 86) we are reading an absurdity in Spanish that implies that we like dangerous diseases. The original is "The gout or tooth-ache, though exquisitely painful, excite very little sympathy; more dangerous diseases, though accompanied with very little pain, excite the highest". (Smith 1982, I.ii.I.9, 30).

23 Certainly, we see that, although the concepts of *simpatía* and *empatía* are similar as they both relate to emotions, there is still a difference. The antonym of the word "*simpatía*" is "*antipatía*"; the antonym of *empatía* is "*insensibilidad, indiferencia, desafecto, embotamiento, frialdad* ", which is closer to the antonym of the English word sympathy.

Bibliography

Alonso-Cortés Alonso, Á. (2008) *Comercio y Lenguaje: La Retórica de la Persuasión en Adam Smith*. Available online at: http://eprints.ucm.es/7999/1/COMERCIO_Y_LEN GUAJE._MS_1_wpd.pdf (last accessed 13 July 2014).

Álvarez Junco, J. (1996) "The nation building process in nineteenth century Spain," in Clare Mar-Molinero and Angel Smith, *Nationalism and the Nation in the Iberian Peninsula*, Oxford: Oxford International Publishers, pp. 89–106.

Binmore, K. (1994) *Game Theory and the Social Contract, Playing Fair*, vol. 1, London, MIT Press.

Calero, A. (2003) "La teoría de los sentimientos morales y una investigación sobre la naturaleza y causas de la riqueza de las naciones: Troprezar dos veces con la misma piedra." Available online at: www.econ.uba.ar/www/institutos/epistemologia/marco_ archivos/trabajos_XV_archivos/CALERO~1.PDF (last accessed 13 July 2014).

Argemí, L. "Adam Smith y teoría de los sentimientos morales." Available online at: www.bduimp.es/archivo/conferencias/pdf/03-05_83_10030_03_Argemi_Adam_idc52564.pdf (last accessed 13 July 2014).

Bejar, H. (2001) "Filantropía democrática y sentimientos morales," *Isegoría*, 25: 91–113.

Bel, G., Joan C. and Xavier F. (2006) "Liberalización y competencia en España: ¿Dónde Estamos?" *Información Comercial Española*, 829: 123–144.

Calderón, R. (2000) "Difusión de la doctrina de la riqueza de las naciones en España. Nuevos apuntes acerca de la traducción de 1794 y de su traductor, Josef Alonso Ortiz. La hipótesis del 'funcionario ilustrado'," *Revista Empresa y Humanismo*, III, 1/01: 75–100.

Carrasco, M.A. (2004) "Adam Smith's reconstruction of practical reason," *Review of Metaphysics*, 58 (1): 81–116.

Carrasco, M.A. (2006) "Adam Smith: filósofo de la razón práctica," *Estudios Públicos*, 104: 113–148.

Carrasco, M.A. (2009) "De hutcheson a Smith: un sentimentalismo sofisticado," *Revista de Filosofía*, 65: 81–96.

Carrión, G. (2008) "Imaginación y economía. fundamentos gnoseológicos y antropológicos en el pensamiento de Adam Smith," *Cuadernos Empresa y Humanismo*, 103: 1–253.

Casanova, J. (1994) "Spain: from state church to disestablishment," in *Public Religions in the Modern World*, Chicago, IL: University of Chicago Press, pp. 75–91.

Chaves, J.A. (2002) "Ética y economía: la perspectiva de amartya sen," *Estudios Filosóficos*, 51 (146): 5–37.

Darwall, S. (1998) "Empathy, sympathy, care," *Philosophical Studies*, 89 (2): 261–82.

Darwall, S. (1999) "Sympathetic liberalism: recent work on Adam Smith," *Philosophy and Public Affairs*, 28 (2): 139–64.

Dwyer, J. (1987) *Virtuous Discourse: Sensibility and Community in Late Eighteenth-Century Scotland*, Edinburgh: John Donald Publishers.

Dwyer, J. (1998) *The Age of the Passions: an interpretation of Adam Smith and Scottish Enlightement Culture*, East Linton: Tuckwell Press.

Eisenberg, N. and Strayer, J. (1987) "Critical issues in the study of empathy," in N. Eisenberg and J. Strayer (eds), *Empathy and Its Development*, Cambridge: Cambridge University Press, pp. 3–13.

Elton, M. (1989) "Rousseau y la fundamentación moral del contrato social," *Estudios Públicos*, 36: 273–308.

Elton, M. (2006) "Benevolencia y educación pública en Adam Smith," *Estudios Públicos*, 104: 217–45.

Elton, M. (2009) "El concepto de justicia negativa en Adam Smith y sus raíces en el iusnaturalismo moderno," in J. García-Huidobro, H. Herrera and M. A. Huesbe (eds), *Lo Jurídico y lo Político*, Cuadernos de Extensión Jurídica, Universidad de los Andes, pp. 97–109.

Fernández Tresguerres, A. (2007) "Sobre la compasión," *El Catoblepas Revista Crítica del Presente*, 61: 3.

Fontaine, P. (1997) "Identification and economic behaviour: sympathy and empathy in historical perspective," *Economics and Philosophy*, 13: 261–280.

Fontaine, P. (2001) "The changing place of empathy in welfare economics," *History of Political Economy*, 33 (3): 387–409.

Heilbroner, R. (1982) "The socialization of individual in A. Smith," *History of Political Economy*, 14: 427–39.

Griswold Jr., C.L. (1999) *Adam Smith and the Virtues of Enlightenment*, Cambridge: Cambridge University Press.

Guisán, E. (1994) "Sentimiento moral," in *Diez Palabras Clave en Ética*, Dir. Adela Cortina, Estella: Verbo Divino, p. 406.

Hume, D. (1964) *A Treatise of Human Nature Being an Attempt to Introduce the Experimental Method of Reasoning into Moral Subjects and Dialogues Concerning Natural Religion, The Philosophical Works*, in T.H. Green and T.H. Grose (eds). Vol. 2 [first edition 1886, London, Scientia Verlag].

Hurtado Prieto, J. (2003) "La teoría del valor de Adam Smith: la cuestión de los precios naturales y sus interpretaciones," *Cuadernos de Economía*, 21 (38): 15–45.

Hurtado Prieto, J. (2003b) "The risks of an economic agent: a Rousseauian reading of Adam Smith," *Colombian Economic Journal*, 1 (1): 193–220.

Hurtado Prieto, J. (2004) "Bernard Mandeville's heir: Adam Smith or Jean-Jacques Rousseau on the possibility of economic analysis," *European Journal of the History of Economic Thought*, 11 (1): 1–31.

Hurtado Prieto, J. (2005) "Pity, sympathy and self-interest: review of Pierre Force's self-interest before Adam Smith," *European Journal of the History of Economic Thought*, 12 (4): 715–23.

Hurtado Prieto, J. (2006a) "El sistema de la simpatía de Adam Smith: una alternativa liberal olvidada por John Rawls," *Documento CEDE* 2006-17.

Hurtado Prieto, J. (2006b) "Rawls y Smith. de la utilidad de la 'simpatía' para una concepción liberal de la justicia," *Estudios Públicos*, 104: 89–111.

Hurtado Prieto, J. (2006c) "Dr. Mandeville's licentious system: Adam Smith on Bernard Mandeville," in E. Schliesser and L. Montes (eds), *New Voices on Adam Smith*, Abingdon: Routledge, pp. 221–46.

Kirman, A. and Teschl, M. (2010) "Selfish or selfless? the role of empathy in economics," *Philosophical Transactions of the Royal Society B*, 365: 303–317.

Lázaro Cantero, R. (2001) "Adam Smith: Interés particular y bien común," *Cuadernos Empresa y Humanismo*, 84: 1–69.

Lazzari, G. and Simonetta, M. (eds) (2006) *Héroes de la Libertad: Pensadores que Cambiaron el Rumbo de la Historia*, Buenos Aires: Fundación Friedrich A. Hayek.

Levy, D.M. and Peart, S.J. (2004) "Sympathy and approbation in Hume and Smith: a solution to the other rational species problem," *Economics and Philosophy*, 20: 331–49.

Martín, V. (1998) "La ética del propio interés mitigado por la simpatía," *Revista de Libros*, 15: 15.

Martínez-Echevarría, M.A. (2004) "Adam Smith," *Juristas Universales*, 52, Rafael Domingo (ed.), Vol. II, Madrid: Marcial Pons.

Montes, L. (2003a) "Das Adam Smith problem: its origins, the stages of the current debate, and one implication for our understanding of sympathy," *Journal of the History of Economic Thought*, 25 (1): 64–90.

Montes, L. (2003b) "Smith and Newton: some methodological issues concerning general economic equilibrium theory," *Cambridge Journal of Economics*, 27 (5): 723–47.

Montes, L. (2004a) *Adam Smith in Context: A Critical Reassessment of Some Central Components of his Thought*, New York: Palgrave Macmillan.

Montes, L. (2004b) "Adam Smith: ¿Liberal o Cristiano?," *Centro de Estudios Públicos*, 93: 103–129; reprinted in *Libertas*, 41: 99–136.

Montes, L. (2004c) "De la tolerancia, su contexto y una posible relación con el 'nombre general' de propiedad en John Locke," *Revista de Ciencia Política*, 24 (2): 142–58.

Montes, L. (2006a) "Smith and Newton: Closer than we thought," in *New Voices on Adam Smith*, L. Montes and E. Schliesser (eds), London: Routledge, pp. 247–70.

Montes, L. (2006b) "Sobre el Newtonianismo y la teoría del equilibrio económico general de Adam Smith," *Centro de Estudios Públicos*, 104: 247–78.

Montes, L. (2006c) "Tras la huella de Adam Smith: su relevancia hoy," *Centro de Estudios Públicos*, 104: 5–24.

Montes, L. (2006d) "Adam Smith: real Newtonian," in *A History of Scottish Economic Thought*, A. Dow and S. Dow (eds), London: Routledge, pp. 102–21.

Montes, L. (2008a) "Newton's real influence on Adam Smith, and its context," *Cambridge Journal of Economics*, 32 (4): 555–76.

Montes, L. (2008b) "Adam Smith as an eclectic stoic," *Adam Smith Review*, 4: 30–56.

Montes, L. (2008c) "The origins of das Adam Smith problem and our understanding of sympathy," in *The Street Porter and the Philosopher: Conversations on Analytical Egalitarianism*, S. Peart and D. Levy (eds), Ann Arbor, MI: University of Michigan Press, pp. 158–78.

Montes, L. (2009a) "Adam Smith on the standing army versus militia issue: Wealth over virtue?" in *The Elgar Companion to Adam Smith*, J. Young (ed.), London: Edward Elgar, pp. 315–35.

Montes, L. (2009b) "La influencia de Newton en Adam Smith," *Anuario Filosófico*, 42: 137–58.

Montes, L. and Schliesser, E. (eds) (2006a) *New Voices on Adam Smith*, London: Routledge.

Mossner, E.C. and Simpson Ross, I. (1987) *The Correspondence of Adam Smith, The Glasgow Edition of the Works and* Correspondence *of Adam Smith, vol. VI*, Indianapolis, Oxford University Press, Liberty Classics.

Nieli, R. (1986) "Spheres of intimacy and the A. Smith problem," *Journal of the History of Ideas*, 47 (4): 611–24.

Pack, S.J. (1991) *Capitalism as a Moral System: A. Smith Critique of the Free Market Economy*, Aldershot, Elgar.

Pena, J.A. and Sánchez, J.M.S. (2006) "Altruismo, simpatía y comportamientos prosociales en el análisis económico," *Principios*, 4, p. 67.

Pena, J.A. and Sánchez, J.M.S. (2007) "Los fundamentos morales de la economía: una relectura del problema de Adam Smith," *Revista de Economía Institucional*, 9 (16): 63–87.

Perdices, L. (1999) "The wealth of nations and the Spanish economists," in *Adam Smith Across Nations. Translations and Receptions of the Wealth of Nations*, C.C. Lai (ed.), Oxford: Oxford University.

Perdices, L. (2000a) "The wealth of nations and Spanish economists," *Adam Smith Across Nation*, Oxford: Oxford University Press.

Perdices, L. (2000b) "La riqueza de las naciones y los economistas Españoles," *Economía y Economistas Españoles*, vol. 6, Barcelona: FUNCAS, Galaxia, Gutenberg.

Perdices, L. and Fuentes, E. (1997) *Edición de la Investigación de la Naturaleza y Causa de la Riqueza de las Naciones Realizada por José Alonso Ortiz en 1794*, Salamanca: Junta de Castilla y León.

Perdices, L. and Reeder, J. (2003) "Smith (Adam) en España, La recepción de," in *Diccionario de Pensamiento Económico en España* (1500–2000), Madrid: Fundación ICO, Editorial Síntesis, pp. 762–6.

Perdices, L. and Reeder, J. (2010) "Estudio preliminar: La riqueza de las Ideas de Adam Smith" in A. Smith, *Investigación sobre la Naturaleza y Causas de la Riqueza de las Naciones*, Madrid: Fundación ICO-Editorial Síntesis.

Pfefferkorn, R. (2008) "Adam Smith, un liberalismo bien temperado," *Revista Sociedad y Economía*, 14: 227–38.

Ramos Torre, R, (2001) "La más melancólica de las reflexiones. Simpatía, virtud y fortuna en *La Teoría de los Sentimientos Morales* de Adam Smith," *Política y Sociedad*, 37: 21–46.

Raphael, D.D. (2007) *The Impartial Spectator: Adam Smith's Moral Philosophy*, Oxford: Oxford University Press.

Reeder, J. (1997) *On Moral Sentiments: Contemporary Responses to Adam Smith*, Bristol: Thoemmes Press.

Reeder, J. and Cardoso, J.L. (2002) "Adam Smith in the Spanish and Portuguese speaking world," in K. Tribe (ed.) *A Critical Bibliography of Adam Smith*, London: Pickering and Chatto.

Rodríguez Braun, C. (1984) "Ambigüedad de Adam Smith sobre la cuestión colonial," *Moneda y Crédito*, 171: 55–65.

Rodríguez Braun, C. (1989) *La Cuestión Colonial y la Economía Clásica. De Adam Smith y Jeremy Bentham a Karl Marx*, Madrid: Alianza Editorial.

Rodríguez Braun, C. (1992) "Pownall on Smith on colonies," *Storia del Pensiero Economico*, 23: 3–10.

Rodríguez Braun, C. (1997) "Early Smithian economics in the Spanish Empire: J. H.Vieytes and colonial policy," *European Journal of the History of Economic Thought*, 4 (3): 444–54.

Rodríguez Braun, C. (2006) "Adam Smith," *La Ilustración Liberal. Revista Española e Americana*, no. 27, Retratos, pp. 111–15.

Scalzo, G.R. (2009) "Génesis del concepto de interés propio," *Cuadernos Empresa y Humanismo*, 108, pp. 7–107.

Schwartz, P. (1978) "El ensayo de José Alonso Ortiz: Monetarismo Smithiano en la España de los vales reales," in A. Otazu (comp.), *Dinero y Crédito (Siglos XVI al XIX)*, Madrid: Moneda y Crédito.

Schwartz, P. (1990) *La Recepción Inicial de la "Riqueza de las Naciones" en España*, Madrid: Banco de España, Servicio de Estudios.

Schwartz, P. (1992) "La moral del amor propio y los fundamentos éticos del capitalismo en el pensamiento de Adam Smith," in R.R. de Urquía and E.M. Ureña (eds), *Economía y Dinámica Social*, Publicaciones Universidad Pontificia Comillas, Madrid.

Schwartz, P. (2000) "La recepción inicial de la riqueza de la naciones en España," in *Economía y Economistas Españoles, vol. IV, La Economía Clásica*, E. Fuentes Quintana (ed.), Barcelona: Galaxia Gutenberg.

Schwartz, P. (2001) "The wealth of nations censored: Early translations in Spain," in A.E. Murphy and R. Prendergast (eds), *Contributions to the History of Economic Thought: Essays in Honour of R.D.C. Black*, Abingdon: Routledge.

Smith, A. (1941) *Teoría de los Sentimientos Morales*, introduction by Eduardo Nicol, trans. Edmundo O'Gorman, México: Fondo de Cultura Económica.

Smith, A. (1982) *Theory of Moral Sentiments*, in D.D. Raphael and A.L. Macfie (eds), *Vol. I of the Glasgow Edition of the Works and Correspondence of Adam Smith*, Indianapolis, IN: Liberty Fund.

Smith, A. (1992) *Investigación sobre la Naturaleza y Causas de la Riqueza de las Naciones*, 7th ed., México, DF: Fondo de Cultura Económica.

Smith, A. (1995) *Lecciones sobre Jurisprudencia*, Granada: Editorial Comares.

Smith, A. (1998) *Ensayos Filosóficos*, Madrid: Ediciones Pirámide.

Smith, A. (2004) *Teoría de los Sentimientos Morales*, trans. Carlos Rodríguez Braun, Madrid: Alianza [1997].

Smith, R.S. (1957) "The wealth of nations in Spain and hispanic America, 1780–1830," *Journal of Political Economy*, 4: 104–25.

Sugden, R. (2002) "Beyond sympathy and empathy: Adam Smith's concept of fellow-feeling," *Economics and Philosophy*, 18: 63–87.

Trincado, E. (2001) "El iusnaturalismo no utilitarista de Adam Smith," *Información Comercial Española*, 789: 95–9.

Trincado, E. (2003a) *Crítica a la Doctrina de la Utilidad y Revisión de las Teorías de Hume, Smith y Bentham*, Madrid: Universidad Complutense de Madrid.

Trincado, E. (2003b) "Adam Smith: crítico del utilitarismo," *Télos. Revista Iberoamericana de Estudios Utilitaristas*, 12 (1): 43–62.

Trincado, E. (2004) "Equity, utility and transaction costs: on the origin of judicial power in Adam Smith," *Storia del Pensiero Economico*, 1: 33–51.

Trincado, E. (2005) "Utility, money and transaction costs: authoritarian vs libertarian monetary policies," *History of Economic Ideas*, 13 (1): 57–77.

Trincado, E. (2006) "Adam Smith criticism of the doctrine of utility: a theory of the creative present," in L. Montes and E. Schliesser, *New Voices on Adam Smith*, New York: Routledge, pp. 313–27.

Trincado, E. (2007) "Costes de transacción vs costes de jerarquía en la provisión de bienes: una interpretación de la teoría Smithiana," *Revista de Historia Económica. Journal of Iberian and Latin American Economic History*, 2: 261–92.

Trincado, E. (2008) "Economía del desarrollo vs economía del bienestar: distintas filosofías de la vida," *Revista de Economía Mundial*, 18: 141–54.

Trincado, E. (2009) "Teorías del valor y la función empresarial," *Investigaciones de Historia Económica*, 14: 11–38.

Trincado, E. (2011) *Las Teorías del Tiempo*, Berlin: Editorial Académica Española.

Trincado, E. and Ramos, J.L. (2011) "John Stuart Mill and nineteenth century Spain," *Journal of the History of Economic Thought*, 33 (4): 507–26.

Van Holthoon, F.L. (1993) "Adam Smith and David Hume: With sympathy," *Utilitas. A Journal of Utilitarian Studies*, 5 (1): 35–49.

French translations and re-translations of Smith's *Theory of Moral Sentiments*

The unbearable lightness of (re)translating

Michaël Biziou

Introduction

The author of these lines took part in the French translation of Adam Smith's *Theory of Moral Sentiments* published in 1999.[1] Translating the *Theory* into French during the very last years of the twentieth century conveyed to me the feeling of something like an unbearable lightness of translating. This bizarre expression is coined from the title of a famous novel by the Franco-Czech writer Milan Kundera.[2] In this book, the main character, Tomas, bestows a deep philosophical meaning to a common German saying, which comes to his mind as he has an important decision to take:

> There is no means of testing which decision is better, because there is no basis for comparison. We live everything as it comes, without warning, like an actor going on cold. … *Einmal ist keinmal*, says Tomas to himself. What happens but once, says the German adage, might as well not have happened at all. If we have only one life to live, we might as well not have lived at all.[3]

Thus, since Tomas knows that he will live each situation and will take each decision only once, his existence seems both to have 'lightness', because what happens in the ephemeral singularity of one only time is a free act of creativity, and to be 'unbearable', because in this ephemeral singularity the whole of his being is each time at stake. Now let me explain here that, similarly, '*einmal ist keinmal*' could also fit perfectly as a motto for the 1999 French translation of the *Theory* and therefore that his translator too felt this curious feeling of 'unbearable lightness'.

In order to do so, I begin with methodological considerations on the status of translation as retranslation, for the 1999 translation has indeed to be located within a multi-secular history of successive retranslations of the *Theory* into French. I plead the necessity of studying any (re)translation in relation to what I call its objective context and its subjective project. Then, as a second step, I endeavour to spell out what were the objective contexts and the subjective projects of each of the French translations of the *Theory* which preceded that of 1999. The statement of these contexts and projects allow me to account in detail for several specific and technical translation choices made by the past translators. As a third and last step, I proceed in the same way for the last translation.

I. From translation to retranslation

If '*einmal ist keinmal*' could fit as a motto for the 1999 French translation of the *Theory*, and if therefore its translator felt a feeling of 'unbearable lightness' upon this occasion, it is because this work was not so much a translation as a retranslation.[4] Indeed, before this latest French translation, several others had already been already achieved, as detailed below. Even though I only deal here with the limited case of those translations and retranslations of Smith's *Theory* into French, one might even go as far as to say that '*einmal ist keinmal*' could be a motto for all retranslations in general and, consequently, that there is an 'unbearable lightness' which is bound to be felt through any act of retranslating.[5]

The 'unbearable lightness' of retranslating is linked to what could be called a publishing paradox, inversely symmetrical to the existential paradox of Kundera's character. These two paradoxes consist of a certain relationship between contingency and responsibility. It is because Tomas lives only once each situation, and therefore cannot find anything to which each of his decisions can be compared, that he experiences this feeling. The contingency of the singular situation gives him 'lightness', since he can invent his life as he wishes, but, on the other hand, this contingency makes him face his own and full responsibility, and it is this which can appear as 'unbearable'. Such is the existential paradox: the more contingent is the situation, the more it requires from Tomas to take his responsibilities; so, the more there is lightness, the more it is unbearable. Symmetrically, and inversely, the retranslator is aware that his work is only one attempt amongst others, which can be compared to previous translations, and will be to those following. This is what brings him 'lightness', because he knows that his work is bearing the hallmark of contingency, so that he does not have to feel in charge of the overwhelming burden of revealing once and for all the allegedly absolute meaning of the text to be translated. But, on the other hand, the retranslator, by the very fact that he has committed himself to redo a translation that others before him had already undertaken, shows that he pretends to do better than them, or at least that he hopes to bring something important that his predecessors had not told. This responsibility makes his task sometimes, somewhat, 'unbearable', whether it be on account of his grand vocation or of his high pretentiousness.

To put it another way, the feeling of an 'unbearable lightness' appears when the act of retranslating is seen as it is, an historical practice, to be set in its historical dimension. Indeed, it would be a naive illusion to think that a retranslation could be a direct and immediate jump back to the original text, skipping over the history of previous translating attempts.[6] This is also true whether or not the retranslator is aware of this history. This history exists anyway, and it necessarily produces its effects on the present time, and therefore on the culture and on the choices of the retranslator. One might even support the paradox that the first translation of a text is already, in some way, a retranslation. Indeed, if the translator innovates with this particular translation, he nonetheless belongs to the whole history of translation in general: no translation can be considered, unless one lapses into mythology, as the first one in human history.[7] The meaning of a text to be translated is therefore elaborated progressively, through successive layers of interpretation, and consecutive translating attempts, which follow one another in history. It is not a hidden treasure, immutable and an-historic, waiting to be discovered at last by the good translator, that is to say a translator which would be miraculously free from all the historical influences resulting in the prejudices and concerns of his own time. If the translator is in fact a retranslator, he has to be seen not only as an heir inheriting a legacy from the author he translates, but also and no less as the last offspring of a lineage of translators.

Consequently, to go back to the limited case with which I am dealing here, it is impossible to understand fully what is at stake in a French translation of the *Theory* published in 1999 without making reference to the preceding translations in the same language. Thus, I begin by drawing a brief sketch of the publishing history of the French translations of this book. For reasons that I do not need to investigate here, the *Theory* (initially published in 1759, with a sixth and last much augmented edition in 1790) has never been as worldwidely renowned as Smith's other great work, the *Inquiry into the Nature and Causes of the Wealth of Nations* (first published in 1776, third definitive edition in 1784, with minor corrections until 1789).[8] The latter found as quick as widespread a fame, so that translations of it appeared in many European languages as soon as in the eighteenth century. On the contrary, to read a complete version of Smith's *Theory* in their own idioms, such countries as Italy or Spain had to wait until the end of the twentieth century.[9] However, this was definitely not the case of France, a country that entertained a close relationship with Great Britain, and with Scotland in particular, during the Enlightenment. Smith himself sojourned in France for two years, from 1764 to 1766, seizing many opportunities to be introduced to the local intellectual world.[10] Accordingly, France begot no less than four translations of the *Theory* in the second half of the eighteenth century. During the same period, up to seven French translations of the *Inquiry* were offered to the public.[11] Then the translating process – one would dare to say the translating frenzy – stopped, for the two books alike. It stopped for about two centuries, the nineteenth and twentieth being mostly in France centuries of re-editions. It was only in the very last years of the twentieth century that a contemporary translation of the *Theory*, accompanied by two new translations of the *Inquiry*, were published.[12]

Within this history, what specific significance can be ascribed to the latest translation of the *Theory*? In other words, what are the particular historical determinations that could account for the feeling of 'unbearable lightness' that this retranslation occasioned? To answer these questions, we need to compare in some detail the latest translation to its predecessors. I propose to do so by examining, for each translation, two different aspects. I shall call them, respectively, the objective context and the subjective project of the translation.[13] Both of these aspects are necessary to make sense of the history of the successive translations. First, each translation emerges inside what could be called an objective context: by which I mean the state – whether it be intellectual, political, economic, etc. – of the society in which the translation is bound to be published. Second, each translation is motivated by a subjective project: by which I mean the various goals – whether they be intellectual, political, economic, etc. – that the translator sets to himself, in other words, the reasons why he wants to share with the public this particular text at this particular time. It is only after having considered these two general aspects that, subsequently, specific and technical remarks concerning particular points of a given translation – that is to say, the way it chooses to translate such or such word, such or such phrase – can be fully meaningful.

Accordingly, the next part of my essay is dedicated to the eighteenth-century French translations of the *Theory*, and aims to explain their respective objective contexts and subjective projects. The third part does the same for the latest translation. On the basis of these different contexts and projects, I discuss successively in each of these two parts specific and technical problems of translating Smith into French.

II. Contexts and projects of the eighteenth-century translations

The first French translation of the *Theory* is by the hand of Marc-Antoine Eidous.[14] He publishes it in 1764, under the title of *Métaphysique de l'âme, ou Théorie des sentiments moraux* which reads as 'Metaphysics of the Soul, or Theory of Moral Sentiments'. This is quite disconcerting. For, of course, as any Smith scholar knows, there is no decisive mention of 'metaphysics', nor of the 'soul', in the original English text. Smith's intention in his book is to found morals on sentiments, rather than on reason. He speaks of a 'theory of sentiments' and not of 'metaphysics', of 'human nature'[15] and not of the 'soul' – a choice of vocabulary connected to his rejection of moral rationalism and his adoption of moral sentimentalism. Smith himself does declare to be mortified by this translation.[16] Should we then consider that such a title, which appears to be so far away from Smith's own philosophical categories and interests, is a mere aberration? Is Eidous such a calamitous translator? And, consequently, should the potential retranslators be allowed to think that this first translation is so hopeless that it will be pretty easy to do better?

The answer is not so simple, and this is where we have to take into account what I have called the objective context of the translation. More precisely, I am talking here of an intellectual context, concerning the state of philosophy in France at that time. In 1764, French moral philosophy was still largely rationalist, following in Malebranche's wake.[17] Thus, it is not absurd, far from it indeed, to put some key words of the rationalist tradition in the title of a new book on morals, to catch the attention of the French public. This was the very first translation of a text then quite recent, only five years after the publication of the original, and it had to find some efficient way to strike its potential readers' minds. In that light, the terms 'metaphysics' and 'soul' created an appropriate framework, because they were familiar, to introduce a theory that founds morals on 'sentiments', which to say the least was then unusual in France. From the consideration of this objective context, what I have called the subjective project of the translator can be roughly guessed, in the absence of precise declarations.[18] Eidous was certainly no faithful disciple of Smith and no fiery advocate of moral sentimentalism. He was not out to bring to France a new doctrine that could challenge, shake and crumble its philosophical tradition. More probably, he was rather trying to bring to the public something new and stimulating, but not too disconcerting, that could meet happily with the spirit of the time. To some extent, the title 'Metaphysics of the Soul' might well be, besides an ingenious first attempt to acclimate a foreign produce to the local ground, some clever promotional argument.[19]

A second French translation appeared ten years later, in 1774–1775, by the Abbé (Father) Jean-Louis Blavet.[20] It bears the more expected and strictly literal title of *Théorie des sentiments moraux*. It is commissioned by the circle of the Marquise de Boufflers, mistress of the Prince de Conti, of whom Blavet was the librarian, famous anglophile salonière, friend of David Hume, Samuel Johnson, Horace Walpole, and of Adam Smith himself. Such is the objective context that is relevant to make sense of Blavet's translation: an intellectual context very much open to British influence. However, this does not make of him the mouthpiece of Scottish moral sentimentalism confronting French rationalism. Indeed, in the 'Preface' of his translation, Blavet exposes in the following terms what I see as his subjective project as a translator:

> I consider this book as a faithful mirror where men of all times, and of all countries, can recognize themselves with pleasure, and at the same time it is a pure and fertile spring where they can draw the most beautiful lessons and find the noblest incentive to virtue.[21]

Two things are striking in this sentence. First, it totally denies the possibility of any cultural differences between the original text and its translation. The book is said to be able to speak universally and indistinctly to 'men of all times, and of all countries'. To extend Blavet's revealing metaphor, if the book is a 'mirror', then its good translation is supposed to be totally transparent. If everything works well, according to Blavet, the passage from one language to another, therefore from one philosophical culture to another, does not require asking the question of a change in the reader's point of view. But that is a presupposition far from being self-evident. It is highly liable to leave unnoticed many differences between Smith's philosophy and what the French readers of the time believe they can understand of it.

As to the second striking point in Blavet's sentence, it precisely concerns Smith's philosophy and its interpretation. Blavet explains that, apart from being a 'mirror'; that is, a description, Smith's book is a 'spring' where one can draw 'lessons' and an 'incentive to virtue', i.e. exhortation. But that way of praising the *Theory*, thus insisting upon its two qualities of description and of exhortation, leaves definitely aside a third aspect, no less important: the explanatory aspect of Smith's theory. Indeed, the philosophical originality and value of Smith greatly consist in the way he explains the existence of moral standards by founding them on sentiments. Now, it is no wonder that Blavet does not talk about this primordial aspect, because the explanation elaborated by the Scottish philosopher is exactly what is most foreign to French moral rationalism. A rationalist philosophy can accept the description of the virtuous and vicious actions or characters presented in the *Theory*; it can echo the author's exhortation to promote the ones and to oppose the others but it cannot, for weighty theoretical reasons, consent to the sentimentalist explanation that Smith gives of the foundation of morals. It is clear that conveying this sentimentalist explanation does not belong to the translating project of Blavet, who does not even mention it.

The third translation has never been completed, nor published, and its manuscript has never been found. We have heard of it only through Smith's correspondence with the person who had undertaken it, Louis Alexandre de La Rochefoucauld.[22] He decided to put an end to his enterprise when Blavet published his own translation.[23]

The fourth translation is the work of Sophie de Grouchy, Marquise de Condorcet.[24] She was the wife of the Marquis de Condorcet, the famous philosopher and politician, who himself was well acquainted with Smith's thought.[25] She published her translation in 1798, under the strictly literal title of *Théorie des sentiments moraux*, as did Blavet. However, she adds a long subtitle of her own: 'An analytical essay upon the principles of the judgments that men naturally pass, first on the actions of other people, then on their own'.

Two points are worth noticing about this new version. First, as shows her subtitle, the Marquise obviously takes very seriously what I have called the explanatory aspect of Smith's philosophy, i.e. the way he explains the existence of moral standards by founding them on sentiments. Unlike Blavet, who, as we have seen, leaves aside this explanatory aspect and is only interested in the *Theory*'s descriptive and exhortative aspects, the Marquise considers the book as an 'analytical essay' that expounds the 'principles of the judgments'. To analyse principles is, indeed, to do something more that to describe actions or characters, and to exhort to virtue. Second, if the Marquise acknowledged this explanatory aspect in Smith, she nonetheless considered it as a partial failure. So much so that she felt the need to publish, in the same volume containing her translation, a long addendum of approximately 150 pages commenting on Smith's philosophy, usually referred to as *Letters on Sympathy*.[26] These letters are supposed to amend and extend Smith's theory where it proves too limited and shallow according to the Marquise.[27] As she writes bluntly: 'Smith did not go further than establishing the existence of [sympathy] and showing its principal effects. I was sorry that he had not done more, had not penetrated its first cause, nor explained how it must belong to all beings capable of sensation and reflection. As you will see, I have been bold enough to correct these omissions'.[28] I think that the Marquise's position towards Smith, very attentive and very critical at the same time, can be understood only if one takes into account, there again, the objective context and the subjective project of her translation.

The objective context can be considered from both a political and an intellectual point of view. Politically, the context is the French Revolution and, more specifically, the years immediately following the fearsome times of the Jacobin Terror. The

Condorcet couple, though sincerely in favour of the Revolutionary cause, were persecuted during the Terror, which finally cost the Marquis his life in 1794. Thus, the Marquise worked on her translation and on her *Letters* in a time that happened to be divided between the enthusiasm of moulding a new society along democratic ideals and the consternation caused by the bloody excesses of the fight between political factions pretending to serve these ideals. As to the intellectual context, it is enough to say that, as most French thinkers of the period, and despite her anglophilia, the Marquise still belonged to the rationalist tradition of French moral philosophy.

If we come now to the subjective translation project that arises inside this objective context, it appears to be, too, both of a political and of an intellectual nature. Politically, the Marquise is eager to bring to the public of Revolutionary France a text showing how society can gain stability and avoid violence through the harmonization of individual judgements referring to commonly shared moral standards. Smith's severe criticism towards the 'animosity of hostile factions' and the 'ferocious' character of some patriots in 'a nation distracted by faction'[29] should necessarily seem of a momentous importance to a woman who was just a victim of them. More generally speaking, the newborn French Republic had rid itself of the traditional transcendent principles of social unity such as God and the sacred right of kings. It was then in need of new principles, immanent and human. This is exactly what Smith's *Theory* offered, when it explained that sentiments, through the psychological process of sympathy, could found the moral standards to which the judgements of men in society refer. Therefore, the *Letters* pretend to amend and extend Smith's doctrine of sympathy to allow all the consequences useful to the Republic to be drawn from it. They end up proposing a programme of social reforms – in the political, legal or educational fields – that noticeably drifts away from the original preoccupations of the *Theory*.[30] The Marquise translates, so to say, the theory of moral sentiments into a theory of republican sentiments.

The subjective translation project of the Marquise is also of an intellectual nature; that is to say, it depends on the kind of moral philosophy prevailing in France at her time. The Marquise regrets that such a politically useful book does not go philosophically far enough in the explanation it gives of the foundation of morals. This is why the *Letters* rework the concept of sympathy, which is indeed the central concept used in the *Theory* to explain how moral standards are founded on sentiments. On the one hand, the Marquise roots sympathy in a sensualist physiology, thus ascribing to the psychological process a bodily basis.[31] On the other hand, and most importantly, she claims that the process of sympathy must be extended with the reflexions of reason to be able to come to moral judgements: sentiment 'is necessarily modified through reflexion; and it is these modifications that lead us to the idea of moral good or evil'.[32] Accordingly, virtue comes to be defined as 'actions giving to others a pleasure that is approved by reason'.[33] In the same manner, rights are founded on 'a preference required by reason itself in favour of an individual'.[34] Smith grounds moral standards on sentiments, but this sentimentalist foundation is not enough: reason is needed too. Thus, the Marquise's translation tends to interpret once again, as do the previous ones, Scottish moral sentimentalism through the framework of French moral rationalism.

Now, bearing in mind all the general remarks above concerning the objective context and the subjective project of translation, it becomes possible to make sense of several specific and technical translation choices, particularly those points that seem today to be surprising or unsatisfying. Of course, one could choose to see these seeming anomalies only as resulting from the search for elegant style at the expense of literality, or from a mere lack of attention, or again from a relative linguistic incompetence. However, I maintain that they are better understood and more interesting, so that they can be made fully meaningful, if they are seen in the light of the objective context and subjective project of translation. I offer here some examples taken from the Marquise's translation.

For example when Smith, at the beginning of the *Theory*, writes that 'the most hardened violator of the laws of society is not altogether without [pity]', the Marquise translates with some licence that '[pity] still exists in some degree in the heart of men who were the boldest to violate the laws of society'.[35] How to account for the differences? The transformation of 'hardened' into 'bold' can be explained by the Marquise's thesis that sympathy has to be educated by reason in order to be able to produce moral judgments. In her educational and rationalist perspective, a 'bold' violator can still be amended, because if someone needs boldness to perform an action, by definition that action has not yet become a habit. The bold man can still be brought back to reason. On the contrary, a 'hardened' villain is practically lost to virtue, because his bad habits are so strongly ill-bent that reason and education are no more able to correct them. Besides, in this sentence the Marquise adds on her own initiative references to the 'heart' and to 'some degree' of pity. These additions follow the same logic as before. According to the Marquise, pity belongs to the 'heart', a passive faculty of feeling, which has to be activated by reason, an active faculty of reflexion. This activation, through education, allows passing from a 'degree' of pity still pre-moral and merely sentimental, to a superior 'degree' of pity, moral and approved by reason.

Talking about the 'degree' of sentiments, the Marquise fails entirely to under-stand what Smith means when he actually mentions it. In Smith's theory, men can adopt common moral standards because sympathy makes them share their respective sentiments, and moreover equilibrates the 'degree' of these.[36] Not only does sympathy allow us to feel the pain, the joy or the indignation of the others, but it also lets us feel these sentiments at a degree approximately equal to theirs. Now, when the Marquise uses the word 'degree', as I have just given an example of it, she often commits a philosophical misinterpretation. Instead of understanding 'degree' as an intensity to be regulated, she conceives it as a potentiality to be deve-loped. She does not see it in relation to a process that allows the equilibration of the intensity of sentiments between several persons. She rather interprets it in relation to the transition, thanks to the intervention of reason, from a virtue still potential to a virtue fully accomplished. It sounds more like a finalist metaphysics of virtue – somewhat similar to Aristotle's, for whom virtue consists in going from potentiality to actuality, through the exercise of reason – than like a theory of moral sentiments. That is probably why the Marquise so often leaves aside the vocabulary of 'proportion', 'measure', 'pitch' or 'point', unable to realize how essential these words are to express the sympathetic process of equilibrating the intensities of sentiments. Smith's 'extravagant and out of proportion' becomes 'unfounded and without reason'.[37] 'Measure' is rendered by 'rule' or 'we judge'.[38] 'Pitch' is several times omitted[39] or turned into a 'degree of sympathy'.[40] The 'point of propriety' is understood as a 'character of propriety'.[41]

The result of this misinterpretation of the sympathetic process of equilibrating the intensity of sentiments is that the Marquise also misunderstands the effect produced by this process. That effect is the creation, inside the mind of all men, of an internal authority dictating moral standards. It is commonly called moral conscience but Smith prefers to name it the 'impartial spectator'.[42] What Smith means is that there is, inside each of us, an imaginary spectator who observes and morally judges us. For this imaginary spectator to be morally legitimate, he has to be impartial. And impartiality is precisely defined, for Smith, as the equilibration through sympathy of the degree of our sentiments with the degree of the sentiments of the others. Now, if the Marquise properly discerns that the moral authority in Smith's theory is presented as a 'spectator', she does not give much importance to his being 'impartial'. For her, what is important is more to be reasonable than to be impartial. Indeed, according to her, morality stems from the reflexions of reason operating upon the process of sympathy, as we have seen, not from sympathy itself equilibrating the intensity of sentiments, since she does not even grasp that this equilibrating process takes place. Consequently, the Marquise sometimes just forgets to translate 'impartial' in the phrase 'impartial spectator', or she even goes as far as erasing the whole phrase itself.[43]

Another trend in the Marquise's work is to reconstruct what she calls, like Eidous, the first French translator of the *Theory*, a 'metaphysics of the soul'.[44] She readily names, separates and classifies various faculties and principles, as if she were drawing some metaphysical chart of the human soul. On the contrary, the original text adopts a much more continuist and operative conception of the mind. It describes processes, rather than faculties, and these processes are seen as following the ones from the others, rather than being each of them ascribed to its own specific principle. I have already implicitly alluded to this aspect, when noticing the introduction by the Marquise of a reference to the 'heart'[45] to distinguish passive sensibility from active reason. In the same way, when Smith writes about 'some principles … which interest him in the fortune of others', it is rendered by 'a principle of interest towards what happens to others'.[46] Thus, the plurality of various undetermined principles is transformed into the unity of one specific principle, and is arbitrarily named 'principle of interest'. Also, Smith's 'fellow-feeling with any passion whatever' clots into a faculty: 'the faculty to share others' passions, whatever they be'.[47] In another passage, Smith makes an analogy between 'the eye of the body' and 'the natural eye of the mind', but the Marquise translates 'the eyes of our body' and 'the glance of our intelligence'.[48] Not only is the symmetry of the two phrases lost but the choice of 'intelligence' instead of 'mind' also deviates towards a rationalist interpretation. 'Mind', in this context, can be indistinctively reason and sentiments (both being opposed to the 'body'); whereas 'intelligence' is nothing else than reason.

III. Context and project of the twentieth-century translation

In spite of all the points which appear today as an unfortunate lack of precision, if not as a series of philosophical misinterpretations, the Marquise de Condorcet's translation remained as a reference in France for two centuries. Until the very last years of the twentieth century, it was the only translation of Smith's *Theory* available, being republished three times during this period: in 1830, in 1860, and lastly in 1982.[49] Considering what I could pleasantly call the long reign of the Marquise, three questions are to be asked. First, why did this translation so easily overshadow the preceding ones? Second, why did it satisfy for so long the French public? Third, what motivated the publication of a new translation?

As to the first question, it can be answered that the Marquise was the only translator who came late enough in the eighteenth century to have the opportunity to work on the sixth and last edition of the *Theory*, that of 1790. Considering the importance of the revisions that Smith brought to the last edition, this simple chronological fact is enough to outdate objectively the Marquise's predecessors.[50] Moreover, Eidous and Blavet's translations have been pointed to by several critics of their time for their lack of accuracy and elegance whereas, by comparison, the Marquise's work benefited from a good reputation on these points as soon as it was issued.[51]

Regarding the second question, it appears that the interpretative distortions that are imposed on Smith's philosophy by the Marquise's translation were simply not a problem for generations of French-speaking readers. To put it very scantily – for being more precise would take us far beyond the scope of our present topic – one can distinguish, in two centuries of French intellectual life, two broad periods corresponding to two main reasons why the Marquise's translation was not seen as inaccurate.

During the first half of the nineteenth century, it can be said that the readers of the *Theory* in French shared the same moral rationalism as that of its translator. Thus, some French philosophers of the period, as Théodore Jouffroy and Victor Cousin, do give much attention to Smith's moral philosophy when elaborating their own doctrine.[52] But if they are appreciative of Smith as an eminent member of what they term the 'Scottish school of philosophy', their favourite author in this so-called school is much rather Thomas Reid. Indeed, they consider that Reid's commonsense theory gives a more appropriate place to reason in morals than the Smithian theory of sympathy. According to them, in accordance with their interpretation of Reid, what Smith calls the 'impartial spectator' and points out as the source of all moral standards is, in fact, nothing else but reason itself.[53]

Then, from the second half of the nineteenth century to the late twentieth century, in France people almost stopped reading Smith as a moral philosopher. More precisely, when one still read the *Theory*, it was very rarely for the explanation it provided of the foundation of morals. There were some exceptions of course, like the philosopher Henri Bergson, who questioned the concept of 'impartial spectator' in the light of his own moral theory.[54] But on the whole, if the readers of the first half of the nineteenth century did not consider the Marquise's translation as inaccurate because they shared with her the same moral rationalism, those of the second half of the nineteenth century to the late twentieth century did not consider it as inaccurate because they were not much interested in the confrontation between moral rationalism and moral sentimentalism. During that period, most French readers came into contact with the *Theory* only for the sake of its connection with the economics of the *Inquiry into the Nature and Causes of the Wealth of Nations*, which was from then on considered as Smith's masterpiece. In other words, one looks no more in the *Theory* for an enquiry upon the foundation of morals, but for a point of view upon economics.

Thus, the French take interest in what the German are to call '*das Adam Smith Problem*': the problem of the intriguing relationship that Smith's moral theory, which is based on sentiments and gives a large role to altruism, sustains with his economic theory, which is based on interest and seems to rely only on selfishness.[55] Several commentators wonder then if Smith does not contradict himself from one book to another, or at least if he did not change his mind when ceasing to be a moral philosopher to become an economist. Economist Henri Baudrillart, editor of the 1860 re-edition of the Marquise's translation, starts his 'Introduction' to the book by stating: 'it could be hard to believe that the same philosopher wrote both the *Theory of Moral Sentiments* and the immortal *Inquiry into the Wealth of Nations*'.[56] Baudrillart, however, does not adhere to the idea that the two books contradict one another, and goes on showing the existence of several links between them. He even ascribes to them a 'common inspiration',[57] which he finds in the concept of 'universal harmony'.[58] What Smith wants to prove from one book to the other, according to Baudrillart, is that a harmony universally and naturally takes place between the sentiments of men (in morals), as between their interests (in economics). So sympathy, in the *Theory*, is just another name for harmony. In this interpretation, the 'impartial spectator' becomes quite an abstruse and tortuous concept, which Smith had had better replaced by the concept of reason: 'This ideal spectator that we carry inside us ... Smith should have given him right away his real name, which is reason, instead of trying to explain it as an artificial production of sympathy alone'.[59] Baudrillart thus adopts the moral rationalism of the French tradition, just as Cousin and Jouffroy a few years before[60] – even if his insistence on the concept of harmony (both of sentiments and of interests), more than on that of reason, shows that his interest lies mainly in the connection between morals and economics, rather than in the question of the foundation of morals as such. This is indeed why Baudrillart is satisfied with the Marquise's translation, through which, he says, Smith's thought 'is always conveyed with the utmost precision'.[61] He also publishes the Marquise's *Letters* alongside his re-edition of the *Theory*, considering that 'the philosophical theory upon which these *Letters* are grounded does not noticeably differ from Adam Smith's'.[62]

Other French readers of the period were not directly interested in '*das Adam Smith Problem*' but studied the *Theory* in order to deal with broader issues such as utilitarianism, liberalism or individualism. One can give the examples, at the very beginning of the twentieth century, of Elie Halevy[63] or Albert Schatz.[64] On the scale of these vast inquiries in the history of moral, political and economic ideas, recounting the constitution of intellectual traditions along several generations of thinkers, the minute explanation elaborated by Smith to found moral standards upon sentiments is only a detail of little weight. What interests these readers of the *Theory* is much less the philosophical principles of morals than the social consequences of morals. Here again, the *Theory* is considered as noteworthy only inasmuch as it can bring a supplementary dimension to the understanding of the *Inquiry*, which is viewed as Smith's most remarkable contribution to the history of ideas. From this angle, the Marquise's translation remains entirely satisfying.

At last, a new French translation of the *Theory* appeared in the very extremity of the twentieth century. What motivates such an enterprise, after two centuries of supremacy of the Marquise? According to my precedent line of argument, a new translation supposes a new objective context and, consequently, a new subjective project.

The objective context is double, as in the time of the Marquise: it is both political and intellectual. Politically, the new translation was initiated less than ten years after the fall of the Berlin Wall, in a period where free-trade economics seemed to be no longer challenged in Europe by the radically adverse ideology of communism. Free-trade economics was, however, shaken by several economic crises affecting the free market in its process of globalization, and confronted with accusations of immorality, cynicism and injustice launched by socialism or social democracy. If, on the one hand, free-trade economics seems to be firmly established in Europe, on the other hand its perimeter is restricted by an appeal to the welfare state to fight against inequalities and to ensure policies of social justice. As to the intellectual context, the new translators are historians of philosophy whose academic training has made vigilant concerning the problem of the foundation of morals, and consequently concerning the debate between sentimentalism and rationalism. The preceding generation of French historians of philosophy, in the end of the 1970s and in the beginning of the 1980s, published several important studies on David Hume, the philosopher who certainly influenced the most Smith's moral philosophy.[65] However that generation did give much attention to Smith and this task was quite naturally taken up by the next generation. Besides, this natural transition from Hume to Smith was greatly helped by the development, in France at the same period, of studies on the Scottish Enlightenment.[66]

The subjective translating project connected to this objective context can be inferred both from the 'Introduction' that the translators wrote for their translation of the *Theory*, and from the various writings they published shortly before or after it.[67] It also appears to be both of a political and of an intellectual nature. Politically, what is at stake is first to see if studying the moral philosophy of one of the founding fathers of free-trade economics can help to clarify the accusations of immorality, cynicism and injustice directed at this doctrine. More generally speaking, the *Theory* can allow us to question certain concepts amongst the most decisive for our contemporary political reflexion. For example, can Smith's conception of society fit our contemporary concept of 'civil society' as opposed to the 'state'?[68] Can his distinction between justice and benevolence help us to understand the contemporary category of 'social justice'?[69] Does his definition of prudence as the virtue of self-love mean that even self-interested commercial transactions should have a moral dimension?[70]

The intellectual aspect of the subjective project; that is, its more abstract philosophical dimension concerning the foundation of morals, aims at providing an understanding as accurate as possible of the way Smith advocates his moral sentimentalism. In opposition to all the preceding French translations, and informed by a precise knowledge in the history of philosophy, the new translation presents Smith as the inventive and rigorous heir of the Scottish sentimentalism of Francis Hutcheson and David Hume, not as some rationalist using ambiguous expressions. Moreover, to stay as close as possible to Smith's concepts and arguments, complexity of vocabulary and of syntax is not to be avoided, should it affect the elegance of style. After all, the *Theory* is a rewriting of the lectures that Smith used to give at the University of Glasgow,[71] and it is allowable to retain all its technical characteristics while translating it. All the more so since the expected readership of this translation is mostly composed of researchers, teachers and their students. If the Marquise de Condorcet dreamed that her translation might reach a large public of citizens eager to build in common a new Revolutionary France, the new translators, aware enough of the present-day state of academic publications, do not fancy such a vast influence.

It is on the general basis of this objective context and of this subjective project that the specific and technical translation choices made by the contemporary translators can be presented and justified – just as the choices of the Marquise that seem apparently surprising or unsatisfying were explained above. Here, I provide two series of examples that are particularly representative.

First, it goes without saying that much attention is given to the various characteristics of the process of sympathy, since it is no less than the core of Smith's sentimentalist explanation of moral standards. Thus, unlike what the Marquise did, in the new translation the variations in intensity of the sentiments are clearly marked through the literal translation of words such as 'degree', 'high', 'low', 'pitch', 'mediocrity', 'to enliven', 'to alleviate',[72] etc. Another important characteristic of the process of sympathy consists in various movements of sentiments. The important point here is to be able to express the way sentiments can be communicated from one person to another, coming from the outside to the inside or, reversely, going from the inside to the outside. These movements are expressed literally, even if one should concede that the result can sometimes sound unusual in French: 'to enter into',[73] 'to go along with',[74] 'to bring the case home to oneself',[75] etc. A third remarkable characteristic of the process of sympathy is the way Smith describes it as a kind of psychological or social stage, with its spectators and actors, the ones watching the others and, sometimes, exchanging their respective points of view. Accordingly, the vocabulary of the theatre and that of the various points of view is insisted upon: 'spectator', 'actor', 'applause', 'the light in which it is seen'[76], etc.

A second series of examples can be articulated around what can be called the different languages used in the *Theory*. Smith's moral philosophy is expressed with words that, in the eighteenth century, already have a long history, that belong to intellectual traditions bestowing upon them a large part of their conceptual density and of their various meanings. Smith's innovations are often, in fact, reinterpretations of traditional themes in the history of philosophy. The seventh part of the *Theory* which, under the title 'Of systems of moral philosophy', offers a vast methodical history of moral philosophy, shows that Smith is quite aware of his numerous borrowings and influences. It appears of the highest importance for the translators to identify these philosophical references and to render them so as to form coherent patterns. It is these patterns that constitute, from page to page, what can be called different languages. There is, first of all, the language of empiricism, inherited directly from Hume's science of human nature. Humean echoes definitely have to be heard when are translated such words as 'common',[77] 'association',[78] 'fancy',[79] 'to conceive',[80] 'understanding',[81] etc. Then there is the language of the moral sentiments tradition, which has mainly been elaborated successively by Shaftesbury, Hutcheson, and Hume.[82] For example, the translation of the English word 'sense' is problematic, since the French word *'sens'* does not always have the same connotations. As in English, the French *'sens'* can be a bodily organ providing physical sensations, or even a faculty of judgment such as the common sense; but sometimes the correct translation is rather the French *'raison'*, which is 'reason' in English.[83] However, for want of a better choice, the translators always render the English 'sense' as the French *'sens'*, for example when translating the phrases 'moral sense'[84] or 'sense of propriety'.[85] Thus, they deliberately have to take the risk that Smith's sentimentalism might be misread as some kind of sensualism similar to that of Condillac or to that of the Marquise in her *Letters*. 'Self-love' is also a problem in the language of the moral sentiments tradition, since the French can potentially offer two words for it: *'amour de soi'* and *'amour propre'*.[86] The translators decide to choose *'amour de soi'*, according to a long philosophical tradition. As it is the case for the English 'self-love', the French *'amour de soi'* has no negative meaning in itself, whereas *'amour propre'* is often disparaged in the vocabulary of philosophers.[87] A third reference with which Smith's text is impregnated is the language of stoicism. In this case Smith's choice of English words deliberately refers to the vocabulary of Greco-Latin philosophy. They have to be translated into French words that allow one to perceive this underlying vocabulary thanks to common linguistic roots. 'To recommend' refers to the Latin *commendatio* (and to the Greek *okeiôsis*),[88] 'propriety' to the Latin *convenientia* (and to the Greek *katekon*),[89] 'decorum' is Latin in itself (and corresponds to the Greek *prepon*),[90] 'good offices' recalls Cicero's title *De officiis*,[91] etc.

Lastly, it should be added that this new translation is accompanied by many footnotes, which of course reflect its translation project. This does not mean that theses footnotes put forward interpretations or commentaries on Smith's philosophy. Such interpretative footnotes call too much for criticism and, besides, nothing ages as rapidly as those kinds of notes according to the variations in intellectual fashions. It would have been too much of a risk to make the interest of the translation depend on the validity of an interpretation or on the 'sell-by' date of a commentary. Therefore, the footnotes are only designed to give precise references to Smith's philosophical sources and point out the use of what I have called various languages; to explain the historical context of Smith's allusions to certain people or events; to show the connections between the different parts of the *Theory*, or between the *Theory* and Smith's other writings; to give explanations on the evolution of the text along its successive editions; and to vindicate those of the translation choices that need an explicit justification. To put it differently, whereas the translation project of the Marquise de Condorcet led her to write the *Letters on Sympathy* in order to amend and extend Smith's theory, the translation project of the contemporary translators induced them to add a scholarly apparatus composed with the methods of the history of philosophy.

Conclusion

To refer to categories that are commonly used in translation studies,[92] should we conclude that the twentieth-century translation of the *Theory* is 'source-oriented', because it tries to accommodate in French the 'guest language' and the 'guest culture', allowing them to retain their own characteristics? Should we add that the eighteenth-century translations are, conversely, 'target-oriented', because they rather aim at forcing the text into an interpretation suiting the 'host language' and the 'host culture'?

Such a theoretical opposition, although enlightening, may nonetheless be too abstract to be able to account precisely for concrete cases. In the case of the French translations of the *Theory*, it corresponds only imperfectly to the actual translators' practices, and to the goals they seem to pursue. The *Theory*'s translators – and one can probably say so of almost all translators, apart from dogmatic ones that strive to apply at all costs a theory of translatology – certainly did not choose to be 'source-oriented' or 'target-oriented' as such, just for the sake of being 'source-oriented' or 'target-oriented'. Each of these two approaches obviously has its advantages and its disadvantages and a translator is led to seek the advantages of the one and to tolerate the disadvantages of the other, or possibly to mix the two approaches in a pragmatic manner, only because he is motivated by something else more concrete. It is this something else that I have described, above, as the subjective project of the translator inside his objective context. Therefore, rather than saying that the Marquise de Condorcet is 'target-oriented', which indeed is not inaccurate at a certain level of abstraction, it is better to explain that she hopes to contribute, with her translation, to the edification of a democratic France where the moral sentiments of citizens could be guided by reason. Instead of asserting that the twentieth-century translators are 'source-oriented', which indeed is not inaccurate either, it is better to show that they try to examine the possible moral foundation of free-trade economics through the methods of history of philosophy.

Now that I think I have demonstrated clearly enough the importance of taking into account the objective context and the subjective project that characterize each of the successive French translations of the *Theory*, it is time to come back at last to the feeling of 'unbearable lightness' that I mentioned at the beginning of this chapter. What is the connection between this paradoxical feeling and what has been explained above concerning the objective context of the translation and its subjective project? What is the link between, on the one hand, the contingency and the responsibility that are constitutive of the paradox of the 'unbearable lightness' and, on the other hand, the context and the project that are constitutive of the act of translating? I would answer that in my case the 'lightness' of translating comes from the objective context and its contingency, whereas its aspect sometimes and somewhat 'unbearable' stems from the subjective project and the responsibility it implies.

Indeed, on the one hand, translating is not heavy when one realizes that one is supported by a whole historical context, that the questions one asks to the text are those of one's time. One knows that one's contemporaries are driven too to ask the same questions, and that they can only welcome one's enterprise with a certain interest. To overstate it a little: who, around the end of the twentieth century, amongst the public liable to read a translation of Adam Smith, would not be interested to know more about free-trade economics and its possible moral foundation? Who would not appreciate that a translation of Smith's *Theory* should help to search in this direction? This is where 'lightness' proceeds from. But, on the other hand, to feel supported by one's context and to know that one asks questions that interest one's contemporaries does not prevent from feeling anxiety when one gets down to work. The concern for literality – with its will for technical rigor and its fear of mistranslation – and the requirements of the history of philosophy – in its search for sources and its apprehension about anachronism – can turn into a tiring obsessive activity. This is where, sometimes, the somewhat 'unbearable' aspect comes from. Therefore, the 'unbearable lightness' means simply that (re)translating is not exempt from the common lot of all human activities in history, torn as they are between the creative joys of contingency and the anxieties of responsibility.

Notes

1   Adam Smith (1999). The book benefited a pocket and revised edition four years later in 2003. This translation was worked out by a team of three people but, here, I speak only for myself. The following reflections upon our common work, especially in the third part and in the conclusion of this paper, do not necessarily express the point of view of my two colleagues and friends.

2   Milan Kundera (1984): *The Unbearable Lightness of Being.*

3   Milan Kundera (1984), p. 9. Kundera explicitly presents this vision in connection with Nietzsche's doctrine of 'eternal recurrence'. Out of this philosophical context, '*einmal ist keinmal*' means literally 'once is never'. The phrase can be used either as an excuse for doing something again after the first try (it then means 'once doesn't count' or 'once is not enough') or as a way to assure that something is not usual (it is then understood as 'once will not hurt' or 'what happened just once does not make a habit'). Walter Benjamin, author of a famous essay on *The Task of the Translator* [1921], quotes several times this saying in his writings, as it is noted by Robert Kahn and Catriona Seth (2010), p. 7.

4   Although translation has certainly been a much studied field for a long time, the specific concept and practice of retranslation began to get the attention it deserves only relatively recently, since the 1990s (see note 5). Even the word 'retranslation' is

relatively uncommon and its meaning is floating. A retranslation can be a second translation (e.g. two successive translations from English to French – as it is the case of the successive French translations of the *Theory* which are examined here) or a double translation (e.g. someone translates from English to French a book that is already an English translation from the German – this was the case for some German works by Hannah Arendt, translated into French via their English version) or even a retro-translation (e.g. someone translates from French to English a book that had already been translated from English to French – this is the case for the *Complete Works of Jeremy Bentham*, edited in 1838–1843 by John Bowring, which partly retranslates into English the French translations made by Bentham's Swiss disciple Etienne Dumont).

5   On the problems of retranslation, many particular case studies have been published but one can find general reflections on the topic in these following references: Paul Bensimon (1990); Antoine Berman (1990); Yves Gambier (1994); Patrizia Pierini (1999); Bernard Rousset (2000); Annie Brisset (2004); Lawrence Venuti (2004); Outi Paloposki (2004); Siobhan Brownlie (2006); Juan Jesús Zaro Vera (2007); Jean-Pierre Lefebvre (2008); Robert Kahn and Catriona Seth (2010); Yves Chevrel (2010); Enrico Monti (2011); Jean-René Ladmiral (2011); Yves Gambier (2011).

6   This disregard of history is what Yves Gambier (1994) reproves as a 'logocentric vision' or a belief in the 'immanence of the meaning' (p. 414, translation supplied). In this case, 'the blindness of the first translators would be outmatched by the denials of the later ones, in their endeavour to reach the source' (ibid.).

7   Thus, Henri Meschonnic (1999) can declare: 'Translating, even what has never been translated before, is always retranslating. Because translating is preceded by the history of translating.' (p. 436, translation supplied).

8   On the international reception of Smith's writings (in Germany, Russia, Poland, Italy, France, Spain, Japan, etc.) see two collections of essays: Hiroshi Mizuta and Chuhei Sugiyama, eds. (1993); Keith Tribe, (ed.) (2002). More specifically on the international reception of the *Theory*, see Alec Lawrence Macfie and David Daiches Raphael (1976), p. 29–33.

9   In Italian, see Adam Smith (1991). In Spanish, see Adam Smith (1997). Before these full-text translations, there were partial Italian and Spanish versions, which were parts of anthologies. But still, these were only published during the twentieth century. In Italian, see Adam Smith (1974). In Spanish, see Adam Smith (1941) – this partial translation, selecting around 170 pages, whereas the original text is around 400, is made from the classical collection by Lewis Amherst Selby-Bigge, (ed.) (1897).

10 Smith's sojourn in France was certainly decisive for the influence that the French Enlightenment had on the Scottish philosopher, and reciprocally. For a detailed analysis on this point, refer to Smith's intellectual biographies, particularly John Rae (2006), ch. 12–14, p. 174–231; Ian Simpson Ross (2010), ch. 13, p. 209–33; Nicholas Phillipson (2010), ch. 9, p. 180–99.

11 For a history of the reception of Smith's works in France from the eighteenth to the twentieth centuries, see Gilbert Faccarello and Philippe Steiner (2002). For the reception of Smith's works during the more restricted but highly interesting period of second half of the eighteenth century, see Harvey Chisick (2004), and the pages dedicated to Smith in Alexander Broadie (2012). For the reception of the *Theory* in France, see Takaho Ando (1993) and Ruth Scurr (2009). For the reception of the *Inquiry* in France, see Kenneth Carpenter (1995) and Kenneth Carpenter (2002).

12 The two contemporary translations of the *Inquiry* are Adam Smith (1995) and Adam Smith (2000–2005).

13   This distinction between an objective context and a subjective project is inspired, not without some latitude, from the analysis of Antoine Berman (1995), p. 74–82. Berman proposes in fact a triple distinction between the 'translation position', the 'translation project' and the 'translator's horizon'. The 'translation position' is a 'compromise between the way the translator perceives, as a subject led by the translation drive, the translating task, and the way he has internalized the ambient discourse concerning translation' (p. 74–75, translation supplied). The 'translation project' is 'the way in which the translator, on the one hand, performs the literary transfer, and, on the other hand, chooses a mode of translation' (p. 76). The 'translator's horizon' is 'the set of linguistic, literary, cultural and historical parameters that determine how the translator feels, acts and thinks' (p. 79). What I call 'objective context' is inspired from Berman's 'translator's horizon', while the 'subjective project' obviously corresponds to his 'translation project'. However, I do not take up the idea of 'translation position' because, on the one hand, that would require an analysis of the various theories of translation in eighteenth-century France and, on the other hand, there are no sufficient hints allowing to explain the 'translation drive' of most of the translators I am talking about here. I do not deny at all the relevance of Berman's category of 'translation position' in general but I consider that it falls out of the range of the present essay.

14   Adam Smith (1764). Marc-Antoine Eidous [1724–1790], a prolific translator and a regular collaborator of Diderot and d'Alembert's *Encyclopaedia*, also translated several works by Francis Hutcheson. See his biographical note in Louis-Gabriel Michaud and Joseph-François Michaud, eds. (1811–1828), vol. 12 [1814], p. 575.

15   Adam Smith (1976), VII, iii, 2, § 5, p. 319.

16   Adam Smith (1977), February 1772, p. 161 (translation supplied): 'It was a great mortification for me to see the way my book (*Theory of Moral Sentiments*) had been translated … Your generous kindness has relived me of such a sorrow, and has done me the greatest favour one can do to a man of letters.' Smith writes (in French) to the Marquise de Boufflers, to tell her how grateful he is that she should have taken the initiative for a new translation of his book, that will be published in 1774–1775 – see below. He might be exaggerating his disappointment towards Eidous' translation, in order to emphasize his gratitude towards the 'generous kindness' of his friend the Marquise.

17   For a general presentation of French moral philosophy in the eighteenth century, see Lester G. Crocker (1963) and Jacques Domenech (1989).

18   Eidous writes only a very brief 'Foreword' to his translation, see Marc-Antoine Eidous (1764). He praises the 'success' of the book 'in England', the 'clarity and simplicity of its style', the way 'the most abstract metaphysical matters are presented at the common readers' level' (p. vii–viii).

19   In the context of a first translation, to change the title of a book, or of a movie to be more in harmony with the taste and culture of the public might not be a bad move. To take a meritorious example, think of the way Marcel Proust's famous literary cycle, *A la recherche du temps perdu* [1913–1927], was first translated into English as *Remembrance of Things Past* by Charles Kenneth Scott Moncrieff – see Proust (1922–1931). It is a line taken from Shakespeare's *Sonnets* ('When to the sessions of sweet silent thought / I summon up remembrance of things past'), which has the advantage to convey immediately to the cultivated English reader of the time the feeling of nostalgia that saturates Proust's narrative. The literal translation, *In Search of Lost Time*, has come to be preferred by a later generation of translators under the supervision of Christopher Prendergast – see Proust (2002). It suits contemporary readers much

better acquainted with what is by now a long-studied book: 'search' has an analytical or experimental connotation that is much more philosophical than a mere musing 'remembrance', and 'lost time' has the bitter flavour of wasted time, whereas 'things past' is just nostalgically sweet. In the same manner, Scott Moncrieff cautiously translated the title of one of Proust's volumes as *Cities of the Plain*, instead of the literal *Sodom and Gomorrah*. It is an obvious concession to the Puritanism of the time, which might have been shocked by an implicit allusion to sodomites, but it cleverly retains the Biblical reference (it is a quotation from Genesis, 19, 29, referring indeed to the cities of Sodom and Gomorrah). Taking into account the contemporary evolution of morals, the new 2002 translation uses the literal translation.

20 Adam Smith (1774–1775). Jean-Louis Blavet [1719–1809], librarian of the Prince de Conti, royal censor, friend of François Quesnay and of the Physiocrats, also published a translation of Smith's *Inquiry* in 1779–1780. See his biographical note in Louis-Gabriel Michaud and Joseph-François Michaud, eds. (1811–1828), vol. 5 [1823], p. 576–7. Smith writes (in French, translation supplied) to Blavet that he is 'very satisfied' with his translation of the *Theory*, and 'even more' with that of the *Enquiry* – see Adam Smith (1977), 23 July 1782, p. 260.

21 Jean-Louis Blavet (1774–1774), p. viii, translation supplied.

22 Louis Alexandre, Duc de La Rochefoucauld [1743–1792], president of the Royal Academy of Sciences, deputy in the Estates-General and in the Constituent Assembly during the French Revolution, is the grandson of François, Duc de La Rochefoucauld, author of the *Maxims* [1664], whom Smith refers to in the *Theory* – see Adam Smith (1976), VII, ii, 4, § 6, p. 308. One can learn about of his intellectual background in a study dedicated to the salon of his mother: Daniel Vaugelade (2001).

23 See La Rochefoucauld's letter written four years after giving up his project, in Adam Smith (1977), 3 March 1778, p. 233 (translation supplied): 'I had just achieved to translate the first part [of the *Theory*] when Father Blavet's own translation was published, and thus I was compelled to relinquish the pleasure to bring in my language one of the best works written in yours'. La Rochefoucauld also offers to Smith to translate the fifth revised edition of the *Theory*, but this project fails too, see his letter in ibid., 6 August 1779, p. 238.

24 Adam Smith (1798). Sophie de Grouchy, Marquise de Condorcet [1764–1822], has a renowned salon during the Old Regime. Though she belongs to the nobility, she is in favour of the democratic ideals of the French Revolution. Several biographies of her are available; see, for example, Thierry Boissel (1988).

25 On the relationship between Smith and the Marquis de Condorcet, see Horst Dippel (1981) and Emma Rothschild (2002).

26 The original title is in fact 'Lettres à C*** sur la *Théorie des sentiments moraux*', see Marquise de Condorcet (1798). In this title 'C***' most probably stands for the philosopher Pierre-Jean-Georges Cabanis – thought it is not altogether impossible that the Marquise might rather refer to her deceased husband Condorcet. Cabanis (1980), X, p. 549, explicitly pays tribute to the Marquise's criticism and modification of Smith's theory of sympathy. Three critical editions of the *Letters on Sympathy* are available: Marquise de Condorcet (1994), Marquise de Condorcet (2010) and, translated into English, Marquise de Condorcet (2008).

27 The Marquise de Condorcet's translation of the *Theory* and her *Letters on Sympathy* have interested several scholars, amongst whom Takaho Ando (1983); Takaho Ando (1993); Jean-Paul de Lagrave (1994); Evelyn L. Forget (2001); Deidre Dawson (2004); Jean Delisle (2004); Marc André Bernier (2009); Jeanne Britton (2009); Ruth Scurr

(2009); Catriona Seth (2010a); Catriona Seth (2010b); Daniel Dumouchel (2010); Michel Malherbe (2010); Marc André Bernier (2010); Eric Schliesser (2014); Spiros Tegos (2014).

28   Marquise de Condorcet (1798), letter I, p. 357, translation supplied.

29   Adam Smith (1976), III, 3, § 43, p. 155. See also ibid., VI, ii, 2, § 12–17, p. 231–234, and VI, iii, § 12, p. 241–242. The criticism of factions is common in British political philosophy of the time, in connection with the English Revolutions of 1641 and 1688. However, it is not altogether impossible to think that Smith, when he writes these lines, might refer to the beginnings of the French Revolution in 1789. The paragraphs of VI, ii, 2, § 12–17, and VI, iii, § 12, belong to the sixth edition of the *Theory*, published in 1790, and its manuscript has been delivered to the publisher at the beginning of winter in 1789 – as we know from Dugald Stewart (1980), p. 238.

30   Marquise de Condorcet (1798), letter VIII, p. 490. More generally, the republican project of the Marquise is mostly displayed in the letters VI, VII and VIII.

31   On this sensualist reworking of the concept of sympathy, see especially ibid., letter I. Note that, for the Marquise, rationalism (in morals) does not exclude sensualism. All rationalism is not necessarily idealist, or at least it is a question of definition.

32   Ibid., letter V, p. 440, translation supplied. On the role of reflexion towards sentiment, see also *id.*, letter II, p. 370–371.

33   Ibid., letter V, p. 441, translation supplied.

34   ibid., letter VI, p. 453, translation supplied.

35   Adam Smith (1976), I, i, 1, § 1, p. 9. In French: '*[La pitié] existe encore à quelque degré dans le cœur ... des hommes qui ont violé le plus audacieusement les lois de la société*'.

36   Ibid., I, i, 4, § 7, p. 21–22.

37   Ibid., I, i, 3, § 9, p. 19. In French: '*sans fondement et sans raison*'.

38   Ibid., I, i, 5, § 10, p. 26, and I, i, 3, § 10, p. 19. In French: '*règle*', '*jugeons*'.

39   Ibid., I, i, 4, § 7, p. 22; I, i, 4, § 9, p. 23; I, i, 5, § 8, p. 26, etc.

40   Ibid., I, ii, Introduction, § 1, p. 27. In French: '*degré de sympathie*'.

41   Ibid., I, ii, Introduction, § 2, p. 27. In French: '*caractère de convenance*'.

42   Ibid., I, i, 5, § 4, p. 24, and *passim*.

43   Ibid., I, i, 5, § 8, p. 26 (in French 'impartial' is omitted); III, 3, § 4, p. 137 ('the eye of the impartial spectator' is rendered by 'our conscience', in French: '*notre conscience*'); III, 3, § 28, p. 148 ('he enjoys ... the applause of every candid and impartial spectator' becomes 'he applauds himself', in French: '*il s'applaudit lui-même*'); III, 3, § 42, p. 154 (in French 'impartial' is omitted); etc.

44   Marquise de Condorcet (1798), letter V, p. 435–436.

45   Adam Smith (1976), I, i, 1, § 1, p. 9. In French: '*le cœur*'.

46   Ibid., I, i, 1, § 1, p. 9. In French: '*un principe d'intérêt pour ce qui arrive aux autres*'.

47   ibid., I, i, 1, § 5, p. 10. In French: '*la faculté de partager les passions des autres, quelles qu'elles soient*'.

48   Ibid., III, 3, § 2, p. 134–5. In French: '*yeux de notre corps*' and '*regards de notre intelligence*'.

49   Adam Smith (1830). Then Adam Smith (1860), with an introduction and footnotes by Henri Baudrillart. Lastly Adam Smith (1982), a reprint of the Baudrillart edition including its introduction and footnotes.

50   On the importance of Smith's extensive revisions of the sixth edition of the *Theory* in 1790, see David Daiches Raphael (2007), ch. I, p. 1–11: 'Two versions'; and Ryan Patrick Hanley (2009), ch. III, p. 82–99: 'The what and how of TMS VI'. The numerous

changes and additions bring up the questions of Smith's judgment upon commercial society (*Theory*, I, iii, 3), of the significance of his theory of virtues (ibid., VI), of his position towards religion (ibid., II, ii, 3), of the importance he gives to Stoicism (ibid., VI, iii and VII, ii, 1), or of a possible alteration in his concept of impartial spectator (ibid., III, 2). It is true that the philosophical significance of these revisions was neglected for a long time – that is to say before the publication of works in the history of philosophy such as the two books I have just mentioned. However, their mere quantitative importance (more than 100 added pages, constituting a totally new part of the book), is obvious enough to recommend to the public a translation based upon the last edition.

51 Related quotations taken from such journals as the *Correspondance littéraire, philosophique et critique* [1747–1793] or *La décade philosophique* [1794–1807] or, from the correspondence of various critics of the time, can be found in Gilbert Faccarello and Philippe Steiner (2002) and Catriona Seth (2010a).

52 See Victor Cousin (1840), vol. II, p. 99–183; Théodore Jouffroy (1858), vol. I, p. 406–27 and vol. II, p. 1–55.

53 On the interpretation of Smith's moral philosophy in France during the first part of the XIXth century, see Jean-Pierre Cotten (1991); Jean-Pierre Cotten (1992); and Laurent Jaffro (2007).

54 See Bergson (1977), chap. I; and Bergson (2003–2006), vol. I, lesson LXVI.

55 The rise of '*Das Adam Smith Problem*' amongst German scholars is exposed by Alec Lawrence Macfie and David Daiches Raphael (1976), p. 20–5; and David Daiches Raphael (1985), ch. V, p. 86–90.

56 Henri Baudrillart (1860), p. v–vi, translation supplied. Baudrillart exposes similar views in a book published at the same time, see Henri Baudrillart (1883), p. 97–8.

57 Henri Baudrillart (1860), p. vii, translation supplied.

58 Ibid., p. xi, translation supplied.

59 Ibid., p. x, translation supplied.

60 Ibid., p. viii, where Baudrillart refers to the works of Jouffroy and Cousin above mentioned.

61 Ibid., p. xiii, translation supplied.

62 Baudrillart's footnote in Adam Smith (1860), p. 434.

63 Elie Halevy (1928), vol. I, ch. 3.

64 Albert Schatz (1907), part I, ch. 4.

65 See Didier Deleule (1979); Michel Malherbe (1980); Yves Michaud (1983); Michel Malherbe (1984); Jean-Pierre Cléro (1985).

66 French studies on Scotland notably ended up to the creation, in 2000, of the *French Society for Scottish Studies* and its website.

67 Claude Gautier (1993); Michaël Biziou, Claude Gautier and Jean-François Pradeau (1999); Michaël Biziou (2000); Michaël Biziou (ed.) (2000); Michaël Biziou (2003); Magali Bessone and Michaël Biziou (eds) (2009).

68 Adam Smith (1976), II, ii, 3, § 1-4, p. 85–6. On this question, see Claude Gautier (1993).

69 Adam Smith (1976), II, ii, 1, § 1–10, p. 78–82. On this question, see Michaël Biziou (2009).

70 Adam Smith (1976), VI, i, § 5–6, p. 213. On this question, see Michaël Biziou (2003), p. 140–8.

71 As is stated in Alec Lawrence Macfie and David Daiches Raphael (1976), p. 1–5.

72 Adam Smith (1976), *passim*. In French: '*degré*', '*haut*', '*bas*', '*hauteur*', '*médiocrité*', '*aviver*', '*atténuer*'.

73   Ibid., I, i, 1, § 4, p. 10, and *passim*. In French: '*entrer dans*' (rather than the more usual but less literal '*partager*').

74   Ibid. and *passim*. In French: '*accompagner*' (rather than the more usual but less literal '*ressentir aussi*').

75   Ibid., and *passim*. In French: '*ramener en soi le cas*' (rather than the more usual but less literal '*s'imaginer*').

76   Ibid., *passim*. In French: '*spectateur*', '*acteur*', '*applaudissement*', '*le point de vue duquel il est vu*'.

77   Ibid., I, i, 3, § 8, p. 18, and *passim*. In French: '*commun*' (rather than the less humean '*courant*').

78   Ibid., VI, ii, 1, § 12, p. 222, and *passim*. In French: '*association*' (rather than the less humean '*lien*').

79   Ibid., I, i, 1, § 3, p. 10, and *passim*. In French: '*fantaisie*' (rather than the less humean '*imagination*').

80   Ibid., I, i, 1, § 1, p. 10, and *passim*. In French: '*concevoir*' (rather than the less humean '*se représenter*').

81   Ibid., I, i, 5, § 6, p. 25, and *passim*. In French: '*entendement*' (rather than the less humean '*compréhension*').

82   On the successive elaboration of the moral sentiments tradition through Shaftesbury, Hutcheson, Hume and Smith, see Michaël Biziou (2000).

83   For example, *Sense and Sensibility* [1811] by Jane Austen is never literally translated into French as '*Sens et sensibilité*'. The French '*sens*' would sound too bodily or carnal (as in the 'realm of the senses'), or much too abstract or philosophical ('*sens*' is also 'meaning', so that '*sens de la vie*' is 'meaning of life'). This title was translated as *Raison et sensibilité* ('reason and sensibility'), see Austen (1814); or as *Le cœur et la raison* ('heart and reason'), see Austen (2009).

84   Adam Smith (1976), III, 4, § 5, p. 158, and *passim*. In French: '*sens moral*'.

85   Ibid., I, ii, 3, § 8, p. 38, and *passim*. In French: '*sens de la convenance*'.

86   Bernard Mandeville, an author that Smith knew very well, uses 'self-liking' in contrast with 'self-love' in a way somewhat similar to the two French words '*amour de soi*' and '*amour propre*'. See Bernard Mandeville (1924), vol. II, 3rd dialogue, p. 130. But Smith does not make use of 'self-liking'.

87   The two words '*amour de soi*' (from the Latin '*amor sui*') and '*amour propre*' (from '*amor proprius*') were originally used to differentiate two opposed meanings of the Greek '*philautia*', such as can be found in Aristotle. Indeed, Aristotle distinguishes two '*philautiai*', one virtuous and the other vicious. See Aristotle (2009), IX, 8, 1168b12–1169a17: '[The good man] is most truly a lover of self, of another type than that which is a matter of reproach, and as different from that as living according to a rational principle is from living as passion dictates, and desiring what is noble from desiring what seems advantageous.' In eighteenth-century France, for Jean-Jacques Rousseau for example, '*amour de soi*' is a natural instinct of self-preservation and is not vicious, whereas '*amour propre*' is a social sentiment that presupposes a comparison with the others, and that quickly leads to vice. See Jean-Jacques Rousseau (1964), note XV, p. 219. As to Smith, when he talks about what becomes of 'self-love' when arises a comparison with the others, he uses the words 'pride', 'love of praise' or 'vanity', see for example Smith (1976), I, iii, 2, § 1, p. 50–51, and III, 2, § 1–3, p. 113–14.

88   Ibid., VI, 1, § 1, p. 212, and *passim*. In French: '*recommander*' (which is closer to the Latin word than '*désigner à l'attention de*').

89 Ibid., I, i, 3, § 1, p. 16, and *passim*. In French: '*convenance*' (which is closer to the Latin word than '*bienséance*').
90 Ibid., I, ii, 1, § 11, p. 30, and *passim*. In French: '*décorum*' (which is closer to the Latin word than '*cérémonial*').
91 Ibid., II, i, 2, § 4, p. 70, and *passim*. In French: '*bons offices*' (which is closer to the Latin word than '*bienfaits*').
92 See especially Jean-René Ladmiral (1986). Ladmiral calls 'source-oriented' these translators who 'focus on the signifier of the language of the source-text that has to be translated', whereas he considers as 'target-oriented' those who 'aim at respecting the signified (or, more exactly, the meaning and value) of the speech that is to appear in the target-language' (p. 33, translation supplied). This opposition can already be found in Friedrich Schleiermacher's conference *On the Different Methods of Translating* [1813]: 'Either the translator leaves the writer in peace as much as possible and moves the reader toward him; or he leaves the reader in peace as much as possible and moves the writer toward him.' – see Friedrich Schleiermacher (2000), p. 49. In the first case, the translator sees to it that the reader can perceive, as beneath the surface of his translation, the underlying presence of the source-language; in the second case, the translator tries to create the illusion that the author himself has written his text directly in the target-language.

Bibliography

Ando, T. (1983) 'Mme de Condorcet et la philosophie de la "sympathie"', *Studies on Voltaire and the Eighteenth Century*, 216: 335–6.
Ando, T. (1993) 'The introduction of Adam Smith's moral philosophy to French thought', in H. Mizuta and C. Sugiyama (eds) *Adam Smith: International Perspectives*, pp. 207–9.
Aristotle (2009) *Nichomachean Ethics*, translated by William David Ross, Oxford: Oxford University Press.
Austen, J. (1814) [1811] *Raison et sensibilité*, translated by Isabelle de Montolieu, Paris: Arthus-Bertrand.
Austen, J. (2009) [1811] *Le cœur et la raison*, translated by Pierre Goubert, Paris: Gallimard.
Baudrillart, H. (1860) 'Introduction', in *Adam Smith* (1860): v–xvi.
Baudrillart, H. (1883) [1860] *Des rapports de la morale et de l'économie politique*, 2nd edition, Paris: Guillaumin et Compagnie.
Bensimon, P. (1990) 'Présentation', *Palimpsestes*, 4: ix–xiii.
Bentham, J. (1838–1843) *The Complete Works of Jeremy Bentham*, Edinburgh: William Tait.
Bergson, H. (1977) [1932] *The Two Sources of Morality and Religion*, translated by R.A. Audra and C. Brereton, Notre Dame, IN: University of Notre Dame Press.
Bergson, H. (2003–2006) [1885–1888] *Leçons clermontoises*, Paris: L'Harmattan.
Berman, A. (1990) 'La retraduction comme espace de traduction', *Palimpsestes*, 4: 1–7.
Berman, A. (1995) *Pour une critique des traductions: John Donne*, Paris: Gallimard.
Bernier, M.A. (2009) 'Sophie de Condorcet, lectrice française d'Adam Smith', *Travaux de littérature*, 22: 227–36.
Bernier, M.A. (2010) 'Rhétorique et politique des émotions physiques de l'âme chez Sophie de Grouchy', in *Marquise de Condorcet* (2010), pp. 167–78.
Bessone, M. and Biziou, M. (eds) (2009) *Adam Smith philosophe. De la morale à l'économie, ou philosophie du libéralisme*, Rennes: Presses Universitaires de Rennes.
Biziou, M. (2000) *Le concept de système dans la tradition anglo-écossaise des sentiments*

moraux, 1699–1795. De la métaphysique à l'économie politique (Shaftesbury, Hutcheson, Hume, Smith), Lille: ANRT.

Biziou, M. (ed.) (2000) *Adam Smith et la théorie des sentiments moraux*, issue of the *Revue philosophique de la France et de l'étranger*, 4.

Biziou, M. (2003) *Adam Smith et l'origine du libéralisme*, Paris: PUF.

Biziou, M. (2009) 'Libéralisme économique, pauvreté et inégalités sociales selon Adam Smith', in M. Bessone and M. Biziou (eds) *Adam Smith philosophe. De la morale à l'économie, ou philosophie du libéralisme* (2009): 183–200.

Biziou, M., Gautier, C. and Pradeau, J.-F. (1999) 'Introduction: structure et arguments de la *Théorie des sentiments moraux*', in *Adam Smith* (1999): 1–13.

Blavet, J.-L. (1774–1775) 'Préface', in *Adam Smith* (1774–1775), vol. I: vii–xii.

Boissel, T. (1988) *Sophie de Condorcet, femme des Lumières, 1764–1822*, Paris: Presses de la Renaissance.

Brisset, A. (2004) 'Retraduire ou le corps changeant de la connaissance: sur l'historicité de la traduction', *Palimpsestes*, 15: 17–45.

Britton, J. (2009) 'Translating sympathy by the letter: Henry Mackenzie, Sophie de Condorcet, and Adam Smith', *Eighteenth-Century Fiction*, 22, 1: 71–98.

Broadie, A. (2012) *Agreeable Connexions: Scottish Enlightenment Links with France*, Edinburgh: John Donald.

Brownlie, S. (2006) 'Narrative theory and retranslation theory', *Across Languages and Cultures*, 7 (2): 145–70.

Cabanis, P.J.G. (1980) [1802] *Rapports du physique et du moral de l'homme*, Geneva: Slatkine.

Carpenter, K. (1995) 'Recherches sur la nature et les causes de la richesse des nations d'Adam Smith et politique culturelle en France', *Economies et Sociétés*, 10: 5–30.

Carpenter, K. (2002) *The Dissemination of the Wealth of Nations in French and in France, 1776–1843*, New York: The Bibliographical Society of America.

Chevrel, Y. (2010) 'Introduction: la retraduction – *und kein Ende*', in R. Kahn and C. Seth (eds) *La retraduction*, Mont-Saint-Aignan: Publications des Universités de Rouen et du Havre, pp. 11–20.

Chisick, H. (2004) 'The representation of David Hume and Adam Smith in the *Année Littéraire* and the *Journal Encyclopédique*', in D. Dawson and P. Morère (eds) *Scotland and France in the Enlightenment*, pp. 240–263.

Cléro, J.-P. (1985) *La philosophie de passions chez David Hume*, Paris: Klincksiek.

Condorcet, Marquise de (1798) 'Lettres à C*** sur la *Théorie des sentiments moraux*', in *Adam Smith* (1798), vol. II: 355–507.

Condorcet, Marquise de (1994) [1798] *Lettres sur la sympathie, suivies des Lettres d'amour*, Montreal: L'Etincelle.

Condorcet, Marquise de (2008) [1798] *Letters on Sympathy*, translated by Karin Brown and James E. McClellan III, Philadelphia, PA: American Philosophical Society.

Condorcet, Marquise de (2010) [1798] *Les 'Lettres sur la sympathie' (1798) de Sophie de Grouchy, Marquise de Condorcet*, Oxford: The Voltaire Foundation.

Cotten, J.-P. (1991) 'La réception d'Adam Smith chez cousin et les éclectiques', *Corpus*, 18/19: 51–60.

Cotten, J.-P. (1992) 'La réception d'Adam Smith chez les derniers idéologistes et dans la 'nouvelle philosophie', in J.-P. Cotten, *Autour de Victor Cousin. Une politique de la philosophie*, Paris: Les Belles Lettres, pp. 117–43.

Cousin, V. (1840) *Cours d'histoire de la philosophie morale au XVIIIᵉ siècle*, Paris: Ladrange.

Crocker, L.G. (1963) *Nature and Culture: Ethical Thought in the French Enlightenment*, Baltimore, MD: Johns Hopkins University Press.

Dawson, D. (2004) 'From moral philosophy to public policy: Sophie de Grouchy's translation and critique of Smith's *Theory of Moral Sentiments*', in D. Dawson and P. Morère (eds) *Scotland and France in the Enlightenment*, Lewisburg: Bucknell University Press, pp. 264–83.

Dawson, D. and Morère, P. (eds) (2004) *Scotland and France in the Enlightenment*, Lewisburg: Bucknell University Press.

Deleule, D. (1979) *Hume et la naissance du libéralisme économique*, Paris: Aubier.

Delisle, J. (2004) 'La Marquise de Condorcet: l'aristocrate républicaine, la traductrice militante et la philosophe', in J.-P. Beaulieu (ed.) (2004) *D'une écriture à l'autre. Les femmes et la traduction sous l'Ancien régime*, Ottawa: Presses de l'Université d'Ottawa, 243–64.

Dippel, H. (1981) *Individuum und Gesellschaft, soziales Denken zwischen Tradition und Revolution: Smith, Condorcet, Franklin*, Göttingen: Vandenhoeck und Ruprecht.

Domenech, J. (1989) *L'éthique des Lumières. Les fondements de la morale dans la philosophie française du XVIIIe siècle*, Paris: Vrin.

Dumouchel, D. (2010) 'Une éducation sentimentale: sympathie et construction de la morale dans les *Lettres sur la sympathie* de Sophie de Grouchy', in Marquise de Condorcet, *Les 'Lettres sur la sympathie' (1798) de Sophie de Grouchy, Marquise de Condorcet*, Oxford: The Voltaire Foundation, pp. 139–150.

Eidous, M.-A. (1764) 'Avertissement', in *Adam Smith* (1764), vol. I: vii–viii.

Faccarello, G. and Steiner, P. (2002) 'The diffusion of the work of Adam Smith in the French language: an outline history', in K. Tribe (ed.) *A Critical Bibliography of Adam Smith*, London: Pickering & Chatto, pp. 61–119.

Forget, E.L. (2001) 'Cultivating sympathy: Sophie Condorcet's *Letters on Sympathy*', *Journal of the History of Economic Thought*, 23 (3): 319–37.

Gambier, Y. (1994) 'La retraduction, retour et détour', *Meta. Translators' Journal*, 39 (3): 413–17.

Gambier, Y. (2011) 'La retraduction, ambiguïtés et défis' in E. Monti and P. Schnyder (eds) *Autour de la retraduction. Perspectives littéraires européennes*, Paris: Orizons, pp. 49–66.

Gautier, C. (1993) *La naissance de la société civile. Lectures anglo-écossaises: Mandeville, Smith, Ferguson*, Paris: PUF.

Halevy, E. (1928) [1901–1904] *The Growth of Philosophic Radicalism*, translated by Mary Morris, London: Faber and Gwyer.

Hanley, R.P. (2009) *Adam Smith and the Character of Virtue*, Cambridge: Cambridge University Press.

Jaffro, L. (2007) 'Raison et sentiment. L'histoire des théories du sens moral vue par Jouffroy', in E. Arosio and M. Malherbe (eds) *Philosophie française et philosophie écossaise, 1750–1850*, Paris: Vrin, pp. 137–150.

Jouffroy, T. (1858) [1834] *Cours de droit naturel*, 3rd edition, Paris: Hachette.

Kahn, R. and Seth, C. (eds) (2010) *La retraduction*, Mont-Saint-Aignan: Publications des Universités de Rouen et du Havre.

Kahn, R. and Seth, C. (2010) 'Avant-propos: une fois ne suffit pas', in R. Kahn and C. Seth (eds) (2010): 7–10.

Kundera, M. (1984) [1984] *The Unbearable Lightness of Being*, translated by Michael Henry Heim, New York: Harper and Row.

Ladmiral, J.-R. (1986) 'Sourciers et ciblistes', *Revue d'esthétique*, 12: 33–42.

Ladmiral, J.-R. (2011) 'Nous autres traductions, nous savons maintenant que nous sommes mortelles…', in E. Monti and P. Schnyder (eds) *Autour de la retraduction. Perspectives littéraires européennes*, Paris: Orizons, pp. 29–48.

Lagrave, J.-P. de (1994) 'Sophie de Condorcet, Marquise des Lumières et adepte de la sympathie', in Marquise de Condorcet *Lettres sur la sympathie, suivies des Lettres d'amour*, Montreal: L'Etincelle, pp. 17–44.

Lefebvre, J.-P. (2008) 'Retraduire', *Traduire*, 218: 7–13.

Macfie, A.L. and Raphael, D.D. (1976) 'Introduction', in *Adam Smith* (1976), pp. 1–52.

Malherbe, M. (1980) *Kant ou Hume*, Paris: Vrin.

Malherbe, M. (1984) *La philosophie empiriste de David Hume*, Paris: Vrin.

Malherbe, M. (2010) 'Justice et société chez Sophie de Grouchy', in Marquise de Condorcet, *Les 'Lettres sur la sympathie' (1798) de Sophie de Grouchy, Marquise de Condorcet*, Oxford: The Voltaire Foundation, pp. 151–61.

Mandeville, B. (1924) [1705–1729] *The Fable of the Bees*, Oxford: Clarendon Press.

Meschonnic, H. (1999) *Poétique du traduire*, Lagrasse: Verdier.

Michaud, L.-G. and Michaud, J.-F. (eds) (1811–1828) *Biographie universelle, ancienne et moderne*, Paris: Michaud Frères.

Michaud, Y. (1983) *Hume et la fin de la philosophie*, Paris: PUF.

Mizuta, H. and Sugiyama, C. (eds) (1993) *Adam Smith: International Perspectives*, New York: Saint Martin Press.

Monti, E. and Schnyder, P. (eds) (2011) *Autour de la retraduction. Perspectives littéraires européennes*, Paris: Orizons.

Monti, E. (2011) 'Introduction: La retraduction, un état des lieux', in E. Monti and P. Schnyder (eds) *Autour de la retraduction. Perspectives littéraires européennes*, Paris: Orizons, pp. 9–27.

Paloposki, O. (2004) 'A thousand and one translations: revisiting retranslation', in G. Hansen, K. Malmkjær and D. Gile (eds) *Claims, Changes and Challenges in Translation Studies*, Amsterdam: Benjamins, pp. 27–38.

Phillipson, N. (2010) *Adam Smith: An Enlightened Life*, New Haven: Yale University Press.

Pierini, P. (1999) 'La ritraduzione in prospettiva teorica e pratica', in P. Pierini (1999) *L'atto del tradurre. Aspetti teorici e pratici della traduzione*, Roma: Bulzoni, 51–72.

Proust, M. (1922–1931) [1913–1927] *Remembrance of Things Past*, translated by Charles Kenneth Scott Moncrieff, New York: Henry Holt.

Proust, M. (2002) [1913–1927] *In Search of Lost Time*, translated by Christopher Prendergast, London: Allen Lane.

Rae, J. (2006) [1895] *The Life of Adam Smith*, New York: Cosimo.

Raphael, D.D. (1985) *Adam Smith*, Oxford: Oxford University Press.

Raphael, D.D. (2007) *The Impartial Spectator. Adam Smith's Moral Philosophy*, Oxford: Oxford University Press.

Ross, I.S. (2010) [1995] *The Life of Adam Smith*, 2nd edition, Oxford: Oxford University Press.

Rothschild, E. (2002) *Economic Sentiments: Adam Smith, Condorcet, and the Enlightenment*, Cambridge, MA: Harvard University Press.

Rousseau, J.-J. (1964) [1755] *Discours sur l'origine et les fondements de l'inégalité parmi les hommes* in Jean-Jacques Rousseau (1964) *Œuvres complètes*, Paris: Gallimard, Bibliothèque de la Pléiade, vol. III.

Rousset, B. (2000) 'La retraduction et le problème de la langue première d'une pensée philosophique', in O. Bloch and J. Moutaux (eds) *Traduire les philosophes*, Paris: Publications de la Sorbonne, pp. 247–56.

Schatz, A. (1907) *L'individualisme économique et social: ses origines, son évolution, ses formes contemporaines*, Paris: Armand Colin.

Schleiermacher, F. (2000) [1813] 'On the different methods of translating', translated by Susan Bernofsky, in Lawrence Venuti (ed.) (2000) *The Translation Studies Reader*, Abindgon: Routledge, 43–63.

Schliesser, E. (2014) 'Sophie de Grouchy, Marquise de Condorcet: Wisdom and Reform between Reason and Feeling', in E. O'Neill and M.P. Lascano (eds) *Feminist History of Philosophy: The Recovery and Evaluation of Women's Philosophical Thought*, Dordrecht: Springer, forthcoming.

Scurr, R. (2009) 'Inequality and political stability from the Ancien Régime to the revolution: the reception of Adam Smith's *Theory of Moral Sentiments* in France', *History of European Ideas*, 25: 441–9.

Selby-Bigge, L.A. (ed.) (1897) *British Moralists, being Selections from Writers Principally of the Eighteenth Century*, Oxford: Clarendon Press.

Seth, C. (2010a) 'Adam Smith retraduit par Sophie de Condorcet', in R. Kahn and C. Seth (eds) *La retraduction*, Mont-Saint-Aignan: Publications des Universités de Rouen et du Havre, pp. 61–72.

Seth, C. (2010b) 'Un double service rendu à la postérité: la *Théorie des sentiments moraux* par Adam Smith, suivie des *Lettres sur la sympathie*', in Marquise de Condorcet, *Les 'Lettres sur la sympathie' (1798) de Sophie de Grouchy, Marquise de Condorcet*, Oxford: The Voltaire Foundation, pp. 127–37.

Smith, A. (1764) [1759] *Métaphysique de l'âme, ou Théorie des sentiments moraux*, translated by Marc-Antoine Eidous, 2 vols, Paris: Briasson.

Smith, A. (1774–1775) [1759] *Théorie des sentiments moraux*, translated by Jean-Louis Blavet, 2 vols, Paris: Valade.

Smith, A. (1798) [1759] *Théorie des sentiments moraux*, translated by the Marquise de Condorcet, 2 vols, Paris: Buisson.

Smith, A. (1830) [1759] *Théorie des sentiments moraux*, translated by the Marquise de Condorcet, Paris: Barois aîné.

Smith, A. (1860) [1759] *Théorie des sentiments moraux*, translated by the Marquise de Condorcet, introduction by Henri Baudrillart, Paris: Guillaumin et Compagnie.

Smith, A. (1941) [1759] *Teoría de los sentimientos morales*, translated by Edmundo O'Gorman, introduction by Eduardo Nicol, Mexico: El Colegio de México.

Smith, A. (1974) *Morale dei sentimenti e ricchezza delle nazioni*, translated by Ida Cappiello, Napoli: Guida.

Smith, A. (1976) [1759] *Theory of Moral Sentiments*, Oxford: Oxford University Press.

Smith, A. (1977) *Correspondence of Adam Smith*, Oxford: Oxford University Press.

Smith, A. (1982) [1759] *Théorie des sentiments moraux*, translated by the Marquise de Condorcet, introduction by Henri Baudrillart, Plan de la Tour: Editions d'aujourd'hui, series Les introuvables.

Smith, A. (1991) [1759] *Teoria dei sentimenti morali*, translated by Cesare Cozzo, introduction by Adelino Zanini, Roma: Istituto della Enciclopedia Italiana Treccani.

Smith, A. (1995) [1776] *Enquête sur la nature et les causes de la richesse des nations*, translated by Paulette Taïeb, Paris: PUF.

Smith, A. (1997) [1759] *Teoría de los sentimientos morales*, translated by Carlos Rodríguez Braun, Madrid: Alianza.

Smith, A. (1999) [1759] *Théorie des sentiments moraux*, translated by Michaël Biziou, Claude Gautier and Jean-François Pradeau, Paris: PUF, series Léviathan; revised pocket edition Paris: PUF, 2003, series Quadrige.

Smith, A. (2000–2005) [1776] *Recherches sur la nature et les causes de la richesse des nations*, translated by Philippe Jaudel, Paris: Economica.

Stewart, D. (1980) [1794] 'Account of the life and writings of Adam Smith', in Adam Smith (1980) *Essays on Philosophical Subjects*, Oxford: Oxford University Press, pp. 269–351.

Tegos, S. (2014) 'Sympathie morale et tragédie sociale: Sophie de Grouchy lectrice d'Adam Smith', *Noesis*, 22, forthcoming.

Tribe, K. (ed.) (2002) *A Critical Bibliography of Adam Smith*, London: Pickering & Chatto.

Vaugelade, Daniel (2001) *Le Salon physiocratique des La Rochefoucauld, animé par Louise Elisabeth de La Rochefoucauld, Duchesse d'Enville, 1716–1797*, Paris: Publibook.

Venuti, L. (2004) 'Retranslations: The creation of value', *Bucknell Review: A Scholarly Journal of Letters, Arts and Sciences*, 47 (1): 25–38.

Zaro Vera, J.J. (2007) 'En torno al concepto de retraducción' in Francisco Ruiz Noguera and Juan Jesús Zaro Vera (eds) (2007) *Retraducir: una nueva mirada. La retraduccion de textos literarios y audiovisuales*, Málaga: Miguel Gómez Ediciones, pp. 7–29.

Symposium

Smith and China

A 'third culture' in economics?

An essay on Smith, Confucius and the rise of China

Carsten Herrmann-Pillath

Towards the sinicization of economics?

Concomitant with China's rise as an economic power, we observe an increasing impact of China on economic thinking. Currently, this happens mostly by the force of example. China's rise questions some established standards in economic theory, especially in contrast to certain basic assumptions of the so-called Washington consensus in development economics (Rodrik 2006). China's experience was an important input into the careful revision of certain ideas about strategies of development, summarized in the *Growth Report* (Commission on Growth and Development 2008), which has been also recognized by the World Bank, the major foreign adviser to Chinese economic policy after 1978. This special role of China was also reflected in the appointment of a Chinese economist as World Bank Chief Economist, Justin Lin Yifu, who is currently promoting a 'New Structural Economics' as an innovative framework for development economics (Lin 2010). Beyond this power of example, recently, China also has begun to submit proposals for reforms of the international economic order, especially with regard to the international monetary system.

These observations raise the question of whether China can also emerge as a major source of ideas about economics and economic policy in the near future. This question can be framed in two different ways. One is to ask whether Chinese economists will contribute to the development of economic science, as it stands. This will necessarily happen, and certainly already happens, reflecting the increasing internationalization of Chinese scholarship as a result of the past history of the massive 'studying abroad' phenomenon, among other factors. The other perspective on the question refers to the deeper level of the underlying philosophy and ideology of economics. For a long time, this question would have been seen in the light of the traditional and now obsolete contrast between modern economics and Marxism. Today, the ideological foundations of modern Chinese economic development are obscure and mostly seen as non-existent, in the sense of the diagnosis of endemic pragmatism and, possibly, even political cynicism, since what seems compatible with maintaining the current political system also appears to be acceptable as economic policy, as long as the policy fosters economic growth.

In this chapter, I wish to focus on this second perspective, yet at an even deeper level. This is the question how far Chinese *culture* could be a source of novelties in modern conceptions about the fundamentals of economics and economic policy (for my approach to Chinese culture in general, see Herrmann-Pillath 2006, 2009a). This inquiry is different from the search for specific economic ideas emerging from reflections on the rise of China, because it refers to both the domain of economic and philosophical thinking and the domain of general values and conceptions of economic life as embedded into society (for an anthropological view on this relation, see Gudeman 1986). The latter dimension is of interest in the context of economics, because one of the commonplaces of cultural analysis in economics is the assignment of China to the set of so-called 'collectivist' cultures in the world. The distinction between 'individualism' and 'collectivism' is standard lore in the management sciences (Hofstede 1991) but has been also introduced into economics, especially in the context of research into the long-run determinants of economic development (Greif 1994, Greif and Tabellini 2010). This notion does not refer to ideological components of Chinese culture but mainly to behavioral patterns, in the sense of a confluence of social-psychological tendencies and social-structural facts. Behavioral patterns have been in the focus of many theories about economic development, such as Max Weber's famous protestantism hypothesis. Very often, they are seen as building blocks of general sets of cultural values which ultimately also find expression in ideologies, such as economic liberalism, which emphasizes the importance of individual liberty and entrepreneurship. Recently, many economists are therefore inclined to highlight long-run legacies of past endowments with institutions, such as different patterns of colonial rule, and therefore tend towards a theory of cultural determinism in economic development (La Porta *et al.* 1997, Acemoglu *et al.* 2001, Acemoglu *et al.* 2002, Guiso *et al.* 2006; with reference to China: Landes 2006).

There is no doubt that China is undergoing landslide social changes, which will also affect those behavioral patterns, and that there is a lively exchange of ideas between China and the world. In this chapter, I wish to explore the potential of these changes as far as China's role as a source of inspiration in economic thinking is concerned, in the sense of basic conceptions of economic policy and the relation between the economy and society (that is, I do not talk about economics specifically as a scientific discipline). So, I do not venture to identify the existing impact of China but I explore the field in a creative way, as a project in transcultural communication and synthesis. My question is whether we can imagine a 'third culture' in economics, in the sense in which this term is used in the theory of cross-cultural communication (Casmir 1999; for an earlier attempt, see Herrmann-Pillath 2010). However, this creative exploration builds on a series of facts about China that seem to be neglected especially in those approaches, which emphasize collectivism as a major cultural feature. I put together two perspectives on China. One is the behavioral perspective on collectivism. This mainly refers to fundamental conceptions about economic behavior and social interaction in Chinese popular culture, especially in the rural society; that is, the 'little tradition' in anthropological parlance. Considering social change in China today, the dominating force is urbanization and rural change, which will also increase the impact of traditional ways of life on the modern economy; for example, in the context of family business (and not just trigger the modernizing force of urbanization, to which rural society would passively adapt) (for a programmatic statement on this, see Yang 2008). The other perspective sheds light on the 'great tradition'; that is, in a very broad sense, the meaning of Confucianism in the context of the economy. There is a revival of Confucianism in China today but this might mostly reflect political expedience and the search for national identity after Marxism lost its legitimacy. My interest in classical Chinese thinking flows from my project of creative interpretation: Can we imagine to make sense of certain Confucian principles in the modern world? This exercise is similar to Amartya Sen's (2009) approach to employ terms from classical Indian philosophy to build a modern theory of justice. Such an approach aims at writing a de-centered intellectual history of the world that does not claim actual lines of impact in the history of ideas, but that reconstructs this history in search for commonalities, shared questions and the potential for future conceptual innovations that arise from those ideational discoveries. That being said, it is important to recognize that common views on 'modernization as Westernization' systematically misperceive the factual impact of flows of ideas from East to West throughout history (Hobson 2004).

How can we succeed in both endeavours and establish a common framework? There are few theoretical approaches that fuse intellectual history and behavioral analysis, in the sense of historical anthropology and social history. One of them is the work by the sociologist Norbert Elias (1969), who argued that changing patterns of behavior in Western Europe eventually also resulted in principled ideological conceptions about the separating line between the individual and 'society' as an abstract idea. Once those conceptions were established, they also gave rise to corresponding narratives about large-scale social and intellectual changes, which have always come close to teleological ideas about progress towards modernity, liberty, individualism, and democracy. In this context, global intellectual history was also implicitly truncated to reflect this self-conception of the West.

A foremost example is Adam Smith, whom I also put in the center of this chapter, for that very reason. In doing this, my argument is a companion to Arrighi's (2007) book, provocatively entitled *Adam Smith in Beijing*. However, whereas Arrighi emphasizes certain structural characteristics of China's 'Smithian' economic system, past and present, I concentrate on the cultural dimension. Smith is regarded as the father of modern economic thinking, especially in terms of its ideological foundations of individualistic liberalism. At the same time, Smith was a behavioral scientist, and his ideas about the economy were rooted in empirical observations about human behavior, especially of the moral kind. Recently, economists have revived their interest in Smith as a behavioral scientist, and have therefore rediscovered his magisterial *Theory of Moral Sentiments* (Ashraf *et al.* 2005; Smith [1759] 1976). Indeed, in the history of economic thought, we notice a bias, if not a distortion in claiming Smith as the father of economics, as he was a moral philosopher in the first place. The complexity of his behavioral theory stays in stark contradiction with his reception in economics, and was perceived as the 'Adam Smith problem' for a long time (finally settled in the 1976 Glasgow edition; see Raphael and Macfie 1976). I interpret the history of the 'Adam Smith problem' as an indicator of the fundamental issue of how far the reception of past ideas is actually a part of the narrative that renders current developments meaningful. If that is the case, a new question looms large: How far can we reach a reassessment of Western intellectual history if we see it in the light of an entirely different and mostly autonomous culture? In other words, reading Smith through the lense of Confucius, what do we see? And how far can what we see contribute to conceptual innovation in the future? Especially, what are the implications for the idea of a liberal economy and society?

Classical Chinese thinking was mainly moral philosophy, and so we may ask what are the commonalities and differences between Confucianism and Smith, the moral philosopher? The results of this inquiry are also important for analyzing the behavioral aspects of Chinese culture. As a first step, we can ask in which way Smith's notions of morality were compatible with related conceptions in Chinese popular culture. In the second step, we have to notice the complex interaction between 'little tradition' and 'great tradition' in China. Here, the meanings of the term 'Confucianism' are ambivalent, reaching from certain elements of popular culture to the philosophical viewpoints of different groups of scholars and eventually to the official ideology of the Chinese empire. On all levels, Confucianism is a construct which in fact synthesizes different ideas stemming from Daoism, Buddhism or the ancient doctrine of Legism with different weights and emphasis, respectively. Official Confucianism adapted elements from popular culture, but often also stood in contrast to it, aiming at the moral transformation of society (for example, regarding the family, see Ebrey 1991). These tensions were part and parcel of Chinese folk religion and popular beliefs about society (see, for example, Feuchtwang 1992). At the same time, Confucian 'social engineering', especially with regard to the extended family and its underlying values, was a major force in shaping the homogeneity and resilience of traditional culture in China, ultimately showing the way to an indigenous, yet close to modern national identity already in Ming times (Faure 2007).

In this chapter, owing to the limited space available, I can only sketch a rough argument. I begin with an inspiring, although controversial, recent contribution by a Chinese economist and intellectual, who argues that China's rise may be linked with the global transition to cosmopolitanism, and that this has historical roots in classical Chinese thinking, which he sees as a direct precursor to modern economics as it has been seminally shaped by Adam Smith. In the next section, I put these reinterpretations of classical Chinese thought in the context of our current revisionist view on Chinese economic and social history, which describes Imperial China as a market economy and society *sui generis*. I then sketch the cultural legacy of this historical structure salient in the 'little tradition' of rural China today. Finally, I pull all the threads of the argument together in a synopsis of family resemblances between Confucianism and Adam Smith. I conclude with some observations about the emerging 'third culture' in economics that can be discerned from these observations.

China and cosmopolitanism: a view on the Chinese origins of modern economic thought

To entice readers to open up their minds to what follows, I wish to introduce a viewpoint that was developed by the Chinese economist Sheng Hong in the past two decades (Sheng 2010). Until recently, Sheng Hong was Director of the Unirule Institute at Beijing, an autonomous think tank in economics. The Unirule Institute was established in 1993 by a number of leading Chinese intellectuals and economists under the leadership of Mao Yushi, himself originally an economist with a focus on the United States and, later, an influential voice in the Chinese public, who heralded the need to find a synthesis between economic growth and moral principles, both in his writings and in his many grassroots activities. The name of the institute is more expressive in Chinese, *Tianze yanjiusuo*. The use of *tianze* 天则 refers to the 'principles of the heaven' and is inspired by a citation from one of the oldest Confucian classics, the Shijing: *tian sheng zheng min, you wu you li* 天生烝民，有物有则, which roughly translates as 'Heaven generates humankind, with matter and rules', meaning that all human beings follow naturally endowed rules. The use of the term *tianze* in the title of an economics research institute signals the idea that there are natural principles according to which the economy operates, which should not be disturbed by external interventions, beyond the establishment of institutions, which are mainly seen as evolving endogenously. In this sense, the name of the institute reflects a liberal position in economic policy, with a special emphasis on the perspective of institutional economics. Even more so, the philosophical implications of the motto come close to the fundamental principles of the Scottish Enlightenment.

In his works, Sheng Hong consistently strives to reconcile Chinese tradition with modern economic development and modern economics. His recently published book makes accessible some of his papers that were published in the 1990s in influential journals such as *Du shu* ('*Reading*') and *Guanli shijie* ('*Management World*'), so reaching a broad audience in the intellectual elites. In these papers, Sheng argues that classical Chinese thinking was not only compatible with modern economics, but even presaged it and exerted impact on it. Sheng boldly asserts that certain fundamental notions of modern economics stemmed from China, at least implicitly and indirectly, but certainly in terms of fundamental philosophical stances.

I do not want to discuss the philological validity of these propositions, beyond a few remarks below. What is important is that an influential Chinese scholar discusses in great detail the question of a possible synthesis between Chinese thinking and the Western tradition, especially with regard to basic notions such as the liberal economic order (for a related report and analysis on current Chinese views, see Barbalet 2011). Sheng proposes that this synthesis could reflect a transcultural exchange in a multicultural world, which would not assign the exclusive status of modernity to one of them. He calls this synthesis 'ecumenical'. The word 'ecumene' is sometimes used in English translations of the Chinese *tianxia* 天下, which Sheng refers to in his call for *tianxia zhuyi*, hence 'ecumenical thinking/ecumenism', which he confronts with 'globalism' *shijie zhuyi*. In

European history, the term 'ecumene' shows a similar vacillation of semantics as the Chinese *tianxia*, denoting the reach of human civilization in Greek times and the empire in Roman times. To avoid these semantic repercussions, and yet without stretching the argument, I would propose to translate *tianxia zhuyi* as 'cosmopolitanism', in the sense of current scholarly debates, especially in the context of Adam Smith (Forman-Barzilai 2010; auspiciously, there is also a similar use of the term 'cosmopolitanism' in the context of Europe, see Beck 2009). This is because, in the etymology of the term, the word *tianxia* refers to two overlapping, but different meanings. Originally the term referred to the land that was controlled by the Chinese emperor, including the territories that were aligned to the empire via tribute relations. Later, the term turned more abstract and referred to the reach of human civilization. This is also the sense of the famous dictum *tianxia wei gong* 天下为公 in the calligraphy by Sun Yatsen, which became part of the staple of catchwords in the global green movement (there, implying that 'the Earth belongs to all'). Sheng uses the term in this broader sense, so that we can say that *tianxia zhuyi* is the idea of a global civilization that encompasses a diversity of cultures. In fact, this interpretation matches with the historical evolution of the Chinese empire, which was a multiethnic body politic based on certain universal civilizational principles and artifacts such as the Chinese script (Schmidt-Glintzer 1997).

It is essential to recognize why Sheng makes that distinction. He claims that globalism, which he considers to be a Western term, is actually violating basic principles of economic liberalism in opting for trade liberalization but containing international migration. So, globalism is a conceptual framework which still builds on the conception of the nation state and hence economic nationalism. Sheng argues that Chinese traditional culture was embracing cosmopolitanism, but had to develop into nationalism to fence off Western nationalisms. He distinguishes between Western 'expansionary nationalism' and Chinese 'defensive nationalism', and is worried about the legacy of the latter for the future development of China. According to him, the tension between traditional cosmopolitanism and nationalism left China in an awkward position, and the only solution would be the realization of cosmopolitanism of a truly global scale, which he hopes will happen with the rise of China. With such grand views on secular trends, Sheng stands in the tradition of influential Chinese thinkers of the late and early twentieth century: For example, the Confucian intellectual Liang Shuming (who experienced the first decade of Chinese economic reforms and who passed away in 1988) had argued in the 1920s that China could only survive if the world were to be 'sinicized' in cultural terms, which would also help to overcome the many deficits of Western culture that were so obvious to Chinese intellectuals after the tragedy of World War I (Alitto 1979). Ideas about the transition from the 'nation state' to a new political order based on culture and civilization continue to flourish among Chinese intellectuals until today (see, for example, 21 *shiji jingji daobao* 2004).

In this context, Sheng also discusses economics. The bridge between economic liberalism and cosmopolitanism, Chinese style, is built when the fact is recognized that, according to Sheng, China actually played an important role in shaping modern economic thought. In this, he refers to the work by Quenays, *Despotisme de la Chine*, well aware of the fact that Adam Smith did not see China in the same light. Smith already manifests the incipient change in the perception of China during the later stage of the Enlightenment. Whereas the early thinkers saw China as a model government, already in Smith we see the emphasis on relative decline (for example, Smith 1976: 111ff.). In Smith, this was related to the paramount policy issue with which Smith himself was also concerned, namely the liberalization of foreign trade. Smith recognized the high level of economic productivity China had achieved, but also argued that with different institutions that level could have been surpassed. China was stuck in a stationary situation, simply because it could rely on a large internal market. In contrast, Quesnay emphasized the benevolent despotism of China, which was open to economic activity, and so contributed to prosperity. He realized that Chinese practice was close to the physiocratic analysis of the economic process, and exploited China as a model (Priddat 2001: 87ff.). After all, his nickname was the 'Confucius of Europe'. Quesnay's viewpoints reflected a broad tendency in the Enlightenment to see China as a model for good government that Europe should emulate (for a survey, see Mungello 1999: 87ff.).

Sheng does not claim that there was a Chinese impact in the details, but saw a strong relevance of the Chinese notion of a natural order on physiocratic thought and, in this respect, also on Adam Smith, as far as the laissez-faire doctrine is concerned. With the stylized picture of China that was crafted in the early Enlightenment, certain fundamental notions emerged of a natural process in the economy that should not be disturbed by strong interventions of government. The hypothesis that European economic thinking was influenced by China has been confirmed recently in attempts to write a global intellectual history (Hobson 2004). As today, this worked mainly via the example of China (and much less via the transfer of specific intellectual contributions), which was not only reported in many influential Jesuit texts and compilations of geographic knowledge, but was also visually present in millions of pieces of Chinese porcellain depicting the Eastern Arcadia. The Chinese doctrine of *wu wei* 无为 was a conceptual centerpiece of physiocratic movements and was presumably put into practice for the first time in the newly established Swiss federation, in a transformation which was achieved, among others, by the influential writer of *Staatsromane* (novels of government) Albrecht von Haller in extending the *wu wei* principle to commerce (Gerlach 2005). So, we have evidence of a diffuse, yet broad impact of Chinese ideas on economics, and even on policies on the eve of European industrialization.

In his argument, Sheng concentrates on specific concepts in modern economics, which he traces back to classical Chinese thought in the Warring States period, and puts together a syncretic view of different authors, reaching from Master Kong to Lao Zi. In this, he makes a very strong claim, namely that classical Chinese thought already presaged many concepts of modern *institutional economics*. He starts from one point that certainly deserves attention: This is the concept of the limits of knowledge, which is especially strong in Daoist thought, and which he interprets also as a precursor of the Scottish views on the limitations to human constructivist rationality. Further, he points out that the early thinkers already emphasized the importance of property rights in a peaceful society, and that government has the responsibility to protect them. Differences among people are essential for society, which Sheng interprets as an early indication of the division of labour, and, indeed, in classical conceptions the notion of universal cooperation based on reciprocity looms large. The government is obliged to prepare the preconditions for that, and, at the same time, has to refrain from claiming too many resources from the people. By these means, the government would contribute to maintaining the natural order of society. So, Sheng concludes that there is much common ground between classical Chinese thought and modern economics, which he sees as a precondition for China and Chinese economists becoming a force of transforming globalism into cosmopolitanism in the future.

Sheng Hong's viewpoint certainly highlights important and neglected points in the interpretation of the classical literature, but it also seems to blur the semantical boundaries between the traditional views on inequalitity and distinctiveness in social hierarchies and the modern notion of diversity in the division of labour and the marketplace. He also downplays the distinctions between physiocratic thinking, both Chinese and European style, and modern economics. In our context, these issues are not as important as the more basic point: In principle, it is possible to create a reconciliation between institutional, which means, ultimately, Smithian economics and classical Chinese thought. In a creative, if not provocative argument, Sheng shows the way how a 'third culture' in economics might look like, which would reflect a truly cosmopolitan perspective on fundamental principles and values underlying economics as a science and a political doctrine.

China's traditional 'Smithian' market economy

A few remarks seem to be in place to clarify the historical background of Chinese thinking about the economy during imperial times. When Western observers emphasize the role of Confucianism in Chinese political culture and society, this presents a very distorted picture of historical facts. It is amazing to notice that, until the late twentieth century, the fundamental tension in Chinese political culture was that between 'progressivist etatism' and 'conservative liberalism'. This leitmotif was firmly established in one of the most influential economic texts in Imperial China, the 'Discourses about Salt and Iron' *Yantie lun* (Loewe 1974: 93ff.; Schefold *et al.* 2002), which reports on a policy debate at the Han Imperial Court that took place in the year 81BC. Here, the legist view recommended state monopolies on salt and iron and an elaborate system of government interventions into markets to increase the prosperity of the people and the riches of the empire. Legist thought was also in favour of industry and commerce, albeit with strong goverment regulation. These ideas continued to exert a strong influence on government practice throughout the empire, and they were still implicit in modernist thought in the twentieth century. The Confucians strongly criticized this approach and argued that government should refrain from interfering with natural processes in the economy, especially if this would also be connected with the explicit pursuit of wealth on the part of the imperial administration (which establishes a family resemblance with the anti-mercantilist thinking of Quesnay and Smith). For them, government should be based on moral order, and the economy should be left in a natural state, in which agriculture is the only source of economic riches (agriculture as the root, *nongben* 农本).

As we see, compared with Europe, the peculiarity of the Chinese ideological development lies in the combination between liberalism and conservatism on the one hand, and modernism and etatism on the other. The Western combination of modernism and liberalism did not occur in China, and even today seems to be relatively weak. However, as we shall see, this assessment calls for second thoughts. One is to recognize the convergence between Smithian and Confucian views on the role of morality in human society, which I discuss in subsequent sections of this chapter. The other is to relate the ideological development in Imperial China to the factual historical changes that took place until China was confronted with Western imperialism, and which have motivated Arrighi (2007) to qualify the Chinese economy in Imperial times as 'Smithian'.

In the past four decades, our views about the socioeconomic structure of the Chinese empire have undergone a revision, if not a revolution, heralded by Mark Elvin's (1973) magisterial analysis of the 'medieval economic revolution' under the Song emperors (these revisions have been synthesized in brilliant early surveys by the doyen of American China studies, John King Fairbank [1978], and summarized in his posthumously published 'new history' of China [1992], but they continue to be fleshed out until today, also challenging conventional wisdom about the 'European miracle'; e.g. Wong 1997, Pommeranz 2000, Zelin 2009). Previously, our views were directly shaped by Chinese historiography which provided a 'great tradition' view on Chinese history. That is, political and social change was interpreted in the light of Confucian orthodoxy and, hence, mainly from the view of the government, which even includes a distorted picture of its own legist practice (so, for example, the eminent French historian, Etienne Balazs [1964: 13ff.] spoke of China as a 'permanently bureaucratic society', although he already was aware of the upcoming revisions of the historical picture). Today, we have a much more precise view on popular culture and socioeconomic structure beyond the reach and scope of the imperial state (e.g. Eastman 1988), which have also changed our ideas about the relation between the 'great' and the 'little tradition'. This has also gone hand in hand with the increasing recognition of geographical and subcultural diversity in Imperial China, for example, in emphasizing the uniqueness of the Jiangnan region as the most socioeconomically advanced region in China (Naquin and Rawski 1988).

This is not the place to discuss details, but we need to recognize that the classical debate about 'salt and iron' was already a 'modern' one, in the sense that it was centered around the phenomenon of declining feudalism and the emergence of market relations during the preceding Warring States period. Confucius's conservativism was directly opposing these social changes, while recognizing beneficial aspects on general prosperity. Other thinkers emphasized other aspects of these changes, but eventually one ideological conflict remained in the center of the further intellectual developments of the Chinese empire, between Legism (often, but wrongly translated as 'legalism') and Confucianism, which was even invoked again under Mao's rule. Legism was the philosophical foundation of authoritarian bureaucratic rule, with a deep mistrust against human nature, whereas Confucians started out from the primacy of a natural moral order as the foundation of government.

Interestingly, although Confucianism looked down on merchants in moral terms, in fact it proposed a duality of moral values for the 'gentleman' *junzi* and the ordinary people *xiao ren*, the 'little ones'. Economic activity of ordinary people was seen as perfectly legitimate, and the government even had to protect and support it, a claim that was firstly made by Confucius's disciple Mencius in a systematic fashion. Indeed, in the history of Confucianism, there were significant strands of thought in which markets and their social context were seen in a very positive light, such as the Zhejiang school of Confucianism, which, until today, is one of the Chinese provinces with the highest share of private entrepreneurship in the economy. Interestingly, this so-called 'pragmatic' (*shigong xue* 事功学) school already emerged during Song times, simultaneously with the establishment of the Neo-Confucian orthodoxy, and branched out into different strands which remained especially strong in the Jiangnan region, epitomized as Yongjia School, with *yongjia* 永嘉 referring to nowadays Wenzhou (Wang Xiaoyi *et al.* 1996: 10ff; at today's Ningbo city, there is a museum devoted to this school, and Zhejiang University has established a Center for Confucian Entrepreneurs). The recognition of markets as a fundamental organizational principle in society also affected government policies, which became much less interventionist under the Qing emperors, and there was a shift from direct to indirect policies, for example, even in emergency actions taken against floods and famines, such as providing relief not in kind but in specie' so that markets would have done the job of allocating the resources to those who were in need (Will 1990). The imperial bureaucracy was highly professional in assessing the relative efficiency of markets and administrative measures in particular contexts.

These ideological developments reflected an economy and society which looked very different from the picture of 'oriental despotism' that was dominant in Western perceptions until the 1960s, and in many popular conceptions until today (for an excellent overview, see Zelin 1990, and for a systematic exposure of faulty contrasts between Europe and China in terms on institutions and marketization, see Pommeranz 2000; for a critical view, see Brenner and Isett 2002). Considering Sheng's arguments, which did not refer to historical developments, they may make much more sense in reference to those historical facts than in the interpretation of the early thinkers. This is essential for the grand view of global trends, which recently emphasizes the reemergence of China as a leading economy of the world, after almost two centuries of social havoc, internal strife, foreign invasions and war. At the height of her endogenous development, China had a government which aimed at minimizing the burden for her citizens, explicitly keeping taxes low and striving for the rationalization of procedures (Ma 2011). Merchants may not have counted much in the 'great tradition', but they were in fact highly regarded elites in local communities, with the lineage (the Chinese form of the extended family) as the primordial unit which integrates different social roles and strata, especially scholar-officials and merchants (a landmark volume triggering this shift of perspective was Esherick and Rankin 1990, followed by in-depth studies such as Faure 2007). Self-organization in townships and cities became increasingly important, with local government officials mainly playing the role as coordinators and moral leaders. Even essential government functions such as taxation were delegated to self-organizing bodies of local merchant communities (Mann 1987).

In fact, economic historians today no longer see strong and interventionist bureaucratic government as the main cause of the failed transition to industrialization, but an increasingly weak government which could not provide for the necessary public infrastructure (Jones 1988). This relative inactivity directly reflects the classical preferences for indirect rule, mainly relying on the natural order, against the background of growing demographic and ecological strains on infrastructure (Robertson 1999: 16ff.). In the economy, the government did not directly regulate private activities, which were guided by informal customary law (Huang 2006a,b). But the government heeded attention to this customary law and actively contributed to its enforcement. Traditional China was a contractarian society to a much higher degree than Europe in its past (Hansen 1995). All important matters were regulated by private contracts following customary law, and if necessary, those contracts were enforced also by the local courts (for a view on the contemporary relevance of these customs, see Cohen 1992). This customary law was the breeding ground for the unfolding of a division of labour that was repeatedly described by Western travellers to China who, until the late eighteenth century, emphasized the relative prosperity of China as compared to Europe.

Classical thinking saw the family at the center of the society. Interestingly, Sheng Hong also argues that familism can be the foundation for cosmopolitanism, opposing to nationalism. Yet, throughout the twentieth century, the traditional family was not mainly recognized as the breeding ground of Chinese entrepreneurship, but as a major obstacle to modernization, because it allegedly blocked the transition to the modern corporation. Again, our picture is undergoing significant changes (surveyed in Zelin 2009). The traditional Chinese family unit included large-scale corporate entities, the lineages and their funds, which underwent an autonomous transition to more professional and accountable forms of governance and professional management. Lineage organization with shareholding arrangements also served as a pattern that was followed by non-kin-based merchant organizations. In acknowledging these facts, it is increasingly difficult to assign causal primacy to cultural factors in China's failed endogenous modernization (such as in Landes 2006), especially when considering the endemic instability of the government under pressure from foreign impact. Further, it is essential to differentiate between political and ecological factors in China's development, and institutional factors. Recent revisionist economic history has emphasized the former against the latter, and highlighted the similarity of market mechanisms between China and Europe (such as Rawski 1989, Pommeranz 2000). In other words, past assessments of Chinese development were distorted by the limited view on the collapse of the 'great tradition', and the systematic neglect of the 'little tradition'. However, the term 'little tradition' may be misleading in this context, as we refer in fact to relatively homogenous features of Chinese culture which unified society across all strata, and which was inherited across generations also in the twentieth century, especially in the rural areas (Cohen 1994, Yang 2007, Faure 2007, Herrmann-Pillath 2009b).

To summarize, we can say that Imperial China was a market economy with a strong reliance on endogenously evolving institutions and relatively weak direct government intervention, which was supportive to markets. This economy was driven by entrepreneurial activity in the context of highly differentiated local, regional and national market systems. Especially, Chinese agriculture was commercialized to a high degree, with the most prosperous Jiangnan region as the developmental spearhead. Given this historical pattern, what are the implications for the reconstruction of Chinese culture with regard to the value foundations of behavior and social action?

The essence of Chinese culture: the view from modern behavioral sciences and Chinese anthropology

What is the core of Chinese culture, especially in relation to the economy and social interactions? I analyze this question in two steps. First, I give an overview about certain principles of social interaction and behavioral patterns that have been established in recent anthropological research, social psychology and cognitive sciences (for a more extensive treatment, see Herrmann-Pillath 2009c). In doing this, I criticize the common uses of the term 'collectivism' in economics and emphasize the individualistic and entrepreneurial values in popular culture, which have been characteristic for China over centuries, if not millenia. In the next section, I move on to interpret these observations in a grand synthesis of Adam Smith and Confucius, which, as I have said, is intended to be a transcultural synthesis in a similar vein as Sheng Hong's.

In recent research in cognitive and social psychology, the standard notion of collectivism has been questioned (for a survey, see Brewer and Chen 2007). Today, a minimal distinction is that between 'relational collectivism' and 'categorial collectivism' (my term, Brewer and Chen use 'group collectivism' which I deem confusing). In both cases, the collective refers to a group, but with essentially different characteristics. In relational collectivism, the group consists of people with whom an individual interacts in a particular context. Categorial collectivism refers to abstract collectives such as the nation or the company. Clearly, the categories can overlap in concrete cases, because the company is also a set of people who interact. But almost always, and even in this case, the two groups are not co-extensive (we only interact with a subset of employees of a company). In cross-cultural comparisons, the importance of this distinction results from the fact that the two collectivisms run across standard dual oppositions. So, for example, Americans may score highly in individualism (e.g. entrepreneurship) but also in categorial collectivism (e.g. loyalty to the company). This observation shows that the Western emphasis on individualism may be misleading, because individualism cannot be defined independently from the proper delineation of the boundaries between the individual and the group, which is a cultural phenomenon in itself.

Regarding China, the interesting observation is that relational collectivism corresponds with earlier philosophical and sociological characterizations of Chinese culture being a culture of 'interdependent individualism' or 'interdependent personalism' (Metzger 1977, King 1994). The resulting ambiguity reflects certain features of traditional conceptions of social relations which can be best understood when analyzing the ubiquitous role of *guanxi* in Chinese society, namely particularistic webs of relations which can be exploited for mutual gain (for a recent collection of research papers on *guanxi*, see Gold *et al.* 2002). This analysis starts with a caveat: The scholarly treatment of *guanxi* reaches from its elevation to a fundamental principle to its treatment as a transitory phenomenon in communist China (Yang 1994 versus Guthrie 1998), and also in Chinese indigenous conceptualizations these different attitudes can be found, both scholarly and in folk culture (see the discussion in Chang 2010). Yet, the concept is of sufficient generality so that its analysis is useful to identify some universal structural features which eventually are also independent from this concept in the narrow sense; this is why it also plays a central role in recent attempts to characterize Chinese business behavior (Li 2007). Therefore, subsequently I will no longer use the term, but just speak of 'social relations' as reflected in indigenous conceptions (for a discussion of contemporary transformations of *guanxi*, see Wank 1996, 2002).

What makes Chinese social relations special, in comparison with Western conceptions, is the emphasis on embeddedness and relatedness as primary forces of social action (Gabrenya and Hwang 1996; for consequences in management, see e.g. Chua *et al.* 2009). This is accompanied by the notion of concentric circles, with family and friendship at the core, and their expansion with decreasing degrees of familiarity and mutual trust. However, these circles are not naturally determined, beyond the inner circles, but can be actively shaped in social interaction. The central determinant is a specific mix between emotions and instrumental reason (Jacobs 1982, Kipnis 2002). A stable social relation is grounded in shared emotions, mostly based on perceived similarities among individuals, and common interests in reciprocal exchange. The emotional basis is the precondition for the long-term sustainability of the relationship, which at the same time allows for the decoupling of reciprocity. A sustainable social relationship builds on imbalanced reciprocity and the moral commitment to exchange benefits through time. Until very recently, in Chinese villages, these abstract norms were cast into an explicit system of social accounts. Social relations are managed with great effort by everybody, and they are also public to a certain degree. They are embodied in a flow of gifts at the many occasions throughout the life cycle of an individual (Kipnis 1996, Yan 1996). Although it is very difficult to demonstrate a long run of continuity of these patterns in the Chinese past, there are intriguing findings about gift exchange among Confucian elites in Imperial China, which reveal the same patterns as in contemporary villages (on the 'social art' of the Ming artist Wen Zhengming, see Clunas 2004, with explicit comparisons to the recent anthropological research).

Against this background, it is essential to recognize two aspects. The first is that the individual stands at the center of its unfolding social relations. The second is that the individual invests in social relations, so that relations are often linked with shared endeavours (Chen and Chen 2004). Both aspects stay in stark tension with standard views on collectivism. In Chinese conceptions, the ego is not simply entangled in a web of social relations that dominate his interests (I use 'his' intentionally, as there are certainly gender differences in this respect), but plays an active role in shaping them. Especially, the set of relations is not a given, but there is much space for social creativity in starting new relations. In that sense, managing social relations is an entrepreneurial activity that comes close to invest into the formation of social capital (actually, Chang 2010 reports that the farmers at her fieldsite refer to the management of social relations as 'raising pigs', *yang zhu*). This is most evident from the calculatory nature of the relations, which, in spite of being emotionally grounded, are conceived in instrumental terms.

When considering the public nature of social relations, this refers to their observability in terms of embodied signs, in particular the flow of gifts. But even more so, the public character results from the moral framework in which they take place. Chinese language distinguishes between two kinds of emotions, the individual feelings *ganqing* 感情 and the socially approved emotional commitments, the *renqing* 人情. So, all social relations are guided by a moral code which makes the measure of fulfilment public. This is why the flow of gifts is also called the exchange of *renqing*, even referring to cash as *renqing* (Wilson 1997). The public nature of social relations is also evident from the pivotal role of 'face' in Chinese social interactions, where a clear distinction between social status *mianzi* 面子 and moral reputation *lian* 压 is made (Hwang 2006). The exchange of *renqing* is a matter of moral reputation. For our subsequent discussion of Smith, it is essential to recognize that, in Chinese social interaction, the concern for face encompasses both Ego and Alter, that is, not only does Ego care for his face, but Ego also cares for the face of Alter. The latter presupposes the capacity to take Alter's position. This switch of positions is a major precondition for implicit communication, which has been consistently emphasized as a hallmark of East Asian cultures in general (see Hall's 1976 notion of 'high-context cultures').

In traditional rural society, this role of social relations was mainly focused on non-agnatic kinship, which always, and today increasingly, includes non-kin as 'quasi-kin' (Chang 2010, Xiao 2010). The common picture of China as a patriarchal Confucian society fails to depict in sufficient detail the fact that a major expansion of social relations takes place via marriage. In this context, Skinner's (1964/65) seminal analysis of traditional Chinese society as a market-centered – as opposed to a village-centered – society is of central importance. Very often, marriage relations transcended village borders and were mediated via the market towns. So, non-agnatic social relations also followed the market-based patterns of interactions.

In her most recent extensive ethnography of a Chinese village, Chang (2010) has developed a conceptual framework which goes beyond the conception of *guanxi*, the *lishang wanglai* 礼尚往来 model. This highlights two essential elements of popular wisdom about social relations in China. One, the *wanglai*, refers to the idea that social relations are created and emerge from recurrent social interchange, without preconceived positions of the individuals involved. These interactions are embedded into *lishang*, which are the local conceptions of propriety. What is proper behavior is not simply determined by a given codex, but can be further analyzed in terms of different sources of justification, such as human feelings (the *renqing*) or rational calculation. This can result into different forms of social relations, such as generous, expressive or instrumental. *Guanxi* are just a subset of this comprehensive set of possible kinds of relations. It is important to recognize that this framework even includes religious behavior, as people also maintain social relations with their ancestors. So, on the one hand the individual is seen as being entangled in vast web of clearly specified relations, but at the same time it remains at the center of these relations and can shape them actively.

The relevance of these social structures and interactional patterns for economic processes comes to the fore in many ways. One example is the role of embedded governance in the provision of public goods in Chinese villages, which has been empirically scrutinized by Tsai (2002, 2007). Tsai shows that the degree of accountability of local cadres managing infrastructure differs vastly across Chinese villages, even if 'all else is close to equal'; that is, with similar levels of development, close proximity, and so on, depending on the strength and structure of traditional social interactions, such as in lineages and temple organizations. A central intermediating variable is the role of of moral reputation and the resulting commitment of cadres towards the local community. Indeed, popular religion and its related social interaction patterns also played a significant role in Taiwanese economic development and business organization (Pennarz 1992). This mutual embeddedness of religious and business activities continues to exist and even is strenghtening in many places of China today (for the intriguing case of a rapidly modernizing region in Zhejiang province, Wenzhou, which is dominated by private business, see Yang 2007).

To summarize and generalize, recent research into the psychology and sociology of Chinese social interaction has clearly shown that the individualism–collectivism divide is seriously misleading, which is informing most economics and theory-based literature on comparative institutional and economic development until now (e.g. Greif and Tabellini 2010). Chinese culture features a complex pattern of relational collectivism and interdependent individualism, which is revealed in anthropological studies on rural society. On a more abstract level, the differences between China and Western societies may be located in differences of cognitive style, which in turn interact with differences of social ecology (Nisbett 2003). This leads us back to differences in the intellectual history of the West and the East. Chinese cognition scores highly in indicators of field-dependence, which means is context-sensitive and holistic, whereas the average Western individual tends to be more field-independent and analytic. This has consequences for the perception of social relations, as field dependence evidently relates with relational collectivism and interdependent personalism, whereas field independence implies more emphasis on categorial separations (for corresponding experiments on different cognitive stances towards semantic classification, see Ji *et al.* 2004).

So far, my claim is that Chinese culture reflects a co-evolution of behavioral patterns and structural characteristics of the imperial market economy, which provides the scaffold on which the rise of China as an economic power could firmly rely. Confucianism as a moral and political world view was a part of this long-run historical process. These two dimensions, the research into behavioral patterns and the view on intellectual history, can now be merged in our discussion of Adam Smith, the moral philosopher. China's 'great tradition' always interacted with her 'little tradition', and so we can ask whether eventually the economic success of Chinese business all over the world, which is deeply rooted in her 'little tradition', may also be an indicator for a Smithian dimension in classical thought, which has been pinpointed by Sheng Hong's provocative ideas.

Confucian family resemblances in Adam Smith's thought

It is straightforward to put the previous sections together into one single picture in which the historical fact of a Chinese market economy corresponds with behavioral patterns which emphasize the entrepreneurial management of social relations. Chinese popular culture is compatible with a market-based society, as it was already emerging in China during the time of Confucius. Now, can we see Confucius in the light of Adam Smith, and vice versa?

Recently, Adam Smith has received much attention in China, even at the highest level of government, with Premier Wen Jiabao referring to Smith repeatedly (see, for example, Financial Times 2009). There are extensive commentaries on Smith (see, for example, Luo Weidong 2005). The reason is the continuing reception of the *Theory of Moral Sentiments*. Indeed, a closer look demonstrates that the book reveals many commonalities between Smithian and Confucian thinking. When I use the latter term, I do not refer to Confucius himself, but to the amalgam of ideas that can be seen as being constitutive for the 'great tradition', in a similar vein as in Sheng Hong's argument. This can include, for example, notions from Buddhism in later times.

The common ground between the two lines of thought is naturalism. Smith does not deduce moral principles from first principles, either established by reason or by religious fiat, but claims to ground them in observations of human nature. This is essentially a Confucian viewpoint, which also implies that both perspectives converge on the view that there is a natural inclination of human beings to behave in a moral way. It is also fascinating to notice that the ancient Chinese notion of 'Heaven', *tian*, comes very close to Smith's deism, which actually depersonalizes the role of the Creator to the largest possible degree, while keeping the idea that nature follows certain principles that were ultimately established by Him, in the sense of nature being the causal root of all human behavior, but being directed towards a final end which is transcendental, hence divine (Long 2006). Both the Confucians and Smith would agree, however, that, for the understanding of human life, it is not necessary to rely on the Creator himself or itself, but on those principles. In this sense, moral philosophy is based on natural facts.

Smith and the Confucians add the important idea of education and individual development. Fully developed morality is the result of moral development in real social interactions. Here, Smith even concurs with the Confucians in seeing the family as the natural and most important domain where this development takes place. Indeed, Smith clearly has the notion of circles of sympathy, which provide the context for morality, such that the link between the potential universalistic standpoint of the impartial spectator and the specific cultural context is never fully broken (Forman-Barzilai 2006).

Based on naturalism, Smith starts his moral theory with the fundamental concept of 'sympathy'. Sympathy is a special and well-developed notion which, in this detail, does not seem to have a direct correspondence with Chinese concepts (for penetrating analyses, see Sugden 2002 and Broadie 2006). On the other hand, the notion introduces a perspective which is in fact much closer to Chinese ideas than the abstract conceptions of egoistic individualism which were later highlighted in European intellectual discourse. In Smith, sympathy reflects the fundamental sociality of human nature, and it denotes the capacity to take the position of others. I propose to relate this idea to the fundamental Confucian notion of *ren* 仁. *Ren* refers to the essential twosomeness of any form of human existence, and it relates to the capacity to act together.

According to recent philological research (Ge Zhaoguang 2001: 95ff.), *ren* is a simplified merger of the two characters for 'heart' and 'body', which was later streamlined into the combination of the Chinese character radical 'man' and the character 'two'. So, two different semantic fields are activated. One is, in the original meaning, that one can understand the body through the heart, and the other, that human existence is always twosome. Both meanings connect with each other, as the heart is seen as enabling a human being to be together with others via a fundamental capacity for mutual understanding. This meaning should be contrasted with the many Western attempts at translating the concept, sometimes ending up with notions such as 'love', whereas more careful translators refrain from providing too much content, such as 'humanity' (Chan 1967). Clearly, whereas the former directly transfers Western meanings into the Eastern concept, the latter is overly broad. I venture to propose that Smithian 'sympathy' might be a proper translation of *ren*, if we exclude later Neo-Confucian extensions of the term into the metaphysical unity of subject and object.

Ren shares with sympathy one important property: It is not just 'sympathy' in the modern sense, and it is not unconditional altruism. In the Confucian framework, *ren* is abstract and concrete at the same time. Its concreteness stems from the fact that in Chinese social thinking, sociality is always a concrete phenomenon, as we have seen in the discussion of relational collectivism. That is, there is no reference to any sort of abstract collective, but primordially to the system of social circles centering around an individual, with the family at the core. That is, even though *ren* is an abstract principle, it cannot serve directly as a conceptual tool to derive moral obligations. This presupposes a specific social context. However, it is also important to notice that, in Chinese thinking, *ren* also emerges as a universalistic principle, because all Confucian concepts are ultimately rooted in certain meta-physical and cosmological conceptions that relate to the cosmos as such and human civilization as a part of it (in the sense of *tianxia*). Of course, civilization itself served as a benchmark to distinguish between the humans and the barbarians, as in all other high cultures, including Western cultures, until most recently. But, in principle, all human beings are seen as being equal in terms of the potential for moral and civilizational development. Then, in Chinese thinking, the moral order of society is directly reflected in the natural order of the cosmos, which implies the universality of the moral order. This is why moral failure, in particular of the rulers, causes disruptions of natural processes, such as floods. Smith, as an empiricist, does not have such magical beliefs about nature and society, but, at the same time, he adopts a special version of deism which assigns an almost metaphysical role to order, akin to a sort of prestabilized harmony imposed by Him in defining the starting points of the process of evolution, especially human nature.

However, given the multiplicity of particular values and behaviors, *ren* does not suffice as an absolute benchmark for morality. Smith and the Confucians converge in the view that the complementary fundamental principle is 'justice'. In classical Chinese, there were two concepts jointly defining the semantic field of justice, and which both show close resemblance to Smithian notions (Roetz 1992). One is *yi* 义, the other is *gong* 公. *Gong* is the opposite of *si* 私 and can be found in modern Chinese in composites such as public ownership (*gong you*) versus private ownership (*si you*). In the original meaning, *gong* comes very close to 'impartiality' as opposing partial interest *si*. For example, these concepts were applied in the recurrent discourse about irrigation systems and water control in China thoughout imperial times, with *gong* reflecting the interest of local and regional communities in maintaining lakes and reservoirs for water management, whereas *si* referred to the equally essential partial interest in expanding agricultural land by impoldering (Schoppa 1989).

So, the classical Chinese notion of justice was directly referring to the notion of impartiality, which stands at the center of Smith's thought. *Gong* appears in most modern words referring to justice, such as *gongzheng* or *gongping*. In comparison, *yi* in *zhengyi* has a stronger component of contextuality, especially in the sense that in the classical Chinese view, equal treatment has to be modified by social structure, such that social actions are valued differently from the viewpoint of different social roles, such as father and son (if the son murders the the father, this is of a different moral value than when the father murders the son, such that 'equality' would imply different punishments). Again, there is a related concept in Smith, which is 'propriety'. Yet, the conjunction of the two concepts also implies that there is a transition possible to universalistic notions of equality. In this sense, the Chinese conception of morality builds on the conception of a plurality of perspectives, though materialized in the specifically Chinese social setting, and which can be synthesized into a universalistic view via moral development.

At this point, the distinction between conventional and post-conventional morality comes into play (Roetz 1992). One the one hand, justice, especially as *yi*, relates with the notion of ritual, *li* 礼, which reflects the hierarchical nature of society, so that justice implies the unequal treatment of different positions and perspectives. But on the other hand, the majority of Confucian thinkers believed that the resultant social order is only 'just' in the sense of *gong* if it serves the interests of everybody, thus being impartial in terms of the ultimate outcomes. This is the use of *gong* in Sun Yatsen's calligraphy *tianxia wei gong*.

In the Confucian view, sociality is based on reciprocity, and the terms of reciprocity are guided by ritual (as we see, the folk wisdom epitomized in the *lishang wanglai* conception actually reflects Confucian thinking). Reciprocity is conceived as direct reciprocity in the terms of exchange, especially retribution, denoted as *bao* 报. In the unfolding of Chinese thinking, this was later merged with Buddhist ideas about retribution (Yang 1957). However, reciprocity is also extended into the Chinese version of the Golden Rule (denoted with the term *shu* 恕), which implies a universalization in the Kantian sense. This transition can be seen as showing family resemblances with Smith's conception of the impartial spectator, even though the latter is a much more complex notion (on its Kantian dimensions, see Tugendhat 2004). This is because the evolution of the spectator's position is based on the reciprocal evaluation of symphatic feelings of resentment and the implied calculation of relative weights of actions and counteractions in moral behavior. This calculatory venue towards impartiality is similar to the moral accounting involved in the ideas about retribution in China. As we have seen, in folk customs, this is directly applied to evaluating the flow of gifts, which is partial, but at the same time is seen as constitutive for the local community as a universalistic reference.

There is clearly a much stronger rule of rites in China, as compared with Smith. Classical Chinese thinking accepts natural hierarchies in society, and it defines reciprocity relative to them. However, when reading Smith in detail, this thinking does not appear to be strange to him. This is for two reasons. The first is that the Chinese approach actually means that morality cannot be defined independently from social context. This is a major unresolved issue in Smith's conception of the impartial spectator, as, ultimately, this inner voice cannot be independent from any reference to the established moral norms in a given society. In this sense, the circles of sympathy necessarily stay in tension with an entirely universalistic impartiality (Forman-Barzilai 2010). For Smith, eventually, this means that he adopted a critical, if not pessimistic attitude to society. On the one hand, he saw moral development in the context of concrete societies. But, at the same time, he believed that the driving force of emulation will misguide individual behavior, as social status does not necessarily coincide with moral status. So, Smith implicitly distinguished between social status (*mianzi*) and moral status (*lian*), and proposed an ethics of virtue, which is certainly Confucian in essence (although Aristotelian in terms of the genesis of ideas; see Hanley 2006). The most dangerous force working against a moral order is deceit (Gerschlager 2005). High-status individuals display signs of status, society strives to attain them, and eventually follows wrong moral standards. The disjunction between moral status and social status was the most critical issue in Smith's thinking, which, in the end, even induced him to think in pessimistic terms about the market society. Only two forces could stop this downward spiral. One is that elites take the responsibility of moral leadership, the other is the establishment of law and institutions that put a limit to the negative effects, especially via competition, which contains the accumulation of power (and, of course, even creates the positive drive for economic growth).

Adam Smith is a true Confucian in this emphasis on moral leadership. Confucians did not uphold hierarchy and rites at any price. On the contrary, a central concern of Confucius himself was moral disorder, which he perceived as the dissociation between assigned status and moral essence. Rites without moral essence are without value, and in this sense, rites even obtain a critical potential (in claiming the 'rectification of names'). For this very reason, Confucians throughout Chinese history acted as critics of the Emperor even on the highest level, and they displayed deep mistrust of the concentration of power. The ideal-typical person of high moral standing, the *junzi*, would always keep a distance to the powerful, and his main task is to uncover moral failure in society, especially in the highest ranks. Moral tension was the defining feature of the Confucian scholar-official (Metzger 1977). In this context, its also significant to realize that Smith concurs with Confucian views in rejecting 'utility' as a possible justification of ethical statements (Shaver 2006). There is a parallelism between the Confucian acceptance of the ordinary interest in prosperity and the Smithian appraisal of material progress, but also in the juxtaposition between 'utility' and virtue, and the exclusive focus on the latter when the moral foundation of human society is at stake.

This brief comparative sketch reveals many family resemblances between Smith and classical Chinese thinking. I have not discussed Smith's economics in the narrow sense, as we can certainly discover many parallels in the sense of Sheng Hong's reconstruction. As Arrighi (2007) has argued in much detail, Smithian economics appears to be the proper theoretical framework of the Chinese stationary, but highly competitive market economy in imperial times, also in the sense that Smith eventually failed to fully appreciate the transformative nature of capitalism, China failed to generate endogenous forces to a full transition to capitalism, after a headstart of eight centuries during the Song medieval economic revolution. What is essential is that the view from Confucianism puts Smith back into the right proportions between economic and moral reasoning. Smith saw morality as an essential and defining element of a civil society centering on the market (Evensky 2005). His focus on individual interest in *The Wealth of Nations* reflects a complex philosophical position in which the question is raised: On which constellation of interests can institutional development in complex societies be based (compare the discussion by Mehta 2006)? That is, reference to partial interest is justified by public interest, or justice. Confucians agree on that, in expecting the government to heed attention to particular interests, and even taking their fulfilment as a yardstick to assess good governance. But government itself cannot be based on any kind of conjunction of partial interests, a view which Smith would certainly endorse.

Conclusion: defining the 'third culture' in economics

By way of conclusion, let me now venture to sketch a conceptual synthesis of Smith and Confucius, asking for the relevance of both the 'little' and 'great' tradition' of China for a global conception of a market-based society, or, in Sheng Hong's sense, market-based cosmopolitanism. The core concepts of this perspective are embeddedness and contextuality, both of which have a positive and a normative dimension. In the positive dimension, Chinese popular culture highlights a fact that has been rediscovered by economics only in the past three decades, namely that trust and social capital matter most for entrepreneurial success and the sustainability of the market society (Platteau 1994). Relational collectivism and interdependent personalism emphasize the social nature of individual entrepreneurship. Against the background of the never-ending series of regulatory failures and governance problems in modern capitalism, the Chinese tradition emphasizes personal responsibility and moral commitment, and highlights the role of the family as a primary unit of society and business. Especially in the context of emerging markets and catch-up processes, this role of the family business deserves much more attention also in economics and economic policy.

Asking how trust and social capital can be generated, the role of moral leadership is especially salient (Casson 1991). This is very significant against the background of the strong interaction between the new institutional economics and management science in recent decades, which start from the Williamsonian view on opportunism as a fundamental human feature (Ghoshal 2005). Confucians disagree, in the sense that, together with Smith, they have an optimistic view on human malleability through education. Economic theory as well as management science and education have to include morality into their framework. It is important to emphasize that this is not endogenous morality, which is mostly emphasized by individualistic social theory, claiming that markets create the morals that they need (Baurmann 1996). Both Smith and the Confucians believe that markets are a hotbed for moral failure. Thus, morality is exogenous to market society.

The emerging 'third culture' in economics also has consequences for policy conceptions and policy design. The infamous Chinese 'pragmatism' can be reinterpreted as contextualism in the sense of the cognitive science concept of field dependence. Following a distinction that has been made recently by Armatya Sen (2009), the Chinese view and the Western approach of the past can be seen as juxtaposing 'realization-focused comparisons' on the one hand and 'transcendental institutionalism' on the other hand. The latter emphasizes reference to idealized and theoretical conceptions of systems, whereas the former puts progress relative to the status quo into the center of attention. This leads us back to the initial observations about development economics. The naive versions of the Washington consensus were mainly decontextualized, reflecting the belief of economists into the universality of their theories. There was a lack of medium-level theorizing linking theory with specific circumstances in time and place (compare Little's 1992 philosophy of science view on Chinese studies). This does not imply questioning fundamental tenets of economics, but, in the sense of Justin Lin's (2010) *New Structural Economics*, to heed attention to changing conditions of application in the course of economic development. This implies a cautious approach to government intervention, mainly because of the awareness that the informational requirements for targeting policies are complex and rarely possible to fulfil. So, a 'third culture' in economic policies does not put most emphasis on criteria of efficiency, but, as Sheng Hong emphasizes, on the limits of knowledge. The measure of success in policy making is not how we make best use of what we now, but how we minimize possible damage from what we do not know.

A 'third culture' in economics will also rethink the notion of consumer sovereignty. This question was raised recently in the context of behavioral economics, leading towards notions of 'libertarian paternalism' and related ideas about how to influence consumption decisions to the best of the imperfectly informed consumer plagued by so-called 'anomalies' in rational decision making (McFadden 2006, Thaler and Sunstein 2009). A Smithian and Confucian view emphasizes personal development towards responsibility through education, which includes a critical approach to consumption, which is always seen as a possible source of moral failure through deceit and self-delusion.

These are some flashlights on a 'third culture' in economics. The main task in this endeavor is to recognize the plurality of developmental trajectories today, and to aim at putting this into a truly cosmopolitian view on the history of ideas on the economy, the polity and society. Economic policies, especially in complex fields such as health care or the regulation of public utilities, are always guided by certain foundational conceptions about values and principles, as instrumentalist economic theorizing rarely leads to unequivocal recommendations and solutions. In this domain, we enter the realm of philosophy. In this domain, reflection upon past thinkers can be an extremely powerful source for new ideas.

Bibliography

21 *shiji jingji daobao* (ed.) (2004) *Zhongguo shiji. Xin de kaishe he jiyu*, Hong Kong.

Acemoglu, D., Johnson, S. and Robinson, J.A. (2001) 'The colonial origins of comparative development: an empirical investigation', *American Economic Review*, 91(5): 1369–1401.

Acemoglu, D., Johnson, S. and Robinson, J.A. (2002) 'Reversal of fortune: geography and institutions in the making of the modern world income distribution', *Quarterly Journal of Economics*, 117: 1231–94.

Alitto, G.S. (1979) *The Last Confucian: Liang Shu-ming and the Chinese Dilemma of Modernity*, Berkeley, CA: University of California Press.

Ashraf, N., Camerer, C.F. and Loewenstein, G. (2005) 'Adam Smith, behavioral economist', *Journal of Economic Perspectives* 19(3): 131146.

Balazs, E. (1964) *Chinese Civilization and Bureaucracy: Variations on a Theme*, New Haven, CT: Yale University Press.

Barbalet, J. (2011) 'Market relations as wuwei: traditional concepts in analysis of China's post-1978 economy', *Asian Studies Review* 35(3): 335–54.

Baurmann, M. (1996) *Der Markt der Tugend: Recht und Moral in der liberalen Gesellschaft. Eine soziologische Untersuchung*. Tübingen: Mohr Siebeck.

Beck, U. (2009) 'Understanding the real Europe: a cosmopolitan vision', in Chris Rumford (ed.), *The SAGE Handbook of European Studies*, Los Angeles, CA: SAGE, pp. 602–36.

Brenner, R. and Isett, C. (2002) 'England's divergence from China's Yangzi delta: property relations, microeconomics, and patterns of development', *Journal of Asian Studies*, 61(2): 609–62.

Brewer, M.B. and Ya-Ru, C. (2007) 'Where (who) are collectives in collectivism? Toward conceptual clarification of individualism and collectivism', *Psychological Review*, 114(1): 133–51.

Broadie, A. (2006) 'Sympathy and the impartial spectator', in K. Haakonssen (ed.) *The Cambridge Companion to Adam Smith*, Cambridge: Cambridge University Press, pp. 158–89.

Casmir, F. (1999) 'Foundations for the study of intercultural communication based on a third-culture building model', *International Journal of Intercultural Relations*, 23(1): 91–116.

Casson, M. (1991) *The Economics of Business Culture: Game Theory, Transaction Costs, and Economic Performance*, Oxford: Clarendon.

Chua, R.Y.J., Morris, M.W. and Ingram, P. (2009) 'Guanxi vs. networking: Distinctive configurations of affect- and cognition-based trust in the networks of Chinese vs American managers', *Journal of International Business Studies*, 40: 490–508.

Clunas, C. (2004) *Elegant Debts. The Social Art of Wen Zhengming*, Honululu: University of Hawai'i Press.

Cohen, M. (1992) 'Family management and family division on contemporary rural China', *China Quarterly*, 130: 357–77.

Cohen, M. (1994) 'Being Chinese: the peripheralization of traditional identity', in T. Wei-ming (ed.), *The Living Tree: The Changing Meaning of Being Chinese Today*, Stanford, CA: Stanford University Press, pp. 88–109.

Commission on Growth and Development (2008) *The Growth Report. Strategies for Sustained Growth and Inclusive Development*, Washington DC: World Bank.

Eastman, L.E. (1988) *Family, Fields, and Ancestors. Constancy and Change in China's Social and Economic History*, New York: Oxford University Press.

Ebrey, P. (1991) 'The Chinese family and the spread of Confucian values', in: R. Gilbert (ed.) *The East Asian Region. Confucian Heritage and Its Modern Adaptation*, Princeton, NJ: Princeton University Press, pp. 45–83.

Elias, N. (1969/1990) *Über den Prozeß der Zivilisation. Soziogenetische und psycho-genetische Untersuchungen. Erster Band: Wandlungen des Verhaltens in den weltlichen Oberschichten des Abendlandes*, Frankfurt: Suhrkamp.

Elvin, M. (1973) *The Pattern of the Chinese Past*, Stanford, CA: Stanford University Press.

Esherick, J.W. and Rankin, M.B. (eds) (1990) *Chinese Local Elites and Patterns of Dominance*, Berkeley, CA: University of California Press.

Evensky, J. (2005) 'Adam Smith's theory of moral sentiments: on morals and why they matter to a liberal society of free people and free markets', *Journal of Economic Perspectives*, 19(3): 109–30.

Fairbank, J.K. (1978) 'Introduction: the old order', in J.K. Fairbank (ed.) *The Cambridge History of China. Volume 10. Late Ch'ing 1800–1911*, Cambridge: Cambridge University Press, pp. 1–34.

Fairbank, J.K. (1992) *China. A New History*, Cambridge: Belknap.

Faure, D. (2007) *Emperor and Ancestor: State and Lineage in South China*, Stanford, CA: Stanford University Press.

Feuchtwang, S. (1992) *The Imperial Metaphor: Popular Religion in China*, London: Routledge.

Financial Times (2009) 'Transcript of interview: Wen Jiabao', *Financial Times*, 9 February.

Forman-Barzilai, F. (2006) 'Smith on "connexion", culture and judgment', in L. Montes and E. Schliesser, *New Voices on Adam Smith*, London: Routledge, pp. 89–114.

Forman-Barzilai, F. (2010) *Adam Smith and the Circles of Sympathy. Cosmopolitanism and Moral Theory*, Cambridge: Cambridge University Press.

Gabrenya Jr., W.K. and Hwang K.-K. (1996) 'Chinese social interaction: harmony and hierarchy on the good earth', in M.H. Bond (ed.) *The Handbook of Chinese Psychology*, New York: Oxford University Press, pp. 309–21.

Ge Zhaoguang (2001) *Zhongguo sixiang shi* [*The History of Thought in China*], Shanghai: Fudan daxue chubanshe.

Gerlach, C. (2005) *Wu-Wei in Europe: A Study of Eurasian Economic Thought*, in Working papers of the global economic history network 12/05. London: London School of Economics.

Gerschlager, C. (2005) 'Beyond economic man: Adam Smith's concept of the agent and the role of deception', *Cahiers d'Économie Politique*, 49, Spring: 31–49.

Ghoshal, S. (2005) 'Bad management theories are destroying good management practices', *Academy of Management Learning and Education*, 4(1): 75–91.

Gold, T., Guthrie, D. and Wank, D. (eds) (2002) *Social Connections in China: Institutions, Culture, and the Changing Nature of Guanxi*, Cambridge: Cambridge University Press.

Greif, A. (1994) 'Cultural beliefs and the organization of society: a historical and theoretical reflection on collectivist and individualist societies', *Journal of Political Economy*, 102(5): 912–50.

Greif, A. and Tabellini, G. (2010) 'Cultural and institutional bifurcation: China and Europe compared', *American Economic Review: Papers and Proceedings*, 100: 135–140.

Gudeman, S. (1986) *Economics as Culture. Models and Metaphors of Livelihood*, London: Routledge and Kegan Paul.

Guiso, L., Sapienza, P. and Zingales, L. (2006) 'Does culture affect economic outcomes?', *Journal of Economic Perspectives*, 20(2): 23–48.

Guthrie, D. (1998) 'The declining significance of Guanxi in China's economic transition', *China Quarterly*, 154: 254–82.

Hall, E.T. (1976) *Beyond Culture*, New York: Doubleday.

Hanley, R.P. (2006) 'Adam Smith, Aristotle and virtue ethics', in L. Montes and E. Schliesser (eds) *New Voices on Adam Smith*, London: Routledge, pp. 89–114.

Hansen, V. (1995) *Negotiating Daily Life in Traditional China: How Ordinary People Used Contracts, 600–1400*, New Haven, CT: Yale University Press.

Herrmann-Pillath, C. (2006) 'Cultural species and institutional change in China', *Journal of Economic Issues*, 40(3): 539–74.

Herrmann-Pillath, C. (2009a) 'China's path-dependent transition: Culture mediating between market and socialism', in J. Kornai and Q. Yingyi (eds) *Market and Socialism in the Light of the Experiences of China and Vietnam*, International Economic Association Conference Volume 146, London: Palgrave, pp. 110–34.

Herrmann-Pillath, C. (2009b) 'Social classes in "old society" (before 1949)', in D. Pong (ed.), *Encyclopedia of Modern China*, New York: Charles Scribner's Sons/Gale Cengage.

Herrmann-Pillath, C. (2009c) 'Social capital, chinese style: individualism, relational collectivism and the cultural embeddedness of the institutions–performance link' *China Economic Journal*, 2(3): 325–50.

Herrmann-Pillath, C. (2010) 'Adam Smith and Confucius: a tour d'horizon towards a transcultural foundation of institutions', *Fudan Journal of the Humanities and Social Sciences*, 3(3): 91–126.

Hobson, J.M. (2004) *The Eastern Origins of Western Civilization*, Cambridge: Cambridge University Press.

Hofstede, G. (1991) *Cultures and Organizations: Software of the Mind*, London: McGraw-Hill.

Huang, P.C.C. (2006a) 'Civil adjudication in China, past and present', *Modern China*, 32(2): 135–80.

Huang, P.C.C. (2006b) 'Court mediation in China, past and present', *Modern China*, 32(3): 275–314.

Hwang, K.-K. (2006) 'Moral face and social face: contingent self-esteem in Confucian society', *International Journal of Psychology*, 41(4): 276–81.

Jacobs, J.B. (1982) 'The concept of Guanxi and local politics in a rural Chinese cultural setting', in S. Greenblatt, R.W. Wilson and A.A. Wilson (eds) *Social Interaction in Chinese Society*, New York: Praeger, pp. 209–36.

Jones, E.R. (1988) *Growth Recurring*, Oxford: Oxford University Press.

King, A.Y.-c. (1994) 'Kuan-hsi and network building: A sociological interpretation', in T. Weiming (ed.) *The Living Tree: The Changing Meaning of Being Chinese Today*, Stanford, CA: Stanford University Press, pp. 109–26.

Kipnis, A. (1996) 'The language of gifts: managing Guanxi in a north China village', *Modern China*, 22(3): 285–314.

Kipnis, A. (2002) 'Practices of Guanxi production and Ganqing avoidance', in T. Gold, D. Guthrie and D. Wank (eds) *Social Connections in China: Institutions, Culture, and the Changing Nature of Guanxi*, Cambridge: Cambridge University Press, pp. 21–36.

La Porta, R., Lopez–de–Silvanes, F., Shleifer, A. and Vishny, R.W. (1997) 'Legal determinants of external finance', *Journal of Finance*, 52: 1131–1150.

Landes, D.S. (2006) 'Why Europe and the West? Why not China?', *Journal of Economic Perspectives*, 20(2): 3–22

Li-Jun, J., Nisbett, R.E. and Zhiyong, Z. (2004) 'Is it culture or is it language? Examination of language effects in cross-cultural research on categorization', *Journal of Personality and Social Psychology*, 87(1): 57–65.

Li, P.P. (2007) 'Guanxi as the Chinese norm for personalized social capital: toward an integrated duality framework of informal exchange', in H.W.-C. Yeung (ed.) *Handbook of Research on Asian Business*, Cheltenham: Edward Elgar, pp. 62–83.

Lin, J.L. (2010) *New Structural Economics. A Framework for Rethinking Development*, Policy Research Working Paper 5197, Washington: World Bank.

Little, D. (1992) *Understanding Peasant China. Case Studies in the Philosophy of Social Science*, New Haven, CT: Yale University Press.

Loewe, M. (1974) *Crisis and Conflict in Han China 104 BC to AD 9*, London: Allen & Unwin.

Long, B. (2006) 'Adam Smith's natural theology of society', *Adam Smith Review* 2: 124–48.

Luo, W. (2005) *Qinggan, zhixu, meide. Yadang Simi de lilun xue shijie* [*Sentiments, Order, Virtue. The World of Ethics in Adam Smith*], Beijing: Zhongguo renmin chubanshe.

Ma, D. (2011) 'Rock, scissors, paper: the problem of incentives and information in the traditional Chinese state and the origin of the great divergence', Paper presented at the 16th International Economic Association World Congress, Beijing.

Mann, S. (1987) *Local Merchants and the Chinese Bureaucracy 1750–1950*, Stanford: Stanford University Press.

McFadden, D. (2006) 'Free markets and fettered consumers', *American Economic Review* 96(1): 5–29.

Mehta, P.B. (2006) 'Self-interest and other interests', in K. Haakonssen (ed.) *The Cambridge Companion to Adam Smith*, Cambridge: Cambridge University Press, pp. 246–69.

Metzger, T.A. (1977) *Escape From Predicament. Neo-Confucianism and China's Evolving Political Culture*, New York: Columbia University Press.

Mungello, D.E. (1999) *The Great Encounter of China and the West, 1500–1900*, Lanham, MD: Rowman & Littlefield.

Naquin, S. and Rawski, E. (1988) *Chinese Society in the Eighteenth Century*, New Haven, CT: Yale University Press.

Nisbett, R. (2003) *The Geography of Thought: How Asians and Westerners Think Differently... and Why*, New York: Free Press.

Pennarz, J. (1992) *Mazu, Macht und Marktwirtschaft. Die religiöse Organisation im sozialen und ökonomischen Wandlungsprozeß der ländlichen Gesellschaft Taiwans*, München: Akademischer.

Platteau, J.-P. (1994a) 'Behind the market stage where real societies exist. Part I: The role of public and private order institutions', *Journal of Development Studies*, 30(3): 533–77.

Platteau, J.-P. (1994b) 'Behind the market stage where real societies exist. Part II: The role of moral norms', *Journal of Development Studies*, 30(4): 753–817.

Pommeranz, K. (2000) *The Great Divergence. China, Europe, and the Making of the Modern World Economy*, Princeton, NJ: Princeton University Press.

Priddat, B.P. (2001) *Le Concert Universel: Die Physiokratie. Eine Tranformation-sphilosophie des 18. Jahrhunderts*, Marburg: Metropolis.

Raphael, D.D. and Macfie, A.L. (1976) 'Introduction to Adam Smith', in D.D. Raphael and A.L. Macfie (eds) *The Theory of Moral Sentiments*, Oxford: Clarendon Press, pp. 1–52.

Rawski, T.G. (1989) *Economic Growth in Pre-War China*, Berkeley, CA: University of California Press.

Robertson, P. (1999) *Economic Change in China, c. 1850–1950*, Cambridge: Cambridge University Press.

Rodrik, D. (2007) *One Economics, Many Recipes. Globalization, Institutions, and Economic Growth*, Princeton, NJ: Princeton University Press.

Roetz, H. (1992) *Die konfuzianische Ethik der Achsenzeit. Eine Rekonstruktion unter dem Aspekt des Durchbruchs zu postkonventionellem Denken*. Frankfurt: Suhrkamp.

Schefold, B., Mende, E.v. and Vogel, H.U. (2002) *Huan Kuan. Yantie lun. Vademecum zu dem Klassiker der chinesischen Wirtschaftsdebatten*, Düsseldorf: Verlag Wirtschaft und Finanzen.

Schmidt-Glintzer, H. (1997) *China: Vielvölkerreich und Einheitsstaat. Von den Anfängen bis heute*, München: Beck.

Schoppa, K.R. (1989) *Xiang Lake – Nine Centuries of Chinese Life*, New Haven, CT: Yale University Press.

Sen, A. (2009) *The Idea of Justice*, Cambridge: Belknap.

Shaver, R. (2006) 'Virtues, utility, and rules', in K. Haakonssen (ed.) *The Cambridge Companion to Adam Smith*, Cambridge: Cambridge University Press, pp. 189–213.

Sheng, H. (2010) *Wei wan shi kai taiping. Creating Peace Forever. Yi ge jingji xuejia dui wenming wenti de sikao*, Beijing: Zhongguo fazhan chubanshe.

Skinner, G.W. (1964/65) 'Marketing and social structure in rural China', *Journal of Asian Studies*, 24: 3–43, 195–228, 363–99.

Smith, A. ([1759] 1976) *The Theory of Moral Sentiments*, Oxford: Clarendon Press.

Smith, A. ([1776] 1976) *An Inquiry Into the Nature and Causes of The Wealth of Nations*, Oxford: Oxford University Press.

Sugden, R. (2002) 'Beyond sympathy and empathy: Adam Smith's concept of fellow-feeling', *Economics and Philosophy*, 18: 63–87.

Thaler, R.H., and Sunstein, R.C. (2009) *Nudge: Improving Decisions about Health, Wealth, and Happiness*, Harmondsworth: Penguin.

Tsai, L.L. (2002) 'Cadres, temple and lineage institutions, and governance in rural China', *China Journal*, 48: 1–28.

Tsai, L.L. (2007) *Accountability without Democracy, Solidary Groups and Public Goods Provision in Rural China*, Cambridge: Cambridge University Press.

Tugendhat, E. (2004) 'Universalistically approved intersubjective attitudes: Adam Smith', *Adam Smith Review*, 1: 88–104.

Wang, X. and Zhu, C. (1996) *Zhongguo xiangcun de minying qiye yu jiazu jingji. Zhejiang sheng Cangnan xian Xiangdong cun diaocha, Dangdai Zhongguo de cunzhuang yu cunluo wenhua congshu*, Vol. 5, Chen Jiyuan and He Mengbi (Carsten Herrmann-Pillath) (eds), Taiyuan: Shanxi jingji chubanshe.

Wank, D. (1996) 'The institutional practice of market clientelism: Guanxi and private business in a South China City', *China Quarterly*, 144: 820–38.

Wank, D. (2002) 'Business-state clientelism in China: decline or evolution?' in T. Gold, D. Guthrie and D. Wank (eds) *Social Connections in China: Institutions, Culture, and the Changing Nature of Guanxi*, Cambridge: Cambridge University Press, pp. 97–115.

Will, P.-E. (1990) *Bureaucracy and Famine in Eighteenth-Century China*, Stanford, CA: Stanford University Press.

Wilson, S. (1997) 'The cash nexus and social networks: mutual aid and gifts in contemporary Shanghai villages', *China Journal*, 37: 91–115.

Wing-Tsit, C. (1967) 'The story of Chinese philosophy', in C. Moore (ed.) *The Chinese Mind: Essentials of Chinese Philosophy and Culture*, Honolulu: University of Hawai'i Press, pp. 31–76.

Wong, R.B. (1997) *China Transformed. Historical Change and the Limits of European Experience*, Ithaca, NY: Cornell University Press.

Xiangqun, C. (2010) *Guanxi or Li shang wanglai? Reciprocity, Special Support Networks, Social Creativity in a Chinese Village*, Taipei: Airiti Press.

Xiao-Ping, C. and Chao, C.C. (2004) 'On the intricacies of the Chinese Guanxi: A process model of Guanxi development', *Asia Pacific Journal of Management*, 21: 305–24.

Xiao, L. (2010) *Xia cun shehui. Zhongguo Jiannan nongcun de richang shenghuo he shehui jiegou (1976–2006)*, Shanghai: Sanlian chubanshe.

Yan, Y. (1996) 'The culture of Guanxi in a north China village', *China Journal*, 35: 1–26.

Yang, L.-s. (1957) 'The concept of Pao as a basis for social relations in China', in J.K. Fairbank (ed.) *Chinese Thought and Institutions*, Chicago, IL: University of Chicago Press, pp. 291–309.

Yang, M.M.-h. (1994) *Gifts, Favours and Banquets: The Art of Social Relationships in China*, Ithaca, NY: Cornell University Press.

Yang, M.M.-h. (2007) 'Ritual economy and rural capitalism with Chinese characteristics', in D. Held and H.L. Moore, (eds) *Cultural Politics in a Global Age: Uncertainty, Solidarity and Innovation*, London: OneWorld, pp. 226–33.

Zelin, M. (1990) 'The structure of the Chinese economy during the Qing period: Some thoughts on the 150th anniversary of the opium war', in K. Lieberthal, J. Kallgren, R. MacFarquhar and F. Wakeman Jr. (eds) *Perspectives on Modern China: Four Anniversaries*, Armonk, NY: M. E. Sharpe, pp. 31–67.

Zelin, M. (2009) 'The firm in early modern China', in *Journal of Economic Behavior & Organization*, 71: 623–37.

Emotion and sympathy in Confucius and Adam Smith

Henrique Schnieder

In a recent paper, the Chinese philosopher, Liu Yuedi, indirectly questioned the comparative approach to Confucius and Adam Smith proposed by Zhang Weibin (2000) concerning emotion, sympathy, and their respective role in human society.

Liu analysed the role of emotions (情, *qing*) as ontology in Confucian political philosophy, focusing on the question of how they are transmitted from 'inside the self' to 'outside the self' and how they relate to human nature or to factual realities. Liu concludes that emotions are developed in self-cultivation, through aesthetical education, and then expanded to society through families and kinship. However, this is not a factual judgement but a logic necessity, since society would not function if emotions were not transposed and did not establish 'social morality' and thus social harmony. It was among his goals to show a distinct propriety of Confucian philosophy and to contrast this with Western approaches, which he calls 'rationalist'. In this very broad sense, this paper concurs with Liu's position – except for his treatment of Adam Smith.

Liu acknowledges some similarities with the Confucian position in Smith's *Theory of Moral Sentiments* (*TMS*). He stresses, however, that Smith considers emotions to be a corrective to self-interest. Thus, Smith's social philosophy lacks a proper ontology of emotions.

In this chapter, a different reading of the *TMS* is proposed. It highlights the similarities of Smith's concept of emotion and sympathy with Confucius, while maintaining Liu's conclusion that Smith lacks a proper ontology of emotions. Reading moral self-cultivation as inherent to Smith's theory is the cornerstone of this analysis. In the first section, the relevance and central positions of the *TMS* are outlined; in the second section, they are contrasted with Confucius's propositions; a final section answers the question of whether Liu's judgement of Adam Smith can be rectified.

The goal of this chapter is to examine the parallels of both philosophies, not to concur with the philosophical quality of their arguments.

Adam Smith and the *Theory of Moral Sentiments*

In this section, Smith's argument for sympathy in the *TMS* is outlined and submitted to an analysis from a contemporary perspective.

Sympathy and the impartial spectator

> When the original passions of the person principally concerned are in perfect concord with the sympathetic emotions of the spectator, they necessarily appear to this last just and proper, and suitable to their objects.
>
> (*TMS* I.i 3.1)

The first chapter of the *TMS* carries the title 'On Sympathy', and, if names indeed serve to denote meanings, then the title itself has something important to say not only about the chapter, but about the book it introduces. Sympathy – its precise definition has yet to be provided – takes a prominent place in Smith's moral and social theory. This is immediately shown in the introduction to the *TMS*. Smith begins with all elements he deems essential for the account of an action's morality: the pair agent–spectator and the sympathetic sentiments.

> The sentiment of affection of the heart, from which any action proceeds and upon which its whole virtue or vice must ultimately depend, may be considered under two different aspects, or in two different relations: First, in relation to the cause which excites it or the motives which give occasion to it, and second, in relation to the end which it proposes or the effect it intends to produce. In the suitableness or unsuitableness, in the proportion or disproportion which the affection seems to bear to the cause or objects which excite it consists the property or impropriety, the decency or ungracefulness of the consequent action. In the beneficial or hurtful nature of the effects which the affection aims at, or tends to produce, consists the merit or demerit of the action, the qualities by which it is entitled to reward or its deserving punishment.
>
> (*TMS* I.i.3.5–7)

Smith then proceeds with the moral relevance of an action founded on the 'sentiment of affection' situated in the 'heart' of the agent; in other words, in the feelings or, in a more modern diction, in the propositional attitudes of the agent. The philosopher is less interested in the logical account of the action, but rather in the intentions of the agent and the acceptance of the action as well as the agent's intentions by others. Smith's argument for judging the moral value of an action follows these lines:

A spectator observes an action. He knows what has prompted the agent to act or think of acting. The spectator imagines himself in the agent's place and notes whether he would be prompted to act likewise. In other words, the spectator finds that he 'sympathizes' with the agent. Moral judgements begin with the reaction of spectators to the actions and the motives of other people. The spectators in question are normal fellow members of society. And for the most part, Smith writes about social cohesion and about what 'we' feel and think about the conduct of other people. Most importantly, moral judgements begin with a relationship of sympathy between the spectator – or the member of the community – with the agent.

Sympathy means putting oneself in the agent's shoes and imagining what it would mean to act likewise.

Smith begins to stress the impartiality of the spectator only when he comes to theorize about the effect on the agent of the reactions of spectators. Smith's spectator is first called impartial in the chapter that distinguishes between the amiable and the respectable virtues, the virtues of humanity on the one hand, and self-command on the other. Humanity is a more-than-average degree of sympathetic feeling and is the result of an effort by the spectator to heighten his sympathy in order to match the experience of the person principally concerned. Self-command is conversely a virtue of the 'person principally concerned' and is the result of an endeavour to restrain natural emotion and to lower its pitch to that which the ordinary spectator feels by sympathy (*TMS* I.i.5.4).

> When I endeavour to examine my own conduct, when I endeavour to pass sentence upon it, and either to approve or to condemn it, it is evident that, in all such cases, I divide myself, as it were, into two persons; and that I, the examiner and the judge, represent a different character from that other I, the person whose character is examined into and judged of.
>
> (*TMS* III.i.5.1)

Sympathy holds things together. Sympathy keeps people in their own orbit and in harmony with others (the general theory of morality paralleling Newton's general theory of physics). Sympathy occurs through the objective part of man that Smith calls the impartial spectator. Whereas one person can judge one agent, how is the person to account for their own action? The agent has to 'divide' himself into two: an agent in its proper sense and a supposed spectator, which is called impartial, for it is the part that is self-judging. Impartiality, however, does not rule out sympathy. It is indeed sympathy that allows us to judge as an impartial spectator, since this is a common feature of all members of the community.

By using the impartial spectator to examine one's own and others' actions, a person separates him- or herself into two: the examiner and the examined. As to the way in which the impartial spectator is supposed to work, Recktenwald (1986: 23) schematizes as shown in Figure 1.

Smith's theory is that the spectator can only determine whether an action is good or bad if he is, at the same time, aware of the causes and effects of an agent's actions and the motives and aims of his own actions. How is he to know both? The effects are easily analyzed by the materialization of the action. The agent's motives, however, are more difficult to penetrate. Putting oneself in someone else's shoes may be easier to talk about than to do. Just by thinking about the inclinations I might have had if I had been the agent does not necessarily lead to finding out what motives the agent had. The only thing one would find out would be what inclinations one would have if one were the agent. How, then, can someone find out what an agent actually thinks?

Here, Smith refers to two principles that he deems necessary conditions for a human society. He first presupposes that all members of the community share the

Real (existing) impartial spectator	or	Imagined (postulated) impartial spectator
observes		
alien behaviour (the other)	or	own behaviour (myself)
and judges whether		
cause and effect	or	motives and aims
of the action		
a) are commensurable with the constrains or sentiments	and	b) are commensurable with the objects they intended to reach

Figure 1 Rechtenwald's scheme of the impartial spectator

same values, and, second, he equally presupposes that they train themselves to adhere to these values; that is, he imagines all members of society cultivating common values.

> To be amiable, and to be meritorious; that is, to deserve love and to deserve reward, are the great characters of virtue; and to be odious and punishable, of vice. But all these characters have an immediate reference to the sentiments of others. Virtue is not said to be amiable, or to be meritorious, because it is the object of its own love or of its own gratitude; but because it exercises those sentiments in other men.
>
> (*TMS* III.1.7)

The argument in which morality is a means of self control rests largely on Smith's notion of self-command as an essential precondition for human society. However, his philosophy is finer grained, since morality is not only self-command, but a constitutive principle.

> Although it may be true, therefore, that every individual, in his own breast, naturally prefers himself to all mankind, yet he dares not look mankind in the face and avow that he acts according to this principle.
>
> (*TMS* II. ii.1–11)

For Adam Smith, conscience is a social product, a mirror of social feeling. Without society, Smith wrote, a man 'could no more think of his own character…of the beauty or deformity of his own mind, than the beauty or deformity of his own face'. For both he needs a mirror. The mirror in which he can view his character 'is placed on the countenance and behaviour of those he lives with' (*TMS* III.1.3). In this sense, putting oneself in someone else's shoes means going back to this common conscience and asking whether there are motivations that are compatible or that emanate from the principled values shared by the community.

Summarizing Smith's approach, there are two points to be noted: First, the 'impartial spectator' is introduced as aiming to relate with others or asking how their actions can be reflected by one's self and others. Here, the observer is positively relating one's actions with one's morality, making it compatible with the overall sense of ethics. The cultivation of values as well as the self-inculcation of values is a necessary condition for being able to use the impartial spectator as a tool to evaluate one's actions. This instrument, however, does not apply on an individual basis; its chief aim is to relate individuals with each other, hence making sympathy a sufficient condition for its application. Only if people relate positively with each other can the impartial spectator unfold his use; this positive relation is crucially determined by sympathy.

Second, Smith considers social harmony not only to be a product of individuals using the impartial spectator, but also a precondition for its application, since overall values and 'moralities' are supposed to be something shared by all of society. In a context in which each has different sentiments, the impartial spectator would lead not to social desiderata, but only to the rationalization of individual value judgement. Smith aims at self-cultivation and thereby at the inculcation of common sentiments that enable virtue.

Smith's TMS, a modern evaluation

Even from today's perspective, Smith stands apart from his contemporary philosophers. As for the value of Smith's *TMS* Frantz puts it nicely:

> Smith was among a group of writers who were reacting against the rapidly changing, confusing, and potentially corrupting nature of the growing 'society of strangers'. Smith wanted to understand how social bonds are created and maintained, and how one can live a virtuous life under those circumstances. He saw a solution in an individual suppressing the ego and entering into the feelings of another.
>
> (Frantz 2000: 8)

According to Haig (2011), Smith made a persuasive case for the statement that 'moral sentiments' are the foundation of ethical behaviour in his 1759 book. Sympathy in the *TMS* is best described by the metaphor of mirrors reflecting mirrors; we see ourselves through others' eyes, who see themselves through others' eyes.

In a neuroeconomical experiment, Zak (2011) reveals that the embeddedness of individuals is important for their moral behaviour, claiming that 'live history matters, institutions matter, organizations matter, and happiness happens (2011:

10–11)'. Going further, he appropriates a quote of the *TMS* illustrating his own results: 'As we have no immediate experience of what other men feel, we can form no idea of the manner in which they are affected, but by conceiving what we ourselves should feel in the like situation' (2011: 9).

Firth characterizes Adam Smith's personal point of view: 'Smith's moral world is peopled by groups who are ranked according to their regard for true virtue. At the apex of the moral hierarchy are a small minority who are dedicated to moral and virtue' Firth (2007: 115). In this sense, she classifies Smith's moral philosophy as spiritual self-discipline.

Carsten Herrmann-Pillath works on family resemblances between Adam Smith and Confucianism, especially the Zhedong School. He states that Smith perceives cognitive processes as linking up with social context via the specific construction of the 'spectator', who is by definition 'the other' in the sense of a third party (Herrmann-Pillath 2008, 10–11). The cognitive process appears to be an ongoing refinement of this interaction between the positions of the observer and the observed via deliberation. The objects of deliberation are innate conceptions of the other, which means that Smith proposes a non-reductionist naturalistic approach, which assigns culture as a repertoire of cognitive tools a crucial role. Thus, mental processes are inexplicably enmeshed with external symbolic communication.

Remarkably, this capability is itself a complex construct of emotions and cognitions, because Smith identifies a sentiment that supports the bridge to the other, namely sympathy (Ashraf 2005, 24).

Through the transition from the spectator to the 'impartial spectator', the virtue of 'justice' emerges (*TMS* II.i 5.11.ff.). As has been emphasized by several commentators, Smith's notion of justice does not argue from the viewpoint of its effects on society, but is also based on sympathy, namely sympathy with resentment (Schliesser 2006). The virtue of justice arises from a purification of sympathy by way of being processed by the impartial spectator.

The foundation of justice lies in the sympathy with the resentment of an aggrieved individual. However, whether this feeling is itself appropriate can only be assessed by weighting the merits of the respective actions, which, of course, also involves a balancing with the sympathy for the actor and the aggrieved person. This is achieved by looking at the situation from the perspective of the impartial observer. Thus, the virtue of justice does not arise from some axiomatic deduction, but is an emergent property of the process of moral development, ending up in universalistic standards of approval and disapproval.

Confucius, morals and self-cultivation

In this section, some of the main features of Confucian philosophy are highlighted and contrasted with Adam Smith's theory. To provide an answer to the question initially posed, Confucianism will be described as outlined in Liu Yedi's paper.

Moral self-cultivation and mode of association

According to Liu (2010), Confucian philosophy is empirically grounded in a private sphere of 'emotion' in a more general sense, so the ontology of *qing* (情, *qing*, emotion) becomes its cornerstone. Emotion deals with communal as well as individual harmony. In Liu's account, although both David Hume and Adam Smith single out 'sympathy' as a forceful moral motivation, Confucianism goes further to conceive the sympathy-oriented *ren* (仁, *ren*, humanity) as the origin of emotion and life and to attribute *ren* to the 'integrity with heaven and earth'.

Confucian morality takes an approach consisting of two elements: moral self-cultivation and the mode of association. First, self-cultivation is an individual's moral cultivation to attain inner harmony; the main idea being training oneself in virtue, piety and rites through self-cultivation. Second, through the sentiment of sympathy, meaning 'to feel others in oneself', the private experience of self-cultivation is put in a perspective of 'inter-subjectivity' for mutual empathy. This is spread throughout the family to the whole of society, eventually becoming 'transcendent' to all. This is also the specific difference between Chinese and so-called Western civilization, which Liu calls the 'different mode of association'.

This specific difference in Chinese society is described by Liu using a model of concentric cycles. It is a continuum from the self and family, through the state, and to the universe. This approach of putting oneself in others' shoes corresponds to the differential mode of association.

The hierarchical structure of Confucian politics is sustained by this continuum, the philosophy of which can be found in the saying that

> If you yourself desire rank and standing; then help others to get rank and standing. You want to turn your own merits to account, then help others to turn their account in fact, the ability to take one's own feeling as a guide – that is the sort of thing that lies in the direction of Goodness.
>
> (Analects 6:28)

Rank and standing are obtained through experience in learning and in the moral cultivation of the self. However, as learning is a precondition for advancing in rank and standing, the content of what is to be learnt is also defined by the place an individual takes in society. Learning and rank are mutual enablers. Learning is also 'learning in order to take a given place in society or to achieve a desired rank'. Learning in order to do the correct thing is something cherished by Confucius himself.

> At fifteen I set my heart on learning. At thirty I had formed my character. At forty I had no doubts. At fifty I knew the mandate of heaven. At sixty nothing disturbed me. At seventy I could follow my desires without trespassing the boundaries of right.
>
> (Analects 2:4)

Confucian ethics are a system in which virtues and rules fall out of an under-standing of the self as constituted by the roles determined by the relationships in which a person stands, like a focal point, a field of social activities and relations (Nuyen 2009: 2). For Confucians, social relationships are characterized by social position, or roles and social positions are defined in terms of obligations. To each role there is an attached set of obligations, and to take a social role is to be under a set of obligations. Which obligations go with which role is determined by more or less explicit social expectations. For the key social roles, these are encoded in the rites, *li* (禮).[1] *Li* describes both the factual and the ethical. There is a close connection between *li* and *yi* (义, *yi,* righteousness, literally justice; meaning the moral disposition to do good, or, as Cheng Chung-ying describes it, basic morality; Cheng 1972: 269 – 280), a connection spelled out in the Analects. 'The gentleman is on the side of *yi*.' (Analects 4,10) and 'takes *yi* to his essence and acts in accordance to *li*' (Analects 15,17). In a Confucian system, a person is a person by virtue of standing in a network of social relationships, being it parenthood, friendship, husbandry, or others.

Note here that Smith also acknowledges the 'role' someone has in society. Although he seems to be more flexible regarding rank and standing, an individual's advancement, as well as *li*; through the impartial spectator, Smith accepts that everyone has a place in a network of social relationships. The spectator judges the agent's action in the light of overall values but also in the light of what one ought to do. This, in itself, is deeply influenced by the place the agent has in a given situation, but also in society at large. In a similar way that Confucius sees it, Smith conceives the impartial spectator as ethical as well as factual; he does not separate two different realms of actions. *TMS* takes the situation of the agent in a given social network to be co-determining the ethical value of his actions in a determined context. The similarity to Confucian thinking is, here again, given.

Thus, in the Confucian context, to know one's obligations is to know who one is in the network of social relationships and what this entails. Such knowledge requires self-cultivation, which, in turn, requires dedication, hard work and making choices. Self-cultivation consists of learning to rectify names (正名, *zhengming*; to use a name that fits what is named) and to be sincere.

The Confucians posited that moral development of the individual never takes place in insolation, so that the educational process in natural societies instils the individual with proper norms. In a typical metaphor, *ren* means to understand the body through the heart; that is, to access the other's feelings through one's heart to arrive at harmony among people.

Especially here, the similarity to Smith's *TMS* is rampant. His concept of sympathy (for example, in *TMS* I.i.5.5 or as argued above) seems at least to work in the same way that *ren* does, although the two are not very much alike. Both principles have two dimensions, the individual and the societal. Both principles claim the that the individual has to work on him- or herself regarding his or her standing in a communal network or his or her position towards others, as well as on his or her primary values and virtues. Again, both principles claim to transfer one's self into society, understanding one's actions through the other members of that society.

In Adam Smith, as in Confucius, sympathy does not tame self-interest but is a precondition for the self to judge the moral actions of others as well as its own. For both, sympathy is a social concept that enables one to transcend the self and to put the spectator in someone else's stead to develop social harmony. People's possibilities for forming societies and for developing ethically therein are dependent on the application of sympathy, and this is dependent on the self-inculcation of what sympathy entails for individual actions. This relation between the inner and outer aspect of sympathy, moral self-cultivation, and self control is explored further in the next section.

Keji *and* li

Confucius constantly reminds his disciples that the essence of marksmanship (or archery) does not lie in the physical strength to pierce the hide, but in the self control for doing so (Analects 3.16), and that a fine steed should not be praised for its strength, but only for its *de* (德, virtue, Analects 14.33). Confucius thought that the person seeking others' approval, yet negligent of his own inner growth, is the single most serious enemy of virtue (Analects 17.12; 14.24). What is then, according to Confucius, the correct way of balancing inner growth and outer appearance? As the Analects put it, none. Confucius' greatest passion was to cultivate the self to the extent that one becomes a *junzi* (君子, gentleman, superior person, exemplary person) who refuses to embrace a strict inner/outer and private/public distinction (Analects 8.4).

Confucius' point is that when unmediated by the *li*, the borderline between virtue (candour) and vice (rudeness) is blurred. Their distinction is completely subject to the differing (often contrasting) subjective interpretations of the persons involved, which is troubling from both the moral and the political perspective. It is for this reason that ritual propriety must be incorporated in the process of self-transformation alongside self control (*keji*, 克己), which initially reconstructs moral agency. Together, these two practices complete the Confucian notion of self-cultivation. 'To return to the observance of the *li* through self control (*keji*) constitutes *ren* (Analects 12.1)'.

Kim (2009) seems to follow a path similar to Liu and tries to point out the difference between Confucius and Smith. He states that the Analects' central claim is that which makes Confucian self-transformation so distinctive and unique; and it is the incorporation of the practice of ritual property within it, whereas liberal[2] self-transformation that relies heavily on a method of self-control comes back to the problem it originally set out to overcome.

Here, however, an interesting inversion of Kim's and Liu's case against the similarity with Smith can be made. Liu states that although sympathy is mentioned by Smith, its sole purpose is to control self-interest and the self's overbearing appetite for its own goals. In Confucius, *li* and *keji* seem to fulfil this role. If individual discretion is to be granted,[3] then there will always be a risk of misinterpretation and misguided actions, even if the motives are good. To prevent this, self-cultivation has to be corrected by self control as a sort of 'back-up mechanism'. Self-control is entailed in Smith's impartial spectator and explicit in Confucius' argument. The often made confusion is to assert that sympathy only serves self-control in the *TMS*. As seen above, self-control is as minimal for *TMS* as it is for Confucius. Indeed, self-control can be interpreted as being more important to Confucius than to Smith, since the former dedicates important parts of the Analects to it, whereas the latter does not.

For both, the primary issue is not control but transformation. What is so attractive about Smith's impartial spectator and the Confucian *li* is that they not only perform a self-transformative function that simultaneously resolves social conflicts but, because they are not as rigid as legal arrangements, they allow room for the moral discretion of the agent.

According to Chen (2010), the *de* (德, virtue) of Confucius has two emphases. On the one hand, it is the foundational or universal aspect of virtue; on the other hand, it is the practical application and development of the requirements of the social system of that time. The former has primarily an ethical meaning, while the latter includes political and social meanings (Chen 2010: 277). In this sense, established criteria are needed to guide behaviour in a specific manner and *ren* is not only a *de* but also a *dao* (道, way). Remembering the basal notion of *ren*, 'do not impose on others what you do not desire' (Analects 12.2), the similarity to Smith's impartial spectator is complete: He is the one taking care of the agent act on motives and aiming effects compatible with one's own virtues.

Similarly, Smith's 'sympathy' is not only a virtue, but a way of organizing the realms of the self and those of society. Sympathy is an overall principle entailing self-cultivation, socially shared values and the possibility of acting in the sense of these virtues. Action and moral judgement are performed by the agent and the spectator or the impartial spectator, both requiring the ability of the individual to put him or herself in someone else's shoes. Therefore, at the principle level as well as at the practical level, there are similarities between Confucius and Smith that go beyond using similar concepts. The philosophical systems behind the concepts are very much alike, too.

There are, however, differences. The first being a difference in style. Whereas Confucius spells out the single levers of his system, Smith is often obscure, using metaphors and comparisons to make his point. This could lead and has led to misinterpretations of his *TMS*. The second difference is more important and concerns the mode of association. According to Liu's argument, Confucianism follows the model of concentric circles, associating first through the family, then to kinship, thus becoming universal and transcendent. Smith's mode of association is individual. He assumes every member of society to share the same values, and, therefore, association is a role change in the performing or judging of an action based on these values.

Third, and here is the specific difference between Smith and Confucius stressed by Liu: Smith lacks the ontology of sentiments. He is not concerned with the nature of sympathy; he is concerned with its content. Indeed, he assumes it to exist, without saying how it exists or interacts with the world. Smith is more interested in epistemic questions than in how to recognize and act accordingly. Therefore, Smith's sympathy cannot be transcendent as Liu argues are the Confucian *qing*.

Confucius versus Adam Smith?

In this chapter, it has been argued that Adam Smith and Confucius are philosophically concerned with emotions and make emotions a cornerstone of their social philosophy. Smith's and Confucius' approaches can be considered similar, are based on the moral self-development of individuals in a society. These respective philosophies see in emotions the link from the individual towards society, considering that social harmony is essential and inherent to the system.

It has also been argued that there are two differences between the philosophers. Although both acknowledge emotions and sympathy to be pivotal for the individual as well as for social morality, Confucius considers *ren* to be the origin of emotion and life. Based thereon, he develops an original ontological approach. Smith, on the other hand, has no such aspirations. Although moral sentiments can be read as ontological facts as well as epistemic conditions, he does not see them separated from human life as such or from society. He also does not provide the mechanism to explain how sentiments necessarily link individuals to society. Smith's solution for achieving social harmony – an interest that runs throughout his various works – includes the use of prudence and what we generally call intuition; Smith called it sympathy and the impartial spectator.

Does this make Liu's (2010) argument wrong? Considering that Liu was contrasting Confucian moral ontology with 'Western' thought in general, the point made in this paper does not falsify Liu's main theme, whereby 'Western' philosophy opts for a 'rationalist' approach in social philosophy, while Confucians opt for an 'emotional' path. Holding to this frame of interpretation, this chapter has drawn attention to Adam Smith's philosophy as possibly unique and as similar to Confucian thinking. This does not challenge Liu's argument concerning 'Western' thought, but explains an exception to his overall considerations.

There may be, however, another point in answering to Liu's thesis. By focusing this argument on one philosopher's work, this chapter has opted for a methodological approach to comparative philosophy based on individual concepts and their similarities. Liu chose another concept: comparing general traits attributed to 'Western' and 'Eastern' philosophy. His approach is prone to three different types of difficulty. First, at an ontological level, Liu's approach might entail the claim of a 'unifying entity' that makes 'western' philosophy 'Western' and 'eastern' philosophy 'Eastern'. This, however, leads to the task of identifying and proving the existence of this 'unifying entity'; a task that might seem too difficult to fulfil. The comparison of 'Eastern' and 'Western' philosophy can also take a less problematic path by claiming only an epistemic similarity within both groups. Still, this might be too difficult to hold, since there is little epistemic similarity between, for example, the logical-analytical philosophy of Saul Kripke and the thinking of Plato. Depending on what 'Eastern' is supposed to mean, it seems difficult to subsume India's Vedic philosophy into the same group as Chinese Mohism (see Harrison 2013). The third type of difficulty may be encountered even by the weakest claim, namely a practical separation of 'Eastern' and 'Western' for the sake of schematization or simplicity. Here again, the criteria for such can be critically challenged. Even if creating such groups is practical, there still is the need to describe how it advances research, especially since the outcomes of such a research cannot be extrapolated to the whole group, since the groups are created artificially. For example: even if 'Chinese Philosophy' is a practical label, finding out that some 'Chinese philosophers' believed in the Way does not allow for a generalization of the sort 'all (or most) Chinese philosophers believe in the Way'.

The methodology of this chapter, however, addresses this last difficulty. Claiming some sort of practical similarity is useful, if it is taken simply as a point of departure. Comparative philosophy would, therefore, mean comparing two (or more) philosophers (or even two ideas) of different philosophical backgrounds, whereby assigning a background to the authors would base on the practical criteria grouping them. The outcomes of a comparison, however, cannot be extrapolated to the whole background. The outcomes are only valid in the direct comparison of the authors; the practical criteria are just employed as 'background identifiers'. By applying this methodology, comparative philosophy would avoid ontic or epistemic generalizations and therefore would lose much of its ambition, but it gains in insight and granularity by directing research to deeper analysis, gaining, thus, in academic rigour.

Bibliography

Ashraf, N., Camerer, C. and Loewenstein, G. (2005) 'Adam Smith, behavioral economist', *Journal of Economic Perspectives*, 19(3): 131–46.

Cheng, C. (1972) 'On yi as a universal principle of specific application in Confucian morality', *Philosophy East and West*, 22: 269–80.

Chen, L. (2010) 'Virtue ethics and Confucian ethics', *Dao*, 9: 275–87.

Firth, A. (2007) 'Adam Smith's moral philosophy as ethical self-formation', in G. Cockfield, A. Firth and J. Laurent (eds) *New Perspectives on Adam Smith's The Theory of Moral Sentiments*, Cheltenham: Edward Elgar, pp. 106–24.

Frantz, R. (2000) 'Intuitive elements in Adam Smith', *Journal of Socio-Economics*, 29: 1–19.

Haig, D. (2011) 'Sympathy with Adam Smith and reflexions on self', *Journal of Economic Behavior & Organization*, 77(1): 4–13.

Harrison, V. (2013) *Eastern Philosophy: The Basics*, Abingdon: Routledge.

Herrmann-Pillath, C. (2008) 'Adam Smith and Confucius: a tour d'horizon towards transcultural foundations of institutions', background paper from Creative Destruction 2008. *Cultural Science*. Available online at: http://cultural-science.org/FeastPapers2008/Carsten1Bp.pdf (last accessed 15 July 2014).

Liu, Y. (2010) 'Emotions (Qing) as ontology in Confucian political philosophy', *Proceedings of the Conference on Chinese Philosophy*, Beijing: Renmin Daxue, pp. 65–76.

Kim, S. (2009) 'Self-transformation and civil society: Lockean vs. Confucian', *Dao*, 8: 383–401.

Nuyen, A.T. (2009) 'Moral obligation and moral motivation in Confucian role-based ethics', *Dao*, 8: 1–11.

Raphael, D.D. (2007) *The Impartial Spectator: Adam Smith's Moral Philosophy*, Oxford: Clarendon Press.

Recktenwald, H. (1986) *Über Adam Smiths The Theory of Moral Sentiments*, Darmstadt-Düsseldorf: Verlag Wirtschaft und Finanzen.

Smith, A. (1789) *The Theory of Moral Sentiments* [6th ed., submitted 1789, printed 1790], edited by D.D. Raphael and A.L. Macfie (1976) Oxford: Clarendon Press.

Schliesser, E. (2006) 'Articulating practices as reasons. Adam Smith on the social conditions of possibility of property', *Adam Smith Review*, 2: 69–97

Zak, P.J. (2011) 'The physiology of moral sentiments', *Journal of Economic Behavior & Organization*, 77(1): 53–65.

Zhang, W. (2000) *On Adam Smith and Confucius: The Theory of Moral Sentiments and The Analects*, Huntington: Nova Science Publishers.

Symposium

Adam Smith in Kirkcaldy

Introduction

The Right Honourable Gordon Brown

The town I come from, Kirkcaldy, is also the home of Adam Smith. While he is thought by many to be the prophet of modern capitalism, he is, in fact, the moral philosopher who wrote of our obligations to others.

Visit the town and its one-and-a-half mile long promenade and you will understand how the sea that dominates the town shaped his view of the world. You cannot understand Adam Smith without understanding the community in which he was born, grew up and to which he returned to write his two great books, *The Wealth of Nations* and *The Theory of Moral Sentiments*.

In Smith's time, Kirkcaldy was a major port, which specialised in trade between the United Kingdom and the European continent. From his home overlooking the sea, Adam Smith, born the son of the local customs officer, would look out and every day witness some of the 100 or so merchant ships that came in and out of the harbour.

Kirkcaldy flourished by exporting its goods and importing others. This is how Smith came to understand that trade was the engine of growth and that the economy prospered through the specialisation of labour.

But Adam Smith grew up in what was also a strong, cohesive community. The church in which he was baptised and the school he attended were but only a few yards from where he lived. And the Adam Smith of the invisible hand was also the Adam Smith of the helping hand and, indeed, for Smith, his thoughts on moral sentiments were even more important than his theories on the wealth of nations.

He wrote of our capacity to put ourselves in other peoples' shoes, and thus to consider their interests and needs, and he wrote of the 'circle of sympathy' starting with family, friends and compatriots, a sense of obligation that diminished, he said, with distance. Understandably, we felt less obligation to strangers. But this view was conditional upon three forces of importance then that are of less importance now: our limited knowledge of strangers, our restricted ability to make contact and communicate with them and our smaller sense of mutual obligation. If Adam Smith were writing now, he would be showing how distance had ceased to be a barrier to knowledge, how contact and communication with strangers was possible and how we had developed a stronger sense of mutual obligation based on our interdependence.[1] He might even be writing of us being able to feel, however distantly, the pain of others and of us being capable of believing in something bigger than just ourselves and those nearest to us.

I am delighted that the colloquium 'Smith in Kirkcaldy' was convened in June 2012 to help launch the new Adam Smith Global Foundation. Our great thanks go to Fonna Forman for organising the event, to Liberty Fund and the International Adam Smith Society for their support, and to *The Adam Smith Review* for welcoming these papers here.

Note

1   See Fonna Forman, *Adam Smith and the Circles of Sympathy* (Cambridge: Cambridge University Press, 2010).

Adam Smith from Kirkcaldy, via Glasgow University to Panmure House, Edinburgh[1]

Gavin Kennedy

The five biographies of Adam Smith 1793–2010

First, I shall outline certain essentials relating to the life of Adam Smith in Kirk-caldy (22 years), Glasgow (15 years) and Edinburgh (15 years), his main places of residence. Although he spent most of his life in Scotland, he also spent some years and months visiting Paris, Toulouse, Bordeaux, Geneva and London.

There are five serious biographies of Adam Smith, of which Professor Dugald Stewart wrote the first. He knew Smith personally, as a family friend through his father, Professor Michael Stewart, who was a student at Glasgow with Adam Smith. After Smith died in 1790, Dugald Stewart read the eulogy to the Royal Society of Edinburgh in 1793. It was published in 1795 by Smith's literary executors, Joseph Black and James Hutton, and was reproduced in many nine-teenth-century editions of Smith's *Theory of Moral Sentiments* and *The Wealth of Nations*; it remains in print today.[2]

John Rae wrote the second biography, *Life of Adam Smith* (1895).[3] Rae bene-fited from the scant surviving correspondence to and from Adam Smith. He also accessed Adam Smith's papers archived at Glasgow University. His was the standard full biography of Smith until 1995, although various derivative, small volumes appeared in the nineteenth century that contained nothing new.[4]

William Robert Scott contributed new materials in his 'Adam Smith as Student and Professor' (1937),[5] as a result of mining Glasgow University archives from when Smith attended, first as a student (1737–40) and later after his appointment as Professor of Logic (1751) and then Professor of Moral Sentiments (1752–64). Scott's extracts serve scholars unable to visit Glasgow. Interestingly, Smith's credible administrative role as a reliable confidant of the Principal while at Glasgow reveals a competence and attention to detail that belies anecdotes about his supposed 'other worldly' and disorderly manner, mainly sourced from Alexander Carlyle[6] and still widely circulating throughout the twentieth century.

Ian Simpson Ross wrote *The Life of Adam Smith* (1995; 2nd ed. 2010),[7] which, in my view, is the definitive biography. Ross combines a masterly and detailed account of Smith's whole life and of his works. He also provides interesting details of Smith's relationships with his mother, Margaret Douglas Smith, his lifelong friends and his scholarly accomplishments. Ross makes excellent use of source materials, those known to previous biographers, and also much that is relatively new, to give us a complete portrait of those who influenced him and whom he influenced in the eighteenth-century context in which he lived, including his surviving correspondence, also co-edited by Ian Ross.[8]

Ross also discusses Smith's lesser-known publications, such as his *History of Astronomy* (1744–c.58), *Origins of Language* (1761), *Lectures on Rhetoric* (1762–3), his *Lectures on Jurisprudence* (1762–63 and '1766') and several other fragments.[9] These materials played a larger role in his thinking than is sometimes realised today.

No survey would be complete without mentioning Nicholas Phillipson's intellectual biography: *Adam Smith: An Enlightened Life* (2010).[10] It is a formidable tour de force of Adam Smith's ideas, especially on his still neglected work as a moral philosopher. The real problem of the so-called 'Adam Smith Problem' is that many critics of his political economy have not read his *Theory of Moral Sentiments*. Phillipson's intellectual biography of Smith is an excellent remedy for that deficiency.

Together, these scholarly biographies give distinctive accounts of Adam Smith's contributions to the Scottish Enlightenment in the last decades of the eighteenth century. Collectively, their authors trawled with fine-mesh nets through the extant sources. Smith's published and unpublished books, essays and correspondence are widely available as a complete set in the *Glasgow Edition of the Works and Corres-pondence of Adam Smith* from Oxford University Press. Liberty Fund's exact copies of the *Glasgow Edition of Smith's Works* bring Smith's entire corpus within the budgets of most libraries, scholars and general readers.

Adam Smith in Kirkcaldy

Adam Smith was baptised on 5 June 1723, possibly soon after he was born.[11] His father had died six months earlier, in January 1723. He was brought up an 'infirm and sickly boy' by his widowed mother, Margaret Douglas Smith, who, by contem-porary accounts (Dugald Stewart) 'indulged him', creating a loving bond between them that he cherished throughout his life. She died in 1784 at Panmure House, aged 90, leaving Smith emotionally distraught. He replied to enquiries of when his publisher could expect corrected proofs from Smith for the fourth edition of *The Wealth of Nations* explaining that he was delayed by the death of his mother, whose funeral he had recently attended.[12] He said of his relationship with her, '[she] loved me more than any other person ever did or ever will love me, and whom I certainly loved and respected more than I shall either love and respect any other person'.[13]

Margaret Douglas Smith was very religious and her piety impressed Adam (and all those who knew her) so greatly that despite his scepticism of 'revealed religion', since he attended Oxford University, he ensured that nothing he said or did in public would embarrass her from his making public his loss of faith in 'revealed religion'.[14]

Smith's mother's house in Kirkcaldy High Street was demolished in 1834. However, her walled garden remains intact, fronting on to the Firth of Forth. The organisers of the Colloquium[15] plan to restore the walled garden and a small building beside it for visitors seeking information about Kirkcaldy's most famous son.

At the Colloquium, we had the opportunity to visit the site of Margaret Douglas Smith's house (now 220 High Street) and its walled garden, to which Adam Smith, as a distinguished retired professor, returned in 1767 after his visit to France in 1764–66. While teaching as a professor, he had already begun making notes and short drafts of what become his *Wealth of Nations* (the originals are in Glasgow University's archives).[16] Other sections of the *Wealth of Nations* include verbatim extracts from his *Lectures on Jurisprudence* (note 7), showing that he had lectured on his ideas on political economy at Glasgow University in 1762–63, and probably for several years before, even perhaps when he delivered his Edinburgh Lectures in 1748–51.[17]

The relatively close proximity of the three important places for him in his childhood in Kirkcaldy's is evident from short walking tours when led by local expert guides, well briefed on Smith's life at Kirkcaldy. The offices of the newly formed Adam Smith Global Foundation, located in the restored building beside his mother's garden is developing an 'Adam Smith trail' passing relevant sites demonstrating Smith's deep relationship with Kirkcaldy. The Colloquium took place in the 'Old Kirk' that Smith attended with his mother as a child and man. The Old Kirk's square bell tower, with its magnificent views of Kirkcaldy's environs, is all that remains of the Old Kirk today. The rest of the building burned down. Its large, restored central hall is now a viable conference venue and the Old Kirk's original graveyard remains as it was in Smith's day and is well maintained. The eighteenth-century minister regularly visited the Smith household in the course of his duties to teach young boys of Adam age the Calvinist catechism, prior to their acceptance into the (moderate) Calvinism of the local Kirkcaldy Kirk. From Smith's studious and retentive memory, noticed early in his youth and throughout his life, we can be sure that he had no problems in reciting it.

From the Old Kirk, visitors can take a short 100-yard walk downhill to the site of the two-room Kirkcaldy grammar school attended by Smith from 1731 to 1737, then under the attentive care of David Millar, a teacher of 'sufficient reputation' from nearby Cupar.[18] However, all that is left today of the old school is a small, tarred-over car park.

Proceeding 200 yards further down the hill, we join Kirkcaldy High Street where, almost diagonally opposite, is the building on the former site of his mother's house (adorned with a small plaque). Smith spent his youthful years in Kirkcaldy within the compact nearness of his home, his school and his Kirk. He also visited his maternal grandparents and other relatives in their farms at nearby Strathendry, a few miles outside Kirkcaldy.

His mother's walled garden, fronted directly on to the foreshore of the Firth of Forth (owing to land reclamation, the shore now extends about 100 yards further into the sea). Because of the geography of the bay at Kirkcaldy, its prospect is not directly towards the City of Edinburgh; instead, it looks outwards directly to the open North Sea. His father, who died in January 1723 (before Smith was born in June), was the local Kirkcaldy Customs official. He was probably still remembered during Smith's youth, which may have encouraged the young Adam to visit its busy port, yards from his mother's house, and to mix among the ship's crews, porters and merchants by the harbour, giving him an indelible insight into the excitements of trade between Scotland and the Baltic, and elsewhere, which remained with him when considering the mutual benefits of international trade.

At Kirkcaldy grammar school, Smith proved to be proficient, particularly in Latin, such that he joined the third level, not the beginners' Latin class, at Glasgow University in 1737. At the time, professors delivered their lectures in Latin, although the 'never to be forgotten'[19] Professor Francis Hutcheson delivered his moral philosophy lectures in English, as did Smith when he took them over in 1752. Nevertheless, competence in Latin was regarded as an essential mark of university education in Scotland and for many decades through to the twentieth century.

Oxford

Smith left Glasgow in 1740 without graduating but with a coveted Snell Exhibition to Balliol College, Oxford University. He was never happy there, spending six years away from his family in Kirkcaldy. The annual vacations were insufficient time for him to ride eight days each way to visit Kirkcaldy and return to Oxford.[20] This is confirmed in Balliol College's 'Battel' accounts, which he personally signed for his daily sustenance, showing that, except for under two weeks of each year, he was in residence at the College during each year from August 1740 to 1746.

We know that he visited the Duke of Argyll's residence in nearby Adderbury and also perhaps London with his cousin, William Smith, who was in service with the Duke.[21] Absent from the influence of his mother and his church, he seems to have drifted gradually away from his intention to graduate and be ordained into the Church of England and return to Scotland to serve as a minister in the Episcopalian Church of Scotland. He switched courses in 1744 from ordination to jurisprudence and, when he left Oxford in 1746, he never returned. Thirty years later, Smith remained deeply critical of Balliol's academic life ('prayers twice a day and lectures twice a week') compared with Glasgow's more challenging intellectual demands of daily lectures, tutorials and essays from 7.30 a.m., six days a week. He added that, at Oxford, the faculty 'have given up even the pretence of teaching'.[22]

Smith returns to Scotland

On his return to Kirkcaldy, Smith set about finding a career. Two influential family friends, Henry Home (the future Lord Kames, a Scottish judge and moral philosopher) and James Oswald, a Member of Parliament, proposed that Smith should deliver a series of public lectures (not at the university) on rhetoric in Edinburgh, for course fees. The plan worked and Smith earned up to £100 a year from 1748 to 1751 from these subscriptions, a considerable sum indeed for a young man not yet a professor at a university. Smith added some lectures on jurisprudence, including political economy. More important, his public reputation from demonstrating his academic abilities as a teacher helped him to succeed in 1751 in his application for the post of Professor of Logic at Glasgow University and, in 1752, as Professor of Moral Philosophy, where he taught from 1751 to 1764.

As a professor, he took his mother with him to live in Professor's Close in the university, and his cousin, Janet Douglas, to be his mother's housekeeper – a role she performed over the next 36 years until she died at Panmure House in 1788. His income of £300 a year meant that his family enjoyed relative affluence as his reputation grew at Glasgow and elsewhere. His 16 years at Glasgow as student and professor, well documented by W. R. Scott, as discussed above, provides much material to make Glasgow University a potentially attractive part of a possible future 'Three-City Adam Smith Scottish Heritage Trail', joining the three main centres of his life in Kirkcaldy, Glasgow and Edinburgh.

Smith's Glasgow teaching experiences ended in 1764 when he was persuaded to take the young Henry Scott (the new Duke of Buccleuch), who had recently left Eton, to France for two years. It was in France that Smith confirmed his tentative decision to write what became *The Wealth of Nations*. When Adam Smith returned in 1766 from the French tour with the young Duke of Buccleuch, he stayed in London until 1767 before returning to his mother's home in Kirkcaldy. Altogether, it took over 12 years from his tentative efforts in France to research, compose and write his classic work,[23] the bulk of which he composed in its final form in his mother's house in Kirkcaldy.[24] Her rear garden was large enough for him to pace in solitude and deep thought, somewhat oblivious of others (some saw this habit as his 'absent mindedness'),[25] but in the long solitudes of his mother's garden he was able to turn his mind solely to the mammoth task of compiling the source materials and refining his arguments for his world-famous classic.

Smith took his manuscript to London in 1773[26] to see it through the press. We know that Smith 'was very zealous in American affairs' in London from 1773 to 1776.[27] The political events in North America intruded and delayed publication of *The Wealth of Nations* until March 1776 and also his return to Kirkcaldy in June 1776.

This left him with the dilemma of what do next? He did not have any immediate fixed ideas, although he had plenty to do to fulfil his already advertised intentions since 1759, in the *Theory of Moral Sentiments*, of completing a book on the 'science of jurisprudence'. The events in the British colonies in North America may have caused Smith to hesitate from fulfilling his 1759 promise. In 1762, he had lectured to his students that 'Jurisprudence is the theory of the rules by which civil governments ought to be directed', indicating that a theory of jurisprudence had to cover a very long swathe of history, including possibly the American events.[28] At the very least, he would have to respond to questions about them.

If British colonists had succeeded in rejecting a constitutional monarchy, he would have to cover these events, knowing that he had to beware of possible problems arising for him from his writing. Subsequent events after the 1783 Declaration of Independence would have exacerbated his dilemma because he could not write on the 'science of jurisprudence' without confronting such a problem head-on. But, by saying nothing at all and by postponing the completion of his proposed book on jurisprudence, and by destroying the unfinished manuscript, such postponement resolved his problem, however unsatisfactory it remains for posterity. He gave strict orders to his executors from his deathbed in 1790 that most of his papers, which included his draft 'Jurisprudence' manuscript, were to be burned 'unread' and 'without any examination'.[29]

The new constitution may have fitted well with Smith's teachings on jurisprudence and the wealth of nations, such as the separation of powers, the separation of church and state, habeas corpus, trial by jury and judges appointed for life and good behaviour.[30] However, whatever appeal the US constitution might have had for Smith, he could not openly condone a rebellion against King George. Smith was a Hanoverian in matters of rebellions against the king in 1715 and 1745. Thus, Smith's major problem in post-1776 Britain was to avoid offending the legitimacy of the British sovereign. However he wrote 'Jurisprudence', he had to address the American rebellion and the ideas behind the rejection of George III by the former colonists.

Smith, in late 1776, still had to find something else to do and also to move from Kirkcaldy to Edinburgh, where the intellectual life was most appealing to him. In the event, in 1777, that opportunity presented itself in the form of a vacancy at the Scottish Customs Board. Smith decided to apply for the post to Sir Grey Cooper, Secretary to the Treasury. His long-time friend, the Duke of Buccleuch, aided independently by his mother, the Duchess, became active in pursuing his support for Smith's appointment. By coincidence, Smith had written to Sir Grey Cooper in support of an individual for a vacant post of a collectorship at Grenville harbour, and which Sir Grey said showed marked enthusiasm for that candidate in contrast to the 'phlegm, composure and indifference' of his own application for the post of Scottish Custom's Commissioner. Grey told Smith, at the time acting as consultant on tax affairs for Lord North (premier), that he did not need 'yours or any other great man's recommendation' and he 'will, if I am not much mistaken soon be appointed a Commissioner of the Customs in Scotland'.[31] Now the demands of being a full-time Commissioner fortuitously precluded his finishing a major work on jurisprudence. I suggest that this event became his perfect excuse for silence (John Rae [1895] almost hints as much).[32]

On his appointment, Smith moved his family from Kirkcaldy to Edinburgh in February 1788, where he leased Panmure House, in the Canongate. He moved for several family reasons. On the personal side, his mother, now in her eighties, was frail and he probably wanted to spend time with her, as she had in spending much of her youth looking after him, both when he was a sickly child and as a young professor. Moving to Edinburgh meant that his mother and his cousin, Janet Douglas, would be very comfortable with him at Panmure House. Also, his new appointment fortuitously required residence in Edinburgh. He could easily afford the move, following his sharply increased affluence (£600 a year from his Custom's salary and the £300 life-pension from the Duke of Buccleuch). It also brought Smith into satisfying proximity with many of the other leading figures in what we know now as the Scottish Enlightenment.

Smith's appointment as a Commissioner of Scottish Customs was no sinecure.

His appointment, however attracted light mockery from his friend, Edmund Gibbon (*Decline and Fall of Rome*), who wrote about a 'strange' and 'so very extraordinary report' he had heard that 'my particular friend' (Adam Smith) was taking a post as a 'Customs Commissioner in Scotland'.[33]

For Smith, his appointment was consistent. He made his thinking about tariffs clear in *The Wealth of Nations*, if not to all modern historians. He said that the idea of total free trade was 'absurd' because some tariff incomes were necessary to maintain government expenditure for its proper purpose (defence, justice, and public works), without which the prosperity of an economy would be threatened. Existing taxation was not sufficient to cover government expenditure in the war-torn eighteenth century and 'income tax' had not yet been invented. Smith also asserted that it was 'utopian' to believe that absolute free trade could ever be implemented 'in England' without some tariffs (*WN* IV.ii.43: 480). He objected to the tariffs inspired by 'merchants and manufacturers' seeking monopolies to protect themselves from foreign competition and force consumers to pay higher prices. Punitive tariffs against neighbouring countries from 'jealousy of trade' led to the expense of unnecessary wars.

Smith's assiduousness in exercising his Customs House duties is revealing. Minutes show that he attended four days a week from January 1778 to 1790, chairing meetings and administrative work, except when on official duty in London at the request of government ministers for advice, combined, on occasion, with visits to his publisher to guide new editions through the press. His regular attendance at the Customs House resulted in his signature on over eighty per cent of the official letters and minutes during his tenure. He chaired a Commissioner's meeting for the last time on 8 April 1790, just weeks before he died on 17 July.

Revival of interest in Adam Smith

There has been a notable flurry of promising activities in recent years regarding scholarly attention to the historical background of Adam Smith's life and works.

The preparation and publishing of a *Glasgow Edition* of all of Adam Smith's works for the bi-century, starting with *The Wealth of Nations* and *Theory of Moral Sentiments* in 1976 by Oxford University Press, by a team of Smithian scholars, mostly from Glasgow University, boosted interest in the man and what he stood for. The academy around the world responded with scores of books, journal articles and academic conferences, all of which continue in the twenty-first century.

The International Adam Smith Society was formed in 2004 and attracted a large number of scholars interested in Adam Smith. It publishes the annual *Adam Smith Review*. Its current President, Professor Ryan Hanley, and Editor, Professor Fonna Forman, and various contributors and reviewers were also present at the Kirkcaldy Colloquium in 2013.

In Edinburgh, the erection of a specially commissioned bronze statue of Adam Smith, cast by Alexander Stoddard, a Scottish sculptor (from private subscriptions arranged by the Adam Smith Institute in London) in July 2008, drew on worldwide support from the revival of interest in Adam Smith. It stands, 19-feet tall, beside

St Giles Cathedral, opposite the Edinburgh City Chambers that were once the offices of the Customs and the Salt Duty Commissioners where Adam Smith worked from 1778 to 1790. Professor Vernon Smith, who also attending the 2013 Colloquium, unveiled the statue and a short informal meeting was attended by forty scholars in one of the public rooms in Panmure House (recently aquired by Edinburgh Business School, Heriot-Watt University) and there was a public debate later in Edinburgh's Old Town, which Smith frequented with other leaders of the Scottish Enlightenment.

The Principal of Glasgow University, Professor Anton Muscatelli, a distinguished Scottish economist, has taken steps to celebrate Glasgow University's intimate connections with Adam Smith by rebranding several faculty posts and in renaming its management programmes as the Adam Smith Business School. The University also made accessible its excellent archival collections relating to Smith when he attended, both as a student and later as a professor. The archives relating to Adam Smith are important. He wrote his *Theory of Moral Sentiments* (1759) in Glasgow and the context of his teaching and tutorial courses were significant to his approach.

Adam Smith at Panmure House

Professor Anton Muscatelli, formerly the Principal of Heriot-Watt University, 2007–09, the home of Edinburgh Business School, which was founded in 1997 and led by Professor Keith Lumsden (an economist). Edinburgh Business School acquired Panmure House in 2008 from its own funds, with the necessary political support of Professor Muscatelli in the university, and embarked on an ambitious fundraising programme to undertake the daunting task of renovating and restoring the disused, near-derelict building.

Panmure House is important not just because Adam Smith lived there for twelve years. It is more than a tourist attraction. Similarly, after Glasgow and his tour of France, he wrote the bulk of *The Wealth of Nations* in Kirkcaldy, including thinking through his ideas in his mother's garden, which survives today.

At Panmure House, from 1778 to 1790, Adam Smith hosted regular Sunday suppers, to which leading figures in the Scottish Enlightenment were invited to join him at his table. Also, although his weekdays were taken up by his administrative duties at the Customs House, a short walk uphill from Panmure House along the Royal Mile, he found time to socialise at weekends with his fellow contributors to the ongoing ferment of ideas across their fields of expertise in natural science, moral philosophy, political economy and the literary arts. Visitors to Edinburgh from the Continent and London were invited to join his friends, most of who lived nearby. They discussed topics of mutual interest to philosophers. These were 'conversations among friends', perfectly safe from mockery or troublesome censure. They partook of a typically frugal meal (though Smith had a passion for strawberries for breakfast and for sugarlumps at any time) or they enjoyed a drink or two at a local tavern, often in meetings of the Oyster Club (known among them as 'Adam Smith's Club'). Visitors were welcome, provided they did not try to dominate the exchanges, like a Mr Bogle who Smith said 'talked so much' he 'spoiled the evening'.[34]

Smith valued these meetings and the discussions where everybody spoke freely. Exercising care in private freedom of speech was taken more seriously in the eighteenth century than some scholars appreciate today. There was the ever-present threat from zealots in the Church of Scotland, who made life uncomfortable for those they judged to be without due piety towards their strict interpretations of the scriptures. In a significant passage written in 1759, Smith described an admonition that he operated throughout his adult life: 'a certain reserve is necessary when we talk of our own friends, our own studies, our own professions…a philosopher is company to a philosopher only; the members of a club, to his own little knot of companions' (*TMS* I.ii.2.6: 33–4).

At his table in Panmure House and in meetings of the Oyster Club, Smith relaxed with his fellow philosophers and they with him. Dugald Stewart's eyewitness report of Smith with his philosopher friends reveals the real Smith, much at variance with the misleading anecdotal tales of such as Alexander Carlyle of Inveresk.[35] Stewart said of Smith that 'in the society of those he loved, his features were often brightened with a smile of inexpressible benignity' (Stewart V.12–27). A short list of Smith's regular dinner and social companions (beer and wine were safer in those day than tap water) indicate the importance that the conversations with his companions at Panmure House and the Oyster Club were for the Scottish Enlightenment.

Among his regular visitors meeting weekly 'in a most enlightened and agreeable, cheerful and social company' were:[36] William Robertson, historian, Principal of Edinburgh University, moderate-leaning Calvinist and Moderator of the Church of Scotland; Professor Joseph Black, chemist, discoverer of latent heat and investor in agricultural manufacturing (one of Smith's executors); James Hutton, a groundbreaking founder of scientific geology, especially on the age of the Earth ('No vestiges of a beginning, no prospect of an end'); Hugh Blair, local minister, became Professor of Rhetoric at Edinburgh University (he used Smith's Edinburgh lecture notes); Adam Ferguson, who wrote the *History of Civil Society*, Professor at Edinburgh University and credited as a pioneer of early sociology; William Cullen, Professor of Medicine at Edinburgh University, founder of medical degrees for practitioners (Smith's physician); Dr. Swediaur, a Paris physician, in Edinburgh in 1784 as a medical researcher with Cullen; John Home, dramatist and author hounded out of his ministry by Presbyterian zealots violently opposed to plays and actors; George Clerk Maxwell, agricultural improver and fellow Customs Commissioner; Henry Mackenzie, lawyer and novelist; John Playfair, Professor of Mathematics at Edinburgh University; Dugald Stewart, who held chairs in mathematics and moral philosophy at Edinburgh University and was a close family friend; Walter Smellie, antiquarian printer and naturalist; James Edgar, classicist and poker club member; Robert Adam, leading UK classical style architect; John Clerk of Eldin, inventor of a new system of naval tactics; Lord Daer – the 'noble youthful Daer' – who was the first lord that Robert Burns ever met, and who taught the poet that, in a lord, he had after all but 'met a brither', with nothing uncommon about him. Visitors from outside Scotland included Edmund Burke, parliamentarian; and Samuel Rogers, a leading English poet.

These were representative of what we call, the 'Scottish Enlightenment'. Of course, other leading lights, like David Hume, possibly Europe's leading eighteenth-century philosopher and Smith's close friend and collaborator, had passed on before Smith came to reside at Panmure House. But, for much of the time that he spent there, the men who made up the Enlightenment mixed, socialised, exchanged ideas and cross-fertilised those ideas in a productive and the encouraging, because unthreatening, company of each other.

Adam Smith died at Panmure House on 12 July 1790. He is buried in the graveyard of the Canongate Parish Church, a few yards from Panmure House.

Postscript

The latest report (2013) of the plans for the post-renovated Panmure House (built in 1697) include its role as a major international academic centre of excellence in moral philosophy and political economy in the twenty-first century (as well as other applications of Adam Smith's interests in history, rhetoric, humanities, origins of language, jurisprudence, the arts, the spread of opulence, problems of current societies and the roles of government). There will also be an international commitment to economics and philosophy for pre- and post-university education.

The Edinburgh city authorities and Scottish Heritage finally approved the plans, with a nine-month plan of work starting in July 2014.[37] An international appeal for funding commenced with ambitious targets for the renovation and for an Endowment Fund with the establishment of 'Friends of Panmure House' as a charity in the USA and the UK.

Notes

1   Delivered at the Colloquium, Kirkcaldy, 7–8 August 2012.
2   Stewart, D. [1793]. 'Account of the Life and Writings of Adam Smith, LLD'. *Transactions of the Royal Society of Edinburgh*, 1793, in Smith, A. 1980. *Essays on Philosophical Subjects*. Oxford: Oxford University Press.
3   Rae, J. 1895. *The Life of Adam Smith*. London: Macmillan & Co. Reprinted 1965 and 1977. 'Introduction and Guide to John Rae's Life of Adam Smith' by Jacob Viner.
4   See, e.g. R. R. Haldane, M.P. 1887. *Life of Adam Smith*, London: Walter Scott.
5   Scott, W. R. 1937. *Adam Smith as Student and Professor, with Unpublished Documents, Including Parts of the 'Edinburgh Lectures', A Draft of The Wealth of Nations, Extracts from the Muniments of the University of Glasgow and Correspondence.* Glasgow: Jackson, Son & Company, publishers to the University.
6   Carlyle, A. 1910. *The Autobiography of Dr. Alexander Carlyle of Inveresk*, (ed.) John H. Burton. London: T. N. Foulis.
7   Ross, I. S. 2010. *The Life of Adam Smith*, 2nd ed. Oxford: Oxford University Press. Originally published 1995.
8   Smith, A. 1977, 1987. *The Correspondence of Adam Smith*, Ernest. Campbell Mossner and Ian Simpson Ross, (eds). Oxford: Oxford University Press.

9   See, e.g. Haldane, *Life of Adam Smith.*
10 Scott, 'Adam Smith as Student and Professor'.
11 Carlyle, *The Autobiography of Dr. Alexander Carlyle of Inveresk.*
12 Ross, *The Life of Adam Smith.*
13 Smith, *The Correspondence of Adam Smith.*
14 A recent fad for insisting on changing the dates in Smith's life and his materials prior to 1752, when Britain switched to the Gregorian calendar, by omitting 11 days, adds avoidable confusion to no great purpose when citing the existing archives all in the old dates. Pedants who write pointless letters that Adam Smith was born/baptised on '16th' not the '5th of June' 1723, as recorded on his Baptism certificate and on correspondence in the old calendar, demonstrate the empty art of pedantically insisting on distinctions without a difference, except where they add confusion.
15 I found no trace of her burial at the Canongate Church records (National Records of Scotland). Perhaps she was buried in her family's graves at Strathendry in Fife, which question local Kirkcaldy historians may wish to follow up.
16 Smith to William Strahan, 10 June 1784, Correspondence, no. 137, p. 275.
17 Kennedy, G. 2011. 'Adam Smith on Religion', *Journal of the History of Economic Thought*, vol. 33. (3). I am also inclined to the view, hinted at by Dugald Stewart (1980, pp. 349–50) that Smith not marrying may have been occasioned by his mother's reaction to his taking a wife who would intrude on her domestic intimacies with her only son. Stewart met the lady in the early 1800s. (Stewart's biography, 'Note K, p. 326'; see note 2.)
18 Ross, *The Life of Adam Smith*, 18.
19 Smith, *The Correspondence of Adam Smith*, p. 309. Letter no. 274 to Dr Archibald Davidson, Principal, Glasgow University, 16 November 1787.
20 Ross, *The Life of Adam Smith*, p. 57.
21 Smith, *The Correspondence of Adam Smith*, p. 2. Letter no. 3 to Mrs Smith 23 October, 1741.
22 Smith, A. *The Wealth of Nations.* V.i.f.8: p 761.
23 Smith, A. *The Correspondence of Adam Smith*, Letter no. 82 to David Hume, pp. 101–2. From Toulouse, 5 July, 1764: 'I have begun to write a book in order to pass away the time.'
24 Some materials are included verbatim in *The Wealth of Nations* and came directly from him; e.g. Smith, A. 1762–63. *Lectures on Jurisprudence: Report of 1762–3, Glasgow University Library*, [LJ(A)] VI. 28–49. pp. 338–49.
25 See Ross, *The Life of Adam Smith*, pp. 444–5.
26 Smith, *The Correspondence of Adam Smith*, pp. 168. Letter no. 137 to David Hume, 16 April 1773.
27 Smith, *The Correspondence of Adam Smith*, pp.188–9. Letter no. 149 from David Hume, 8 February 1776.
28 Smith, A. LJ(A), 1762. IX. 1:7. Dec. 24, 1762.
29 Ross, *The Life of Adam Smith*, p. 435. Please note that Ian Ross is not implicated in my interpretations of Smith's motives or behaviours in the above matter.
30 See Kennedy, G. 2010. *Adam Smith: A Moral Philosopher and his Political Economy.* London: Palgrave-Macmillan, pp. 49–51.
31 Smith, A. Correspondence, pp. 227–8. Letter. No. 186, from Sir Grey Cooper, 7 November, 1777.
32 Rae, *The Life of Adam Smith*, ch. XXI.
33 Smith, *The Correspondence of Adam Smith*, p. 228. Letter no. 187 from Edward Gibbon, 26 November 1777.

34   Quoted by Samuel Rogers (another visitor), July 1789. In Clayden, P. W. 1887. *The Early Life of Samuel Rogers*. London: Smith, Elder, p. 92.
35   Smith's careful circumspection probably explains the silent way he behaved in the company of those he did not trust (such as Alexander Carlyle of Inveresk, who did not appreciate Smith's circumspection at all). Carlyle's unflattering anecdotes still circulate today, giving a misleading picture of Adam Smith.
36   Rae, *The Life of Adam Smith*.
37   Brian Healy, 'Conservation of Panmure House gets Underway' Panmure House, Edinburgh Business School, Heriot-Watt University [blog post]. Available online at: www.panmurehouse.org/Panmure-Blog/July-2014/Conservation-of-Panmure-House-gets-underway.aspx (last accessed 30 July 2014).

Adam Smith, James Wilson and the US Constitution[1]

Iain McLean

Introduction

Two men born in Fife, Scotland, helped to shape the US Constitution and Bill of Rights. James Wilson (born Ceres, near Cupar, Scotland, in 1742; died Edenton, North Carolina, USA, in 1798) signed the Declaration of Independence, led the Federalist side in the 1787 Convention in Philadelphia, signed the US Constitution, became an associate justice of the US Supreme Court, wrote one of the first US law texts, and died soon after being imprisoned for debts due to another signer of the Constitution. His Scottish origins, and what they imply for the texts and original public meanings of the Constitution, have only recently started to be explored. Adam Smith's influence on the US Constitution is again a recent subject of study. Not only were they both Fifers but Wilson certainly knew Smith's work. He was probably in Glasgow, borrowing University library books, in 1763–64 and may have attended Smith's class under him or Thomas Young, who taught from Smith's notes after Smith left for France in 1764.

Preliminary: Scottish versus English constitutionalism

Until the 1970s, it was customary to write Scotland out of Anglophone constitutional history not written by Scots. Conventionally, the British Constitution (miscalled the English Constitution by the most influential English writers, such as Bagehot 1865/2001 and Dicey 1915) was given its present shape by the (perhaps Glorious) revolutions of the period between 1628 and 1689. In that time of conflict between kings and parliaments, the final victory of the latter introduced a regime of parliamentary sovereignty. What used to be called the 'Whig interpretation of history' (Butterfield 1931) held that English (glossed as British) constitutional history was a gradual upward progress from despotism to liberty, represented in its finest flowering by the constitution celebrated by Bagehot and Dicey. It is important for what follows that the most intellectual of the American Founding Fathers, Thomas Jefferson and James Madison, were steeped in the Whig history tradition. Of course, their story had a different ending but, for Jefferson, the autocratic rule of the British executive, caricatured in his draft Declaration of Independence (cf Wills 1979) as personal rule by George III, was a temporary obstruction in the road to Whiggish perfection. Such was marked in the USA not by parliamentary sovereignty but by the checks and balances, and hostility to overpowering governments, to be found in the US Constitution and Bill of Rights. The very name of the latter, and some of its contents, recall the English 'Glorious Revolution' of 1688–89, in which a convention parliament deposed James II and invited William and Mary to be parliamentary monarchs constrained by the Bill of Rights Act 1689. Consider, for instance, the following provisions of the US Constitution and Bill of Rights:

> The House of Representatives shall chuse their Speaker and other Officers; and shall have the sole Power of Impeachment.
>
> (US Const. I.2 para 5)

> The Senate shall have the sole power to try all Impeachments.
>
> (US Const. I.3. para. 6)

> All Bills for raising Revenue shall originate in the House of Representatives.
>
> (US Const. I.7)[2]

> The Privilege of the Writ of Habeas Corpus shall not be suspended, unless when in Cases of Rebellion or Invasion the public Safety may require it.
>
> (US Const. I.9)[3]

> Excessive bail shall not be required, nor excessive fines imposed, nor cruel and unusual punishments inflicted
>
> (US Const. Amendment VIII ratified 1791)[4]

These provisions of the US Constitution derive directly from the long struggle between English kings and their parliaments that began in 1628 and culminated in the parliamentary victory of the Glorious Revolution. The Eighth Amendment is an almost word-for-word copy of s.10 of the English Bill of Rights of 1689.

In the last-known letter he ever wrote, Jefferson declined an invitation from the Mayor of Washington DC to attend the city's fiftieth anniversary celebrations of the Declaration of Independence, to be held on July 4 1826.[5] In a letter obviously intended as his personal testament, Jefferson wrote:

> may it [the Declaration of Independence] be to the world, what I believe it will be, to some parts sooner, to others later, but finally to all,) the Signal of arousing men to burst the chains, under which monkish ignorance and superstition had persuaded them to bind themselves, and to assume the blessings & security of self-government. that form which we have substituted, restores the free right to the unbounded exercise of reason and freedom of opinion. all eyes are opened, or opening, to the rights of man. the general spread of the light of science has already laid open to every view. the palpable truth, that the mass of mankind has not been born with saddles on their backs, nor a favored few booted and spurred, ready to ride them legitimately, by the grace of God.[6]

Nothing could be more English Whiggish than that: or could it? But Douglass Adair (1974: 274–88; article originally published in 1952) showed that the imagery of 'saddles on their backs…booted and spurred' came straight from the dying speech of Richard Rumbold, a Whig republican executed in 1685 for treason. Even Adair, however, did not notice that Rumbold and his speech had already been cited in James Wilson's *Lectures on Law*, first published by his son in 1804 (Wilson 1804/2007: I, 477).

But Rumbold was a Scot, executed in Edinburgh. There were two successful British revolutions in 1688–90, not one. After the flight of James VII and II, who had governed England and Scotland separately, both countries summoned convention parliaments; that is, parliaments not summoned by a king, because there was no king to summon them. In Edinburgh, there was a large Jacobite faction but they bolted the parliament to follow the banners of Bonnie Dundee, in the words of Sir Walter Scott:

> To the Lords of Convention 'twas Clavers who spoke.
> 'Ere the King's crown shall fall there are crowns to be broke;
> So let each Cavalier who loves honour and me,
> Come follow the bonnet of Bonny Dundee.[7]

This left the Presbyterian faction in control. They issued an invitation to the same couple as the English Parliament, namely the Dutch Calvinist, William of Orange, and his English wife, Mary, to become King and Queen of Scotland. The Scottish terms were quite different to the English terms. In particular, they demanded that William and Mary recognise the established state of the Presbyterian Church of Scotland, which they did. Accordingly, the Scots confirmed the invitation and passed the Claim of Right Act 1689, which differs from the English Bill of Rights. Among its enumerated grievances against James VII were:

> By levying or Keeping on foot a standing army in tyme of Peace without Consent of Parliament which army did exact localitie free and dry quarters.[8]

And among the promises it had exacted from William and Mary were:

> That Prelacy and the superiority of any office in the Church above presbyters is and hath been a great and insupportable greivance and trouble to this Nation and contrary to the Inclinationes of the generality of the people ever since the reformatione (they haveing reformed from popery by presbyters) and therfor ought to be abolished.[9]

If the Eighth Amendment comes straight from the English Revolution, equally, the Third comes straight from the Scottish Revolution.[10] There were therefore two, not one, Anglophone sources for texts limiting the rights of governments over people, both of them available to the US framers at Philadelphia, and to members of the state and federal congresses who considered and amended the Philadelphia text.

Furthermore, those two constitutions created different regimes in what had become by 1787 a single semi-federal country. The Acts of Union of 1706–07 embodied the relevant provisions of both the English and the Scottish Acts of 1689 for their respective countries. The final Act, the English Act of Union 1706, uses the phrase 'the true Protestant religion' twice: in one section to define the established Church of England and in another to define the established Church of Scotland (McLean 2010: 6). One might have thought that there could be at most one true Protestant religion but the Acts of Union – still, at least until 2014, the fundamental constitutional text for the UK – embed this logical contradiction in constitutional law.

At this point a critic may well say, *This is all very fine, but it was never mentioned in Philadelphia and scarcely in Jefferson's or Madison's voluminous writings. So the fact that the Scottish constitutional settlement of 1689–1707 differed from the English constitutional settlement of the same period is of antiquarian interest only. You cannot show that it had any influence on the Americans.* The rest of this chapter endeavours to meet this challenge by reference to the lives and works of Wilson and Smith.

James Wilson of Cupar

Wilson was schooled in Cupar, at what is now Bell-Baxter High School and, at the early age then customary, went to St Andrews University in 1757 on a bursary. But, apparently for financial reasons, he left early[11] and details of what happened then were, until recently, sketchy. The *American National Biography* has no details of his life between St Andrews and Philadelphia. The (UK) *Dictionary of National Biography* says, 'It has been variously said, but without sustaining evidence, that Wilson was thereafter briefly a university student at Glasgow and Edinburgh' (Conrad 2004). He emigrated in 1765, to Philadelphia, where the College of Philadelphia, now the University of Pennsylvania, soon gave him an honorary degree 'in consideration of his merit and his having had a regular education in the universities of Scotland'. Soon after, he formally studied law under an English-trained lawyer and moved to western Pennsylvania to practise law. Like Thomas Jefferson in Virginia, he was drawn into politics on the issue of whether the UK Parliament had the right to make laws for the American colonies. He argued for a federal solution but nevertheless signed the Declaration of Independence. He opposed the populist Constitution of Pennsylvania and speculated heavily in western lands, before becoming a delegate to the Constitutional Convention in Philadelphia. There, together with Gouverneur Morris, also of Pennsylvania, and James Madison of Virginia, he became one of the three most active delegates on the Federalist side. They may fairly be regarded as the three true Founding Fathers; although their text was, of course, heavily influenced by the need to make concessions to multiple other interests so as to produce a document with a chance of ratification.

In 1790, Wilson led the successful campaign to amend the Constitution of Pennsylvania to incorporate more checks and balances and, in the same year, he was appointed a law lecturer at the (now) University of Pennsylvania. He was already an associate justice of the US Supreme Court, and petitioned President Washington unsuccessfully for the post of Chief Justice. However, his land speculation ended in wartime failure. While still a serving Associate Justice, he was jailed by his creditors at the instance of fellow-framer Pierce Butler, and died bankrupt in 1798. (Jefferson also died bankrupt but, unlike Wilson, had the fortune to die in his own home.)

Wilson's reputation, unlike Jefferson's and Madison's, also went bankrupt and the debt has only recently been cleared. Martin Clagett has recently uncovered the signatures of a James Wilson, strongly resembling the signature of 'our' Wilson, while he was known to have been at St Andrews, in two places: as assistant to the Town Clerk of Cupar in 1761 and as a member of Glasgow University between 1763 and 1765.[12]

> By comparing the signatures here with those on the St Andrews list, with those on the records from the Cupar Council and Burgh Records, with the signatures on the Declaration of Independence and the Constitution, the handwriting is the same. The partial library lending list from the University of Glasgow finds the same signature that appeared in the St Andrews lending lists of 1758 and 1759 and reappeared in the Cupar Register of Bonds in 1761, and showing up in Glasgow's list for 1763–1765.
>
> (Clagett 2012: 164)

Hence,

> there is the intriguing, although not documented, possibility that James Wilson also attended lectures given by Adam Smith, Thomas Reid and John Millar. Thomas Reid followed Adam Smith as the Professor of Moral Philosophy in 1764, modeling his lectures on those both of Smith and his predecessor Francis Hutcheson.
>
> (Clagett 2012: 167)

Adam Smith's final year as Professor of Moral Philosophy was 1763–64, when he left part way through the year to take up a position as travelling tutor to the young Duke of Buccleuch and his brother. His lecture notes for his last two sessions in Glasgow have been preserved by two students. These *Lectures on Jurisprudence* show that Smith's Glasgow class encompassed both the moral philosophy that became his *Theory of Moral Sentiments* (and the political economy that became his *Wealth of Nations*. The jurisprudence that linked the two covered legal and historical sociology, Smith's stadial theory of social development, and comparative public and private law. Late in life, Smith described one of 'two other great works upon the anvil' as being 'a sort of theory and history of Law and Government'.[13] This book, it is reasonable to assume, was being worked up from the middle part of the Glasgow lectures and would have supplied the link between *Theory of Moral Sentiments* and *Wealth of Nations*, of which we now only have the student notes that comprise the *Lectures on Jurisprudence*.

Wilson's borrowings from Glasgow University Library were mostly works of literature and history, not of law or philosophy, so how much of the work of Smith, Reid, and Millar he may have absorbed must remain a matter of speculation. But Glasgow University was a small place; only a year later, Wilson received his Pennsylvania honorary degree on the strength of his knowledge of the Scottish Enlightenment.

Wilson, then, was trained in Scots law through his Cupar apprenticeship before he studied English common law in Philadelphia. He must have encountered the thinking of three giants of the Scottish Enlightenment, including Adam Smith, while in Glasgow. What does this mean for our interpretation of Wilson's constitutionalism?

One of Wilson's successors as a law professor at Pennsylvania has recently considered the impact of Wilson's Scots law background on the drafting of the US Constitution (Ewald 2008, 2010). In May 1787, the Virginia deputation to the Constitutional Convention arrived ten days early and James Madison met Wilson, who was living in Philadelphia. They already knew each other from their service in the Continental Congress – the ineffectual national government that the Constitution was designed to supplant (for instance, they were both involved in an abortive attempt to create a library of French and English-language Enlightenment books for Congress in 1783). Wilson may therefore have helped Madison to draft what became known as the 'Virginia Plan', which was presented to the Convention as soon as it got going (Ewald 2008: 935). In one of his numerous speeches at the Convention, Wilson said, according to Madison's notes:

> [Mr Wilson] entered elaborately into the defence of a proportional representation, stating for his first position that as all authority was derived from the people, equal numbers of people ought to have an equal no of representatives, and different numbers of people different numbers of representatives.
>
> (June 9 1787; Madison 1987: 97)

A month later, Wilson proposed the wording that now forms Article IV.4 of the Constitution: 'that a Republican form of Government shall be guaranteed to each State' (July 18; Madison 1987: 322). He may have been the first delegate to suggest opening the Constitution with the phrase 'We, the People' (Ewald 2008: 988) and of what became Article IV.1: 'Full Faith and Credit shall be given in each State to the public Acts, Records and judicial Proceedings of every other State' (Ewald 2008: 999).

Is that a Scotsman or an Englishman speaking? Consider what sort of Scotland the young law clerk left in 1765. It had an established Church but the semi-federal state of Great Britain guaranteed religious freedom: anyone in England or Scotland oppressed by church establishment there could move to the other country. It had a strong but distant state, where, before 1707, Scotland had had the close and sometimes malevolent state that conspired with the Kirk to hang the 21-year-old Thomas Aikenhead for blasphemy in 1697 (Hunter 2004). That strong but distant state was an essential condition for the Scottish Enlightenment. Only 50 years after

Aikenhead, David Hume could produce his devastating attacks on religion. The writings of the 'infidel Hume' (Witherspoon, quoted by Noll 1989: 39) featured on the reading lists issued by America's most revered educator, John Witherspoon, the Evangelical minister from East Lothian who became President of Princeton and Madison's tutor.

So Philadelphia was quite a lot like Glasgow and Pennsylvania was quite a lot like Scotland. They both had freedom of the press and religion and a remote government. Wilson's first publication was a plea for federalism rather than independence (Wilson 1774/2007). His first legal citation was in denial of the claim to parliamentary sovereignty made by Sir William Blackstone, a precursor of Dicey who was the most studied English lawyer in the American colonies. Sovereignty in America lay, not with the House of Commons, but with the commons themselves – that is, the British people including (in 1774) the people of Pennsylvania (Wilson 1774/2007, pp. 4, 16). The position of the US colonies was not identical to that of Scotland: Scotland, unlike the colonies, was represented in the UK Parliament. But there were useful analogies. This is the context in which to note Adam Smith's comments on America. Although written after Wilson's brush with Smith in Glasgow, they reflect the libertarian free-trading spirit of Smith's Glasgow lectures. Smith was 'very zealous in American affairs' according to a reported comment from the Duke of Buccleuch to David Hume, and was a special advisor, as we would now say, to various UK governments from 1767 to 1778. He takes a robust view of American 'taxation without representation' claims – in his view, the colonists were taking a free ride on the defence services provided for them by the British Empire, from which only they benefited. But in other respects he sympathises with them. In *Wealth of Nations*, he says

> Their manners are more republican, and their governments...have hitherto been more republican too. ...The colonies owe to the policy of Europe the education and great views of their active and enterprising founders; and some of the greatest and most important of them owe to it scarce anything else.
> (*WN* IV.vii.b.53 and 64)

Remarkably, writing in 1776, Smith uses 'republican' as a term of praise. His manner of thinking is exactly the same as Wilson's (McLean 2006: 100–13). The active and enterprising Wilson of Cupar, Glasgow and Philadelphia, is the sort of person Smith has in mind.

Ewald (2008, 2010) and Pfander and Birk (2010) have studied US constitutionalism in the light of scholars' new understanding of the importance of Scotland, Scots law and the Scottish Enlightenment to the American founding. Scots law is based on Roman law and is closer to the continental civil law codes than is English law. Scots lawyers studied in Leiden or Amsterdam and syntheses of Roman-Scots law had been published in the late seventeenth century. Nothing resembling such a codification of the English common law occurred until Sir William Blackstone's textbook was published in 1765. Although Blackstone became highly influential in the USA, the colonies had to reconstruct their legal systems independently of him.

As noted, Blackstone is one of the great advocates of parliamentary sovereignty. The phrase 'We, the people' is not in Blackstone. It is in Wilson and Jefferson. They must have got it from somewhere. Wilson plainly intended to unseat Blackstone when he wrote his *Lectures on Law*. In his pithiest statements:

> I cannot consider him [Blackstone] as a zealous friend of republicanism.
> (Wilson 1804/2007, I: 149)

> The order of things in Britain is exactly the reverse of the order of things in the United States. Here, the people are masters of the government; there, the government is master of the people.
> (Wilson 1804/2007, I: 719)

Pfander and Birk (2011) focus on Article III of the US Constitution, which Wilson, as a member of the crucial Committee on Detail, helped draft. Article III creates and regulates the federal judiciary. It follows the Scots model of hierarchical courts, not the English model of competing courts. In Wilson's time, the Court of Session and the Faculty of Advocates had established the professionalism of Scots law. Specifically, the first draft from the Committee of Detail of what became the Exceptions and Regulations clause is in Wilson's hand (Pfander and Birk 2011: 1677). Apart from specified domains of original jurisdiction, the Supreme Court's jurisdiction: 'shall be appellate, with such Exceptions, and under such Regulations as the Congress shall make' (Madison 1987: 393). Wilson repeats his support for a hierarchy rather than a horizontal competition of courts in his law lectures (Wilson 1804/2007, II: 885–942). The US federal court system derives from Edinburgh rather than London.

Adam Smith of Kirkcaldy

Smith had a much greater influence on the US Constitution than has been recognised (but cf. Fleischacker 2002, 2003). He may have influenced Wilson directly;[14] he certainly did indirectly. More importantly, Smith's work lies behind the Establishment and Free Exercise clauses of the First Amendment: 'Congress shall make no law respecting an establishment of religion, or prohibiting the free exercise thereof'.

Adam Smith was not present at the Philadelphia Convention of 1787. Neither Wilson nor any other delegate seems to have referred in the debates, either to *Theory of Moral Sentiments* or to his *Wealth of Nations*, which includes a full discussion of US politics, nor is he referred to in the standard selections of letters, commentaries and speeches in state ratifying conventions. The online *Founders' Constitution*[15] highlights Smith's argument against David Hume that liberty is best secured by religious pluralism, not by an established church (*WN* V.i.g. 3–19). However, the editors of the *Founders' Constitution* do not trace the link from Smith to the Constitution. This chapter attempts to do so.

Over 60 years ago, Adair (1974) noted that Madison's work made substantial unacknowledged use of the work of that 'infidel Hume' whose work Madison had read under the tutelage of John Witherspoon. Adair's argument was reprised by Wills (1979, 1981). However, the focus of this work on Hume – whom Jefferson misread as 'the great apostle of Toryism' (TJ to Major John Cartwright, 6 June 1824, in Appleby and Ball 1999: 383) – has led scholars to overlook Hume's best friend and argumentative equal.

At one level, it is unsurprising that Smith was not cited in Philadelphia. As an opponent of free riding, his view that the colonists should pay for their own frontier defence had led him to sponsor what became the Quebec Act 1774 (McLean 2006: 101–3), which claimed a border down the Ohio River for the British Empire and seriously damaged the material interest of western land speculators in the colonies, such as George Washington and James Wilson. Although Smith's policy recommendations offended the entire political class in both Great Britain and the United States, it is clear that he respected the colonists' 'republican manners'.

As noted above, the move of the state from Edinburgh to London in 1707 removed the ability of the Kirk to hang Edinburgh undergraduates. The power vacuum in Smith's and Wilson's Scotland had important consequences. At its most banal, it allowed Hutcheson, Smith and Hume to survive and to write (more or less) unmolested. Hutcheson (another of James Wilson's favourite authors) made the first essential move to detach the ethics of the Scottish Enlightenment from their Calvinist foundations. Smith would secularise ethics further; Hume would take religion out of ethics altogether. By 1760, Scottish philosophers had challenged Witherspoon's and the Evangelicals' orthodox Calvinism from both deist (Hutcheson, Smith) and atheist (Hume) standpoints. The deists controlled the Church of Scotland. The 'Moderates' were a group of ministers in Edinburgh who seized control of the General Assembly in 1750 and retained it until the 1830s, when they were overthrown by the majority 'Popular' or 'Evangelical' (that is, orthodox Calvinist) party. The most pungent Evangelical of Hume's generation was Witherspoon, who wielded his sarcastic pen against the Moderates with vigour before emigrating. In *Wealth of Nations*, Smith vividly characterises the Moderates and Evangelicals as 'Loose' and 'Austere', respectively, and offers a Humean natural history of their religions. Austere Calvinists are Austere about drink and sex and, as a result, this appeals to, and benefits, the poor. The poor can be ruined by drink and sex, and they therefore have a material interest in binding themselves to the mast of austerity. The rich can afford to be Loose: drink and sex are superior goods, as economists would now paraphrase Smith's argument (*WN* V.i.g.10–12).

Thus, three recent Scottish models of church–state relations were available to the drafters of the US Bill of Rights: secularist (Humean), Calvinist (Witherspoonesque) and competitive (Smithian). The Bill of Rights was required when several state ratifying conventions tried to make their ratification of the original Constitution contingent on amendments that would protect the individual more fully against the executive than the original document was felt to do. The secularist model (religion is a potential source of trouble, to be controlled by the state in the interests of social peace) is explicit in Hume. It may be implicit in Jefferson's thought at the time but he never stated it in public so far as we know. It was not in contention for polite discussion in America, unlike in France.

A Calvinist model was already in force in Massachusetts and Connecticut: a state church, with ministers appointed by town meetings, which exercised social control on behalf of the state. Unlike 100 years earlier, the state church no longer burnt witches or hanged Quakers and it tolerated the sort of dissenters who had fled and created Rhode Island to escape its clutches. But it remained established. Other states, notably Rhode Island and Quaker-dominated Pennsylvania, protected free exercise and denied establishment. Virginia had had an established Anglican church, whose authority had collapsed at the Revolution, leaving a power vacuum of enormous interest to both Jefferson and Madison (Ragosta 2010). Their first joint campaign in Virginia was against a bill levying a state tax to support teachers of Christianity. It produced Madison's now-famous *Memorial and Remonstrance Against Religious Assessments* (Madison 1999: 29–36).

The first of 15 points offered in support of the remonstrance is also the first prequel, not only of *Federalist* 10 but of the radical interpretation of the Establishment Clause espoused by President Jefferson in his letter to the Danbury Baptist Association of 1802. Point one acknowledges the problem of majority tyranny (it was no doubt designed to appeal to the minority lobby of Baptists in Virginia). It provides that 'Religion…must be left to the conviction and conscience of every man' and that it is 'an inalienable right', echoing article 16 of the Virginia Declaration of Rights. Madison continues, '[N]o other rule exists, by which any question which may divide a Society, can be ultimately determined, but the will of the majority; but it is also true that the majority may trespass on the rights of the minority.'

But Point 7 is pure Adam Smith:

> 7. Because experience witnesseth that ecclesiastical establishments, instead of maintaining the purity and efficacy of Religion, have had a contrary operation. During almost fifteen centuries has the legal establishment of Christianity been on trial. What have been its fruits? More or less in all places, pride and indolence in the Clergy, ignorance and servility in the laity, in both, superstition, bigotry and persecution.
>
> (Memorial 1785, point 7; in Madison 1999: 33)

Madison already knew *Wealth of Nations* in 1785, as he had unsuccessfully lobbied the Continental Congress to buy it in 1783 (see below). Smith's only statement on organised religion is in *Wealth of Nations* Book V, Chapter 1, Part III, 'Of the Expence of publick Works and publick Institutions'. There, he asserts that religion is not the kind of public good that merits government funding, as do the military or education. Quite the contrary, he argues that clergy subsidised by the state 'are apt gradually to lose the qualities, both good and bad, which gave them authority and influence with the inferior ranks of people' and, when confronted with competing sects, 'feel themselves as perfectly defenseless as the indolent, effeminate and full fed nations of the southern parts of Asia, when they were invaded by the active, hardy, and hungry Tartars of the North'. The Scots, and many of the

American colonists of Smith's time, were, he thought, active, hardy and hungry. In fact, Smith continues, a government-subsidised, religious monopoly threatens the security of the state: 'When the authorised teachers of religion propagate through the great body of the people doctrines subversive of the authority of the sovereign, it is by violence only, or by the force of a standing army, that he can maintain his authority'. Compare Madison's point 7 with Smith's:

> [I]f politics had never called in the aid of religion…it would probably have dealt equally and impartially with all the different sects, and have allowed every man to chuse his own priest and his own religion as he thought proper. There would in this case, no doubt, have been a great multitude of religious sects. Almost every different congregation might probably have made a little sect by itself, or have entertained some peculiar tenets of its own. Each teacher would no doubt have felt himself under the necessity of making the utmost exertion, and of using every art both to preserve and to increase the number of his disciples.
>
> (*WN* V.i.g.8)

Religious competition, left alone, is capable of promoting the individual interests of those, including the clergy, who benefit from it; government involvement skews incentives and leads to unintended, adverse consequences.

The second prequel to *Federalist* 10 and Jefferson's letter to the Danbury Baptists is *Vices of the Political System of the United States*, the briefing note which Madison wrote for the Virginia delegation before the Constitutional Convention started. In it, Madison is concerned to see not only why Congress and the states had been unable to coordinate national government but also why the individual states had made bad laws. He identifies two sources of the bad legislation: the representative bodies and the people themselves. The difficulty with the people is that they 'are divided into different interests or factions, as they happen to be creditors or debtors – Rich or poor – husbandmen, merchants or manufacturers – members of different religious sects…&c &c'

Religion fails to impose an adequate constraint on faction. Unlike character, religion fails even to constrain individuals, who may think that it imposes an affirmative duty to force their beliefs on others and to violate the rights of minorities. Madison argues that, when acting on oath, 'the strongest of religious Ties', individuals in popular assemblies have approved acts against which their individual consciences would have revolted. He continues:

> When indeed Religion is kindled into enthusiasm, its force like that of other passions, is increased by the sympathy of a multitude…[A]s religion in its coolest state, is not infallible, it may become a motive to oppression as well as a restraint from injustice. Place three individuals in a situation wherein the interest of each depends on the voice of the others, and give to two of them an interest opposed to the rights of the third? Will the latter be secure? The prudence of every man would shun the danger.
>
> (Madison, *Vices*, in Madison 1999: 78)

Rather than increasing the tendency of legislatures to legislate for 'the general and permanent good of the Community', religion detracts from it.

There is less about religion in Madison's most famous number of *The Federalist,* number 10, which is a hasty rewrite of *Vices* for a different audience: namely, citizens of New York State who needed to be persuaded to ratify the Constitution. But there is enough to show its Smithian origins. Compare this from Madison:

> The influence of factious leaders may kindle a flame within their particular States, but will be unable to spread a general conflagration through the other States: a religious sect may degenerate into a political faction in a part of the Confederacy; but the variety of sects dispersed over the entire face of it, must secure the national Councils against any danger from that source: a rage for paper money, for an abolition of debts, for an equal division of property, or for any other improper or wicked project, will be less apt to pervade the whole body of the Union, than a particular member of it.
>
> (*Federalist* 10, in Madison 1999: 167)

with this from Smith:

> The interested and active zeal of religious teachers can be dangerous and troublesome only where there is either but one sect tolerated in the society, or where the whole of a large society is divided into two or three great sects; the teachers of each acting by concert, and under a regular discipline and subordination. But that zeal must be altogether innocent where the society is divided into two or three hundred, or perhaps into as many as a thousand small sects, of which no one could be considerable enough to disturb the publick tranquility. The teachers of each sect, seeing themselves surrounded on all sides with more adversaries than friends, would be obliged to learn that candour and moderation which is so seldom to be found among the teachers of those great sects whose tenets being supported by the civil magistrate, are held in veneration by almost all the inhabitants of extensive kingdoms and empires, and who therefore see nothing round them but followers, disciples, and humble admirers.
>
> (*WN* V.i.g.8)

Reluctant ratifiers, including some in both New York and Virginia, complained that the Constitution as drafted did not protect individual rights against the state sufficiently. Some states tried to make it a condition of their ratification that a Bill of Rights must be added. In the first US Congress, Madison was the floor leader in the House of Representatives for what became the Bill of Rights: viz., 12 amendments to protect individual rights, of which 10 were ratified.[16] As noted above, the final wording of the first two limbs of the First Amendment is *Congress shall make no law respecting an establishment of religion, or prohibiting the free exercise thereof.* The best-known interpretation of the Establishment and Free

Exercise Clauses, which emerged from Madison's efforts in the First Congress and which has been quoted in US Supreme Court opinions from the beginning of First Amendment jurisprudence as if it were part of the Constitution, is due to Madison's lifelong collaborator, Thomas Jefferson. As President in 1802, Jefferson took a political opportunity to reply to a petition he had received from a committee of Baptists in Danbury, Connecticut. The Baptists were on the wrong side of church establishment in their state, as they had earlier been in Virginia.

> Believing with you that religion is a matter which lies solely between man and his God, that he owes account to none other for his faith or his worship, that the legitimate powers of government reach actions only, and not opinions, I contemplate with sovereign reverence that act of the whole American people which declared that *their* legislature should 'make no law respecting an establishment of religion, or prohibiting the free exercise thereof,' thus building a wall of separation between Church and State.
>
> (TJ to the Danbury Baptists 01.01.1802, in Appleby and Ball 396–7; transcription errors corrected in McLean and Peterson 2010)

Jefferson's complex political motives have been examined elsewhere (McLean and Peterson 2010). For this chapter, the take-home message is that both Jefferson and Madison were true heirs of Adam Smith.

Establishing disputed parenthood

This chapter has compared texts from Smith, Wilson, Jefferson and Madison, and has pointed to family resemblances. But resemblance is not parenthood. How far (if at all) can the texts and views of the Americans be sourced directly from the Scots? Or were the Americans simply fishing in a pool of eighteenth-century commonplaces, fed by many Wilkesite, republican, and/or pro-American pamphleteers in the mid-eighteenth century?

As Fleischacker has said:

> The founders hardly ever discussed their intellectual heritage explicitly, and in their writings, they often failed to let the reader know whom they were quoting. The arguments for Hume's influence on Madison, Hutcheson's on Jefferson, and Reid's on Wilson have been supported almost entirely by identifying verbal echoes, coupled with evidence that the relevant Scottish writings were taught in colleges and owned by American libraries.
>
> (Fleischacker 2002: 898)

If Wilson, Jefferson and Madison had been British, it might indeed be impossible to go further than that. But the Atlantic Ocean may be quite an effective filter of the ideas flowing from the Wilkesite pool. Only what they could read in America (or France, in Jefferson's case), plus whatever mental baggage Wilson brought over from Scotland, can have directly contributed to their intellectual formation.

We cannot prove a negative but, if this or that pamphleteer were not available in the USA, he may be practically ignored as a potential source. For each of the three American targets of this paper, some available lists show what they read or owned (Table 1).

Wilson's law lectures and political works cite various authors in abbreviated forms. His editors have teased out the abbreviations, which refer to works in law, history, philosophy and current affairs. Any classification may be queried but a scheme of classification made for this chapter (available from the author on request) classes 109 of Wilson's sources as legal. Of these, 55 refer to English law, 15 to Scots law and 39 to Roman or civil law. Thus, Wilson's sources are (only) half English and half Roman or Scots. Roman and Scots influences may be detected in other ways. One striking way is the organisation of his law lectures. The most polished part (Part I, which was actually delivered in lecture form) has the chapter headings shown in Table 2.

Does this approach to the subject come from Wilson's studies of English common law under John Dickinson in Philadelphia or from his time as apprentice to the Town Clerk of Cupar? Unlikely, in both cases. Does it come from exposure to Scots public law and jurisprudence? This is much more likely. Note, first, the sequence from II to V. Going from obligation to the law of nature to the law of nations (that is, international law) to municipal (that is, domestic) law is exactly what Smith told his 1763–64 class was the method of 'the civilians', which he would follow in that session, unlike in the previous session (Smith, LJ, 22–7, 401 [source of quote]). The oldest endowed law chair in Scotland is the Regius Chair of Public Law and the Law of Nature and Nations in Edinburgh, founded by Queen Anne immediately upon Union in 1707. The title, both of the chair and of Wilson's lecture sequence, follows that of the best-known contemporary 'civilian' in eighteenth-century Scotland, Samuel Pufendorf, whose *De jure naturae et gentium* (*On the Law of Nature and Nations*) was published in 1672.

Secondly, note that, after his civilian introduction, Wilson devotes lectures VI–IX to the history and sociology of law. This is exactly the same sequence as Adam Smith took in the 1763–64 session, later to be developed more fully by John Millar, who had arrived in Glasgow as Smith's colleague in 1761. Comparative

Table 1 Potential English and Scottish sources for the thoughts of Wilson, Madison and Jefferson

Wilson	Madison	Jefferson
Citations in his Collected Works (Wilson 1804/2007, Bibliographical Glossary, at II: 1205–13)	Purchase recommendations to Congress 1783: *Madison Papers* VI: 62–115. James Madison's library (catalog under construction at Library Thing. Available online at www.librarything.com/ legacylibraries/profile/ JamesMadisonLibrary; accessed 18 July 2014)	Thomas Jefferson's library catalog (Gilreath and Wilson 1989; McLean 2011; Jefferson's Libraries database. Available online at http://tjlibraries.monticello. org; accessed 18 July 2014)

Table 2 Chapter headings in Wilson, *Lectures in Law*, Part I

Chapter	Title
I	Introductory Lecture. Of the Study of the Law in the United States
II	Of the General Principles of Law and Obligation
III	Of the Law of Nature
IV	Of the Law of Nations
V	Of Municipal Law
VI	Of Man, as an Individual
VII	Of Man, as a Member of Society
VIII	Of Man, as a Member of a Confederation
IX	Of Man, as a Member of the Great Commonwealth of Nations
X	Of Government
XI	Comparison of the Constitution of the United States, with That of Great Britain
XII	Of the Common Law
XIII	Of the Nature and Philosophy of Evidence

Source: Wilson 1804/2007, I: vi–vii.

government follows. Lecture XI, reflecting Wilson's experience of contributing to the Declaration of Independence and the Constitution, is the locus of Wilson's attempt to overthrow Blackstone's doctrine of parliamentary sovereignty in favour of popular sovereignty. Common law then just gets a look in, followed by criminal law, both of which Smith treated equally curtly in his 1763–64 lectures (LJ, 24–6). The organisation and content of Wilson's lectures does not prove that he attended or even read the lecture notes from, Smith's class in 1763–64, nor that he audited the classes of Smith and/or Millar. But the intellectual kinship is striking.

In January 1783, Madison and Jefferson, who were both in Philadelphia, collaborated on a booklist which they hoped to persuade the Continental Congress to buy. They failed, as did Wilson (also a member) who moved an amendment 'to confine the purchase for the present to the most essential part of the books' (quoted in Ketcham 1971: 141). But the list is a valuable insight into the minds of Madison, Jefferson and, perhaps, Wilson. They wanted Congress to be enlightened by the radical minds of the French and Scots. The list opens with the French Academy's *Encyclopédie Méthodique*. The next subheading is 'Law of Nature and Nations', in which Hutcheson, Adam Ferguson, Grotius and Pufendorf all feature, ahead of English common lawyers. Likewise, the plain 'Law' subheading puts Justinian and other civil law books ahead of Coke and Blackstone. Under 'History', Madison wants Congress to buy Hume's *History of England*; under 'Politics', the works of the seventeenth-century English republican theorists (Harrington, Sidney, Locke) and the leading contemporary Scots social scientists (Robert Wallace, Hume, Ferguson, Millar, James Burgh, Sir James Steuart, and Smith).[17]

Turning to Jefferson, the primary source available is his library. 'I cannot live without books', he famously wrote (TJ to John Adams, June 10 1815, in Cappon 1987: 443). By analysing the contents of his main catalogs, McLean (2011) attempts to establish the 'Scottishness' of Jefferson's holdings. Out of 5322 books bought by Jefferson, 183 have Scottish imprints. This is five times the proportion that he would have had on the naïve null hypothesis that he was equally likely to own a book published in any country in the Atlantic world of his time (McLean 2011, Table 5). Although, unlike Wilson, Jefferson was not trained in Scots law, he correctly classes his Scots law books under 'Equity and Foreign law' (Scots law being 'foreign' to a Virginian because of its Roman and civil law antecedents; Jefferson's cataloguing scheme is explained in Gilreath and Wilson 1989: 1–13).

How much further, if at all, can we go to attribute direct use of the works of Smith or other Scottish Enlightenment figures, especially against a null hypothesis that the ideas of Wilson, Madison and/or Jefferson derive from swimming in an undifferentiated pool of radical Whig and republican ideas? This would require laborious exclusion of other purported sources. To date, this has been done for the Danbury letter but not for the other American writings discussed in this chapter.

Alternative sources proposed (for example, by Dreisbach 2002; Hamburger 2002) for Jefferson's 'wall of separation' have included Richard Hooker's *Laws of Ecclesiastical Polity*; the writings of Roger Williams, the founder of Rhode Island; Locke's *Letter Concerning Toleration*; and the Scots-born propagandist James Burgh. Study of the purported source texts enabled McLean and Peterson (2010) to eliminate all save Burgh. Burgh was a Scots-born London schoolteacher and journalist who belonged to a radical pro-American circle including Richard Price, Joseph Priestley, and Benjamin Franklin (cf Hay 2004). He writes:

> A church is nothing more than a community of persons united together in affection and esteem, by their holding the same religion, and stands wholly unconnected with secular concerns. The combination of a sect of idle and greedy men, who, supported by power, set themselves up for lords over the consciences of others, and who unite together, under the pretext of being religious rulers, for carrying on a sordid plan of power and riches; is an execrable conspiracy, which all friends of mankind ought to join together to overturn from the foundation...Build an impenetrable wall of separation between things sacred and civil. Do not send a graceless officer, reeking from the arms of his trull,[18] to the performance of a holy rite of religion, as a test for his holding the command of a regiment.
>
> (Burgh 1766: II, 116–19)

Whatever the Danbury Baptists might have made of this sentiment, they would not have liked its expression. Nevertheless, Burgh is a potentially important conduit from the Scottish to the American Enlightenment. He is directly cited by Wilson as the source for Rumbold's 'saddles on their backs' speech (Wilson 1804/2007: I. 477) and by Madison in *Federalist* 56 as an authority on the Parliamentary Union of 1707 (Madison 1999: 324). His *Political Disquisitions* is on Madison's purchase list for Congress. Jefferson recommended the same book to his law student son-in-law in 1790, in a letter which also described *Wealth of Nations* as '[i]n political economy...the best book extant' (TJ to TM Randolph 30 May 1790, in Appleby and Ball 1999 260–3).

Thus, although we cannot prove that Smith and his contemporary Scots thinkers were constantly at the side of the three Americans who did most to shape the Declaration of Independence and the Constitution, it is possible to show that they were all familiar with the main works of the Scottish Enlightenment. At least, arguably, the Danbury letter originated in Kirkcaldy.

Notes

1   This work was facilitated by a Fellowship at the Robert H. Smith Center for Jefferson Studies, Monticello, VA, fall 2010. I acknowledge the generosity of the Thomas Jefferson Foundation in electing me to the Fellowship. I also acknowledge discussant comments at the 2009 Glasgow conference on the 250th anniversary of *TMS* and the Adam Smith Conference in Kirkcaldy, 2012, and the work of my co-author Scot M. Peterson. Earlier versions of some of this material were published in our 'Adam Smith at the Constitutional Convention', *Loyola Law Review* 56: 95–113.

2   Cf. Bill of Rights, sec. 4 1 W. & M., 2d sess., c. 2, 16 Dec. 1689: 4. 'That levying money for or to the use of the crown, by pretence of prerogative, without grant of parliament, for longer time, or in other manner than the same is or shall be granted, is illegal.'

3   Cf. Habeas Corpus Act 31 Car. 2, c. 2 , 27 May 1679.

4   Cf. Bill of Rights, 1 W. & M., 2d sess., c. 2 , 16 Dec. 1689, s. 10. 'That excessive bail ought not to be required, nor excessive fines imposed; nor cruel and unusual punishments inflicted.'

5   In the event, both Jefferson and John Adams died on that day.

6   Jefferson to Roger A. Weightman, 24 June 1826. TJ's spelling and punctuation. Library of Congress. Available online at: www.loc.gov/exhibits/jefferson/214.html (last accessed 16 July 2014).

7   Sir Walter Scott, 'Bonnie Dundee' (original version). The poem has been frequently adapted and parodied; e.g., by Lewis Carroll in Alice through the looking Glass and in a Confederate march written for the Battle of Antietam in 1862. 'Clavers' and 'Bonnie Dundee' both denote John Graham of Claverhouse, 1st Viscount Dundee (1648–89).

8   Cf. US Const. Amendment III. 'No Soldier shall, in time of peace be quartered in any house, without the consent of the Owner, nor in time or war, but in a manner to be prescribed by law.'

9   Claim of Right Act 1689, preamble and c.28. Available online at: www.legislation. gov.uk/aosp/1689/28/contents (last accessed 16 July 2014). Both the Scottish and English Acts are still in force.

10   Also, arguably (but not in this chapter), the Second. For studies of the militia question in Scotland see Fletcher 1997 and the sources cited there.

11   In 1762, according to DNB; after enrolling as a divinity student in 1761, according to ANB. Clagett (2012) has shown that both are wrong. Wilson is recorded in St Andrews only from 1757 to 1759 before returning to Cupar, where he became a legal apprentice to the Town Clerk.

12   Clagett has compared the signatures of three students named James Wilson at Glasgow between 1763 and 1765 with the signatures of James Wilson of Ceres on the St Andrews University Library records and on the US Declaration of Independence and Constitution. He infers that Wilson of Ceres attended, for sure, the class of John Anderson and borrowed library books. There is no firm evidence to link him with the class successively taught by Adam Smith, Thomas Young and Thomas Reid, nor with John Millar's class.

13   AS to le Duc de La Rochefoucauld [d'Enville], 1 December 1785 in *Correspondence of Adam Smith* (Glasgow Edition vol 6) Indianapolis: Liberty Fund, 1987, Letter 248.
14   Wilson's 'Considerations on the Bank of North America' (1785, in Wilson 2007 I: 60–79) quotes *WN* extensively, in a way that is consistent with Wilson having heard Smith's lectures on jurisprudence, from Smith or Young, or from one of the student transcripts that comprise LJ.
15   The Founders' Constitution, edited by Philip B. Kurland and Ralph Lerner. University of Chicago Press and Liberty Fund, 1987. Available online at: http://press-pubs. uchicago.edu/founders (last accessed 16 July 2014).
16   An eleventh, on congressional pay, became the 27th Amendment when ratified in 1992 by the required number of states.
17   Source: J. C. A. Stagg, (ed.) *The Papers of James Madison*, digital edition. Charlottesville, VA: University of Virginia Press, Rotunda, 2010. Vol. 6. Available online at: http://rotunda.upress.virginia.edu/founders/default.xqy?keys=JSMN-index-6-3-72-1-5-1#JSMN-01-06-02-pb-0065 (last accessed 16 July 2014). Titles include *The Wealth of Nations*; Ferguson's *History of Civil Society*; Millar's *Origins of the Distinction of Ranks*; and Burgh's *Political Disquisitions*.
18   As Burgh was a Scotsman, he may have meant 'reeking' in the Scottish sense of 'giving off smoke' but the English sense of 'giving off an unpleasant smell' has the same effect. OED online: *reek*, v.i., senses 1 and 4; *trull*: 'A low prostitute or concubine; a drab, strumpet, trollop'.

Bibliography

Adair, D. (1974) *Fame and the Founding Fathers* edited by T. Colbourn. New York: W. W. Norton. Chapters originally published in various journals in the 1950s. Republished 1998 Indianapolis, IN: Liberty Fund.

Appleby, J. and Ball, T. (eds) (1999) *Jefferson: Political Writings*. Cambridge: Cambrdige University Press.

Bagehot, W. ([1865] 2001) *The English Constitution* edited by Paul Smith. Cambridge: Cambridge University Press.

Burgh, J. (1766) *Crito: or, Essays on Various Subjects*, 2 vols. London: Dodsley.

Butterfield, H. (1931) *The Whig Interpretation of History*. London: G. Bell & Sons.

Cappon, L.J. (1987) *The Adams–Jefferson Letters: The Complete Correspondence Between Thomas Jefferson and Abigail and John Adams*, 2nd edn. Chapel Hill, NC: University of North Carolina Press.

Clagett, M. (2012) 'James Wilson – his Scottish background: corrections and additions', *Pennsylvania History: A Journal of Mid-Atlantic Studies* 79(2): 154–76.

Conrad, S. (2004) 'Wilson, James (1742–1798).' In *Oxford Dictionary of National Biography*, edited by Lawrence Goldman. Oxford: Oxford University Press. Available online at: www.oxforddnb.com/view/article/68676 (last accessed 16 July 2014).

Dicey, A.V. ([1885] 1915) *Introduction to the Study of the Law of the Constitution*, 8th edn with new introduction. London: Macmillan. Also republished in facsimile by Liberty Fund (Indianapolis: 1982).

Dreisbach, D.L. (2002) *Thomas Jefferson and the Wall of Separation Between Church and State*. New York: New York University Press.

Ewald, W. (2008) 'James Wilson and the drafting of the constitution', *University of Pennsylvania Journal of Constitutional Law*, 10: 901–1009.

Ewald, W. (2010) 'James Wilson and the Scottish Enlightenment', *University of Pennsylvania Journal of Constitutional Law*, 12: 1053–114.

Fletcher (of Saltoun), A. (1997) *Political Works* edited by J. Robertson. Cambridge: Cambridge University Press.

Fleischacker, S. (2002) 'Adam Smith's reception among the American founders', *William & Mary Quarterly* 3rd ser. 59: 897–924.

Fleischacker, S. (2003) 'Scottish philosophy and the American founding', in *The Cambridge Companion to the Scottish Enlightenment*, edited by Alexander Broadie. Cambridge: Cambridge University Press, pp. 316–37.

Gilreath, J. and Wilson, D.L. (1989) *Thomas Jefferson's Library: A Catalog with the Entries in his Own Order*. Washington, DC: Library of Congress.

Hamburger, P. (2002) *Separation of Church and State*. Cambridge, MA: Harvard University Press.

Hay, C.H. (2004) 'Burgh, James (1714–1775)', in *Oxford Dictionary of National Biography*, edited by Lawrence Goldman. Oxford: Oxford University Press. Available online at: www.oxforddnb.com/view/article/3992 (last accessed 16 July 2014).

Hunter, M. (2004) 'Aikenhead, Thomas (bap. 1676, d. 1697)', in *Oxford Dictionary of National Biography*, edited by Lawrence Goldman. Oxford: Oxford University Press. Available online at: www.oxforddnb.com/view/article/225 (last accessed 16 July 2014).

Ketcham, R. (1971) *James Madison: A Biography*. New York: Macmillan.

McLean, I. (2006) *Adam Smith, Radical and Egalitarian*. Edinburgh: Edinburgh University Press.

McLean, I. (2010) *What's Wrong with the British Constitution?* Oxford: Oxford University Press.

McLean, I. (2011) 'Scottish enlightenment influence on Thomas Jefferson's book-buying: introducing Jefferson's libraries', Nuffield College Working Papers on Politics. Available online at: www.nuffield.ox.ac.uk/politics/papers/2011/Iain%20McLean_working%20paper%202011_01.pdf (last accessed 16 July 2014).

McLean, I. and Peterson, S.M. (2010) 'Adam Smith at the Constitutional Convention', *Loyola Law Review*, 56: 95–113.

Madison, J. (1987) *Notes of Debates in the Federal Convention*. Bicentennial edition edited by A. Koch. New York: W. W. Norton. Originally published in 1840.

Madison, J. (1999) *Writings*, edited by Jack Rakove. New York: Library of America.

Noll, M.A. (1989) *Princeton and the Republic, 1786–1822*. Princeton, NJ: Princeton University Press.

Pfander, J.E. and Birk, D.D. (2011) 'Article III and the Scottish judiciary', *Harvard Law Review*, 124: 1613–87.

Ragosta, J.A. (2010) *Wellspring of Liberty: How Virginia's Religious Dissenters Helped Win the American Revolution and Secured Religious Liberty*. New York: Oxford University Press.

Smith, A. ([1759] 1976) *The Theory of Moral Sentiments* edited by D.D. Raphael and A.L. Macfie. Oxford: Clarendon Press.

Smith, A. ([1776] 1979) *An Inquiry into the Nature and Causes of the Wealth of Nations*, 2 vols, edited by R.H. Campbell, A.S. Skinner and W.B. Todd. Oxford: Oxford University Press.

Smith, A. (1982) *Lectures in Jurisprudence* (*Glasgow Edition of the Works of Adam Smith*, vol. 5). Indianapolis: Liberty Fund.

Smith, A. (1987) *Correspondence of Adam Smith* (*Glasgow Edition of the Works of Adam Smith*, vol. 6). Indianapolis: Liberty Fund.

Wills, G. (1979) *Inventing America*: *Jefferson's Declaration of Independence*. New York: Vintage Books.

Wills, G. (1982) *Explaining America: The Federalist.* Harmondsworth: Penguin.

Wilson, J. ([1774] 2007) 'Considerations on the nature and extent of the legislative authority of the British parliament', in *Collected Works of James Wilson*, edited by K.L. Hall and M.D. Hall. Indianapolis, IN: Liberty Fund, Vol. I: 3–31.

Wilson, J. ([1804] 2007) 'Lectures in law', in *Collected Works of James Wilson*, edited by K.L. Hall and M.D. Hall. Indianapolis, IN: Liberty Fund, Vol. I: 399 – II: 1214.

Humanomics of Adam Smith[1]

Vernon L. Smith

In 1790, John Kay, eighteenth-century barber turned engraver, left us an endearing sketch of Adam Smith,[2] who he identified as, "The Author of *The Wealth of Nations*" (Smith, 1776; hereafter *Wealth* or *WN* for page references). Kay's portrait was made in the same year that the sixth edition of *The Theory of Moral Sentiments* (Smith, 1759; hereafter *Sentiments* or *TMS* for page references) appeared but, although *Sentiments* had been well received from its first edition to the last, it would be thoroughly eclipsed by *Wealth* for the following two centuries. Kay marks the expression of this truth already in 1790.

Here is a quotation that hints why Smith's first great book would be left in the philosophical shadows by his second: "Smith was highly taken with Pitt, and one evening when dining with him, he remarked to Addington after dinner, 'What an extraordinary man Pitt is; he understands my ideas better than I do myself'" (Rae, 1895, p. 405, quoted from Pellew, 1847, p. 151).

The ideas which Smith is quoted as saying that Pitt understood "better than I do myself" provided the intellectual foundation for the political economy that would nurture what economic historians tell us is the unprecedented takeoff of two centuries of growth in human economic betterment; for the first time in human history, per capita income and wealth would begin its astonishing acceleration. But, as Smith would be the first to emphasize, he was only the messenger – albeit a deeply insightful one – of transformations that grew out of Northern European human experience. McClosky (2010) has taught us that what mattered most in this reformation was a change in attitude at ground level: the widespread acceptance of liberal ideas respecting the dignity of people whose origins were the plainest and most ordinary. The rhetoric of prudence came to include "allowing every man to pursue his own interest his own way, upon the liberal plan of equality, liberty and justice" (*WN* IV.ix.3, p. 664). These liberal principles fuelled Smith's opposition to slavery, mercantilism, empire, colonialism, taxation without representation, and his belief that "the fortune of every individual should depend as much as possible upon his merit, and as little as possible upon his privilege" (Mossner and Ross, 1977, Letter number 143, p 178).[3]

Moreover, his insistence that ideas be ground-tested in experience drew Smith naturally to a habit of close observation and to the forward-looking worlds of science, technology and business that surrounded him. His circle of most intimate personal friends included Joseph Black, a pioneer in physical chemistry.[4] During Smith's tenure at the University of Glasgow (1751–64), James Watt, then 21 years of age, was given an appointment at the university, described in the following words by Joseph Black:

> I became acquainted with Mr. James Watt in the year 1757 or 1758, at which time I was professor of medicine and Lecturer of Chemistry in the University of Glasgow. About that time Mr. Watt came to settle in Glasgow as a maker of mathematical instruments; but being molested by some of the corporations, who considered him as an intruder on their privileges, the University protected him by giving him a shop within their precincts, and by conferring on him the title of Mathematical Instrument Maker to the University.
>
> I soon had occasion to employ him to make some things which I needed for my experiments, and found him to be a young man possessing most uncommon talents for mechanical knowledge and practice, with an originality, readiness, and copiousness of invention, which often surprised and delighted me in our frequent conversations together.
>
> (Muirhead, 1858, p. 58)

Just as Adam Smith became the symbolic intellectual champion of liberalism, Black, Hutton and Watt were practical manifestations and instruments of the science, innovation and "knowledge-how" (Ryle, 1945–46) that was empowered by the liberal attitude that overwhelmed the role of past privilege in shaping who and what a person could become.[5]

Humanomics: Smith's two worlds of sentiments and wealth

Smith's liberal principles that would so capture and leverage the thinking of William Pitt, foreshadowing nineteenth-century Western economic development, began with his first book; the two books together, *Sentiments* and *Wealth*, define what I shall call Adam Smith's two worlds.[6] In both of these worlds, Smith's emphasis is on process and fair play, not on outcomes and equilibrium. In modern economics, this begins most prominently with the long rise of marginal utilitarianism in this 150th anniversary of its beginning.[7]

Sentiments, Smith's world of social commerce

This is the community network of family, extended family, friends and neighbors, nineteenth-century Maine lobstermen and eighteenth-century British whalers, in all of which the rules governing conduct emerge endogenously by consent.[8] These social networks are now global in Facebook and other multi-billion-dollar social media corporations. *Sentiments*, however, frames this world as one that is antecedent to the existence of external civil or criminal enforcement of the rules of fair play but the two worlds live side by side today in continuous adaptation to changing experience and technology.

Decisions are judged in terms of conduct and are disciplined by what other people will go along with, or not go along with. In *Sentiments*, Smith uses the phrase "go along with" 41 times in his text, to bring home to us the sympathetic mechanism by which people – men, the spectator, the fair and impartial spectator – interactively forge the rules of fair play that shape individual behavior. In *Sentiments*, "fair" behaviors always means "not foul", as in the sports metaphor. These rules define "propriety rights" known more commonly as "property rights" by the eighteenth century but Smith clearly is always speaking of rules governed by "propriety", although adhering to the then-current customary use of "property".[9]

In sharp contrast with what has become traditional or mainstream economics, *Sentiments* was concerned to articulate the process whereby these rules emerge rather than to model actions as generating equilibrium based on utilitarian outcomes. In *Sentiments*, Smith denies the possibility of reducing human sociality to an analysis based on utilitarian concepts. For Smith, "social preference" is a contradiction in terms (Wilson, 2010). The rules that emerge must have the feature that anti-social – bad, destabilizing, inimical to efficient – actions do not drive out social – good, stabilizing, efficiency promoting – actions, and *Sentiments* is concerned to enquire as to the mechanisms of evaluation (what is "bad" or "good"), the filtering responses that allow order to prevail, and the impediments that might disallow its emergence. The hypothesis of 'social preference' finesse's all these considerations, accepts the end result, and instills it in a supposed human utilitarian nature.

I have come to believe this is bad social science, and that it is the step-child of the nineteenth-century turn from understanding process to modeling outcomes in terms of the concept of maximize-U equilibrium in outcomes. Worse, it does not enable us to see how the rules that emerged from disinterested social commerce were a natural, widely acceptable, basis for property.[10]

Wealth, Smith's world of economics

The nature and cause of wealth creation is specialization across far-flung communities made possible through long distance (beyond community and even nation) market exchange. Theorem: the division of labor is limited by the extent of the market. This exchange-specialization nexus required a civil order founded on rules of property and therefore upon justice; otherwise the game of "steal" would overwhelm the game of "trade" with anti-social actions in the former driving out social actions in the latter and preventing nations from achieving escape momentum into ever-expanding levels of wealth creation.

This is Smith's "liberal order", an order that grew organically and experientially out of human sociality, but in *Wealth*, Smith does not plagiarize himself to revisit the social psychological processes articulated in *Sentiments* that made that civil order possible. In this crucial sense, *Wealth* builds on *Sentiments*. I believe this explains why economists misread *Wealth* for over two centuries: we had not read and mastered *Sentiments*, and many of us whose comments implied that we had read it, simply did not understand that it was a book-length prolegomena to *Wealth*.

But that "liberal order" was alone not enough to fuel human economic better-ment. Smith needed a fundamental axiom of human behavior and he enunciated it in the form of a *discovery axiom*: "the propensity to truck barter and exchange, one thing for another". This defining characteristic of humans, an integral part of our language and social behavior already embedded in *Sentiments*, is what enabled specialization, innovation and wealth creation to emerge without intention or constructivist reason. Property was only a necessary, not a sufficient condition, for launching Western or any society on a path of wealth creation. What closed the circle was the propensity to trade one thing for another. This *discovery axiom* was essential because – played out in a property environment – it defined a process that would generate prices. But once you had public prices, private opportunity comparisons were inevitable; and private comparisons in turn would lead people to question whether whatever they were doing and however they were spending their time and effort were in their own interest and constituted what they should be doing and spending. Thus were they guided to specialize, re-form and innovate, and no one at the heart of that process had to understand the process for it to wrought miracles.

That prices encourage comparisons and thereby change what people do is clearly and deeply understood by Smith when he states:

> the certainty of being able to exchange all that surplus part of the produce of his own labour, which is over and above his own consumption, for such parts of the produce of other men's labour as he may have occasion for, encourages every man to apply himself to a particular occupation, and to cultivate and bring to perfection whatever talent or genius he may possess for that particular species of business…the very different genius which appears to distinguish men of different professions, when grown up to maturity, is not upon many occasions so much the cause, as the effect of the division of labour…without the disposition to truck, barter, and exchange, every man must have procured to himself every necessary and conveniency of life which he wanted. All must have had the same duties to perform, and the same work to do, and there could have been no such difference of employment as could alone give occasion to any great difference of talents.
>
> (*WN* I.ii. 3–4, pp. 28–9)

Smith on human motivation

Most of the discussion that follows bears on Smith's world of social commerce, although at the end of this chapter I return to economics and to his second book.

In Smith's system, motivation is not utilitarian as in Hume, Bentham, and Jevons; it is not self-love in combination with recognition of our social dependence on each other, which then applies reason to deduce a social contract, as in Hobbes (*TMS* pp. 315–20).[11] Nor does motivation derive from an innate "moral sense" of virtue or vice, beauty or deformity, beneficent or hurtful conduct, as with Smith's great and influential teacher, Francis Hutcheson (*TMS* pp. 321). Nor is it social preferences, allowing other-regarding behavior to be explained as maximizing an other-regarding utility function defined over own and other outcomes, as has become common among both behavioral and experimental economists (see Camerer, 2005, for an excellent summary).

Rather, human motivation concerns the socioeconomic fitness (propriety) of our conduct, and achieving self-command in the humbling of self-love; it is about process, not equilibrium outcomes. If there is a characterizeable equilibrium, it resides in rule selection for "the pleasures of mutual sympathy". "Social preferences" cannot be "preferences" because "The rule that guides fair behavior is not located in an individual's private utility function but instead resides in the connections that the individual has to his cultural environs" (Wilson, 2012, p 410). *Sentiments* is devoted to understanding these connections and the bidirectional pathways between the individual and culture.

Moreover, the rules derive from experience not reason:

> These first perceptions (of right and wrong), as well as all other experiments[12] upon which any general rules are founded, cannot be the object of reason, but of immediate sense and feeling. It is by finding…that one tenor of conduct constantly pleases…and that another…displeases the mind, that we form the general rules of morality…reason cannot render any particular object either agreeable or disagreeable to the mind for its own sake.
>
> (*TMS* VII.iii.2.7, p. 320)

And the resulting order, if efficient, is quite unintended:

> in accounting for the operations of bodies, we never fail to distinguish…the efficient from the final cause, in accounting for those of the mind we are very apt to confound these two different things with one another. When by natural principles we are led to advance those ends, which a refined and enlightened reason would recommend to us, we are very apt to impute to that reason, as to their efficient cause, the sentiments and actions by which we advance those ends.
>
> (*TMS* II.ii.3.5, p. 87)

Motivation: conduct and principles of action

In *Sentiments* the principles, or axioms, of motivation I want to emphasize all derive from human sociability: We desire praise but also to be praiseworthy. Praise is not a source of pleasure ("fellow-feeling") if it is undeserved – given in ignorance or error. We find satisfaction in our praiseworthy conduct, even if no such praise is likely to be bestowed on us (*TMS* III.2.1–5, 113–16).

Conduct through the looking glass: from impartial spectator to self-command

Smith argues that the mature individual learns insensibly from experience to examine his own conduct from the perspective of others as would a "fair and impartial spectator".[13] In this way, we are able to judge our conduct sympathetically and approved or disapprove of it. In effect we screen our actions to insure their compatibility with social norms (*TMS* III.1.2, p. 110). While sympathy is based on feelings and passions the resulting judgments cannot be made independently of the particular context: "the situation that excites it" (*TMS* I.i.I.10, p. 12). Smith carefully distinguishes between the situation, context, or cause that excites our evaluation or judgment of actions, and the outcomes or effects that result from the actions. Our own conduct and that of others, as expressed in actions, can only be read by simultaneously taking account of these two dimensions of human interaction (*TMS* I.i.3.5–8, p. 18). In reading the conduct of others and in examining our own conduct we follow general rules (*TMS* III.4.7, p. 159).

Smith offers an incisive "mental experiment" to establish the proposition that there is no cognitive individual psychology in the absence of a cognitive social psychology: "Were it possible that a human creature could grow up to manhood in some solitary place, without any communication with his own species, he could no more think of his own character, of the propriety or demerit of his own sentiments and conduct, of the beauty or deformity of his own mind, than of the beauty or deformity of his own face" (*TMS* III.1. 3, p. 110). He can experience none of these sentiments because he has no "mirror" to view them. The process of growing up within society provides him with the needed mirror, as people reliably mark their approval or disapproval of his conduct when they encounter him. His mature social mind is achieved through self-command, in which he has learned to "humble the arrogance of his self-love, and bring it down to something which other men can go along with" (*TMS* II.ii.2.1, 83); that is, we "become the impartial spectators of our own character and conduct" (*TMS* III.2.3, 114).

Beneficence, gratitude and trust games

Consider next what I will call Smith's *Beneficence Proposition 1*:

> Actions that are both beneficent and intended alone call for reward because of the "sympathetic gratitude" that they invoke in others.
>
> (*TMS* II.ii. 1.1, 78)

This proposition applies in a straightforward way to laboratory experimental "trust games".[14] Let (Payoff Player 1, Payoff Player 2) define the monetary rewards, respectively, that Player 1 and Player 2 each receives, depending on the options they choose in an extensive form (sequential move) game. These rewards induce final outcome value on each action choice (Smith, 1976). Consider the following game:

Player 1 chooses between two options:

- a. ($20, $20) or b. Pass to Player 2.

- If option "a" is chosen, the game ends and each subject is paid $20 in cash.
- If option "b" is chosen, then Player 2 chooses between:
- c. ($25, $25) or d. ($15, $30); the game ends and the subjects are paid according Player 2's final choice.

The traditional game-theoretic analysis assumes that it is common knowledge that each player is strictly self-loving. It follows that, if given the opportunity, Player 2 will choose "d", the defection outcome ($15, $30); anticipating this response, Player 1, in his self-loving interest, will never pass to Player 2, and therefore the equilibrium outcome is predicted to be "a" ($20, $20).

Not part of the traditional theory is how people come to the state of common knowledge – a topic that is the substance of *Sentiments* because Smith is concerned with the underlying drivers of human social commerce. Consequently, what Smith finds is that, in choosing actions, what people "know" (that is, experience) is gratefulness for beneficent acts, and, by implication, that the facilitators of beneficent action can reasonably expect others to feel gratitude, depending always on circumstances, and therefore with some prediction uncertainty. Against this background, suppose Player 1 passes to Player 2. From *Beneficence Proposition 1*, the latter can see that Player 1 has given up "a", incurring the costly risk of ending up at "d", but enabling both to do better at "c", surely a praiseworthy action, while the choice of "d" almost surely would be blameworthy.[15] Thus, Player 2 can interpret Player 1 as having acted intentionally and beneficially, feel corresponding gratitude and reward that action by choosing "c", the cooperative outcome. Player 1, capable of seeing how Player 2 will interpret the action if she passes to Player 2, will be motivated to choose this option, albeit with more uncertainty than for Player 2.

In this analysis, we note that Smith also makes use of the common knowledge that people are self-loving, but for an entirely different end: such knowledge is necessary for both players to know that Player 1 acted to benefit Player 2. However, such rudimentary "common knowledge" is modified by common social experience, captured in his *Proposition 1* above.

McCabe *et al.* (2003) report the results for 27 pairs of anonymously paired subjects who participate in the above "voluntary trust game". The number of pairs ending play at each of the payoff outcome nodes is: a – 10; c – 11; d – 6. Thus, 17 of 27 Player 1s pass to Player 2. *Beneficence Proposition 1* outscores the equilibrium prediction 17 to 10, and the defection outcome 11 to 6.

Many scholars, however, have explained the choice observations from trust games as a consequence of people's utility maximizing social preferences. In the above game, Player 2 is hypothesized to choose "c" ($25, $25) rather than "d" ($15, $30) because she "prefers" to give Player 1 $10 more while taking $5 less for herself; option "c" yields higher utility for her than option "d" because the loss in "own reward" utility is less than the gain in utility from "other reward" in the range of her choice opportunities.

This prediction as well as that of *Beneficence Proposition 1* are both tested by McCabe *et al.* (2003) in their further report of the results from a variation on the above game, called the "involuntary trust game", in which option "a" is not an available choice for Player 1; both players know that Player 1 must start the game by passing play to Player 2 and gives up nothing; that is, she incurs no opportunity cost. Player 2 then chooses as above between the options "c" ($25, $25) or "d" ($15, $30) and the game ends. From *Beneficence Proposition 1* it is evident that no properly motivated beneficent action can be intended by Player 1. Hence, no gratitude can be felt by Player 2 and the proposition predicts that, in the involuntary trust game, the defection outcome will be supported. The reported outcomes from 27 subjects who play this alternative game are : c – 9; d – 18. Where no gratitude can be felt, defection exceeds cooperation by a two to one margin, almost exactly the reverse of outcomes in the voluntary trust game where gratitude is predicted to be engendered by the game context (that is, the moves available convey intentions).

Comparing the decision results of the two games, the utility maximizing "social preference" prediction is falsified. The experimental results contradict all outcome-based models of decision; in *Sentiments*, however, actions signal conduct, and therefore context and intentions always matter: "To the intention or affection of the heart…all praise or blame, all approbation or disapprobation, of any kind… must ultimately belong" (*TMS* II.iii.3, p 93).[16]

> *Beneficence Proposition 2*:
> Beneficent actions are freely given, and cannot be forced or extorted; the failure of someone to show benevolence may disappoint but does not justify resentment or punishment that people will go along with.
>
> (Sentiments, II.ii.1.3, p. 78)

In the context of the trust games discussed above, this proposition predicts that Player 2 will not feel resentment if Player I chooses equilibrium rather than to "trust" Player 2 to choose cooperation instead of defection. How might we test this prediction? In the voluntary trust game above, suppose we modify Player 1's options so that if she wishes to choose equilibrium, this is accomplished by passing play through Player 2, who then chooses between equilibrium and incurring a cost to punish Player 2. If resentment is felt, we know from the argument in *Sentiments* that it will find expression in the form of costly punishment. For example, the game moves and outcomes could be:

- Player 1 chooses between:
  - pass to Player 2, who chooses between: a1. ($20, $20) or a2. ($18, $18); the game ends.
  - pass to Player 2, who chooses between: c. ($25, $25) or d. ($15, $30); the game ends.

If Player 1 chooses option "a" and Player 2 resents that "b" was not chosen, he can take $2 less, award Player 1 $2 less and thereby punish Player 1 for not choosing beneficently.

Injustice: on resentment, punishment and the evolution of property from propriety

In symmetric opposition to beneficent action we have hurtful action, which is far more significant to Smith, for it forms the basis of his approach to property.

> *Injustice Proposition*:
> Actions that are both intended and hurtful alone deserve punishment because they alone invoke the sympathetic resentment of others.
>
> (*TMS* II.ii.1.2, p. 78)

The significant lesson we learn from *Sentiments* about justice is that it is secured by punishing injustice, not by rewarding acts of justice. Justice is your duty, and duty neither requires or commands reward. Particularly important is the implication that "justice" is not pursued directly as an end, but is what is left over after you have instituted rules discouraging injustice: "Though the breach of justice…exposes to punishment, the observance of the rules of that virtue seems scarce to deserve any reward" (*TMS* II.ii.1.8, pp. 81–2).

No one expects or receives a reward for driving through a green light; you get a citation only for failing to stop appropriately for a red light. To appreciate Smith's vision, think of rules of propriety based on resentment as going "global" beyond the closeknit community in an extended civil order; imagine an immense playing field whose boundaries are defined by specific acts of injustice – murder in its various forms, theft and robbery, violation of contract, bearing false witness, and so on – acts discouraged by making them punishable, where the punishment is proportioned to the severity (resentment) of the infraction; within those bounties, there is freedom to pursue your own interest in your own way. Imagine the large number of ways in which you are free to drive through a green light, but only one way to receive a citation and fine – not stop for a red light. The red light infraction defines a boundary, the green light, an immense region of freedom to explore and create.

Observe also Smith's symmetric treatment of beneficence and injustice: we reward beneficence, but do not punish its want; we punish injustice, but do not reward its want (justice).

Thus: "Among equals…and antecedent to the institution of civil government, (each individual is) regarded as having a right both to defend himself from injuries, and to exact…punishment for those which have been done to him" (*TMS* II.ii.1.7, p. 80). "As the greater and more irreparable the evil that is done, the resentment of the sufferer runs naturally the higher" (*TMS* II.ii.2.2, p. 83).

Smith's world of propriety was the social crucible that birthed property: The sacred laws of justice begin with those that guard our life and call for the most severe penalty; next are those that guard our property and possessions; and last are those which guard what are due us from promises (*TMS* II.ii.2.2, p 84).

But why should punishment be greater for violating possession (robbery) than promises (contract)? The cause of the difference originates in a fundamental characteristic of human emotions: the asymmetry between joy and sorrow from which Smith derives the asymmetry between gains and losses.[17] The specific proposition, as he applies it in this context, is that "Breach of property...theft and robbery...take from us what we are possessed of...breach of contract...only disappoints us of what we expected" (*TMS* p. 84). The general proposition on gain/loss asymmetry is that "We suffer more...when we fall from a better to a worse situation, than we ever enjoy when we rise from a worse to a better" (*TMS* VI.i.4, p. 213; added in 6th edition, 1790). Thus are we naturally oriented to secure the advantages we have already attained and to avoid hazards that risk the loss of fortune and reputation that we have attained.

Conclusion

Consequently, *Sentiments* is about:

1　personal social exchange: antecedent to civil law, property rights first emerge as conventions by mutual voluntary consent that humbles the arrogance of self-love.[18]
2　this experience gave birth to civil law – the world of impersonal market exchange where "Vice (self-love) is beneficial found when its by justice rapt and bound" (Mandeville, 1922). The civil order provides third-party enforcement of the rules of property, thereby reducing, if not eliminating, dependence on interpersonal trust and trustworthiness. This led to *Wealth*; giving life to the calculus of utility maximization and to equilibrium economics for service in long-distance markets, but these concepts both failed in (1) where experimentalists now have recourse to long-lost and forgotten principles found in *Sentiments*.

But Smith's system of natural liberty, as stated in *Wealth*, derived its meaning from *Sentiments*: "allowing every man to pursue his own interest his own way, upon the liberal plan of equality, liberty and justice" (*WN* vol 2, p 664). "Every man, as long as he does not violate the laws of justice, is left perfectly free to pursue his own interest his own way" (*WN* v 2, p. 687).

Notes

1　Jan Osborn and Bart Wilson of the English and Economics Departments teach a Freshman Foundations Course at Chapman University entitled "Humanomics: Exchange and the Human Condition". Their readings from Adam Smith help to define humanomics as a merging of the humanities with economics.
2　John Rae imaginatively describes the context for us: "Kay, standing in his shop over at the corner of the Parliament Close, must often have seen Smith walk past from his house to his office in the morning exactly as he has depicted him in one of his portraits, in a light-coloured coat, probably linen; knee-breeches, white silk stockings, buckle shoes, and flat broad-brimmed beaver hat; walking erect with a bunch of flowers in his left hand, and his cane, held by the middle, borne on his right shoulder..." (Rae, 1895, p. 329).

3   More fully, "That in every profession the fortune of every individual should depend as much as possible upon his merit, and as little as possible upon his privilege, is certainly for the interest of the public. It is even for the interest of every particular profession, which can never so effectually support the general merit and real honour of the greater part of those who exercise it, as by resting on such liberal principles."

4   Smith left the care of his literary papers to his executors, Black and James Hutton, the famous geologist. Earlier, in 1773, Smith had asked his dear friend David Hume, the greatest of British philosophers, to serve in this capacity, but Hume died in 1776. Smith's instruction to Hume concerning his surviving papers were that "there are none worth publishing" (E. Mossner and I. Ross (1977, letter no. 137), although he implied that perhaps an exception could be made for his *History of Astronomy*. In fact, at the urging of Smith on his deathbed, Black and Hutton destroyed all his papers except the one on astronomy (See Dugald Stewart's account in Ross, 1982, pp 327–8).

5   Even in Kay's case, apprenticed as a barber at age 13, his earlier expressed skill as an artist would eventually define how he would leave a monumental mark on Scotch history (Paton, 1837, p. 2).

6   Hayek (1988, p. 18) contrasts the rules of the extended order of exchange with the "instinctual responses, such as "solidarity and altruism," of the small group, but, as I hope to show, *Sentiments* treated the latter at a deeply social-scientific level that provides the property right foundations for the extended order of markets.

7   We learn from the careful scholarship of Howey (1989, pp. 16–18) that, in September of 1862, W. S. Jevons records sending the paper "Notice of a General Mathematical Theory of Political Economy" to the British Association for the Advancement of Science; the paper was read, but only a short abstract was published in the report of the proceedings. This was Jevons' first articulation of the marginal utility and general equilibrium theories of economic equilibrium that created the modern era of (neo-classical) equilibrium economics.

8   See Young (2006), who recognized the significant contribution of *Sentiments* in the conception of property rights as an order that emerged out of human social experience. For a laboratory experimental study of whether and how property rights can arise endogenously in conjunction with specialization and exchange in an environment in which there is no external enforcement of either contracts or possession, see Kimbrough *et al.* (2010). For a now classic study in how neighbors use socially grown rules to govern twentieth-century instances of animal trespass and to settle disputes without recourse to open or closed range law or their shadow, see Elickson (1991).

9   We are informed in Buckle (1991, pp. 172–3) that Locke and other seventeenth-century writers often used "propriety" and "property" interchangeably and that "after showing an initial preference for 'propriety' in much of his work, he (Locke) changed many references to 'property' in later versions". Property was conceived as conformity to conventions that constituted proper (appropriate, approved) behavior.

10 Jeremy Bentham failed to understand these matters, asserting in effect that property comes from the legislature, thereby jump-starting a two-century diversion!

11 "That whole account of human nature, however, which deduces all sentiments and affections from self-love, which has made so much noise in the world, but which, so far as I know, has never yet been fully and distinctly explained, seems to me to have arisen from some confused misapprehension of the system of sympathy" (*TMS* p. 317).

12 In Smith, "experiments" constitute the trial-and-error contextual encounters of each person interacting with others, from which each learns while jointly fashioning the rules of just conduct. Also see *TMS* pp. 152 and 195.

13   Shakespeare expresses a form of this sentiment when Polonius advises his son:

> This above all: to thine own self be true,
> And it must follow, as the night the day,
> Thou canst not then be false to any man.

(Hamlet Act 1, scene 3)

14   See Paganelli (2009) for a discussion of Adam Smith's perspective on 'puzzels' arising in the experimental literature.

15   Hoffman *et al.* (1994) and many others have reported experiments under a "double blind (or anonymity)" condition in which no one, including the experimenter, can identify which subjects made the recorded decision choices. Hence, only the individual subject knows if her action is praise (or blame) worthy. Compared with the standard anonymity of players with respect to each other, subjects choose more self-loving payoffs. Results for double anonymity trust games are reported by Cox and Deck (2005).

16   There are other experimental means of controlling for the expression of intentions as a means of testing the predictive content of *Beneficence Proposition 1*. For example, Coricelli *et al.*, 2000, pp. 253, 288) report trust game results (the payoffs are different than in McCabe *et al.*, 2003) in which both players are humans versus Player 1's choice is made by the computer, while Player 2 is a human. Thus human intentionality is present in the first condition but not in the second. The human-player condition data $(N = 18)$ are $a - 5$; $c - 8$; $d - 5$. The computer-player condition data $(N = 18)$ are $a - 0$; $c - 2$; $d - 16$.

17   The asymmetry between gains and losses is reflected in the study of decision making under risk, perhaps one of the most important empirical findings reported by modern cognitive psychologists (Kahneman and Tversky, 1979).

18   The idea is expressed in Hayek's (1973, p. 162) quote from the third-century Roman jurist, Julius Paulus: "What is right is not derived from the rule but the rule arises from our knowledge of what is right" (Hayek, 1973, p. 162). *Sentiments* articulates a process theory of how we acquire and produce social knowledge of what is right and fashion the rules governing our conduct under that knowledge.

Bibliography

Camerer, C. (2003) *Behavioral Game Theory: Experiments in Strategic Interaction*, Princeton, NJ: Princeton University Press.

Cox, J.C. and Deck, C.A. (2005) "On the nature of reciprocal motives," *Economic Inquiry*, 43: 623–35.

Ellickson, R.C. (1991) *Order Without Law*, Cambridge: Harvard University Press.

Hoffman, E., McCabe, K., Shachat, K. and Smith, V.L. (1994) "Preferences, property rights, and anonymity in bargaining experiments," *Games and Economic Behavior*, 7(3): 346–80.

Howey, R.S. (1989) *The Rise of the Marginal Utility School.* New York: Columbia University Press.

Kahneman, D. and Tversky, A. (1979) "Prospect theory: An analysis of decision under risk," *Econometrica*, 47: 263–91.

Kimbrough, E., Smith, V.L. and Wilson, B. (2010) "Exchange, theft, and the social formation of property," *Journal of Economic Behavior and Organization*, 74: 206–29.

Mandeville, B. (1922) *The Fable of the Bees: or, Private Vices, Publick Benefits*. Oxford: Oxford University Press.

McCabe, K., Rigdon, M. and Smith, V.L. (2003) "Positive reciprocity and intentions in trust games," *Journal of Economic Behavior and Organization*, 52(2): 267–75.

Mossner, E. and Ross, I. (1977) *The Correspondence of Adam Smith. Glasgow Edition of the Works and Correspondence of Adam Smith*, Oxford: Oxford University Press. Letter no. 143: 178.

Muirhead, J.P. (1858) *Life of James Watt with Selections from His Correspondence*, London: John Murray.

Paganelli, M.P. (2009) "Smithian answers to some experimental puzzles," *Elgar Companion to Adam Smith*, edited by Jeffrey Young. Cheltenham: Edward Elgar, pp. 181–92.

Paton, H. (1837/1877) *A Series of Original Portraits and Caricature Etchings by the Late John Kay, Miniature Painter, Edinburgh with Biographical Sketches and Illustrated Anecdotes*, Vol. 1. Edinburgh: Adam and Charles Black.

Pellew, G. (1847) *The Life and Correspondence of the Right Honorable Henry Addington, First Viscount Sidmouth*, Volume 1. London: John Murray.

Ryle, G. (1945–1946) "Knowing how and knowing that: the presidential address," *Proceedings of the Aristotelian Society*, New Series, 46: 1–16.

Ross, I.S. (1982) *Adam Smith Essays on Philosophical Subjects*, Indianapolis, IN: Liberty Fund.

Wilson, B. (2010) "Social preferences aren't preferences," *Journal of Economic Behavior and Organization*, 73(1): 77–82.

Wilson, B. (2012) "Contra private fairness," *American Journal of Economics and Sociology*, 71(2): 407–35.

Young, J.T. (2006) "Adam Smith and new institutional theories of property rights," *Adam Smith Review*, Volume 2, edited by Vivienne Brown. New York: Routledge.

Articles

Adam Smith and the rights of the dead

Alan Lopez

'I have so much to do—
And yet—Existence—some way back—
Stopped—struck—my ticking—through—'

Emily Dickinson

I

Immanuel Kant tells us in his 'Third Definitive Article for a Perpetual Peace' [1795] that the Earth is property shared by all human beings (Kant 1983: para. 358). This argument follows Kant's plea for what he calls a 'cosmopolitan right…of universal *hospitality*' (ibid., emphasis in original).[1] It is the idea that we have a '*right to visit*, to associate', indeed, to 'belong', based on 'our common ownership of the earth's surface' (ibid.). What is notable about Kant's argument for hospitality is that, although originally genetic, in the sense that this right to hospitality is derived from the fact that 'originally no one had a greater right to any region of the earth than anyone else', it becomes clear that Kant's reasons are not simply structural, but ethical (ibid.).[2] Owing to the fact that we share this 'earth' which 'is a globe, [we] cannot scatter ourselves infinitely', must, finally, 'tolerate living in close proximity' (ibid.).[3] It is this idea of toleration to which John Locke appeals in his earlier *Letter Concerning Toleration* [1689], which is not that we should tolerate the conditions in which we live, against which in some instances Locke argues, but that we should tolerate and indeed respect others' rights to be.[4] Locke's is a noble aim, but one that becomes troubled once we recall that we all share this globe. Kant strengthens Locke's claim by arguing that the argument for hospitality should rest not upon moral whim,[5] which in Locke allows refusal of toleration to certain groups, but upon this shared right to the earth, what Kant in his *Metaphysics of Morals*, only two years after 'Perpetual Peace', will call '[t]his rational idea of a *peaceful* [1797], even if not friendly, thoroughgoing community of all nations on the earth…a principle *having to do with rights*' (Kant 1998: 6: 352; emphasis in original).

But while it is one thing to say we share the earth with one other, what does it mean to say we share the earth with the dead?[6] This is the question that Adam

Smith asks in his *Lectures on Jurisprudence*. How 'sacred' should we consider the will of the dead, let alone the 'Will of a dead Friend'? (Corr. Letter 156 from Hume, 3 May 1776).[7] In determining 'how far the right of the dead might extend,' if indeed 'they h[ave] any at all', hence in asking '[w]hat obligation [a]…community [is] under to observe the directions he made concerning his goods' (LJ(A) i.150), Smith anticipates Kant's hospitality, (Smith 1982: LJ(B), para. 169) since in Smith's view this question of obligation can be answered only by answering the even more fundamental question of who counts, as in who counts as 'subjects of a state' (LJ(B), para. 86). One drawback of Kant's right of hospitality is that, despite the wide reach he reserves for equality and the sharing of the earth, the right itself is quite narrow, consisting only of 'the right of an alien not to be treated as an enemy upon his arrival in another's country' (Kant 1983: para. 358).[8] This is notable in its contradistinction to Kant's earlier insistence, in 'Theory and Practice' [1793], that all individuals possess these rights, those of '*equality*' and '*freedom*' and '*independence*', '*a priori*', simply by virtue of our being 'a human being' (Kant 1983: para. 290; emphasis in original), as in 'a being who is in general capable of having rights' (para. 291). Although Kant says that we possess these rights owing to our shared humanity, he also says they are enforceable only to the extent that we are 'a member of the commonwealth' (para. 291). It is only in civil society where these rights are secured and their exercise guaranteed, since it is only in civil society where observation of them can be enforced through what Kant calls 'coercion' (para. 290), thus 'public law' (para. 292). So, for Kant, determining the reach of these inalienable rights, let alone a right of hospitality, similarly becomes a question of who counts as a citizen of the state. Are the dead citizens of the state? If Kant's is our criterion, the dead would seem to have three strikes against them.[9] As Patrick R. Frierson observes, '[t]he dead are not human, not sentient, and not even living' (Frierson 2006: 453). Where, then, does this leave the dead?

Smith insists that the dead have rights, just not of the rational sort identified by Kant; the dead possess what Smith more modestly calls a right to 'piety', known in the ecclesial vernacular as 'a reverence for the will of the dead', the sense 'that the will of the deceased with respect to his goods or heirs should be observed' (LJ(A) i.161). Smith soon enough moves away from this ecclesial foundation in his account of the rights of the dead, loosening the impersonal language of 'should' to the somewhat more convivial and inviting 'regard we all naturaly have to the will of a dying person' (LJ(A) i.150), the 'pleasure' '[w]e naturaly find…in remembering the last words of a friend and in executing his last injunctions' (LJ(B) para. 165).[10] But the point is the same, and it turns on Smith's language of 'last words' and 'last injunctions'. We 'regard' this last 'request' (para. 165), according to Smith, what he earlier calls 'the right we conceive men to have to dispose of their goods after their death' (LJ(A) i.149), not so much because this is 'a piece of piety not to be dispensed with' (i.161), which, while true in some respects, suggests a kind of relenting in favor of avoiding punishment to ourselves, but rather owing to the 'impiety' and indeed 'injury' we 'conceive [would] be done to the dead person' were we 'not to comply with [their] desire' (LJ(B) para. 165), in this instance that slight acknowledgment, itself the basis of testamentary succession at all, that 'the heir of blood is [not] always thought the preferable one' (LJ(B) para. 156). The novelty of Smith's account of succession, meaning most simply his 'found[ing]' it 'on piety and affection to the dead' (para. 89), lies in the very creative way this wrests the right from any jurisprudential foundation. And which is where this right of the dead becomes interesting, hence a matter of jurisprudence, which is when its extension infringes upon the rights of those who are properly subjects of the state – those of the living.[11] And since we are dealing with 'inanimated bodies' (Smith 1982 *TMS*: I.i.13), when we refer to any acts of infringement, from dead to living, we naturally mean those rights possessed when the deceased was alive, what Jean Barbeyrac, in his commentary on Samuel Pufendorf's *Of the Law of Nature and Nations* [1706], calls our appeal to that right that we might have the 'liberty' to 'dispose of [our] Goods at [our] Death', the liberty to 'leave them to such Persons as [w]e love' (Pufendorf 1749: 420 n. 2). These are thus the rights of testamentary succession, or those rights, entails, belonging to what Smith calls '[t]he greatest of all extensions of property' (LJ(B), para. 166). To the extent that we do wish to observe the rights of the dead, what Pufendorf gingerly interprets as the 'Management of what belong'd to the dead', our 'Care of [those]…who are no longer Members of human society' (1749: 420), how far may we extend these rights, the rights of those 'reckon'd as no body in civil Consideration' (418), without infringing upon the rights of those who are, or those of the living? Which is the question: what are the demands the dead may make upon the living?

II

While nowadays testamentary succession is an accepted practice with little fanfare, although gifts bequeathed to universities can be of note, and one has usually heard a story of an individual leaving their estate to beloved family pets, this normalcy was not the case for Adam Smith (Friedman 2009: 75–76). Smith saw as a real challenge the possibility of testamentary succession at all, let alone the question of how far it may reasonably extend, putting it plainly: 'There is no point more difficult to account for than the right we conceive men to have to dispose of their goods after their death. For at what time is it that this right takes place[?]' (LJ(A) i.149). To be fair, the question mark is mine; Smith is not asking a question, to which he already knows the answer, so much as expressing incredulity at the point when this right is understood to take place, which, as he tells us, is '[j]ust at the very time that the person ceases (to have?) the power of disposing of them' (ibid.). This is where Smith's real questions begin.[12] On the one hand, it makes sense why testamentary succession, what Smith calls 'the testamentary heir['s]…claim or right to any of the testators goods', takes place when it does, which, as Smith explains, is not 'untill the moment that he is dead; for till that time he can not even have any reasonable expectation of his possessing them, as the testator may alter his inclination' (ibid.). But then what interests Smith is not the heir's right to the property, but that moment in which the testator transfers possession of this right, which happens to be the same time the testator 'ceases to have the power of disposing of [property]'.

As living and breathing persons, we all possess what Smith calls a natural right 'to dispose of [our] property while [w]e live' (LJ(B), para. 164). But this 'power of disposing of [our] goods (LJ(A) i.149)', what Samuel Pufendorf (1749: 418) calls the 'transferring of Right from one to another Person', does 'suppose the existence of the two Parties at the time of its Date; so that henceforward the thing may be said to be estrang'd from him who thus transferr'd it' (418). This is what Pufendorf means by 'alienation' (418), Smith by disposal of our property, both of which become, in the vernacular of 'transfer[ence of] things by *Testament*', and here Pufendorf appeals to Hugo Grotius' *Rights of War and Peace* [1625], 'the *Alienation of a whole Estate in the case of Death*' (418; emphasis in original). It is here where for Smith this right of property is undone, which is when it attempts to explain those matters, 'On account of Death', where 'things are convey'd from one Person to another' (418). '[S]o long as he draws Breath', Pufendorf tells us, the dying, the '[t]estator', 'retains a full and absolute Right to all his Goods, without the least Diminution' (418). This right is what we appeal to 'in every Act of Alienation', as in those acts, qua alienation, consisting of 'two Parties [in] join[ed] Consents; the one from whom, and the other to whom the thing is transferr'd' (418). Yet 'these Consents', that which 'unit[es]' us 'by [our] conspiring, as it were, together at the same time,' additionally suppose that a transfer can, indeed, 'be made at that time' (418), what Barbeyrac calls the right's 'depend[ance]...upon the mutual Consent of Parties' (418 n. 1). This is complicated somewhat if the time in this instance refers to 'that time, when in respect of the Party who should alienate, nothing can be call'd his own or another's' (418). Yet it is just this time to which testamentary succession refers, what Pufendorf calls our 'Moment of...Death', or that moment we 'loseth immediately all the Right [w]e held whilst alive' (418), and so what Smith himself refers to when he asks, in his jurisprudence lectures, 'how is it that a man comes to have a power of disposing as he pleases of his goods after his death' (LJ(A) i.149–150). This, for Smith, is the stumbling block to testamentary succession, and the difference between it and 'legal succession' (LJ(B), para. 155).[13] The testator 'cannot be said to transferr his right, for the heir has no right in consequence of the testament till after the testator himself have none' (para. 164). By what means, then, does such a thing take place, where one of the parties, dead, does what, 'properly speaking', one should have no right to do? (ibid.)

The idea behind testamentary succession, as in why it takes place when we 'have nothing to do with the things of this World', 'only' when we 'are not in a condition to make it of Force [ourselves]', is the assumption of what Jean Barbeyrac calls the 'reasonable' '[m]an' (Pufendorf 1749: 420 n. 2).[14] Pufendorf reminds us that '[a]lienation' begins with the acceptance as sincere the 'Declarations of a[nother's] Intentions' (419), as in a promise to alienate property, to borrow Hugo Grotius' language, becomes 'mutua[lly] Oblig[ing]' once 'it is...accepted', or 'Acceptance...be signified to the Promisor' (Grotius 2005: 720). Alienation is thus not quite the idea that by simply declaring my intention to transfer I thereby do transfer my property into another's possession, as if without the chance to 'recall' my intentions (Pufendorf 1749: 419). I certainly can recall my intentions, as Grotius for instance tells us, so long as the revoking is done before such acceptance is signified, hence 'before it…obtain[s] its full Effect' (Grotius: 720). But for all intents and purposes, this declared intent to alienate creates what Smith will later call 'a reasonable ground of expectation' in the promisee (LJ(A) ii.56). On account of my acceptance of another's declared intention to alienate, as in my saying or signifying, '*This Engagement shall stand good, if it be accepted; … This shall stand good, if I understand that it is accepted*' (Grotius: 720; emphasis in original), I thereby 'transfer such a Right on the Person towards whom it is directed, that it shall not be disannull'd at the bare Pleasure of the Alienator [myself]' (Pufendorf 1749: 419).[15] This is how alienation works amongst the living: the acceptance as 'valid' (Grotius: 720) one's expressed 'Intent thereby to transfer a proper Right to another' (708), an intent which, once accepted, puts on the promisor an 'Obligation' to deliver, and, on the promisee, a 'Right' to demand that delivery (Pufendorf 1749: 419). It becomes clear what would happen if accepted intent did not, in fact, transfer a right to another: the loss of any 'contracted' 'Obligation' to transfer, nor 'acqui[sition of] any Right' to demand transfer (419). Yet this is the situation in which testator and heir find themselves, a Carrollean 'Promise' understood as, '*You shall have, one time or another, somewhat which I now possess, provided you don't displease me in the mean while; but then you shall have no Right to hinder me from being displeas'd at any time when I think fit, or without any manner of Reason*' (419; emphasis in original).[16] It is the dying's will, or what Barbeyrac calls that 'great Difference between an Alienation by Will, and a bare verbal Declaration of a present Design to give something one time or another, to a certain Person' (418 n. 1). Because the heir's right to the testator's property does not 'commenceth' until 'at the Testator's Death', the heir 'has not, before that Moment, any Right which can be said to depend on the Death of the Party as on a Condition' (419).[17] Since this is our last will and testament, or what '*is mutable and revocable at our Pleasure*', it is a document which only becomes a 'full and perfect Right against' us and our words when we similarly cease to have any possession of either (419; emphasis in original). This is why we can declare an intent to transfer without therefore transferring any right against ourselves, since so long as we do live we never lose this right as testator, as in '[that] most absolute Right of possessing and enjoying [our] Property' while we live (419), which most simply is this right to say, until we can say no more, that 'perhaps the first Opinion was the better' (Grotius: 703). As this is our will, we 'may', if we so choose, 'alienate [our] Goods' to another, 'or [even] strike out those who at present stand Heirs' (Pufendorf 1749: 419), and this, this literal retraction of our declared intent, our 'revok[ing of the] Will' (418 n. 1), 'without any Possibility of Redress' (419), hence 'without the least Diminution' of possession of our goods (419). This is Barbeyrac's 'reasonable man'; it is the assumption that 'no Man Should tie his own Hands', as in do in life what 'Death alone should [do]' (423 n. 3), what Barbeyrac calls this transfer of the 'Power of disposing of our Goods in case of Death' (420 n. 2). For bind our hands is what we would do if we ourselves did transfer this right, which is give to the heir that 'full and irrevocable Right' (418 n. 1) to what we ourselves, '*whilst we live*' (419), 'have Power to enjoy' (418 n. 1), hence to '*revo[ke] at our Pleasure*' (419; emphasis in original).[18]

Smith's answer,[19] as we saw earlier, lies not in the dead's transference of a right, properly speaking, but in the more simple observance of this 'period' itself, the moment of our last words, what Smith calls '[t]hat period…of so momentous a nature that every thing that is connected with it seems to be so also' (LJ(A) i.150).[20] Smith pauses for some time before this moment, explaining his rest by insisting that is when '[t]he advices, the commands, and even the very fooleries of the dying have more effect on us than things of the same nature would have had at any other period' (ibid).[21] In gathering up within ourselves the advices, the commands, and even the fooleries of the dying person, dramatized by Smith as 'a man on his death bed call[ing] his friends together and entreat[ing], beseech[ing], and conjur[ing] them to dispose of his goods in such or such a manner', we find ourselves, 'as it were, forced by [our] piety to the deceased person to dispose of his goods as he desired; [we] imagine what he would think were he to see [us] disposing of them in a manner contrary to what they were so solemnly intreated', as 'if', for instance, 'he should look up from the grave and see things going contrary to what he had enjoined', and that it is out of these imaginative considerations, our supposing what our friend, 'if he was then alive', would feel if he saw things going differently than so intreated, that we aim, as far as we can, to 'dispose of his goods as he desired' (LJ(A) i.151).[22] Although the act is 'illus[ory]', an instance of 'fancy', yet this way we, seemingly quite 'naturally' (*TMS* I.i.1.13), 'chang[e] places in fancy with the sufferer' (I.i.1.3), assume as ours their 'distress…regret…love, and…lamentations' (I.i.2.1), is why, Smith insists, we sympathize, and so why, finally, 'We sympathize even with the dead' (*TMS* I.i.1.13).[23]

Smith is drawing upon imagery in a passage of his in *Theory of Moral Sentiments*, three years before delivery of these 1762–63 lectures on jurisprudence. Smith returns to the passage, in *Moral Sentiments*, in his even later 1766 jurisprudence lectures. Although Smith composes the first edition of *Moral Sentiments* seven years before his 1766 jurisprudence lectures, his is a fondness for *Moral Sentiments*' imagery of death, since we see this imagery in his later lectures on jurisprudence. Although we know we are reading of our piety for the dead, in Smith's lectures, yet we find ourselves drawn back to *Moral Sentiments*, the difference between our present piety for the dead and our earlier sympathy for the dead just so small: that we 'enter as it were into his dead body, and conceive what our living souls would feel if they were joined with his body, and how much we would be distressed to see our last injunctions not performed' (LJ(B), para. 165). And, indeed, the two definitions are close. In *Moral Sentiments* Smith touches death with a light, and most general hand; what we sympathize with, in our sympathy with the dead, is the 'dread of death' (*TMS* I.i.1.13): 'to be no more thought of in this world, but to be obliterated, in a little time, from the affections, and almost from the memory, of…dearest friends and relations' (I.i.1.13). In his lectures on jurisprudence, though, Smith's touch is all the more acute. What in earlier *Moral Sentiments* is an impersonal 'dread of death', and impersonal because it is not loss as such we dread as its certitude, becomes in the lectures the loss that can only come from 'dearest friends and relations': that in our last attempt to stave off death, we would be thwarted, and not by death, but by these same friends. We read, for instance, of the 'distress' we should feel in seeing 'our last injunctions not performed', yet also the 'impiety' and 'injury' (LJ(B), para. 165), and this because these 'last injunctions' happen to be our last will and testament. Although Smith draws no further connection to the paragraph in *Moral Sentiments*, beyond this borrowing of imagery, it is the paragraph we nevertheless find ourselves before as we read its counterpart in his 1766 lectures on jurisprudence. While perhaps unintended by Smith, his arrangement of these passages, in *Moral Sentiments*, 1766 jurisprudence lectures, reveals a larger argument on what for Smith we 'dread' in our 'dread of death', which is not our loss from the world, but loss of our place in the 'affections' and 'memory' of loved ones still in the world. When Smith writes of the 'injury' we should imagine in seeing our goods 'dispos[ed]…in a manner contrary to what they were so solemnly intreated'; hence, when he writes of 'how much we would be distressed to see our last injunctions not performed', we return to that passage in *Moral Sentiments*, and this because the injury Smith refers to is that imagined absence of affection found in *Moral Sentiments*, the idea that if we find 'our last injunctions not performed', it is owing, indeed, to that 'so dreadful a calamity' (*TMS* I.i.1.13), our having been 'forgot by everybody' (I.i.1.13). When present, these are the memories by which a friend assumes as theirs our 'distress…regret…and…lamentations', and so carries out, as if their own, our last injunctions. Hence, they are the memories, when absent, which find us before the contrary, the realization, as we look from our grave, that what we had 'intended', as '[our] last Appointment', 'should be intended in vain' (Pufendorf 1749: 424). Yet, we do extend our hands, and so, in turn, extend the hands of another, even those whom 'Death [has] remove[d]…from all Concerns' (420), since this imagined 'misery' (*TMS* 1.i.1.1), this 'awful futurity' (1.i.1.13), however much 'but a Fiction of the mind' (Hobbes, 2003: 16), is ourselves 'shut out from life and conversation' (*TMS* 1.i.1.13). But if piety is why 'we [allow] prefer[ence for] the person made heir in the testament to the heir at law if he has one' (LJ(A) i.150), why we are 'enclined…to extend property a little farther than a man's lifetime' (LJ(B), para. 165), what do we make of that 'extension of property' (para. 168) belonging to entails, that 'extension of…power' which asks our piety 'to the end of the world'? (para. 166)?[24]

III

What Smith refers to as 'entails' is an ecclesial tradition, after testamentary succession, that enables the dying to restrict the manner in which their property is succeeded and divided by will (LJ(B), para. 167).[25] Smith refers to entails in a few places in his works, though is arguably most clear in *Wealth of Nations*, published a decade after delivery of his 1766 lectures on jurisprudence [1776], where he describes entails as

> the natural consequences of the laws of primogeniture. They were first introduced to preserve a certain lineal succession, of which the law of primogeniture first gave the idea, and to hinder any part of the original estate

> from being carried out of the proposed line either by gift, or devise, or
> alienation; either by folly, or by the misfortune of any of its successive owners.
>
> (Smith 1981: l. 3, ch. 2: 384)

Smith's foreboding language gives us some idea why he reserves for entails the designation of 'greatest of all extensions of property'. On the one hand, entails are similar to normal, testamentary succession; they allow us to place limits on the succession of our goods and property, limits referring to specific heirs.[26] On its face this is innocent enough, and indeed Smith has no qualms in reserving the dying a right to choose their heirs. What troubles Smith, and so where in his mind entails move beyond testamentary succession, is in the incredible reach they allow the dying to restrict this manner of succession, as in this right to insist 'that all gifts of the testator should be valid in the very manner he appointed, and that no one of the heirs c[an] alienate what was entailed to his heirs' (LJ(A) i.163). It is the idea that, to comply with our dying wishes, for instance that our property continue indefinitely and continue exclusively through several generations of sons or daughters, so must we retain this right to forbid any heirs, even the children themselves, from alienating our property.[27] Such a move would violate the intent of our original will to include only lineal sons or daughters, assuming their presence, hence break the stipulated chain of succession.[28] The real purpose for entailing a will becomes clear: to ensure indefinite possession of one's property. Smith, to his credit, observes that 'there can be nothing more absurd than this custom of entails' (LJ(A) i.164). Now, it is again no infringement on our 'reason' or 'piety' to insist '[t]hat a man should have the power of determining what shall be done with his goods after his death' (ibid.).[29] This, after all, as Smith explains, is the 'foundation of testamentary succession', the idea that 'property [should] extend a little farther than a man's lifetime' (LJ(B), para. 165). Where for Smith problems emerge, and why in the end he calls entails, together with the right of primogeniture, an 'unnaturall right' (LJ(A) ii.1), is in this notion that the dying 'should have the power of determining how they shall dispose of it, and so on in infinitum', which, as Smith insists, 'has no foundation in this piety and is the most absurd thing in the world' ((LJ(A) i.164).[30]

What troubles Smith about entails is how they undermine the simplest of all our maxims, which is 'that the earth is the property of each generation' (LJ(A) i.164). Common sense tells us that each generation has the same rights to property as those before or after it, as in the notion that no 'preceding [generation] can have [a] right to bind it up [the earth] from posterity' (LJ(B), para. 168).[31] With the introduction of entails, we find ourselves confronted with a new world view. Now we may reserve for ourselves the right to 'restrict' any generation's subsequent 'use' of our property (LJ(A) i.164). The problems this opens up are many, but one interests us in particular: the erasure of this distinction between past, present, and future possession of property. Once one entails a will, it is no longer possible to distinguish between what is 'altogether' the property of our 'predecessors' and what is the property of 'our[s]', since there is no longer a distinction between the two (ibid.). Such distinctions require not only acknowledgment of the passage of property from one set of hands to another, but a temporal marking of each successive generation's ownership of that property. Entails work by removing these limitations of finitude. But in so doing, entails remove what constitutes our shared humanity as human beings, which is our shared mortality. By 'mortality', I mean not that we do not go on forever, which is more of a structural argument, but rather the responsibility that follows therefrom: that as finite beings on a finite surface we share an obligation to respect the property and rights of others, as in the responsibility to acknowledge our finitude, but also the consequent finitude of any claims of ours to possession of property.[32] This is obviously incompatible with the logic of entails. It is this 'absurd[ity]' Smith refers to when he describes the power of entails as akin to saying 'that our ancestors who lived 500 years ago should have had the power of disposing of all lands at this time', where what we have before us, as Jacques Derrida explains, is a 'conjunction of singularities that partake of, and in the future will continue to partake of, the *same date*' (Derrida 2005: 32; emphasis in original). Entails threaten humanity by indefinitely preserving it.[33]

Owing to this fatal sense of loss, which is the loss of the right to declare ourselves autonomous persons, the question inevitably presents itself: 'to find at what period we are to put an end to the power we have granted a dying person of disposing of his goods' (LJ(A) i.165). But nor is there an easy solution. While we might agree that entails allow the dying too much control in posterity, this does not address the more fundamental problem presented by entails, which is identifying an 'evident time at which this should cease' (ibid.). Smith, however, does arrive at a solution, which returns us to our shared mortality. 'The best rule seems to be', Smith explains, 'that we should permit the dying person to dispose of his goods as far as he sees, that is, to settle how it shall be divided amongst those who are alive at the same time with him' (ibid.). In answering the question of where to draw the line in extending succession, Smith returns us to our mortality, to the fact that we cannot indefinitely extend our hand. But in asking us to consider our finitude, so does Smith return us to our piety. It is our piety to which Smith appeals when he explains why the dying person's property ought to be divided in this way, between those with whom he lived, since it is with these people that 'he may have contracted some affection' (ibid.). This shared affection is what for Smith we appeal to when we say that a dying person has the right 'to settle the succession amongst them' (ibid.). But it is also what for Smith we appeal to when we say that there should be a limit to entails. As it makes sense to limit the powers of entails to those with whom we have shared affection, so is it similarly owing to this logic of mortality that Smith finds it troubling to extend them beyond this point of fellow-feeling, such as to persons 'who are not born' (ibid.). For the question naturally arises: how do we share 'affection' with those from whom there is 'no affection' to share? (LJ(A) i.165).

It is our mortality to which we refer when we entail our will. Since we know that we will not live forever but because we wish to preserve in our posterity some semblance of ourselves, as realized, for instance, in our property, so do we place entails on our will; this allows us to retain possession of ourselves through successive generations. But it is also because of this shared mortality that entails are problematic. In indefinitely securing our rights to our goods and property, we bind the hands of every successive generation to that property. We foreclose anyone else's right to it. This is untenable within this idea that subsequent individuals have the same rights to property and autonomy as the dying did while alive.[34] Our shared mortality, the fact that we do die, addresses the need for a line of demarcation, some understanding that, while in death we acquire this right to extend possession of our property, it is not a right to extend that possession indefinitely, as in to the point that we infringe upon another's own right to own property. The question before Smith is thus one of how far, as in how far the dead may extend their possession of property. It is a question whose answer for Smith returns us to our piety, as in how far we may reasonably permit the dead, on account of our 'reverence' (LJ(A) i.161) for their will, imagined pain to ourselves, to extend their fellow-feeling towards others. And Smith's answer is only as far as those with whom the dead, indeed, has shared 'some' affection, hence shared the same time in life.[35] Beyond this, Smith insists, hence beyond '[t]he utmost stretch of [their]' own mortality, affection 'can not reasonably extend' (LJ(A) i.166). Although piety for the dead's wishes obliges us to extend their affections, hence possession of property, beyond their own lifetimes, it is sympathy with the living's which asks that we limit the reach of that possession, a limit which in Smith's hands becomes no further than those with whom the dead could have shared time and affection, as in no further than ourselves, those who would yet possess a 'fresh' 'memory' of the dead in their 'mind' (LJ(B), para. 168).

Francis Hutcheson reminds us that a contract is a contract insofar as there is '[t]he consent of both parties, of the receiver as well as the giver' (Hutcheson 2007: 161), what Hugo Grotius describes as 'some sufficient Sign to testify [to] the Consent of the Will' (Grotius 2005: 717).[36] Hutcheson insists that this consent, which 'may sometimes be done by a Nod, but generally by Word of Mouth or Writing' (Grotius: 717), 'is necessary in all translation either of property or any other rights' (Hutcheson: 161). It is what Smith himself calls 'voluntary transference' (LJ(A) ii.1). Though Smith distinguishes this from succession by inheritance, which he calls an '[e]xclusive priviledge', and this owing to the fact that '[t]he heir, previous to any other person, has a priviledge of demanding what belonged to the deceased', he does not say this is a strict demarcation (LJ(B), para. 174). Indeed, it is via Smith's language of 'priviledge', rather than right, that he identifies a limit to the reach of the legal heir, whose privilege we will recall may be abrogated by the preference of the dying in testamentary succession (para. 149). Smith's appeal to preference leaves room for alternative measures of property transference, as in voluntary transference. Where this affinity is most close is in Smith's attempt to determine the reach of entails, and so property transference more generally, the 'possession' of which, Smith similarly concedes, 'is not so easy to determine' (para. 170). Smith appeals to at least one aspect of voluntary transference in his account of entails, which in Scotland is its 'use' of 'a symbolical delivery' (ibid.). Delightfully reminding us of the beauty of synecdoche, Smith observes: 'An ear or sheaf of corn signifies the whole field, a stone and turf the estate to the center of the earth, and the keys of the door, the house' (ibid.). These figures are similar to Smith's language of shared 'affection'; they stand in for the word, hence the preference, of the dying. Transference, in testamentary succession, is not reducible to the simple matter, as in legal succession, 'of excluding all others from the possession untill he [heir] determine in whether he will enter heir or not' (LJ(A) ii.27); this presupposes that at stake in this transference is the blood line rather than what is more correctly the preference of the dying; while this preference, as Smith explains, may certainly include 'our ancestors', or the lineal heir, so may it include 'any other person' (LJ(B), para. 149). But as Smith notes, and so where he runs into trouble in following voluntary transference so closely, this is only delivery, and '[b]esides delivery, a charter or writing shewing on what terms the transference was made is also requisite for security' (para. 170). While one may hold in safe keeping, upon arrival of another, a key, and so in this sense, at least symbolically, indicate a 'design' to transfer this right of property to another, Smith reminds us that 'there is no right without possession', possession which in this case of property is 'shew[n]', hence 'distinctly signified' and 'secure[d]', only in this shared act of writing, an act unfortunately requiring 'the will[s]' of both, 'transferrer' and 'transferré'.[37] It becomes clear where the entailed will becomes troubled; this condition of mutual consent, what Gershom Carmichael calls 'concurrent consent' (Carmichael 2002: 103), Pufendorf as what 'is usually made known by outward *Signs*' (Pufendorf 2003: 111; emphasis in original), could not be met if there is no one to reciprocate this consent. Yet this counter-sign is necessary so that there is a contract, a sign, to borrow D. L. Carey Miller's language, 'point[ing] to a mutual intention that ownership should pass' (Miller 1998: 53), and so a sign which would declare that transferrer and transferree indeed shared the same time and affection. It is on the impossibility of this counter-sign, this acceptance of contract, that Smith demarcates the space of the entail, his recognition of what is 'manifestly absurd' in this 'power to dispose of estates for ever', which is the power to do so without consent, the consent, for instance, found in our shared time and affection, and so that consent, figured as those 'principals of testamentary succession', which 'can by no means take place' in 'perpetual entails' (LJ(B), para. 168).[38]

In his reading of Paul Celan's 'Psalm', Jacques Derrida notes that '[t]o address no one is not exactly not to address any one' (Derrida 2005: 42). Although in our moment of death we 'speak to no one' (42), in the sense that those to whom we will speak, the scene, in which we will speak, is yet to arrive, to the extent that we do speak to no one, so do we assume for ourselves the burden, what Derrida calls the '*risk*' (42; emphasis in original), of what it means to offer one's piety and blessings to another, this understanding that when it does come our time to bless, or be blessed, 'there might be no one to bless, no one who can bless' (42).[39] Still, we take consolation in this, telling ourselves, perhaps, 'is this not the only chance for blessing', that blessing arrives as 'an act of faith?' (42). 'What would a blessing be,' we might say, 'that was sure of itself?' (42) Faith is for Derrida the possibility of blessing. Derrida appeals to faith, in a manner of speaking, in order to lift the gift, indeed the '*given[ness]*' of blessing, above the constraints of '[j]udgment... certitude, [and] dogma' (42; emphasis in original), what Derrida calls those 'contestation[s] in the name of "knowledge"', 'proof' (82; emphasis in original). Derrida does this that blessing may remain this interaction of 'someone *engag[ing]* [oneself] with regard to someone else', where the only 'oath' spoken, an oath, of course, 'implicit' (82; emphasis in original), is that this blessing is given as a blessing, as in 'never assured', guaranteed, but '*given*' (42; emphasis in original). But in so doing, so does Derrida ensure that blessing, this 'act of faith without possible proof' (83), will always 'belong to a foreign space' (82), always this question whether 'to *believe* it or *not believe* it' (82; emphasis in original). It is the foreignness found in the blessings of the dying. Inasmuch as these blessings are always yet to arrive, in the sense that theirs is that time only after their own, so do they belong to that time which, though we may imaginatively share with another, could never be a time shared in time with another.[40] Yet, this is also the only way such a blessing could be given, the 'word' (83) of the dead, which, like 'a token, a symbol, a tessera, a trope, a table, or a code', but at any rate a 'word', 'circulates' (40).[41] While this is, on the one hand, the circulation which reveals the word of the dead to be like all other words, as in finite, the finitude, say, which does take the shape of 'ellipsis, discontinuity, caesura, or discretion' (40), so is it, on the other, that circulation which reveals the word of the dead to be unlike any other word.[42] Although all words are given as an 'opened...word' (60), the openness by which they are put into motion as words, the word of the dead, by contrast, 'is, above all, opened' (60), the acknowledgment, ours, that our final words can only be a question.[43]

Acknowledgments

My sincerest thanks to Fonna Forman, for her generous editorial support and encouragement of this essay; anonymous reviewers, who helped make my argument clearer; Rachel Ablow, Branka Arsić, Costica Bradatan, Joseph R. Chaney, Ken Dauber, Susan Eilenberg, Graham Hammill, David E. Johnson, Salah el Moncef bin Khalifa, Ruth Mack, Heather Mezosi, Joel Reed, Ken Smith, and Henry Sussman, for helpful notes, comments, and readings during various stages of the writing process; Maureen Kennedy, Interlibrary Loan Supervisor at Franklin D. Schurz Library at Indiana University South Bend, for generously allowing my use of the library and its services for this project; I am most thankful.

Notes

1   For a lucid account of Kant's political philosophy, see Ripstein (2009).
2   See Seyla Benhabib's disagreement with Jeremy Waldron on this point (Benhabib 2006: 41 n. 16).
3   Locke 1993: 127; Locke 2010: 57.
4   On consent in Locke, see Simmons 1993, especially: 147–192.
5   Locke denies toleration to atheists (Locke 2010: 52–53).
6   I gratefully acknowledge Niamh Reilly's 'Cosmopolitan Feminism and Human Rights' for helping me to ground this discussion (Reilly 2007).
7   Ironically, Smith himself would not honor Hume's last request (Corr. Letter 172 from Smith to William Strahan, 5 September 1776).

8   I am additionally drawing upon Jeremy Waldron's observation 'that the principle requiring hospitality more or less exhausts the content of cosmopolitan right' (Benhabib 2006: 88).

9   In US law, three strikes, or three felonies, are grounds for indefinitely being put 'behind bars' (Kant 1983: 'Perpetual Peace', para. 376).

10 Although chronologically Smith's position here, in his 1762–1763 lectures on jurisprudence, follows the one he gives a few paragraphs earlier, which does not contain the word 'should', and thus would seem the more definitive of the two, it is that previous position and not this one, which shapes my reading of his position on the rights of the dead, since it is that earlier position which is most consistent with his even later claim, in his 1766 lectures on jurisprudence, that what finally 'founds' (LJ(B), para. 165) testamentary succession is simply our 'piety and affection to the dead' (LJ(B), para. 89).

11 My framing of this problem as one of infringement between dead and living draws from Locke's division between church and state in his *Letter Concerning Toleration* (Locke 2010: 12, 23, 13, 23). On how Locke 'violates' his 'attempte[d]…line of demarcation between religion and civil society' (1), see C. Davis and C. Crockett (2007).

12 Ian Simpson Ross and Charles Griswold, offer persuasive arguments on Smith's inability to turn his jurisprudence lectures into a book, a struggle, they show us, unfolded by Smith through letters (Ross 2004; Griswold 2006).

13 Legal, in that for Smith testamentary succession 'is directed [not] by the law…[but] by the testament or the will of the deceased' (LJ(A) i.90).

14 Although this is Barbeyrac's (translated) language, my reading of the 'reasonable man' is indebted, admittedly anachronistically, to Oliver Wendell Holmes Jr's appeal to the term, as in 'what a man of reasonable prudence would have foreseen' (Holmes 1991: 54).

15 Pufendorf's refusal to concede the 'bare pleasure of the alienator' as valid justification for breach of a promise is Francis Hutcheson's later distinction between a lawful and unlawful promise. All things being equal, and thus notwithstanding what Grotius affectionately calls 'the Promises of Madmen, Ideots, and Infants' (Grotius 2005: 709), Hutcheson holds that the only sensible reason for which an 'obligation…can[not] arise from any promise' is if such a promise 'violate[s] directly the reverence due to God, or the perfect rights of others…or …[is] what is not committed to our power' (Hutcheson 2007: 166). Hutcheson's understanding of 'alienation' in promises is helpful in making sense of the distinction between a lawful and unlawful contract. It is an understanding itself indebted to Barbeyrac's appeal to the term in his commentary in Grotius' *The Rights of War and Peace*, which Hutcheson read. Barbeyrac understands by the term 'promise' not 'purely and simply, that a Man should be obliged to stand to the Performance of all he has promised; but only on a Supposition that he has promised what he had a Power to promise'; or, that 'we alienate what we have a power to alienate' (Grotius: 706; 707 n. 7). Grotius refers to Barbeyrac's definition of alienation in his quoting from Aristotle; it is arguably what Pufendorf and Smith have in mind in treating testamentary succession: that my right to promise my 'Property' to another, hence my right to '*Alienat[e]*' myself from the property, turns on my first having '*in [my]Self the Power of Alienation*', hence the power of in fact owning the property in the first place (Grotius: 566; emphasis in original).

16 One imagines this spoken by Humpty Dumpty in Lewis Carroll's *Through the Looking Glass* [1871] (Lopez 2004).

17 Appealing to the subsequent reading of the will, after the testator's death, Barbeyrac notes that this 'imperfect' right does not mean 'that before that [death of testator] 'tis

a vain Act, and of no Force', since 'no other Persons can claim the Goods of the Deceased, until he that is appointed the Heir refuses to inherit' (Pufendorf 1749: 420 n. 2). Though imperfect until the testator's death, 'so long as the Testator has not revoked his Will', hence 'change[d] the Legacies he has made of his Goods', perhaps 'because he flatters himself that he shall have time enough when he comes to die', this 'Right of the Heir continues' (420 n. 1). But since Barbeyrac is referring to that time after the testator's death, the point is consistent with Pufendorf's.

18   My language of 'binding' is gratefully indebted to Frida Beckman and Charlie Blake's 'Editorial Introduction: Shadows of Cruelty: Sadism, Masochism and the Philosophical Muse – part two' (Beckman and Blake 2010).

19   Smith here distances himself from Grotius. For Grotius, there is a proper 'Right of the Deceased', which 'is not extinct' upon the testator's death, but 'is continued in the Person of the Heir to whom it devolves' (Grotius 2005: 684 n. 1). Grotius is referring to lineal succession, which he understands as that 'undoubted Maxim' '[t]hat the Person of the Heir is to be looked upon to be the same as the Person of the Deceased, in regard to the Continuance of Property, either publick or private' (684). Grotius' appeal to 'Continuance', as in his insistence that the testator's right to property 'is not extinct' but merely 'continued', puts him at odds with Smith on succession. In Smith, succession, whether lineal or testamentary, is not of 'continuance' but of 'transference' (LJ(A) ii.1), and this in order to recognize the natural rights possessed by the heir, consent specifically, and autonomy more broadly. It is consent Smith refers to, for instance, when he describes the heir as 'another' in relation to the testator, as in 'another who has the same (? power) of doing with them as (he) pleases as the deceased had' (LJ(A) i.I54). Once we understand the heir as no different than the testator 'in regard to the Continuance of Property', as Grotius insists we do, Smith's position, and succession itself, become impossible. In such a view, Grotius', it makes no sense to speak of the heir as possessing a right 'had' by the deceased, since according to Grotius such a right 'is not extinct' at all but 'continued in the Person of the Heir to whom it devolves'. However, for Smith, it is necessary to recognize an 'extinct[ion]' to the living's right to property, hence to recognize succession as a matter of transfer rather than continuance, and this because unlimited continuance, as allowed by Grotius' position, infringes upon the right of successive heirs to choose, giving flight, for instance, to our problem of entails. While we may decide to maintain property in accordance with the wishes of the deceased, so may we not, at least not to the full extent of the dead's wishes.

20   See, for instance, Ruth A. Miller's reading of our tendency to ascribe to the deceased the 'status [of a] dignified, rights-bearing political subject, at the moment that it is disinterred, moved, exposed, burned, or revealed to have decayed' (Miller 2009: 110).

21   Smith here differs from Pufendorf. While Pufendorf also insists 'that the Right of the Heir to the respective Goods shall not commence 'till the Testator's Decease', the former of which he lauds as an improvement upon biblical succession wherein 'the Right immediately pass'd from the living Parents to the living Children; and the latter were admitted presently, 'twere, into Possession of the Goods', Pufendorf nevertheless chastises appeals to limit succession to such a time when 'Persons…seem to have…more than one Foot in the Grave'; this, Pufendorf explains, leaves no room '[f]or [that] sudden unforeseen Fate [which] frequently either hurries Men out of the world, or however removes them far from their Friends, so as they want Time or Opportunity to express by Mouth their last Resolution' (Pufendorf 1749: 422). Although Barbeyrac insists that Pufendorf errs in his account of biblical succession, the idea 'that the transferring of Property was made among the Living, and, as it were, from hand to

hand' (Pufendorf 2005: 421 n. 1), the same position Smith would develop, I take from Pufendorf his concern for how the dying person delivers those last words, as in what Pufendorf calls the difference between 'dispos[al] of [one's] Goods...while...in Ease and Quiet, and Master of a sound and clear Reason', and disposal of the same 'when...trembling at [the] last Hour, or when [the] Mind [i]s shock'd and weakened by the force of one's Distemper' (422). It is the latter position Smith appeals to, as in what for Smith we ourselves appeal to in extending succession beyond the dead. This rests on Smith's empiricist-based grounding of sympathy, found, for instance, in Smith's restricting piety, hence succession, 'to those who are alive at the person's death' (in other words, Smith's assumption that in one's last hour one would (have time to) gather together one's closest friends) (LJ(B), para.169).

22 I am gratefully indebted to Henry Sussman, for this language of 'gathering' (Sussman 2005: 259). Smith here also anticipates his own last moments (Smith 1980: 327–328).

23 My thinking here is gratefully indebted to Patrick R. Frierson's insight that 'Sympathy with the dead is always sympathy *of the living*' (Frierson 2006: 454; emphasis in original).

24 My quoting of 'we...prefer the person made heir' are the verso notes in LJ(A). See Introduction, 37.

25 On the recent termination of Scotland entails, see the Abolition of Feudal Tenure Act Online: http://www.legislation.gov.uk/asp/2000/5/part/5 (last accessed 8 April 2011).

26 See Legal-Dictionary 2010: http://legal-dictionary.thefreedictionary.com/entail (last accessed 17 July 2014).

27 Compare with the Abolition of Feudal Tenure Act.

28 For an excellent discussion of entails and primogeniture in the Commonwealth state of Virginia, see Baird (n.d.).

29 This, indeed, was not always the case. Part of Smith's founding testamentary succession on shared time and affection is the rather unfortunate implication (which I do not pursue here) that 'this piety to the dead is a pitch of humanity, a refinement on it, which we are not to expect from a people who have not made considerable advances in civilized manners. Accordingly we find that it is pretty late ere it is introduced in most countries' (LJ(A) i.151–152). In this respect, it is interesting to compare the dead to the eighteenth-century orphan, the latter of whom Cheryl L. Nixon reads as that figure who 'critiques society', but also 'reconstruct[s] it, often representing the moral order that must be brought to society, the family, the self...[a figure] forc[ing] the law to articulate its definition of the individual, creating a narrative space [through] which [we] can then interrogate that definition' (Nixon 2011: 30, 31).

30 For an excellent account of fideicomisses and trusts in Roman law, see Johnston (1988).

31 Compare with Locke's insistence that one "cannot by any compact whatsoever bind his children or posterity". It is the idea, as A. John Simmons observes, 'that rights can only be alienated by those who possess them; the consent that transfers rights must be personal consent. Our ancestors or parents cannot bind *us* by their promises and thus deprive us of our rights' (Locke quoted in Simmons 1993: 153; emphasis in original).

32 My reading of this logic of finitude in Smith is gratefully indebted to Martin Hägglund's development of the term in his *Radical Atheism: Derrida and the Time of Life* (2008).

33 For discussion on the dangers entails pose to humanity, see Walker (1866).

34 Although beyond the scope of this essay, Smith also raises commercial objections to entails and primogeniture; these objections appear prominently in *Wealth of Nations*, but are 'hint[ed] at' in Smith's earlier 1762–63 lectures on jurisprudence: 'This right is not only absurd in the highest degree but is also extremely prejudiciall to the

community, as it excludes lands intirely from commerce. The interest of the state requires that lands should be as much in commerce as any other goods. This the power of making entails intirely excludes' (LJ(A) 1.166). Although Smith brackets an appeal to commercial circulation as independent from a sympathetic one, I have tried to cover both bases with this language of 'autonomy', my sense that when Smith declares entails 'absurd' for commercial reasons, he is in fact responding out of the same sympathetic ones: imagining the loss of commerce, definitely, but an imagining which is a loss since it is individuals' loss of autonomy and freedom qua individuals, as in individuals with the freedom to (or not to) engage in commerce. While the present essay additionally does not permit space for treatment of Smith's account of justice in *Theory of Moral Sentiments*, it is interesting to consider the extent to which Smith does appeal to that philosophy of justice in grounding – and limiting – the reach of entails, Smith's defining justice in *Theory of Moral Sentiments* as our 'abstain[ing] from hurting [our] neighbors' (*TMS* II.ii.1.10), what Fonna Forman Barzilai describes as a 'prohibition against inflicting cruelty' (Barzilai 2010: 24).

35   This is again in keeping with Smith's empiricism, his understanding, as Fonna Forman Barzilai explains, that 'our moral horizon fades out at the edges of physical immediacy, affective "connexion" and historical familiarity' (Barzilai 2010: 194).

36   Grotius' appeal to 'sufficiency' is his returning us to his criteria of a valid contract, of which he additionally includes what he calls some sufficient 'Signs of a deliberate Mind' (Grotius 2005: 708). It is what he refers to, for instance, when he marks as 'void' 'the Promises of Madmen, Ideots, and Infants', this idea that a 'Will[ed]' 'Consent' transfers consent, and so is 'obliging', but only if there are 'sufficient' 'Signs of a deliberate Mind', as in signs 'that the Promisor should have the Use of his Reason' (717, 708, 709). Absenting signs of 'Deliberation', the deliberation, for example, by which one offers to another their time and affection, the promisor's predicament in Grotius becomes nearly the testator's in Smith, as in an offered consent which '[has no] Power of obliging at all' (708).

37   Smith LJ(A) ii.1, LJ(B), paras. 169, 170, LJ(A) ii.1, LJ(B), para. 170, LJ(A) ii.2, ii.1.

38   A strict reading of Smith's criterion of fellow-feeling could find us in the awkward position where 'want of that Consent' finds us 'depriv[ed]…of that Right which We hath by Nature to dispose of [our] Goods' (Pufendorf 1749: 420 n. 2). Smith would likely resolve this problem, roughly translated into what Pufendorf calls a 'defective will' (424), by appeal to lineal succession; in this scenario, to borrow Lawrence M. Friedman's language, we would, barring a last-minute (literally) sharing of time and affection, die as if 'intestate' as regards disposal of our 'estate' (Friedman 2009: 76); such would go to a lineal heir or, if impossible, 'fall to the crown' (LJ(A) i.164).

39   Compare, for instance, with Jacques Derrida's: 'Afraid of dying, yes, but that is nothing next to the other terror, I know no worse: to survive my love, to survive you, those whom I love and who know it, to be the last to preserve what I wanted to pass on to you, my love. Imagine the old man who remains with his will, which has just come back to him, in his hands…the old man who remains the last to read himself, late at night' (199). See Derrida (1987). I am quoting from Derrida's *The Post Card: From Socrates to Freud and Beyond*, the former of which, in part, I originally read in Martin Hägglund's *Dying for Time: Proust, Woolf, Nabokov* (Hägglund: 2012: 167). This was, of course, notwithstanding Smith's wish that his remaining papers be 'committed to the flames' (Smith 1980: 327), Smith's predicament with Hume, Smith outlasting his executor, literally, and finding himself, though he would later refuse, as mentioned above, Hume's (Corr. Letter 137 from Smith, 16 April 1773).

40 My grateful thanks to Joseph R. Chaney, for helping me to think 'circulation' as 'transmission' (email *c*. 2006).

41 My reading of this problem of finitude is once more gratefully indebted to Martin Hägglund's *Radical Atheism: Derrida and the Time of Life*.

42 I am quoting Derrida's quoting of Celan's '*Einem, der vor der Tür stand*' (Derrida: 2005).

43 'Open', relative to the heir's right of refusal or acceptance, as in 'that a Man shall not know himself to be Heir 'till the *Will* comes to be open'd upon the *Testator's* Decease. And likewise when the Will is thus open'd, 'tis at the Choice of Heir appointed, whether he will enter upon the Inheritance, or wave and refuse it' (Pufendorf 2005: 418–19; emphasis in original). See also Lyall (1979) for discussion of the relation between contracts and covenants, including the distinction between grace qua covenant and obligation qua contract. Although Smith uses the language of 'piety' and Lyall the language of 'grace' (17), both reach the same conclusion as regards what it means to offer grace to another, which is that 'a person cannot be benefitted against his will' (17).

Bibliography

Baird, R.W. (n.d.) 'Entail', *Bob's Genealogy Filing Cabinet: Colonial and Southern Genealogies*. Available online at: www.genfiles.com/legal/entail.htm (last accessed 8 April 2011).

Benhabib, S. (2006) *Another Cosmopolitanism*, R. Post (ed.) Oxford: Oxford University Press.

Barzilai, F.F. (2010) *Adam Smith and the Circles of Sympathy: Cosmopolitanism and Moral Theory*, Cambridge: Cambridge University Press.

Beckman, F. and Blake, C. (2010) 'Editorial introduction: shadows of cruelty: Sadism, masochism and the philosophical muse: Part two', *Angelaki: Journal of the Theoretical Humanities* 15(1): 1–12.

Carmichael, G. ([1724 edition of Supplements and Observations] 2002) *Natural Rights on the Threshold of the Scottish Enlightenment: The Writings of Gershom Carmichael*, J. Moore and M. Silverthorne (eds), M. Silverthorne (trans.), Indianapolis, IN: Liberty Fund.

Davis, C. and Crockett, C. (2007) 'Editorial introduction: the political and the infinite', *Angelaki: Journal of the Theoretical Humanities* 12.1: 1–10.

Derrida, J. (1987) *The Post Card: From Socrates to Freud and Beyond*, Alan Bass (trans.). Chicago, IL: University of Chicago Press.

Derrida, J. (2005) *Sovereignties in Question: The Poetics of Paul Celan*, T. Dutoit and O. Pasanen (trans.), New York: Fordham University Press.

Friedman, L. (2009) *Dead Hands: A Social History of Wills, Trusts, and Inheritance Law*, Palto Alto: Stanford University Press.

Frierson, P.R. (2006) 'Adam Smith and the possibility of sympathy with nature', *Pacific Philosophical Quarterly*, 87: 442–80.

Griswold, C. (2006) 'On the incompleteness of Adam Smith's system', *Adam Smith Review* 2: 181–16.

Grotius, H. ([1625] 2005) *The Rights of War and Peace*, vols. 1–3, R. Tuck (ed.), Indianapolis, IN: Liberty Fund.

Hägglund, M. (2008) *Radical Atheism: Derrida and the Time of Life*, Palo Alto, CA: Stanford University Press.

Hägglund, M. (2012) *Dying for Time: Proust, Woolf, Nabokov*, Cambridge, MA: Harvard University Press.

Hobbes, T. ([1651] 2003) *Leviathan*, R. Tuck (ed.), Cambridge: Cambridge University Press.

Holmes Jr, O. W. ([1881] 1991) *The Common Law*, New York: Dover Publications.

Hutcheson, F. ([1745; original Latin text; 1747 anonymously translated into English] 2007) *Philosophiae Moralis Institutio Compendiaria, with A Short Introduction to Moral Philosophy*, Luigi Turco (trans.), Indianapolis, IN: Liberty Fund.

Johnston, D. (1988) *The Roman Law of Trusts*, Oxford: Clarendon Press.

Locke, J. ([1689] 1993) *Two Treatises of Government*, M. Goldie (ed.) London: Orion.

Locke, J. ([1689] 2010) *A Letter Concerning Toleration and Other Writings*, M. Goldie (ed.) Indianapolis, IN: Liberty Fund.

Lopez, A. (2004) 'Deleuze with Carroll: Schizophrenia and simulacrum and the philosophy of Lewis Carroll's nonsense', *Angelaki: Journal of the Theoretical Humanities* 9(4): 101–21.

Lyall, F. (1979) 'Metaphors and analogies: Legal language and covenant theology', *Journal of Theology*, 32: 1–17.

Miller, D.L.C. (1998) *A Companion to Justinian's Institutes*, E. Metzger (ed.) New York: Cornell University Press. 'Property', pp. 42–79.

Miller, R.A. (2009) *The Law in Crisis; The Ecstatic Subject of Natural Disaster*, Palo Alto, CA: Stanford University Press.

Nixon, C.L. (2011) *The Orphan in Eighteenth-Century Law and Literature: Estate, Blood, and Body*, Burlington: Ashgate.

Pufendorf, S. ([1673, Latin publication; 1691 translation] 2003) *The Whole Duty of Man, According to the Law of Nature*, A. Tooke (trans.), I. Hunter and D. Saunders (eds), Indianapolis, IN: Liberty Fund.

Pufendorf, S. ([1672, original Latin publication; translated 5th ed. 1749]) *Of the Law of Nature and Nations*, B. Kennet and G. Carew (trans.), London: Lawbook Exchange. Available online at: https://archive.org/details/oflawofnaturenat00pufe (last accessed 25 April 2012).

Reilly, N. (2007) 'Cosmopolitan feminism and human rights', *Hypatia*, 22(4): 180–98.

Ripstein, A. (2009) *Force and Freedom: Kant's Legal and Political Philosophy*, Chicago, IL: University of Chicago Press.

Ross, I.S. (2004) '"Great works upon the anvil" in 1785: Adam Smith's Projected Corpus of Philosophy', *Adam Smith Review*, 1: 40–59.

Simmons, A.J. (1993) *On the Edge of Anarchy: Locke, Consent, and the Limits of Society*, Princeton, NJ: Princeton University Press.

Smith, A. (1976a) *Theory of Moral Sentiments*, D.D. Raphael and A.L. Macfie (eds) Oxford: Oxford University Press; Glasgow edn. Reprinted, Liberty Fund (1982).

Smith, A. (1976b) *An Inquiry into the Nature and Causes of the Wealth of Nations*, R.H. Campbell and A.S. Skinner (eds) Oxford: Oxford University Press; Glasgow edn. Reprinted, Liberty Fund (1982).

Smith, A. (1978) *Lectures on Jurisprudence*, R.L. Meek, D.D. Raphael and P.G. Stein (eds) Oxford: Oxford University Press; Glasgow edn. Reprinted, Liberty Fund (1982).

Smith, A. (1980) *Essays on Philosophical Subjects*, W.P.D. Wightman (ed.) Oxford: Oxford University Press; Glasgow edn. Reprinted, Liberty Fund (1982).

Smith, A. (1987) *Correspondence of Adam Smith*, 2nd ed., E. C. Mossner and I. S. Ross (eds), Oxford: Oxford University Press; Glasgow edn. Reprinted, Liberty Fund (1987).

Sussman, H. (2005) *The Task of the Critic: Poetics, Politics, and Religion*, New York: Fordham University Press.

Walker, A. (1866) *The Science of Wealth: A Manual of Political Economy*, Boston, MA: Little, Brown. Available online at: http://chestofbooks.com/finance/Amasa-Walker/The-Science-of-Wealth/ (last accessed 2 February 2011).

Adam Smith and the social contract

John Thrasher

Adam Smith, with his friend David Hume, is one of the great critics of the social contract. In traditional histories of political and ethical philosophy, Hume and Smith are the beginning of a move away from contract theory and the early development of what would become the rival tradition of utilitarianism.[1] Most political philosophers continue to hold this view.[2] Despite the vintage of this historical narrative, I argue that it has led to a basic misunderstanding in Adam Smith's account of justice. By using the techniques of contemporary contract theory, we can plausibly and profitably interpret Smith as a special kind of contractarian. In so doing, we can helpfully distinguish the notion of impartiality found in Smith from the impartiality of later utilitarians like Henry Sidgwick and contemporary theorists like Amartya Sen and Brian Barry.[3] Indeed, Brian Barry's distinction between justice as impartiality and justice as mutual advantage is central to the claim being made here. Ultimately, I argue that Smith is best understood as a mutual advantage theorist.[4]

The argument for this conclusion proceeds in five parts. Section 1 distinguishes between several forms of contractarianism and argues that the traditional view of Smith as an opponent of the social contract only applies to *original contractarianism* and what, following F. A. Hayek's usage, I call constructivist account of contractarianism. In sections 2 and 3, I present the key elements of Smith's account of justice. What becomes clear is that justice neither arises from, nor is particularly sensitive to considerations of utility or impartiality.[5] With the idea of the contract in place and an account of Smith's understanding of justice, section 4 develops a more precise notion of Smith's standard of mutual advantage or agreement. In section 5, I present a full account of why Smith should be considered a contractarian and what the substance of his version of contractarianism would look like. Ultimately, I argue that understanding Smith as a contractarian is more faithful to his social philosophy as a whole. Additionally, Smith's unique version of contractarianism is superior, in many ways, to other forms of contract theory and, hence, can serve as a model for contemporary contract theorists.

1 Two kinds of contract

In 'Of the Original Contract', Hume argues that no government was founded contractually (Hume, 1784: 487). Furthermore, a contractual basis for government would be neither necessary nor sufficient for creating political obligation. It is not necessary because every government is founded chiefly on opinion, not right. It is not sufficient because a contract of one generation would not be able to bind any other. According to Hume, the social contract is a myth of questionable value. Adam Smith makes much the same point in his *Lectures on Jurisprudence* of 1766 where he is reported to have said: [6]

> Ask a day porter or day-labourer why he obeys the civil magistrate, he will tell you that it is right to do so, that he sees other do it, that he would be punished if he refused to do it, or perhaps that it is a sin against God not to do it. But you will never hear him mention a contract as the foundation of his obedience.
>
> (LJB 12–18, 401–3, Smith 1978)

Smith here is attacking two important claims made by advocates of contract theory in his time. First, he is attacking the factual claim that contract was the foundation of political obligation and the psychological claim that political subjects actually take themselves to be bound to the political authority on the basis of the contract. Second, he is attacking the claim that something like a contract is necessary to establish political obligation.

In substance, Smith's criticism of the idea of the social contract is largely the same as Hume's. Both Smith and Hume are attacking the idea that political obligation did or could have arisen from an original contract. They are attacking a consent-based, historical version of the social contract that we might call, following Gauthier (1979: 12), *original contractarianism*. This is the idea that the original social contract explains political obligation and authority by reference to an original compact in the state of nature. The normative authority of political institutions derives from the free consent of persons to obey those institutions. This version of the social contract is an explanatory as well as justificatory device. It explains and, in so doing, justifies political obligations, duties and the structure of current political authority. Contractual explanations, along original contractarian lines, are alien to Hume's more conventionalist approach. This is especially true when we look at his account of the development of the rules of property, where he argues that there is little difference between superstition and justice except for the fact that justice is useful and that 'all regards to right and property seem entirely without foundation' (*EPM* 3.38: 94–5).[7] For Hume, political authority similarly rests on opinion, not on contract. Smith follows Hume on this general point.

There is no question that both reject original contractarianism. There is, however, a species of contractarianism, the primary purpose of which is not to explain the origins of government and obligation but, rather, to justify or evaluate current systems of justice. This is the social contract as a justificatory device: the *justificatory contract*. Here the contract metaphor is used as a justificatory device to evaluate current or possible systems of interpersonal constraints. As Samuel Freeman points out, the idea of the social contract in ethics is not a substantive view but rather 'a framework for justification in ethics'(Freeman 1990: 122). In the context of Smith's theory, Smith describes justice as the virtue that arises out of the attitude of resentment, to the extent that other persons can *go along with it*, a phrase Smith uses repeatedly in *The Theory of Moral Sentiments* (*TMS*).[8] He writes:

> There is, however, another virtue, of which the observance is not left to the freedom of our own wills, which may be extorted by force, and of which the violation exposes to resentment, and consequently to punishment. This virtue is justice: the violation of justice is injury: it does real and positive hurt to some particular persons, from motives which are naturally disapproved of. It is, therefore, the proper object of resentment, and of punishment, which is the natural consequence of resentment. As mankind *go along with*, and approve of the violence employed to avenge the hurt which is done by injustice, so they much more go along with, and approve of, that which is employed to prevent and beat off the injury, and to restrain the offender from hurting his neighbours.
>
> (*TMS* II.ii.I.5; emphasis added)

So, although justice arises from resentment, for justice and especially the punishment of injustice to be something that others can endorse, they must be able to *go along with it*. This is the basic idea of justice as a kind of agreement that is embodied more fully in the idea of the justificatory social contract.

Justificatory contracts can take a constructivist or non-constructivist form. The constructivist justificatory contract, in this context, is an attempt to specify what would count as an account of justice regardless of historical circumstances and contingencies.[9] This idea is similar to what Amartya Sen has called 'transcendental' accounts of justice. Transcendental and constructivist theorists focus on developing accounts of what ideal political and moral institutions would look like without much concern for what relevant comparisons would be possible in our current world (Sen 2009: 6). For the constructivist, the contractual procedure provides all the relevant justificatory standards, it does not matter, as James Buchanan once put it, that we start from where we are (Buchanan 1975/2000: 101). Wherever we start from, the constructivist contract shows us what is right.

In contrast, the non-constructivist version is a comparative, *testing conception* of the social contract.[10] Here, the social contract is a device for testing whether individuals should reflectively endorse or go along with certain rules of justice. The social contract is a model or an heuristic device for evaluating the reasons that one may or may not have to continue to endorse a set of rules.[11] In any normal society, persons will come together and discuss with one another whether they have legitimate complaints against their institutions and whether some alternative might be preferable (Rawls 1958: 171). They will come together and discuss what they can go along with in their society. These people do not think they are setting up the rules as their society anew, nor are they applying timeless standards against their society as a whole. Instead, they are looking for shared grounds of interpersonal justification. Shared grounds of what would count as a reason to want to continue to endorse or change some institution that concerns them. The contract, in this sense, is a model for what such interpersonal agreement would look like.

The contract then, on the non-constructivist testing conception is consistent with a historical, conventionalist approach in a way that the original contract and the constructivist contract are not. History gives us the institutions we have, but the idea of the contract can serve as an interpersonal standard of justification for helping us determine whether we should reflectively endorse the result of the historical process. The standard of acceptability, the standard of justification, will vary depending on how the deliberative model is set up. Certain requirements, however, will be stable over different models. For instance, only rules that lead to mutual advantage will be acceptable to all parties. Therefore, only rules that meet a mutual advantage test will be something all can go along with. Of course, mutual advantage is a necessary though it may not be a sufficient condition of an acceptable system of rules.[12] Other criteria such as reciprocity between parties or a standard of impartiality or any other number of standards might also be employed.

2 Justice as a negative virtue

Adam Smith sees justice as conformity with a set of rules where the fundamental normative concept is duty. The particular substance of those rules, on a more narrow conception, determines, at least, the rules of justice; typically, prohibitions against acts that tend to excite resentment. The aretaic, positive view of justice, sees justice as a virtue that should be encouraged. Justice is, on this view however, a negative ideal. The point is not to achieve justice so much as to root out and avoid injustice.

Adam Smith identifies the positive approach with the virtue of beneficence and the negative approach with justice proper. For Smith:

> Mere justice is, upon most occasions, but a negative virtue, and only hinders us from hurting our neighbour. The man who barely abstains from violating either the person, or the estate, or the reputation of his neighbours, has surely very little positive merit. He fulfils, however, all the rules of what is peculiarly called justice, and does every thing which his equals can with propriety force him to do, or which they can punish him for not doing. *We may often fulfill all the rules of justice by sitting still and doing nothing.*
>
> (*TMS* II.ii.I.9; emphasis added)

There are many things to note in this passage. First, Smith refers to justice as 'mere' justice. However important justice may be, it is clearly not the only virtue or value that matters. Second, according to Smith, the person who has refrained from acting unjustly may have very little positive merit. For instance, there is no reason to praise Jack for not murdering Jill. Imagine the absurdity of a man walking down the street thanking everyone he passed for not robbing and killing him. Justice, on this negative view is a kind of baseline. Deviations from justice are blameworthy but acting justly is merely avoiding wrong and, therefore, not intrinsically praiseworthy. Third, the negative ideal of justice is clearest in the emphasized portion of the excerpt. Jill can fulfil her duty to justice by sitting in a room and doing nothing.

She in not obliged to fulfil any positive duties.

Smith contrasts justice with another virtue that is important but distinct, namely beneficence. In the section directly before the last excerpt Smith writes:

> Though the mere want of beneficence seems to merit no punishment from equals, the greater exertions of that virtue appear to deserve the highest reward. By being productive of the greatest good, they are the natural and approved objects of the liveliest gratitude. Though the breach of justice, on the contrary, exposes to punishment, the observance of the rules of that virtue seems scarce to deserve any reward. There is, no doubt, a propriety in the practice of justice, and it merits, upon that account, all the approbation which is due to propriety. But as it does no real positive good, it is entitled to very little gratitude.
>
> (*TMS* II.ii.I.9)

Beneficence, being 'productive of the highest good' deserves 'the highest reward' but lack of beneficence is not grounds for punishment. Conversely, the observance of the rules of justice deserves no reward but failing to act justly opens one up to the possibility of punishment. Beneficence, unlike justice, is 'free, it cannot be extorted by force, the mere want of it exposes to no punishment; because the mere want of beneficence tends to do no real positive evil' (*TMS* II.ii.I.3). When someone shows lack of gratitude or charity, they become 'the object of hatred' rather than resentment (*TMS* II.ii.I.4). Resentment, according to Smith, was given to us by nature for 'defense, and for defense only' (*TMS* II.ii.I.4). A terrible emotion, it impels us to retaliate against injustice already committed and to defend against future injustice. While compliance with the rules of justice is necessary for the maintenance of social order, there is no reward for mere compliance.

Nevertheless, justice is of the utmost importance. Smith alludes to this point when he is discussing the 'man of public spirit' who, 'when he cannot establish the right, he will not disdain to ameliorate the wrong; but like Solon, when he cannot establish the best system of laws, he will endeavour to establish the best that the people can bear' (*TMS* VI.ii.2.16). Rooting out injustice, 'ameliorating the wrong', even on the margins, is better than using the force of the state to establish the right in cases where a society can not go along with the heights of virtue. Better to establish the negative ideal of justice than to try to foist a positive standard of beneficence in a way that persons cannot go along with.

Smith's claim that acts of injustice are not only blameworthy but also punishable is striking given what he argues in a later part of the same chapter. According to Smith, individuals do not have the authority to enforce acts of kindness or charity among equals. They do have the authority and the right, however, to enforce justice even 'antecedent to the institution of civil government' (*TMS* II.ii.I.7). In all normal circumstances, Smith seems to be saying, that to use force against another person is unacceptable. It is, at least in principle, acceptable to use force to prevent and remedy injustice, however. Violations of injustice then are special in that they override the normal prohibition against violence. Furthermore, justice is prior to the formation of the state. Smith is claiming that justice does not have its authority because of the state; rather the state has its authority because of justice. There is an external standard by which we can judge our social institutions, namely the standard of justice that everyone can go along with, a contractual standard of justice.

Justice is so important because it stabilizes the conditions of cooperation. Again, we see the contractarian standard of mutual advantage. Insofar as humans want to live together, they tend to want to live on terms that allow for mutual gain. Without social stability, however, cooperation is impossible. As Smith puts it, 'society, however, cannot subsist among those who are at all times ready to hurt and injure one another' (*TMS* II.ii.3.3). The most basic bonds of social concord and cooperation require the establishment and enforcement of justice. Even a society of murderers and robbers requires some form of justice according to Smith (*TMS* II.iii.3). Underneath the shifting institutional framework of particular rules, there is system of 'natural justice' that is generated out of the regularities of sympathy and resentment (*TMS* VII.iv.37). Natural justice is relatively invariant because of certain regularities in the constitution of our moral psychology. The circumstances of justice are built into us in the form of moral emotions. In this way, the institutions of justice are 'natural' in the sense that they are the product of our natural sentiments. They are also 'artificial' in just the way that Hume also suggests because in each particular society, the natural moral emotion of resentment will lead to justice. The particular substance of justice will vary from time to time and place to place. Each bird will build its nest in its own way, though all will build nests (*EPM* 3.2.44: 97). Similarly, the natural attraction of the opposite sex will lead men and women to come together, but the specific institutional structure of marriage will vary widely between different cultures and different times (*LJA* iii.4–49, 141–158). Smith's account of justice separates the negative, social virtue of justice from the positive, personal virtues of beneficence, prudence, and self-command. Justice is the province of resentment and punishment.

We have seen then that Smith sees justice as a system of prohibitions that are backed with sanctions. The origin of these prohibitions is ultimately in the constitution of our moral psychology, specifically our conceptions of resentment and merit. The purpose of our institutions of justice and the role of our moral emotions is to preserve and ensure the requirements of mutual advantage. So far, this is entirely consistent with understanding Smith as a contractarian. To make the case more complete, however, we need to understand more about the substance of Smith's account of justice. Smith thinks of a system of justice as a system of rules rather than a system of principles that one applies to acts (as the utilitarian might) or a collection of stable dispositions to act one way rather than another (as the virtue theorist might). Because of this is it worth looking more closely at the role that rules play in Smith's account of justice.

3 Rules of justice

As we saw in the last section, justice plays an important social role for Smith. It is responsible for defence and forsecuring the background conditions of peace and cooperation. It sets off the boundaries between persons that allow safe and stable social intercourse. To play this role, though, the rules of justice need a specific, determinate form. Even if justice were as important to society as Smith thought, if the rules of justice are vague or indeterminate, enforcement would be difficult. Indeterminacy would lead to disputes that would undermine the social union that justice ensures. Smith argues that although the rules of the other virtues may be indeterminate, justice is different. This distinction between the positive virtues and justice set apart his account of justice from his account of the other virtues. The positive virtues, because of their indeterminacy do not provide effective guidance for action (*TMS* III.6.9).

Even gratitude, Smith's example of a more specific virtue, allows too many exceptions to be a strict rule. The fact that there are many exceptions to gratitude is not, in itself, a problem. It would be a problem, however, if the enforcement of gratitude made use of the police powers of the state (*TMS* VII.iv.37). Beneficence is similar in this regard. Smith admits that the magistrate may 'command mutual good offices to a certain degree' but only to a certain degree (*TMS* II.ii.I.8). The magistrate has some power and duty to establish norms of beneficence but these must be done delicately and rarely, for attempting to institute positive virtues through the law when not appropriate 'is destructive of all liberty, security, and justice' (*TMS* II.ii.I.8). Justice, unlike beneficence, is different in that it admits of precise formulation (*TMS* III.6.9).

The connection between justice and the other virtues is analogous the relationship between grammar and literary style as Smith suggests in a passage that gives the clearest explanation of the importance of justice in Smith's overall system:[13]

> The rules of justice may be compared to the rules of grammar; the rules of the other virtues, to the rules which critics lay down for the attainment of what is sublime and elegant in composition. The one, are precise, accurate, and indispensable. The other, are loose, vague, and indeterminate, and present us rather with a general idea of the perfection we ought to aim at, than afford us any certain and infallible directions for acquiring it.
>
> (*TMS* III.6.9)

Virtue, like style, gives determinacy and character to an individual life. Justice has a pride of place in Smith's system of virtues because of its unique importance for society and because of its precision. It is important to remember, though, that social life is not primarily about justice. Justice is necessary, although not sufficient for the smooth functioning of a society. For that, cultivation of the other virtues is necessary as both a means of making social interaction more fruitful and an antidote to many of the problems that come with modern capitalist society.[14]

Determinacy and precision in a common standard of justice is delivered via general rules of justice. We need general, social rules of justice because we tend to apply our resentment in uneven and partial ways. When we are the judges in our own case, things have a tendency to get out of hand. In those cases, the appropriateness conditions for justified resentment remain unclear and unspecified. To regularize resentment and to generate a common standard, we need to generate specific and generally applicable rules of justice out of attitudes of resentment. We generate these rules first by observing others and noticing their conduct. We then form rules to guide our own behaviour (*TMS* III.4.7). This process generalizes to form the rules of justice as a whole. Smith argues that, 'the general rule…is formed, by finding from experience, that all actions of a certain kind, or circumstanced in a certain manner, are approved or disapproved of' (*TMS* III.4.8). Rules of justice, then, are formed from experience. They arise out of regularities in real and stable attitudes (*TMS* III.4.11).

Justice, although arising out of the natural feeling of resentment, is regularized into a set of general rules. One of the great insights of Smith is that general, interpersonal rules can be generated out of subjective moral attitudes.[15] As Knud Haakonssen puts it, 'Smith's real feat is to show *how* men do have a common moral world with common standards'(Haakonssen 1981: 54; emphasis added). We can look around and see that there is some commonality between codes of justice. Smith's theory of justice is a secular, sentimentalist account of how human beings living together can come to have common standards of justice. This process is at the heart of Smith's entire account of how the impartial spectator works to transform the essentially first-personal point of view of our moral attitudes and transform then into a second-personal standards of appropriate treatment and eventually into third personal general rules of justice and morality (Haakonssen 1981: 56).

Some modern commentators find Smith's method of generating stable common standards of morality out of subjective attitudes unconvincing (Fleischacker 2004: 147; Griswold 1999: 257). These critics seek mind-independent, external standards of right and wrong. Instead, Smith offers common, stable standards of interpersonal assessment. Smith offers a standard of justice that we can all go along with, not necessarily a standard of justice that is true in some mind-independent, fact-insensitive way. The standard of morality that arises from this Smithian process is common, but varied across time and place.[16] There will be regularities in both the moral psychology and the environmental circumstances of humans across societies and time that will generate regularities in standards of justice and morality, but each society will develop sets of generalized rules in different ways.

It is worth noting that modern moral psychology seems to agree with Smith's account of how we generalize and objectify moral principles into rules. The type of developmental process that Smith describes does seem to occur in children. Children are able to distinguish between conventional rules, which typically only apply in a particular institutional context, and moral rules, which apply generally and are not easily overridden by context, between the ages of three and four (Smetana and Braeges 1990). Moral transgressions, typically involving harm or theft, are viewed as more serious than conventional transgressions. Shaun Nichols argues that this development occurs as children begin to organize their emotional responses in terms of general rules, what Nichols calls 'sentimental rules' and is in many ways similar to Smith (Nichols 2007: 16–29).

Once these rules are established as the basis of rules of justice, individuals will generally have a tendency to be motivated to follow the rules. Smith argues that without a 'sacred regard to the general rules, there is no man whose conduct can much be depended upon' (*TMS* III.5.2). We are motivated to follow these rules, to have a sacred regard for a very simple reason: by nature, humans have with an innate desire to please others and to be accepted into society (*TMS* III.2.6). Our natural desire for sympathy with our fellows leads us to seek their approval and hence to be motivated to follow the rules. This desire is not enough, however, because, according to Smith, we desire not only to be loved but also to be lovely (*TMS* III.2.1). That is, we desire to be worthy of the approbation of others as well as self-approbation. This leads us to internalize the rules and to make them the basis of our own self-conception of worth. Once internalized, violations are punished by 'reason, principle, conscience, the inhabitant of the breast, the man within, the great judge and arbiter of our conduct' (*TMS* III.3.4). This 'man within the breast', the impartial spectator, regulates our conduct by generating remorse and guilt after transgressions, resentment and blame at the transgressions of others.

By now, it should be clear that the standard of impartiality of the rules of justice is not the same as the utilitarian or Kantian notions of impartiality. Instead, impartiality is what anyone would have reason 'to go along with'. This is, then, not a utilitarian theory at all.[17] Utility is neither the motive nor the ultimate aim of rule following in Smith (*TMS* III.iii.4). This is important because it shows that both genealogically and motivationally the right indeed precedes the good.[18] The reason to follow rules is not based on utility in the ordinary sense.[19] Regard for the rules of justice is, instead, 'reverential and religious'.[20] He argues:

> It is not the love of our neighbors, it is not the love of mankind, which upon many occasions prompts us to the practice of those divine virtues. It is a stronger love, a more powerful affection, which generally takes place upon such occasions; the love of what is honorable and noble, of the grandeur, dignity, and the superiority of our own characters.
>
> (*TMS* III.iii.4)

Contrast Smith's account of the rules of justice with Smith's account of the other virtues, such as beneficence. Smith argues that with the other virtues, our conduct should ultimately be regulated teleologically. We should 'consider the end and foundation of the rule, more than the rule itself' (*TMS* III.vi.10). These rules are 'rules of thumb' similar to Rawls's *summary view* of rules (Rawls 1955: 19). Rules of justice, for Smith, are much closer to what Rawls has called the *practice view* of rules (Rawls 1955: 26). When following the rules of justice, one must maintain the most 'obstinate steadfastness to the general rules themselves' (*TMS* III.vi.10). This distinction between rules of justice and other rules makes it clear that, at least in terms of justice, Smith is a staunch deontologist. The right, in this case the general rules of justice, restricts the options of choice, regardless of how this restriction affects the pursuit of an individual's good.

For Smith, then, rules of justice have six important properties. They are: (i) The result of appropriate resentment; (ii) antecedent to the formation of civil society; (iii) precise and determinate; (iv) composed of general rules; (v) enforceable; and

(vi) necessary.

The fact that justice is necessary and precise makes it possible to enforce rules of justice. The fact that justice arises from the generalized resentment makes it appropriate for enforcement and punishment but also antecedent to the institutions of civil society. Smith's theory of justice, then, is both sentimentalist and deontological.

The question remains, however, that if the rules of justice are both motivationally and genealogically caused by the sentiments, what work could the social contract possibly play in Smith's account? This is the crux of Smithian contractarianism. Recall that resentment is a personal attitude, while the rules of justice are interpersonal and social. Individuals do not invent their own rules of justice; rather, they enter into a social system where the rules of justice are already established and stable. Their attitudes, being both similar to their fellows and influenced by the need for approbation, will tend to equilibrate to the existing set of social rules, within certain limits. It is not a question of creating the rules *de novo*; instead, it is a question of having reasons to endorse or change the rules that exist. That is the role of the idea of the contract. In the next section, we look in more detail at what properties an agreeable set of rules would have.

4 Modelling agreement

The social contract, in the sense I am using here, represents a system of rules that all have reason to 'go along with'. The justificatory standard is mutual advantage – do members of society see its rules as being a good deal. Mutual advantage, however, does not mean equal advantage. Some may do much better than others given certain rules. Mutual advantage can be modelled as a Pareto condition; that is, if everyone prefers a world with rule X to a world with rule Y, rule Y should not be selected or endorsed as the social rule.[21] Another way to describe the criteria is that a social rule is acceptable if at least one person finds the rule acceptable and no one finds the rule unacceptable. This test is a threshold test of whether everyone can go along with the rule.

This contractual situation can be modelled as a kind of exchange represented by an Edgeworth box. Parties to the contract can be imagined as individuals 'exchanging' rules and sets of rules in a 'market'. For a simplistic example of this model, two agents i and j and two sets of rules, x and y (each set of rules has a continuous interval of particular rules). There is a matrix $M \times N$ of all possible allocations of rules between i and j with the ordered pair $<(x_n,i),(y_n,j)>$ representing one possible allocation. Every feasible allocation is contained within matrix as in an Edgeworth box. For each agent, every point on a higher indifference curve is preferred to every point below that indifference curve. The contract curve represents Pareto optimal allocations and, therefore, points where mutually beneficial and efficient exchange could take place.

If we were using this model to represent the social contract, we would say that any point on the contract curve represent one possible social contract based on the Pareto condition, where social contract means some particular set of rules of justice. These are known as the 'core' solutions and they represent what persons can go along with.[22] We can think of the status quo as the initial endowment of goods or rules, is tested against all possible set of rules. If the status quo does not lie along the contract curve then some person would prefer to move to a social contract on the contract curve. The status quo would not meet the test of mutual advantage – not everyone could go along with it. In this understanding of the social contract, the status quo serves the same function the state of nature serves in original and constructivist contractarian approaches. We always evaluate changes in sets of rules against the baseline of the status quo. The status quo is also, therefore, the 'no agreement' point of the social contract conceived as a bargaining problem.

It is important to note that mutual advantage is importantly different from any version of utilitarianism for two main reasons: 1) it is non-aggregative; and 2) it does not rely on interpersonal comparisons. Smith, together with Hume, is typically identified as utilitarian, so it is worth distinguishing the two ideas here.[23] In traditional utilitarianism, the basic idea is that the utility of each person is summed across the relevant social unit and then an average or other measure of utility is used as the goal of social institutions. Social utility as a total sum or an average (or any number of other standards) is the standard by which institutions are measured. The contractarian idea of mutual advantage differs from the utilitarian standard because it is fundamentally non-aggregative. Each person in the society needs to go along with the rule. A rule is not justified because it advances the sum or product of utility of society as a whole. Because of this, mutual advantage does not require interpersonal comparisons of utility. No sums or products need to be tallied so no interpersonal comparisons are necessary. Given the difficulty with interpersonal comparisons of utility, this is an advantage of the contractarian approach.[24]

The chief disadvantage of any contract theory is indeterminacy. While there may be a set of possible social contracts that meet the mutual advantage criterion, no particular point may be preferred to all others. We may be left with what Amartya Sen calls a *maximal* set of possible allocations, without one particular optimal element.[25] Within that maximal set of contracts, no particular contract is preferred but all are preferred to members outside the set. In these cases, reason does not tell us which option to take. We can call this the *indeterminacy problem*. Furthermore, though mutual advantage may be necessary for the stability and hence the dynamic feasibility of a social contract, it may not be sufficient. After all, we are often concerned with whether a contract is fair, not only whether it is beneficial. Some other criterion besides mutual advantage and the Pareto criterion will be needed to specify what counts as an acceptable social contract. We can call the idea that mutual advantage is insufficient for a complete contractual theory the *insufficiency problem*. I argue, in the next section, that Adam Smith understood as a non-constructivist contractarian has interesting and compelling ways to solve the *indeterminacy problem* as well as the *insufficiency problem*. To see how the Smithian approach to justice can solve these problems we first need to look at his account of justice.

5 Smithian contractarianism

We are now in a position to see why Smith can be profitably considered a contractarian thinker and what is distinctive about his form of contract theory. Smith's evolutionary approach is a move away from the constructivist, threshold contract theory to a developmental, continuous testing approach to the social contract. In traditional contract theories, once the contractual standard is set, all the justificatory work is done. From then on, the relevant political and moral question is about obligation or obedience to justice, not justification. This is not the case for Smith. Each stage of society is a kind of stable contract or equilibrium point that society must go along with.

Adam Smith should be understood as a non-constructivist contractarian that uses the contract idea to test the equilibria that are produced by historical, evolutionary processes. The historical element is essential to Smtih's approach. Smith argues that our institutions are the product of contingent historical processes but also that some institutions are more mutually beneficial than others. In 1803, the editor of the *Edinburgh Review* wrote that Adam Smith attempted to:

> Trace back the history of society to the most simple and universal elements – to resolve almost all that had been ascribed to positive institutions into the spontaneous and irresistible development of certain obvious principles – and to show with how little contrivance or political wisdom the most complicated and apparently artificial schemes of policy might have been created.
>
> (Quoted in Hayek 1978: 267)

After all, 'it is not from the benevolence of the butcher, the brewer, or the baker, that we expect our dinner, but from their regard to their own interest' (*WN* I.ii.2). By individuals acting in accordance with their own perceived interests, as they are naturally inclined to do, society will benefit more than if individuals actually attempted to do good. Reforming our institutions so that they harness the individual pursuit of their perceived interests into mutually beneficial ways is the goal of Smith's project. It is no surprise then that much of the *Wealth of Nations* is practical advice on institutional reform.

This basic idea of attempting to use the contractual standard of mutual benefit to move to better and better sets of social rules can be modelled as a stag hunt. In the basic stag hunt, two players decide whether they will hunt stag or hare for the day. If they choose to hunt stag, they will do better than if both choose to hunt hare. If one player chooses to hunt hare and the other chooses to hunt stag, however, the stag hunter will get very little and the hare hunter will do slightly better. One version of this toy game is shown in Table 1.

There are two pure strategy Nash equilibria: {Stag, Stag} and {Hare, Hare}. The Stag strategy Pareto dominates the Hare strategy by being more mutually beneficial but the Hare strategy is less risky (Skyrms 2002: 410). Players in a stag hunt are trying to move from a suboptimal to a more optimal equilibrium. They are trying to make progress together, to cooperate as members of a society. Smith gives a similar story about the development of market societies and the development of

Table 1 Stag hunt

	Stag	Hare
Stag	9, 9	0, 8
Hare	8, 0	7, 7

justice. In the language of section 4, this is the process of moving, as a society, to more optimal points on the contract curve or core. That is, a point that will act as a stable social contract that all can go along with.

Smith's evolutionary account of the development of justice and social institutions takes the form of his conjectural, stadial theory of history. Smith describes this development in four stages. They are '1st, the Age of Hunters; secondly, the Age of Shepherds; thirdly, the Age of Agriculture; and fourthly, the Age of Commerce' (*LJA* i.27). Smith's conjectural history begins on an island inhabited by few people. It is sufficient for the inhabitants to find food and to hunt what game might be around. Very little social organization is necessary to collect food effectively for a small, hunter-gatherer society. Over time, the population grows and animal husbandry begins. This precipitates a change to the second stage of society, the shepherd phase. In this stage, the population grows and food is more readily available. Although still rudimentary, the institution of property begins developing. In the hunter stage, property exists only ephemerally. One picks a fruit only to eat it or, at most, to bring the fruit home to the family. As Dennis Rasmussen notes, animals begin to be regarded as private property in this stage and inequalities of wealth begin to accumulate (Rasmussen 2008: 96). Smith argues that as these inequalities begin to grow, government becomes necessary to protect property. J. G. A. Pocock highlights that the emphasis on the shepherd stage of society is a novel development in Smith's theory (Pocock 2001: 316–317). The shepherd, in Smith's history precedes the farmer and is the key moment in the development of justice because of the necessity for rules to protect mobile, private property.

One can already see, in this crude presentation of Smith's theory, how it differs from Hume's account of the development of justice. For Smith, justice, property and social institutions in general arise to fulfil a practical human need. As Nicholas Phillipson puts it, for Smith:

> [human] creativity is a function of indigence. He [mankind] learned to cook because he found raw flesh difficult to digest. He learned to make clothes and build huts because he was too frail to live like the beasts. …Smith's profound insights into the importance of security and good government in releasing that love of improvement on which the progress of civilization depended.
>
> (Phillipson 2010: 116)

Regular and effective law secures the gains of improvement. Once individuals can focus their energy on improving their situation without having to worry about the fruits of their improvements being stolen, those improvements will increase. It is not merely the mental process of association that generates the particular social rules and institutions for Smith. Social institutions are adaptations to local conditions.[26]

The development of rules of private property as opposed to the rules of mere possession is the key moment in the development of justice. Following Gerald Gaus, we can compare Locke and Rousseau on the development of the institution of private property to see Smith's key insight. For Locke, property is guaranteed in the state of nature, while for Rousseau, only possession but not property is justified in the state of nature (Gaus 1990: 407–416). In Smith's stadial theory, the state of nature that corresponds most closely to both Locke and Rousseau's notions is the hunter-gatherer stage. Smith would agree, at least in part, with Rousseau that to develop real property we must move out of the hunter-gatherer stage and into the shepherd stage. In this sense, Smith agrees with Rousseau that the development of civil government of some sort is necessary to protect the inequalities of property that arise in the shepherd stage. In fact, Smith makes this point quite forcefully in the *Wealth of Nations* when he writes:

> The affluence of the rich excites the indignation of the poor, who are often both driven by want, and prompted by envy, to invade his possessions. It is only under the shelter of the civil magistrate that the owner of that valuable property, which is acquired by the labour of many years, or perhaps of many successive generations, can sleep a single night in security. He is at all times surrounded by unknown enemies, whom, though he never provoked, he can never appease, and from whose injustice he can be protected only by the powerful arm of the civil magistrate continually held up to chastise it. The acquisition of valuable and extensive property, therefore, necessarily requires the establishment of civil government. Where there is no property, or at least none that exceeds the value of two or three days labour, civil government is not so necessary.
>
> (*WN* V.i.b.2)

Where Rousseau and Smith differ, as Rasmussen makes clear, is that Smith believes this development is natural and beneficial, whereas Rousseau believes that it is unnatural and deleterious (Rasmussen 2008: 97).

Property is a solution to a particular type of problem that causes civil unrest and makes commerce impossible, namely the problem of what counts as legitimate or justified possession and use. Smith argues that this problem is solved conventionally, although similarly across different societies, by the development of stable rules of property and transfer. As Maynard Smith points out, this type of 'ownership' dynamic is quite common in nature, lending credence to the model (Maynard Smith 1982: 95–100). Herbert Gintis applies the model to the development of private property among humans in terms of the development of psychological heuristics like the 'endowment effect' and a basic tendency to territoriality and identification of property, even in young children (Gintis 2007). What this model shows, and what Smith intuited, is that once there is value in a fixed territory, for a bird or a shepherd, non-property conventions are unstable and there is good reason to believe that private ownership norms, property, will develop as a stable solution to the problem. This solution becomes even more regularized and advanced in the fourth, commercial stage.

The development of property, like the development of all social institutions for Smith is the result of humans attempting to solve problems that arise because of social cooperation. The conventional process of the development of human social institutions occurs as individuals innovate and other people either copy or are taught the innovation. In this evolutionary system, ideas are the replicators and human minds or books are the containers of the replicators.[27] Sometimes evolution occurs because of a basic signaling systems and something as simple as an 'imitate-the-best' strategy (Skyrms 2004: 40–41). Smith suggests that something like this may have occurred. Either people in the society who are already considered elites move to the new 'stag' strategy or those that move to the new strategy become the new elites. Either way, if other members of the population begin to imitate the new 'stag' players, the 'stag' strategy will quickly take over the population. Once norms and enforcement mechanisms develop, the new equilibrium can be robustly enforced with minimal punishment of defectors.[28] Similarly, once the population becomes too large, people begin to notice that edible plants can be planted to yield a regular harvest and, hence, agriculture develops. Agricultural societies, being geographically static and relying on even more advanced private property norms, develop sophisticated systems of civil law and enforcement. As agriculture continues to develop, more and more surplus is created and that surplus combined with man's 'propensity to truck, barter, and exchange one thing for another' that the development of commerce slowly arises (*WN* I.ii.1, 26).

At any point in this process, once social institutions have developed, we may still want to ask whether the system of social rules that exists is an acceptable one. To do so, we will need to use the device of the social contract developed in sections 1 and 4 of this chapter to see how the idea of the social contract can be used to test existing social institutions. Before explaining the process of moving from one suboptimal social equilibrium to a more optimal one, it is worth looking at how this contractual test relates to the impartial spectator. There is substantial disagreement about the role the impartial spectator plays in the rules of justice (Fricke 2011: 47–50). It is not my intention to settle that debate here. Instead, I think my approach avoids that question by using a contractual standard as a *social* test meant to appeal to the interests and reason of each individual, it is an open question how that process will work depending on the particular rules of justice in question.

The model we have used of a social equilibrium of rules is a stag hunt. In that game, all of the reasons and interests of the individuals are contained in the payoffs. Now, consider again the example of the stag hunt; each equilibrium stage of social development is either a hare or stag equilibrium. When the possibility of moving from the hunter-gatherer to the shepherd stage is possible, it is the same as a move from suboptimal hare equilibrium to a more optimal stag equilibrium. Once the new equilibrium is achieved, it opens up the possibility to move to a potentially even more optimal equilibrium. Stag hunts are embedded in stag hunts. When choosing between equilibria we are moving to more and more Pareto optimal points on the contract curve – this is the essence of Smith's conventional contractarian theory of justice.

The important point is that the contractarian procedure does not generate the substance of justice. We saw in sections 2 and 3 that the substance of justice arises out of attitudes of resentment regularized generalized into rules. It is the natural, emergent response of our moral psychology to the necessities and dangers of social interaction. The question we are left with is once these institutions have taken form, once we are at a social equilibria, how do we know if we are at a stag or a hare equilibrium?

Members of society need some way of generating reasons to move from one equilibrium to another. They need a device that can serve as an heuristic to show what reason they have to go along with one set of rules versus another. Society for Smith as for Rawls is a 'cooperative venture for mutual advantage' (Rawls 1999a: 4). The role of social institutions in Smith's 'system of natural liberty' is to secure peace by enforcing justice so that people can feel free to engage in beneficial exchange (*WN* IV.ix.51). The more closely the actual social institutions conform to the standards that allow the operation of the 'obvious and simple system of natural liberty' the more mutual advantage free persons in the society will be able to gain from interacting with one another. The social contract as a representational device can be used to determine whether there is reason to want to move to another social equilibrium. In this way, the social contract device can 'test' the current set of social institutions against other, feasible, sets of institutions. Not to generate a set of institutions *ex nihilo*, but as a way of getting leverage on the current set of institutions.

Rawls, of course, proposes that in the representational device of the social contract, individuals will choose his two principles of justice. The Smithian social contract would likely have a different output. To determine what the output would be, we would want to generate our representative persons, parties to the contract, out of the rich moral psychological material that Smith gives us in *The Theory of Moral Sentiments*. For instance, we know that parties to the contract would be motivated by self-interest as well as by a strong, though limited, fellow feeling. Smithian agents are neither egoists nor moral cosmopolitans. They care more about their close associates than those far away.[29] They are also motivated by a strong desire to please and an aversion to offend their fellows (*TMS* III.2.6).

Many elements of the distinctively Smithian agent are important. Each specification helps to determine the specific output of that contractual device. The exact specification of the agents and of contractual output itself is a project for another time. The thing to note here is that the general form of the contractual output would lean heavily on the idea of the mutual advantage of those that are party to the contract. We know this because of what Smith says about the justification of all constitutions. All constitutions, Smith argues, are 'valued only in proportion as they tend to promote the happiness of those who live under them. This is their sole use and end' (*TMS* IV.i.11). Furthermore, we have seen how important the idea of agreement, of what all can go along with, are to Smith. Whatever other important virtue constitutions or social contracts may have, their sole use and end, according to Smith, is to promote the mutual benefit of those who live under them.

We are now able to see the general outline of what we can legitimately call 'Smithian contractarianism'. The evolutionary process of human interaction over long periods generates social institutions. At a certain stage, namely the stage where impersonal exchange through markets is possible, members of the market society will come together to wonder about the optimality of their social institutions. They will ask themselves, 'can we do better?'. To answer that question, they will need to determine what counts as an acceptable criticism or complaint against their current society. To do this in a way that all members of society can 'go along with' requires the use of a social contract as a device of representation. By using this device, members of society will create representative agents out of the material of Smithian practical rationality and moral psychology and then put those agents into a bargaining situation to determine the acceptable form of mutually beneficial social institutions. This differs importantly from utilitarianism in that it is not an aggregative process that requires interpersonal comparisons of utility.

The usual *indeterminacy problem* from section 4 will be solved by the fact of moral psychology and partly by the reduction of the possible solution set of equilibria to those that are feasible from the starting point of the status quo. Some set or core of possible, mutually beneficial equilibria of social institutions will be generated by this device and the facts of the particular culture and history of the agents will, in all likelihood make some equilibria seem more salient than others. This will also solve the *insufficiency problem*. As Rawls points out the agents in the contractual device are only 'artificial creatures inhabiting our device of representation' (Rawls 1996: 28). It is from the point of view of what Rawls calls 'you and me' or from our normal everyday selves living in civil society that we must evaluate the output of the social contract (Rawls 1996: 28). The social contract is a representation that is meant to show us the kind of society that is acceptable for us, the kind of society that we have reason to want to live in.

The direction of social evolution is never certain. Social and cultural institutions develop in an evolutionary fashion as adaptations to the particular problems of a given time and place are tried out and either passed on to the next generation or rejected. The forces of social evolution are like an ocean wave that we can either go along with or swim against. In either case, we cannot divert the path or blunt the force of the wave itself. The idea of the social contract, in this context, is like a surfboard. While we cannot control the wave itself, with a proper instrument, one can ride along the way choosing which direction to go and how. By using the device of the social contract, we are able as a society to help reflectively direct, to some extent, our path through history. Sometimes the forces of social change are little more than a ripple. In these cases, probably the case for most of human history before the development of agriculture, all we can do is keep paddling and wait. In some periods, like much of modern times, it feels like we are riding a tsunami. In either case, all we can do is direct along the ridges of the wave that the forces of social evolution have generated for us.

Adam Smith, as I have argued, does have a social theory that can make use of the idea of the social contract. His conceptions of resentment generating stable, interpersonal rules of justice and of social institutions justified by mutual advantage share many characteristics of modern contractarian approaches to social theory. Furthermore, his use of an evolutionary account of the process of social change helps to solve a problem within contractarian theory, namely how to generate stable, determinate sets of social institutions. While the exact details of the Smithian contract need to be more clearly worked out, it is clear that Smith can profitably be regarded as a kind of contract theorists in the contemporary sense.

Acknowledgments

The author would like to thank many who have read, commented on, or encouraged this work including: Doug Den Uyl, Fonna Forman, Steven Ealy, Chris Freiman, Jerry Gaus, Bill Glod, Keith Hankins, Ryan Hanley, James Hartley, Bobbi Herzberg, Alistair Isaac, Dan Klein, Adam Martin, Chris Martin, Thomas Martin, Chris Nelson, Jim Otteson, David Schmidtz, Emily Skarbek, Kevin Vallier, and especially, Michael Gill, who gave extremely helpful feedback and encouragement during the initial stages of this project. The errors are, of course, mine.

Notes

1   John Rawls, for instance, cites David Hume and Adam Smith (together with Thomas Hobbes) as precursors to the utilitarianism that is found in Jeremy Benthm and ultimately Henry Sidgwick in (1999a: 20 9ff; see also Rosen 2003).
2   Cf. David Gauthier (1979).
3   Amartya Sen discusses the connection between impartiality and objectivity throughout *The Idea of Justice*, often comparing his view to Smith's but also see Sen's discussion of Scanlon and impartiality in (Barry 1989: 4; Barry 1995: 2; Sen 2009: 197–200).
4   Cf. (Griswold, 1999: 244).
5   There is a question, which I do not really go into here, whether Smith could hold a version of utilitarianism as a guide to social policy, while generally being a contractarian. This is a complicated question, but I think some of *The Wealth of Nations* can be read this way. If this were Smith's view, though, his utilitarianism would be much closer to the approach that Russell Hardin describes as 'institutional utilitarianism' and attributes to David Hume. I think the case is stronger for Hume, but it may be that institutional utilitarianism is compatible on some level with contractarianism (Hardin 2007: 165–71).
6   Also see: (*LJA* v.114–118, 315–16) for a similar view.
7   References to (Hume, 1998).
8   Smith uses the phrase 'go along with' at least 42 times in *The Theory of Moral Sentiments*, a fact that was pointed out to me by Vernon Smith in conversation.
9   Notice that the usage of 'constructivist' here is different from its usage in the moral context, especially in the work of John Rawls. Rawlsian constructivism may be either constructivist or non-constructivist in my usage depending on how we interpret Rawls.
10 I am following Gerald Gaus in calling this a 'testing conception' but I do not claim that this is Gaus's view. He uses the term in a different context, although I think there

are some broad similarities between the two views. See Gaus (2011: 424).

11 Rawls described his original position as a 'device of representation'. The idea of the social contract presented here is very similar. See especially, Rawls's defense of the original position against Habermas's criticism in (Rawls 1996: 381).

12 There are two basic reasons why mutual advantage is a necessary criterion of a social contract: (1) mutual advantage is necessary to maintain the stability of the contract. Individuals cannot be expected to maintain a social contract or bargain where they would do better by unilaterally deviating to another point in the feasible set. Therefore, social contracts that are outside of the Pareto set or not mutually beneficial are not feasible in the sense that they will not be stable. (2) Giving reasons is not giving orders. The social contract is not meant to be a suicide pact, no person should be forced to maintain a social order where they are made worse off for the benefits of others if there is another social state where that person would be better off without making someone else worse off. That is, no person should have a state of affairs or a bargain unilaterally imposed on them by others. To allow this would assume that one party to the contract has natural authority over the other party. This idea does violence to the very notion of bargaining or contracting which must occur between persons who each have the ability to walk away from or veto the agreement.

13 Bernard Gert also compares morality, which in his understanding is similar to what Smith means by justice and grammar. See Gert (2005: 4–5) For a good discussion of Smith on this point, see Griswold (1999: 190, 229).

14 The best recent discussion of the role of the virtues besides justice in Adam Smith's moral theory is in Hanley (2009a). I differ from Hanley in not characterizing Smith's overall view as a form of virtue ethics mostly because of the role that justice plays in his system. Hanley is correct that Smith's view does share many of the features of modern virtue ethical approaches to ethics but one key difference is that Smith's positive virtue are constrained by the negative virtue of justice. After all, it is conformity with general rules, not merely the development of general dispositions to behave virtuously that is praiseworthy or blameworthy according to Smith. Contemporary virtue ethics has typically had problems incorporating justice into the virtues for similar reasons, for instance see (LeBar 2009). Whether or not Smith should be considered a virtue ethicist or a deontologist is, in some sense, unimportant. Hanley is right to highlight the important aspects of virtue ethics in Smith's approach and his work has certainly deepened our understanding of Smith's ethics.

15 Arguably, Epicurus and maybe Hobbes had a similar idea (Kavka 1995; Thrasher 2012).

16 For more recent defenses of similar views, see Gaus (2011), Harman (1975), Nichols (2007) and Rawls (1996, 1999b).

17 Rawls lumps together Hume, Smith, Bentham and Mill (and even Hobbes in his essay 'Justice as Fairness') as part of a great utilitarian tradition (Rawls 1999a: vii, 262). While Smith is clearly not a utilitarian in regards to moral theory, Rawls may be closer to the mark with Hume, at least in regards to justice. There is an issue of whether Smith can be considered an 'institutional utilitarian' in the sense that Smith argued, in *The Wealth of Nations*, that social policy should be justified by the effect it has on the average member of society. Still, using something like utilitarianism as the basis of social policy does not imply that Smith's general moral theory or theory of justice is reducible to claims about utility. My claim here is that Smith is best thought of as a social contract thinker rather than a utilitarian. As Rawls points out in *A Theory of*

Justice, it is possible that a utility principle could be the output of a genuinely contractual process. Arguably, Harsanyi's version of utilitarianism is justified contractually in Harsanyi (1955). I think it is an open question whether Smith's contractual theory would lead to something like utilitarian principles.

18   Ryan Hanley argues the opposite, namely that, for Smith, the good precedes the right. His argument, however, is about the methodology of Scottish enlightenment social science, not Smith's theory of justice in particular. He is right to point out that the Scots did not tend to pursue value-free social science in the contemporary style. He is also right to argue that values were a deep part of the Scottish enlightenment social science but this does not imply that the good is prior to the right in a deep sense. Within the range delimited by justice and propriety, the good should be pursued but the right antecedently limits the acceptable means of pursuing the good (see Hanley 2009b: 33). Insofar as Hanley is arguing that, for Smith, the idea of the good life guides our understanding of propriety, he is certainly correct. The difference is that unlike some contemporary virtue theorists and virtually all consequentialists, the good does not determine the content of the right, in this case the rules of justice. Those are determined by a different procedure.

19   Utility in the sense that Hume uses it when he argues 'public utility is the sole origin of justice' (*EPM* 3.3.1).

20   Here, my account seems to follow, at least the conclusion of Christel Fricke's recent discussion of the 'the most sacred rules of justice', at least on the natural authority of the rules of justice (2011: 64–65).

21   There is an important ambiguity in this formulation that there is not space to go into in detail about whether individuals in contract situation have preferences over rules themselves or only over rules insofar as they lead to favorable outcomes. Following Smith's general approach, I think it is reasonable to see Smith as thinking that individuals would have preferences over rules themselves and not merely over outcomes since their sentiments related to resentment are not, fundamentally, outcome based. This is one reason, as I will develop later, why Smith's theory is strongly deontological.

22   An allocation of goods x and y is in the core if for an allocation represented by the ordered pair (X_n, Y_n) the allocation is (1) in the Pareto set and (2) $u_x(X_i, Y_i) \geq u_x(X_j, Y_j)$ i εN and j εN $i \neq j$ – that is, each party would not do better by moving to a different allocation.

23   On this point see: Rosen (2003: ch. 4 and 6).

24   Many have argued that interpersonal comparisons of utility are, contra Lionel Robbins, possible; John Harsanyi, for instance, agues this point in many places (such as Harsanyi 1955). The problem, even if theorists like Harsanyi are right and interpersonal comparisons are possible, is that there are many possible ways of comparing utilities across persons. Utilitarianism, insofar as it requires interpersonal comparisons, must specify one particular and unique way of comparing utilities on a social level. No utilitarians have fully solved this serious problem. The problem also applies to contractarians who want to make specific claims about distributive justice such as Ken Binmore. See, especially, Binmore's discussion of the problem and his proposed 'social index' solution (Binmore 2005: 31–36).

25   See Sen (1997). Sen defines the maximal set as a set of elements in which all of the elements in the set dominate any element outside the set but where none of the elements in the set dominates any of the other elements in the set. More formally, M is a maximal subset of S when $(S) = [x|x \; \varepsilon \; S$ and for no $y \; \varepsilon \; S{:}yPx]$.

26   One way to compare the difference between Smith and Hume on this point is to think of Hume's account of the development of property in the *Treatise* as much more similar

to accounts of evolutionary drift rather than adaptation, whereas, Smith is giving a pretty clearly adaptationist account of social institutions.

27 This account of the development of social practices is similar in general form, although not necessarily in the details to the account found in Sperber (1996).

28 For a detailed explanation see Boyd and Richerson (2005).

29 For an in-depth examination of this aspect of Smith's thought, see Forman-Barzilai (2010).

Bibliography

Barry, B. (1989) *Theories of Justice*, Berkeley, CA: University of California Press.

Barry, B. (1995) *Justice as Impartiality*, Oxford: Oxford University Press.

Binmore, K. (2005) *Natural Justice*, Oxford: Oxford University Press.

Boyd, R. and Richerson, P.J. (2005) 'Punishment allows the evolution of cooperation (or anything else) in sizable groups', in *The Origin and Evolution of Cultures*, Oxford: Oxford University Press, pp. 166–88.

Buchanan, J. (1975/2000) *The Limits of Liberty: Between Anarchy and Leviathan*, Indianapolis, IN: Liberty Fund.

Fleischacker, S. (2004) *On Adam Smith's Wealth of Nations: A Philosophical Companion*, Princeton, NJ: Princeton University Press.

Forman-Barzilai, F. (2010) *Adam Smith and the Circles of Sympathy: Cosmopolitanism and Moral Theory*, Cambridge: Cambridge University Press.

Freeman, S. (1990) 'Reason and agreement in social contract views', *Philosophy and Public Affairs*, 19: 122–57.

Fricke, C. (2011) 'Adam Smith and the "most sacred rules of justice"', *Adam Smith Review*, 6: 46–74.

Gaus, G. (1990) *Value and Justification: The Foundations of Liberal Theory*, Cambridge: Cambridge University Press.

Gaus, G. (2011) *The Order of Public Reason: A Theory of Freedom and Morality in a Diverse and Bounded World*, Cambridge: Cambridge University Press.

Gauthier, D. (1979) 'David Hume, contractarian', *Philosophical Review*, 88: 3–38.

Gert, B. (2005) *Morality: Its Nature and Justification*, New York: Oxford University Press.

Gintis, H. (2007) 'The evolution of private property', *Journal of Economic Behavior and Organization*, 64: 1–16.

Griswold, C. (1999) *Adam Smith and the Virtues of Enlightenment*, Cambridge: Cambridge University Press.

Haakonssen, K. (1981) *The Science of a Legislator: The Natural Jurisprudence of David Hume and Adam Smith*, Cambridge: Cambridge University Press.

Hanley, R. (2009a) *Adam Smith and the Character of Virtue*, Cambridge: Cambridge University Press.

Hanley, R. (2009b) 'Social science and human flourishing: the Scottish enlightenment and today', *Journal of Scottish Philosophy*, 7: 29–46.

Hardin, R. (2007) *David Hume: Moral and Political Theorist*, New York: Oxford University Press.

Harman, G. (1975) 'Moral relativism defended', *Philosophical Review*, 84: 3–22.

Harsanyi, J. (1955) 'Cardinal welfare, individualistic ethics, and interpersonal comparisons of utility', *Journal of Political Economy*, 63: 309–321.

Hayek, F. (1978) 'Adam Smith's message in today's language', in *New Studies in Philosophy, Politics, Economics and the History of Ideas*, London: Routledge, pp. 267–269.

Hume, D. (1784) 'Of the original contract', in E. Miller (ed.) *Essays: Moral, Political, and Literary*, Indianapolis, IN: Liberty Fund, pp. 465–87.

Hume, D. (1754/1998) *An Enquiry Concerning the Principles of Morals*, Beauchamp, T. (ed.) Oxford: Oxford University Press.

Kavka, G. (1995) 'The rationality of rule-following: Hobbes's dispute with the Foole', *Law and Philosophy*, 14: 5–34.

LeBar, M. (2009) 'Virtue ethics and deontic constraints', *Ethics*, 119: 642–71.

Maynard Smith, J. (1982) *Evolution and the Theory of Games*, Cambridge: Cambridge University Press.

Nichols, S. (2007) *Sentimental Rules: On the Natural Foundations of Moral Judgment*, New York: Oxford University Press.

Phillipson, N. (2010) *Adam Smith: An Enlightened Life*, New Haven, CT: Yale University Press.

Pocock, J.G.A. (2001) *Barbarism and Religion, Vol. 2: Narratives of Civil Government*, Cambridge: Cambridge University Press.

Rasmussen, D. (2008) *The Problems and Promise of Commercial Society: Adam Smith's Response to Rousseau*, University Park, PA: Pennsylvania State University Press.

Rawls, J. (1955) 'Two concepts of rules', *Philosophical Review*, 64: 3–32.

Rawls, J. (1958) 'Justice as fairness', *Philosophical Review*, 67: 164–94.

Rawls, J. (1996) *Political Liberalism*, New York: Columbia University Press.

Rawls, J. (1999a) *A Theory of Justice*, rev. edn., Cambridge: Harvard University Press.

Rawls, J. (1999b) 'The independence of moral theory', in S. Freeman (ed.) *Collected Papers*, Cambridge: Harvard University Press, pp. 286–302.

Rosen, F. (2003) *Classical Utilitarianism From Hume to Mill*, London: Routledge.

Sen, A. (1997) 'Maximization and the act of choice', *Econometrica*, 65: 745–79.

Sen, A. (2009) *The Idea of Justice*, Cambridge: Harvard University Press.

Skyrms, B. (2002) 'Signals, evolution and the explanatory power of transient information', *Philosophy of Science*, 69: 407–28.

Skyrms, B. (2004) *The Stag Hunt and the Evolution of Social Structure*, Cambridge: Cambridge University Press.

Smetana, J. and Braeges, J. (1990) 'The development of toddlers' moral and conventional judgments', *Merrill-Palmer Quarterly*, 36: 329–46.

Smith, A. (1976a) *The Theory of Moral Sentiments*, D.D. Raphael and A.L. Macfie (eds), Oxford: Oxford University Press; Glasgow edn. reprinted, Liberty Press (1982).

Smith, A. (1976b) 'An inquiry into the nature and causes of the wealth of nations', R.H. Campbell and A.S. Skinner (eds), Oxford: Oxford University Press; Glasgow edn.

Smith, A. (1978) *Lectures on Jurisprudence*, R.L. Meek, D.D. Raphael and P.G. Stein (eds), Oxford: Oxford University Press; Glasgow edn.

Sperber, D. (1996) *Explaining Culture: A Naturalistic Approach*, Cambridge: Blackwell Publishers.

Thrasher, J.J. (2012) 'Reconciling justice and pleasure in epicurean contractarianism', *Ethical Theory and Moral Practice*, 16: 423–36.

Classical antiquity and reading Adam Smith's *Theory of Moral Sentiments*

Is the sunbathing beggar an allusion to Diogenes the Cynic and Alexander the Great?

Thomas R. Martin

Introduction

The works of Adam Smith reveal his extensive knowledge of the literature, history, and philosophy of classical antiquity.[1] As John Rae eloquently observes, 'all through life [Smith] showed a knowledge of Greek and Latin literature not only uncommonly extensive but uncommonly exact'.[2] The contents of Smith's personal library reveal that he kept at hand editions in the original languages of many Greek and Roman authors.[3] A top-flight education in Smith's time included study in reading ancient Greek and Latin texts in the original and many eighteenth-century intellectuals acquired a considerable depth of knowledge of those sources. Perhaps most remarkable of all was Anthony Ashley Cooper, third Earl of Shaftesbury, Smith's rhetorical *bête noire*.[4] Shaftesbury became fluent in Latin (and perhaps Greek as well) by the time he was eleven years old as a result of the visionary conversational pedagogy that John Locke, a family friend, had recommended for the boy's private tutoring.[5] Smith himself studied Latin and Greek sources so thoroughly that he learned many passages by heart and throughout his life could quote them from memory.[6]

Smith therefore could expect that well-educated readers of his works would be able to recognize references to ancient Greek and Roman literature and history in his writings and draw implications from those connections, even when such references were only allusions rather than direct citations. This expectation existed because Smith and his peers shared a common intellectual discourse that was informed by their deep knowledge of Greek and Latin texts from antiquity, the shared treasury of information that allowed them to chose, at appropriate points, to give additional context and depth to their works through echoes of the classical works in which they had been steeped in their educations.

I am going to suggest in what follows that this shared discourse makes it at least conceivable that, when Smith mentions a sunbathing beggar in *The Theory of Moral Sentiments* (*TMS* IV.1.10) as part of his famous argument about the effect of the invisible hand on the welfare of the poor, he was making an allusion to a famous story from ancient Greek history about an encounter between Diogenes the Cynic philosopher and Alexander the Great, the Macedonian king and conqueror. Since some commentators have criticized Smith's comment in this passage that 'the beggar, who suns himself by the side of the highway, possesses the security which kings are fighting for', it seems worthwhile to present the hypothesis that the meaning of Smith's reference to a beggar at this point in *TMS* might be easier to grasp if the comment does in fact allude to this much-told story from classical antiquity about Diogenes and Alexander. The story, with some variations, appears in a number of Greek and Latin texts that Smith owned in his library. It was also well known to his educated eighteenth-century contemporaries.

To be sure, the hypothesis presented here can be no more than tentative because Smith does not make an explicit reference to the ancient story that I am suggesting his words might have brought to mind for those members of audience who knew the famous stories from the Greek and Roman past as well as he did. My hope, then, is only that this suggestion will seem to deserve consideration because Smith's impressive knowledge of ancient texts makes it possible that appreciation of *TMS* can on occasion be deepened by reference to texts from classical antiquity, even when, as in this case, certainty is unattainable concerning whether Smith in fact intended to point his readers in that direction.

The context in *TMS* of Smith's comment on the sunbathing beggar

The passage on the sunbathing beggar serves as a concluding comment to Smith's discussion in *TMS* Part IV ('Of the Effect of Utility upon the Sentiment of Approbation') of the invisible hand's effect on the distribution of wealth in society.[7] To cap his argument at this point, Smith declares,

> When Providence divided the earth among a few lordly masters, it neither forgot nor abandoned those who seemed to have been left out in the partition. These last too enjoy their share of all that it produces. In what constitutes the real happiness of human life, they are in no respect inferior to those who seem so much above them. In ease of body and peace of mind, all the different ranks of life are nearly upon a level, and the beggar, who suns himself by the side of the highway, possesses that security which kings are fighting for.
>
> (*TMS* IV.1.10)

This section in *TMS* has troubled some modern commentators because on the surface the comparison between a beggar and kings seems difficult to understand. How could a pauper possibly be 'nearly upon a level' with royalty in 'ease of body and peace of mind' and 'security'? Moreover, Smith's remarks in *TMS* about the shame that people generally attribute to poverty and the widespread contempt felt for beggars (on both of which see below) seem to make his culminating comment about the beggar and kings at IV.1.10 even more puzzling. For example, Alexander Gray summed up this 'purple passage' with the conclusion that '[q]uite apart from the doubtful and topical question of Security, this argument certainly endeavours to prove too much'.[8] More recently, Bernard Boxill, in a discussion of utilitarianism and the state of the poor in contemporary society, offers a stinging critique of Smith's description of the sunbathing beggar:

> Smith asks us to imagine a beggar sunning himself on the side of the highway, apparently forgetting that the side of the highway is sometimes icy rather than sunny, and that physical discomforts normally add to unhappiness. But this is the least of his fallacies. He also seems to completely overlook the possibility that the beggar sunning himself on the side of the highway may be mourning the deaths of his children, whom a little money might have saved…. Smith also seems to forget that the poor suffer from knowing how badly others think of them. …Smith may have misunderstood the stolidity of the poor…. But perhaps Smith was not making any claim about the poor in general, but only a claim about beggars sunning themselves on the sides of highways. Such individuals often affect a humility unmixed with any trace of wounded pride and seem to have adopted the Stoic philosophy, which allegedly enables its followers to be happy in whatever circumstances they happen to be in.[9]

Terry Sullivan, in a 2009 online essay on 'Christian Economy Versus *Capitalism* and Versus *Socialism*', follows his rejection of Smith's theory of an invisible hand as a force improving the condition of the poor with this very pointed criticism of comment about the beggar:

> Smith displays a similar complacency about the situation of *the beggar who suns himself by the side of the highway*. Who may not feel so easy in body and mind, after the sun goes down and the rain begins and he remembers that he hasn't eaten for a while. Maybe *The Best Things In Life Are Free* but it usually requires at least bus fare to get to where they are being distributed. Food isn't always free, unless you like grubs.[10]

To be able to assess the possible validity of such criticisms of Smith's comment in *TMS* about a sunbathing beggar and kings and to provide context for the suggestion that at least one of the possible meanings of this comment is easier to understand if one posits an allusion to Diogenes and Alexander, it seems appropriate first to outline some points bearing on the comment that occur immediately preceding in *TMS*.

The mention of the sunbathing beggar appears toward the end of Chapter I of Part IV of *TMS* 'Of the beauty which the appearance of UTILITY bestows upon all the productions of Art, and of the extensive influence of this species of Beauty'. Earlier, near the opening of that same chapter, Smith cites Hume on 'why utility pleases', concluding his summary of Hume's views with the sentence, 'When we visit the palaces of the great, we cannot help conceiving the satisfaction we should enjoy if we ourselves were the masters, and were possessed of so much artful and ingeniously contrived accommodation' (IV.1.2).[11] Smith then presents his own original observation on the nature of 'our' desire to occupy the same station that the great enjoy in life: we yearn, he argues, not so much for the actual conditions of the lives of the great, but rather for what he calls the 'love of system…the same regard to the beauty of order, of art and contrivance' (IV.1.11). As a consequence, people ruin themselves 'by laying out money on trinkets of frivolous utility' and weigh themselves down with 'toys' and 'baubles' (IV.1.6). Smith then elevates this observation to the status of a major determinant of human behavior: 'Nor is it only with regard to such frivolous objects that our conduct is influenced by this principle; it is often the secret motive of the most serious and important pursuits of both private and public life' (IV.1.7).

Smith next discusses the state of the poor. He does not precisely define the financial status of the people he has in mind, but they are not homeless beggars; they live in cottages and ride on horseback. They do, however, yearn for what they imagine the wealthy and great to possess: 'The poor man's son, whom heaven in its anger has visited with ambition, when he begins to look around him, admires the condition of the rich' (IV.1.8).[12] This seems analogous to what Smith has said earlier about the shame commonly attached to poverty:

> The poor man goes out and comes in unheeded, and when in the midst of a crowd is in the same obscurity as if shut up in his own hovel. Those humble cares and painful attentions which occupy those in his situation, afford no amusement to the dissipated and the gay. They turn away their eyes from him, or if the extremity of his distress forces them to look at him, it is only to spurn so disagreeable an object from among them. The fortunate and the proud wonder at the insolence of human wretchedness, that it should dare to present itself before them, and with the loathsome aspect of its misery presume to disturb the serenity of their happiness.
>
> (*TMS* I.iii.2)

Smith seems to be at pains to emphasize the negatives of being poor and, especially, being seen by others to be poor. Everyone, including the poor man, sees poverty as so shameful as to be 'mortifying', a condition that leads mankind 'to conceal our poverty' (I.iii.2.1). So important to Smith is this point that he immediately repeats it: 'The poor man…is ashamed of his poverty. …He is mortified' (I.iii.2.1). The pain of poverty on this score is extreme: 'Compared with the contempt of mankind, all other external evils are easily supported' (I.iii.2.12). Condemned to such a sorry state, then, the ambitious poor man is motivated by the desire to escape the obscurity and the lack of approbation, indeed the active contempt from others that his state of poverty imposes on him (whether deservedly or not).[13]

The reference to heaven in its anger hints that the ambition to improve one's material condition can be far from an unalloyed good. Smith expands on this hint by next devoting two substantial paragraphs (IV.1.8–9) to an emphatic explanation of why this ambition of the poor is deluded and harmful. Smith's description of the nature of the delusion and the harm provides relevant background for understanding the significance of the sunbathing beggar.

First of all, the poor man thinks that, if he could ride in a carriage and be waited upon by a retinue of servants, he would sit still contentedly, and be quiet, enjoying himself in the thought of the happiness and tranquillity of his situation. …he devotes himself for ever to the pursuit of wealth and greatness. To obtain the conveniences which these afford, he submits in the first year, nay in the first month of his application, to more fatigue of body and more uneasiness of mind than he could have suffered through the whole of his life from the want of them.

(*TMS* IV.1.8)

Already at this point, it is clear that on the basis of Smith's argument in this context that a tranquil life and peace of mind trump the value of riches and rank. Smith goes on to reinforce these judgments, adding the crucial point that a man can obtain, purely on his own, the characteristics of life that truly matter:

Through the whole of his life he pursues the idea of a certain artificial and elegant repose which he may never arrive at, for which he sacrifices a real tranquillity that is at all times in his power, and which, if in the extremity of old age he should at last attain to it, he will find to be in no respect preferable to that humble security and contentment which he had abandoned for it.

(*TMS* IV.1.8)

When the poor man does achieve understanding,

he begins at last to find that wealth and greatness are mere trinkets of frivolous utility, no more adapted for procuring ease of body and tranquillity of mind than the tweezer-cases of the lover of toys. …There is no other real difference between them, except that the conveniences of the one are somewhat more observable than those of the other.

(*TMS* IV.1.8)

Smith continues his argument in this same section with the striking claim that the 'conveniency' of 'the palaces, the gardens, the equipage, the retinue of the great' is no more valuable than that of 'a tooth-pick, of an ear-picker, of a machine for cutting the nails, or of any other trinket of the same kind'. All these things are 'subjects of vanity', and the only advantage of the 'magnificence of wealth and greatness' is that money and status, as subjects of vanity, 'more effectually gratify that love of distinction so natural to man'. In the end, however, the 'languor of disease and the weariness of old age' allow a man to see that 'the pleasures of the vain and empty distinctions of greatness disappear'. Smith strengthens his point about the power of this humbling revelation with a vivid metaphor of the great man's life as a machine so stressed that it threatens to blow apart with lethal force:

Power and riches appear then to be, what they are, enormous and operose machines contrived to produce a few trifling conveniences to the body, consisting of springs the most nice and delicate, which must be kept in order with the most anxious attention, and which in spite of all our care are ready every moment to burst into pieces, and to crush in their ruins their unfortunate possessor.

(*TMS* IV.1.8)

These seeming advantages can 'keep off the summer shower, not the winter storm, but leave [the possessor] always as much, and sometimes more exposed than before, to anxiety, to fear, and to sorrow; to diseases, to danger, and to death'.[14] Despite this enduring truth, Smith continues, people still 'in times of ease and prosperity" focus on "those great objects of human desire'. They – indeed, as Smith puts it, 'we' – do not comprehend that 'the real satisfaction' afforded us by 'the pleasures of wealth and greatness' by themselves 'will always appear in the highest degree contemptible and trifling'. We maintain this mistaken view because we confound wealth and greatness 'in our imagination with the order, the regular and harmonious movement of the system, the machine or oeconomy' that produces them (IV.1.9).

Smith ends this reiteration of the principle that he had enunciated earlier with his striking judgment about the crucial role of deception: 'And it is well that nature imposes upon us in this manner. It is this deception which rouses and keeps in continual motion the industry of mankind' (IV.1.10). Smith then prepares the ground for his metaphor of the invisible hand by describing how 'the industry of mankind' has led to agriculture and material progress. Through those 'improvements' over time, it has come to be that 'the proud and unfeeling landlord' provides for his peasant 'brethren', albeit unintentionally and unknowingly, 'that share of the necessities of life, which they would in vain have expected from his humanity or his justice'. In this way, the rich help to support the poor because

[t]hey are led by an invisible hand to make nearly the same distribution of the necessities of life, which would have been made, had the earth been divided into equal portions among all its inhabitants, and thus without intending it, without knowing it, advance the interest of the society, and afford means to the multiplication of the species.

(*TMS* IV.1.10)

Next Smith proceeds to the passage whose context this outline of immediately preceding points was meant to illustrate: 'When Providence divided the earth among a few lordly masters, it neither forgot nor abandoned those who seemed to have been left out in the partition. These last too enjoy their share of all that it produces' (IV.1.10).[15] Here, Smith's language recalls what he said earlier about how, through the mechanism of the invisible hand, the rich 'divide with the poor the produce of their improvements', giving them a 'share of the necessities of life'.

Smith then moves from the material basis of life to the point that he had made so strongly about what is truly most important in our existence: 'In what constitutes the *real happiness* [my emphasis] of human life, they [that is, those who *seemed* poor] are in no respect inferior to those who would *seem* [my emphasis] so much above them'. Here, Smith adverts to his earlier argument about the delusion concerning the value of riches and greatness that most human beings operate under: the appearances of these 'subjects of vanity' are deceiving.

It is at this point in the chapter that the sunbathing beggar appears, when Smith has reached the culmination of his argument about the rich and the poor, and before he moves on to a different implication of his principle, namely the demonstration how 'the same love of system, the same regard to the beauty of order, of art and contrivance, frequently serves to recommend those institutions which tend to promote the public welfare' (IV.1.11).

As mentioned at the start, the concluding statement about the beggar and kings seems on the surface paradoxical because Smith himself has said earlier in *TMS* that the poor exist in a state of obscurity and strenuous disapprobation, and that those poor who have ambition enjoy neither 'ease of body' nor 'peace of mind'. In the pursuit of wealth and rank they toil and labor and wear out their bodies throughout their entire lives, and they are consumed with dissatisfaction at their station in society. How then can someone as poor as a beggar be 'nearly upon a level' in happiness and security with those constituting the highest social rank, with royalty?

The puzzle only seems to deepen when one examines Smith's only previous mention of a beggar in *TMS*. There, he devotes a paragraph to the topic, and his starkly phrased comments also seem to conflict with the apparently positive implications of his mention of the sunbathing beggar. In the earlier passage, he bluntly expresses what he presents as a universal judgment on the 'mere want of fortune, mere poverty' in saying, 'We despise a beggar; and though his importunities may extort an alms from us, he is scarce ever the object of any serious commiseration'.[16] For my argument, however, as, I hope, becomes clear later, it is significant that Smith then offers a very different assessment of 'our' reaction to the state that he calls the 'fall from riches to poverty'. He first expresses his judgment that 'in the present state of society, this misfortune can seldom happen without some misconduct, and some very considerable misconduct too, in the sufferer'. Despite what Smith seems here to regard as the moral failure of people who have lost their wealth and become poor, he goes on to say that, nevertheless, the one who has suffered the 'fall from riches to poverty' usually is pitied to such an extent that his friends and even his creditors support him

> in some degree of decent, though humble, mediocrity. To persons under such misfortunes, we could perhaps easily pardon some degree of weakness; but, at the same time, they who carry the firmest countenance, who accommodate themselves with the greatest ease to their new situation, who seem to feel no humiliation from the change, but to rest their rank in the society, not upon their fortune, but upon their character and conduct, are always the most approved of, and never fail to command our highest and most affectionate admiration.
>
> (*TMS* III.3.18)

This last part will be important to recall when we turn to the life of Diogenes.

Smith's description of the 'decent, though humble, mediocrity' in which this pitiable but somehow sympathetic category of the poor exist still leaves it unclear how a beggar in particular could enjoy 'ease of body', 'peace of mind', and material 'security'. As the modern commentators cited above say, how could a poor beggar have 'nearly' the same level of these qualities as a king when a beggar by definition has no comfortable place to live, no guarantee of food, and therefore no protection from the elements or from hunger or from any other deadly menace (points of course made by the commentators cited above)? Moreover, in his subsequent discussion (VII.ii.1.16) of the philosophy of Zeno, the founder of ancient Stoicism, Smith remarks that poverty is the first of the factors that creates 'pain of body'.[17]

One possible answer deserving serious consideration is that a beggar does possess a type of physical security not possessed by a king: a beggar is free of the fear of being injured or killed in battle. He holds no position of power with the responsibility to defend others or to conduct wars of conquest to acquire glory for himself and his royal line. In other words, the beggar enjoys a literal security from the risk of bodily harm that a king could not have because the monarch would have the responsibility of leading his subjects in time of war, either in defense or conquest.[18] This point about the contrast between the relatively safe existence of a beggar as a non-combatant and the great physical danger to which Alexander was exposed as a king fighting wars does appear in the text of Juvenal, one of the ancient sources to be summarized below, and it certainly cannot be excluded as a plausible explanation of the meaning of security in the passage from *TMS* under consideration here.

At the same time, it also seems reasonable to entertain the possibility that the context of the entire chapter in *TMS* as outlined above suggests that the sunbathing beggar's security refers to one's psychological and emotional state rather than to literal protection from physical harm. This possibility perhaps gains some credence because, not long before the comment on the sunbathing beggar, who is obviously at his ease, Smith emphasizes the 'toilsome pursuits' of the poor man (IV.1.8) and makes clear that ease of body and tranquillity of mind are precisely what people in poverty usually lack. Moreover, the importance to Smith of these ideas about psychological stability is evident from his discussion in *TMS* of the doctrine of the ancient philosopher Epicurus that tranquillity of mind is the state that human beings should strive to achieve rather than material wealth (VII.ii.2.1–17).[19] In Epicurean thought, Smith explains, 'ease of body' and 'security or tranquillity of mind' constitute 'the most perfect state of human nature, the most complete happiness which man was capable of enjoying' (VII.ii.2.7). That is, security is in this context a synonym for tranquillity as a description of the most desirable mental state for a human being. This meaning for security is supported by Smith's thirteen other references to it in *TMS* previous to the appearance of the sunbathing beggar. Ten of these instances employ security to mean, explicitly or implicitly, tranquillity of mind.[20] In only three places, it seems to me, does Smith use security in its common meaning of physical safety and comfort.[21]

It is therefore perhaps plausible to suggest that a most prominent aspect of Smith's argument in the context of Chapter I of Part IV is that 'real happiness' does not depend on riches, power, and (literal) security (in the everyday sense of being safe from want and being able to defend oneself against bodily threats). Smith mentions real happiness at two other places in *TMS* that seem relevant to this suggestion because both these passages explicitly connect to ancient Greek sources. In the first, Smith refers to the philosophy of the Stoics (III.3.30); in the second, he summarizes a conversation between Pyrrhus, the warrior king of Epirus, and a royal 'favourite' about the commander's goals (III.3.31). This passage is an implicit reference to Plutarch's *Life of Pyrrhus* 14, where Pyrrhus has a dialogue on this topic with his ambassador Cineas, who was versed in the philosophy of Epicurus and whose eloquence and wit made him a renowned international ambassador and a source of memorable quotations in antiquity.[22] To the restless Pyrrhus, who was insisting that more military campaigns were the way to happiness (*eudaimonia*) for himself, Cineas directed questions intended to lead the king to admit that his ambitions for happiness could be better satisfied by an Epicurean-like turn to tranquillity rather than by more war. In other words, Smith is alluding to these ancient sources to support his conclusion that '[h]appiness consists in tranquillity and enjoyment' (III.3.30).[23]

In short, happiness depends above all on the mind, as Smith in *TMS* cites Epicurus as saying (VII.ii.2.5) and as he himself explains in his discussion in *WN* of why a coward is more wretched and miserable than a man who is physically disabled (V.i.f.60): 'happiness and misery, which reside altogether in the mind, must necessarily depend more upon the healthful or unhealthful, the mutilated or entire state of the mind, than upon that of the body'. Given this definition of happiness, then, it is possible to see how a beggar, or at least a beggar of a certain remarkable type, could conceivably possess this sort of security, the sort of tranquillity and ease of mind that kings would lack as a result of their elevated position in life and onerous responsibilities. On this interpretation, it might even be said, then, that kings must, metaphorically, fight for mental tranquillity because the circumstances of being a ruler responsible for a kingdom and its wars inevitably make this sort of undisturbed existence so difficult, if not impossible, for a monarch to achieve. In this way, kings fight for (psychological) security.

In any case, it is crucial to say that this possibility does not allow us to conclude that every beggar possesses this security of mind: the only beggar characterized by the possession of such tranquillity is one with the right mental attitude, one who lives his life of poverty as a way to achieve tranquility and who as a result will 'never fail to command our highest and most affectionate admiration'. Could Smith's beggar sunning himself by the side of the highway be just this sort of beggar? As Smith's earlier (and only other) reference in *TMS* to a beggar implies (III.3.18, on which see above), being at leisure is not the conventional conduct of a person in this resource-limited condition.

The beggar at IV.1.10, then, seems to be unusual. Is it possible that the unusualness of this beggar, especially the clue that he is said to be taking the sun, suggests an allusion to an anecdote about an encounter between the philosopher-beggar Diogenes of Sinope and the Macedonian king Alexander the Great that was frequently cited in ancient Greek and Latin texts known to Smith and his well-read contemporaries?

Ancient texts on the encounter between Diogenes and Alexander and on the life of Diogenes

Numerous Greek and Latin authors narrate, or at least advert to, an encounter and exchange of remarks between Diogenes and Alexander.[24] Some of the sources offer slightly differing accounts of the precise posture in which Alexander found Diogenes and of exactly what was said between the two on this occasion (the only one on which they could have met, so far as we can tell from the chronologies of their respective personal histories). That stories about meetings between famous people generate alternate versions, or even that entire incidents can be invented, is of course a phenomenon as familiar in ancient literature as it is in modern celebrity gossip reporting. If the meeting between these two renowned figures actually took place, it would have occurred in 336BC, when Alexander, now King of Macedonia (ruled 336–323BC), made a visit to Corinth in southern Greece.[25] He had come there to address his Greek allies and convince them to recognize him as their supreme leader against the Persian Empire on a military campaign eastward on which he would try to fight his way all the way to the end of the world.[26] Alexander the Great, as he was later called as a result of his victories on that epochal expedition, became the most written-about and debated king of classical antiquity.[27] The meeting took place because, when he visited Corinth, Alexander took the initiative to seek out Diogenes, who by that time was already famous – or perhaps it is more accurate to say infamous – as the original Cynic ('like a dog') philosopher.[28]

To provide what I hope will be adequate context for my hypothesis, I next present summaries of the versions of the encounter between Diogenes and Alexander as found in eleven different ancient Greek and Latin sources that are listed in approximately (certainty is not possible) the chronological order of the date of their composition. These selections were chosen because they contain enough detail to be relevant for the purposes of this paper and also because they come from Greek and Latin texts that it seems likely Smith could have known, to judge from the books that he had in his personal library or that he cites elsewhere in *TMS*.[29] The translations included in the summaries are my renditions of the original texts as literally as possible.

1.   Cicero *Tusculan Disputations* 5.92: In reciting various anecdotes chosen to demonstrate how philosophers do not fear poverty, Cicero reports that when Alexander asked Diogenes to tell him if he needed anything, the latter said, 'Now indeed a little bit away from the sun'. No other details about the encounter are provided. Cicero then adds that Diogenes used to say that he needed nothing, but that the king of Persia (the richest man in the world of Diogenes) would never have enough, and that he had no longing for the pleasures of the Persian king and that the king could never enjoy the pleasures that he Diogenes had.

2.   Valerius Maximus *Memorable Doings and Sayings* 4.3.external 4a (where 'external' indicates a non-Roman story): In a section of anecdotes on examples of abstinence and continence, Valerius reports that Alexander, despite his nickname 'Undefeated' (see Diodorus 17.93.4 and Plutarch *Alexander* 14),

could not defeat the continence of Diogenes. Alexander, Valerius says, approached Diogenes as the latter was sitting in the sun and encouraged him to declare if he wanted anything to be furnished to him. Positioned on the sidewalk, Diogenes replied, 'Soon about other things; in the meantime I would like you not to block me from the sun'. Valerius then interprets this reply as meaning that Alexander was attempting to dislodge Diogenes with his riches but that he was more quickly going to dislodge the Persian king Darius with his armaments.

3. Juvenal *Satires* 14.308–316: In a section of the poem on how the desire for wealth torments human beings and how riches that one has had to toil so hard to win then have to be guarded with yet more misery, Juvenal offers as one of his examples that

> The large clay jars of the Cynic with no clothes do not burn; if you break them, others will be his home tomorrow, and they will remain held together with lead.[30] When Alexander saw the great inhabitant in that piece of clay, he realized how much more fortunate was the one who desires nothing than he who demands the whole globe for himself and is going to experience dangers equal to the things that he achieves. You would have no divine power, if there would be prudence: Fortune, we would not make you a goddess.

It should be noted, as previously mentioned, that Juvenal implies that Alexander admired Diogenes because the philosopher was not exposed to the hazards of war as the price for winning great conquests.

4. Epictetus *Discourses* 3.22.92: In a section on how Cynic philosophers ought to be engaging and witty so as to be prepared to give quick responses on every occasion, Epictetus says that when Alexander was standing over Diogenes while the latter was falling asleep, the king said [quoting Homer *Iliad* 2.24, when the dream-vision sent by Zeus addresses the slumbering King Agamemnon], 'A man who is a decision-maker shouldn't sleep all night long'. Diogenes, still being half-asleep, answered [quoting the very next line of the epic, *Iliad* 2.25], '(The man) to whom the people are entrusted and so many things are matters of care'.[31] No other details of the encounter are offered.

5. Plutarch *On the Fortune of Alexander* 331E–332C: In this essay from the collection known as the *Moralia*, Plutarch discusses whether luck or excellence was responsible for Alexander's success. In this particular section, he is explaining how it is characteristic of a genuinely philosophic soul that it love wisdom and be especially impressed by men who are wise. In this context, he remarks that, as a result of speaking to Diogenes in Corinth, Alexander was so astounded and impressed by Diogenes' way of life and great reputation that often, when the king happened to remember the philosopher, he would say, 'If were not Alexander, I would be Diogenes'. Plutarch then interprets this comment as Alexander meaning, 'I would myself occupy my time with argumentation, if I were not being a philosopher through my deeds'. Plutarch

adds that Alexander did not say, 'If I were not a king, I would be Diogenes', or 'If I were not rich and a member of the Macedonian royal line', because, Plutarch explains, Alexander did not judge luck to be superior to wisdom and his purple robe and diadem to be superior to [the philosopher's] little bag [to hold food] and much-worn cloak. (These items were associated with Diogenes' choice of an unconventional way of life as a penniless beggar, on which see below.) Plutarch repeats the saying 'If I were not Alexander, I would be Diogenes' and then expounds at some length on how it meant that Alexander would have followed the example of Diogenes in his 'easy-to-pay for' style of life (on which see below), were he as king not pursuing the goal of campaigning in the footsteps of Heracles, Perseus, and Dionysus to bring Greek culture to Asia, especially by emulating Diogenes' action in 'adult-erating the currency' (on which see below) by bringing a Greek system of government to the barbarian world (and thereby altering it).

6. Plutarch *On Exile* 605DE: In this essay from the *Moralia*, Plutarch cites the case of Diogenes as an example contradicting the assumption that being forced into exile necessarily leads to the exiled man suffering the loss of his fame. He reports (with no further context offered) that Alexander, seeing Diogenes sitting in sun, stood over him and asked if he needed anything. When Diogenes gave no other order than to remove the shade a little, Alexander was thunder-struck at his spirit and said to his friends, 'If I were not Alexander, I would be Diogenes'.

7. Plutarch *To an Uneducated Ruler* 782AB: In this essay from the *Moralia*, Plutarch argues that it is important for a ruler to acquire philosophical under-standing. Accordingly, Plutarch comments that only the lessons of philosophy can protect us from experiencing what Alexander did when, in Corinth, he saw Diogenes and became enamored of his excellent nature and was amazed at the spirit and greatness of the man. As a result, Alexander remarked, 'If I were not Alexander, I would be Diogenes'. Plutarch then explains that with these words Alexander was not far from saying that he was burdened by his good fortune, distinction, and power as forming a hindrance to excellence and to his having free time, and that he wished he had a little bag and a worn cloak because through these Diogenes was undefeated and unable to be captured, not as he himself was through his armaments and horses and thrusting spears. So (Plutarch imagines Alexander thinking), Alexander by being a philosopher (or, it could also be translated, by practicing philosophy) could be Diogenes in his disposition but remain Alexander in his fortune, and on this account be Diogenes even more just because he was Alexander, who needed a lot of ballast and a great steersman for his great fortune, which faced heavy wind and swell at sea. It should be noted that, in contrast to Juvenal, Plutarch here does not imply that Alexander may have felt any threat to his security from his military endeavors. The Macedonian's belief in himself as unable to be defeated or captured spared him that anxiety.

8. Plutarch *Alexander* 14: In his biography of Alexander, Plutarch reports that after Alexander had been proclaimed the commander of the Greeks against the

Persians at the meeting in Corinth, numerous political leaders and philosophers approached him with congratulations. Alexander expected that Diogenes would be one of them, but the latter took no notice of Alexander and stayed at leisure in Craneion.[32] So, Alexander went to see him and happened upon him lying in the sun. When he saw so many people approaching, Diogenes lifted himself up a little and directed his gaze at Alexander. When the latter spoke to him in greeting and then asked if he happened to need anything, Diogenes said, 'Move over a little out of the sun'. It is said, Plutarch adds, that Alexander was so struck by this and amazed at the man taking him lightly in his [Diogenes'] disdain and greatness that Alexander said to those around him, who as they were leaving laughed and joked [about Diogenes], 'If I were not Alexander, I would be Diogenes'. In this passage, Plutarch does not offer any interpretation of this remark by Alexander, as he does in sources nos. 5 and 7.

9. Arrian *Anabasis of Alexander* 7.2.1–2: Arrian's narrative is the most comprehensive surviving ancient account of Alexander's military expedition. In this passage, immediately after reporting Alexander's meeting with the Indian sages who rejected the ambition to conquer others, Arrian says that Alexander was reported to have been astounded by Diogenes when he happened upon him lying down in the sun on the Isthmus [i. e., at Corinth]. The king stopped with his soldiers and asked if Diogenes needed anything. Diogenes said that he needed nothing else but ordered Alexander and those with him to move out of the way of the sun. Arrian, himself a scholar of philosophy who published the discourses of Epictetus, then remarks that although Alexander was not in every way beyond comprehending those things that were better, he was terribly dominated by fame.

10. Aelian *Historical Miscellany* 3.29: In this collection of anecdotes of various kinds, Aelian records that Diogenes consistently cited Greek tragedy to describe his exile as a penniless, badly clothed beggar and quotes two lines of verse from an unknown (to us) play that the philosopher reportedly used in doing so, but he also says that Diogenes was just as proud of his situation as Alexander was of his rule over the inhabited world after the king had captured the Indians and come back to Babylon.[33] This latter reference would date the anecdote to 323BC near the end of Alexander's life.

11. Diogenes Laertius *Lives of Eminent Philosophers* 6: Laertius in his biography of Diogenes includes several mentions of Alexander the Great. First, he reports in indirect speech, without context or other details, that Alexander said that if he had not been born Alexander, he would have wanted to have been born Diogenes (6.32). Laertius also reports the encounter being considered here, saying that one day Diogenes was taking the sun in the Craneion at Corinth when Alexander came and stood over him and said 'Request of me what you want'. The philosopher replied, 'Remove the shade from me' (6.38). Later in the biography, Laertius records, without further context, that Alexander once stood next to Diogenes and said, 'I am Alexander the great king'. Diogenes then replied, 'And I am Diogenes the dog' (6.60). Later still in his gallery of anecdotes Laertius reports, again without any historical context, that Alexander

stood next to Diogenes and said, 'Are you not afraid of me'? Diogenes responded, 'But what are you? A good thing or bad'? Alexander answered, Good'. Diogenes said, 'Who, then, is afraid of the good'? (6.68).

As these summaries show, the fullest version of the encounter between Diogenes and Alexander appears in Plutarch's biography of Alexander (no. 8 above) from his *Parallel Lives of Greeks and Romans*. Smith attests to knowing the *Parallel Lives* at *TMS* VII.ii.1.31, where he refers to 'the Greek heroes whose lives have been written by Plutarch'.[34] As the summaries also show, the other sources include some variations in the story, including in the case of Epictetus (no. 4) and Laertius (no. 11) different quotations that Plutarch does not cite in his works (nos. 5, 6, 7, and 8). What seems important for the purposes of this paper is to point out that these sources over all do indicate, first, that Diogenes was seen as very poor. In the eleven passages, five of them (nos. 1, 5, 7, 10, and 11) directly or indirectly mention Diogenes' poverty, and none of them even implies that he was anything but a man whose impoverished circumstances were obviously apparent to an observer such as Alexander. Secondly, the sources taken as a whole also indicate, directly or indirectly, that Diogenes was sunning himself when Alexander came up to him (nos. 1, 2, 6, 8, 9, and 11).[35]

Noticing these points, I suggest, might incline an educated contemporary of Smith's time to think of this particular ancient story upon reading *TMS* IV.1.10. It was certainly true that other prominent authors of the eighteenth century discussed Diogenes, Alexander the Great and the encounter between these two famous figures.[36] For example, David Hume, in his *An Enquiry Concerning the Principles of Morals* (London, 1751) ends the section entitled 'A Dialogue' with a comparison between Diogenes and Pascal:

> DIOGENES is the most celebrated model of extravagant philosophy. ...The foundation of DIOGENES's conduct was an endeavour to render himself an independent being as much as possible, and to confine all his wants and desires and pleasures within himself and his own mind. ...The austerities of the GREEK were in order to inure himself to hardships, and prevent his ever suffering'.[37]

Henry Fielding wrote *A Dialogue Between Alexander the Great, and Diogenes the Cynic*, in *Miscellanies* (1743), which imitates Lucian's *Dialogues of the Dead* to offer satirical reflections on the conflict between a ruler's power and philosophical thought.[38] Samuel Johnson, in his short essay in *The Idler* No. 14, Saturday July 15, 1758, used Alexander's uninvited visit to Diogenes to muse on the 'robbery of time' that famous people must endure from importunate visitors.[39] Jean Jacques Rousseau mentioned the meeting between Diogenes and Alexander in his *Discourse on the Virtue Most Necessary for a Hero*.[40] Jean-Louis Castilhon published *Le Diogène moderne, ou le Désabbrobateur* in 1770. This evidence shows that Smith would not have been pointing toward figures from ancient history little known to intellectuals of his era if he was indeed alluding to the meeting between Diogenes and Alexander when at *TMS* IV.1.10 he mentions a sunbathing beggar.

If Smith was in fact making this allusion, then I suggest that the ancient biography of Diogenes perhaps offers hints for understanding how Diogenes as a very special example of a beggar in fact corresponded to Smith's special criteria for those poor who earn approbation instead of contempt, and therefore for understanding why this particular philosopher's life might provide an example, if a highly idiosyncratic one, of how it was possible to achieve tranquillity of mind and real happiness by forsaking the trinkets of frivolous utility that Smith argued most people covet.

As noted above, Laertius' biography of Diogenes occurs in a collection of lives of eminent Greek philosophers, a source that Smith knew (*TMS* VII.ii.1.31, a reference to the life of the philosopher Zeno, which follows soon after that of Diogenes in Laertius' work). As Laertius, tells it, Diogenes started life in Sinope, a city on the Black Sea, as a member of a family that enjoyed a comfortable socioeconomic level. He apparently rose to a position of authority in his hometown, perhaps as a mint official or other magistrate with access to public funds. Subsequently, however, he lost his wealth and his status when he became involved in some sort of financial corruption scandal involving his having 'adulterated the currency'. As a result, he was forced to go into permanent exile (6.20-21, 49, 56), a penalty second in harshness only to execution in ancient Greek society.[41] Now a stateless person, Diogenes journeyed to Athens and became a follower of the philosopher Antisthenes. At some undetermined point, perhaps before Philip II, King of Macedonia and father of Alexander, came to Corinth in 338 BC (Lucian, *How to Write History* 3), Diogenes was captured by pirates and sold as a slave to Xeniades of Corinth to be the pedagogue of his master's sons (6.30–31, 36, 74). He died in Corinth in his late 80s (6.76-77) and was buried in a tomb with a marble sculpture of a dog atop it outside a main gate to that city that was still preserved nearly five hundred years later (6.31, 77–79; Pausanias 2.2.4).[42]

The majority of Laertius' biography consists of vivid details about how Diogenes chose to live his life in exile. When he arrived in Athens, he was a pauper, indeed a beggar (6.49).[43] In Laertius' words, Diogenes elected an 'easy-to-pay for' life (6.21, 37). Taking the lifestyle of a mouse as an inspiration, he owned the absolute minimum of material possessions: a 'little bag' (or 'wallet') in which he kept food and a single threadbare cloak that he also used as bedding (6.22). After observing children drinking and eating with their hands, he even threw away his cup and bowl (6.37). Indeed, Diogenes held in special contempt both possessions and those who sought them (6.24), or had servants to do things they could do for themselves, such as putting on their shoes (6.44). The love of money, he said, was the 'mother city' of all evils (6.50). He literally and scornfully spat in the face of the rich (6.32). For shelter, he found a giant clay storage jar located in the Athenian sanctuary of the Mother of the Gods, which, in keeping with his choice to live in disciplined discomfort, he rolled over hot sands in the summer. In the winter he went around hugging metal statues covered with snow (6.23).

Before he became a slave in Corinth (and therefore supported by his master) and perhaps afterwards as well, he took gifts from friends, but he told them that the money they gave him was what they owed him in recompense (that is, in return for the example he set them by the way he lived his life) and not just alms for which he begged (6.46). When he did ask for money from those who were not his friends, he sometimes did so to make a show of a moral point, to demonstrate that a miser was stingy (6.56) or that a wastrel's spendthrift ways were likely to reduce him to penury (6. 67). In other words, rather than an ordinary beggar piteously beseeching passersby for handouts in his humiliation, he apparently looked everyone in the face with pride and demanded what he insisted was his due.

In addition, Diogenes forged an international reputation for himself through his aggressive flaunting of his disdain for the ideas and conduct of others. He engaged in relentless public derision of any and all whom he regarded as frauds or humbugs, regardless of their fame or their age, from young to old. He more than once mocked Plato, even to his face (6.24–28, 53). In fact, the bulk of Laertius' biography consists of one anecdote after another in which Diogenes upbraids someone or other, from politicians to playwrights to athletes (6.24-69). In addition, Diogenes gained notoriety from the almost antagonistic unconventionality of his personal habits. For example, he went so far in breaking strongly held ancient Greek notions of propriety that he ate in the agora despite being reprimanded for it (6.58, 69). And not only that: he masturbated and moved his bowels publicly there as well, in full view of others gathered in the city's center (6.46, 69; cf. Dio Chrysostom, *Oration* 8.35–36). In short, Diogenes lived, he said, like Heracles, judging nothing to be more important than liberty (6.71).

These characteristics of the life of Diogenes surely make him an unusual beggar by any standard, but I suggest that they would also place him in a special category of the poor described by Smith in an earlier section of *TMS* (III.3.18). There, he refers to individuals who experience a 'fall from riches to poverty' because they were most likely involved in 'some very considerable misconduct' but nevertheless are numbered among 'those who carry the firmest countenance, who seem to feel no humiliation from the change, but to rest their rank in the society, not upon their fortune, but upon their character and conduct' and therefore 'are always the most approved of, and never fail to command our highest and most affectionate admiration'. By 'adulterating the currency' and becoming an exile, Diogenes engineered his fall from wealth to poverty through his own misconduct, but he retained his firm, even fiercely proud countenance and certainly did not feel humiliated by his condition. And his rank in society – his great fame – did indeed rest upon his highly individual character and unconventional conduct. Finally, as the ancient sources about his meeting with Alexander show, the most powerful man in Diogenes' world directly expressed his admiration for the impoverished philosopher's rejection of wealth and possessions.[44] No one could have cared less for trinkets of frivolous utility than Diogenes the Cynic, and Alexander the king as a result regarded the penniless philosopher as great.

Conclusion

I am therefore suggesting that the ancient sources known to Smith reveal that Diogenes possessed the tranquillity of mind representing the kind of security that Smith says constituted real happiness. I further suggest that the type of security embodied by Diogenes could perhaps have been the 'security which kings are fighting for'. On this interpretation, then, it was just this type of security that eluded kings such as Alexander because their elevated but conventional positions of rank brought them what others regarded as the compensation of being the object of constant attention and regard, but in return inevitably exposed them to a 'loss of liberty' because their acquisition of "greatness" caused them to forfeit 'all that leisure, all that ease, all that careless security' (I.iii.2.1). If this seems credible, then Smith is perhaps also hinting that Diogenes' entire life amounted to, as it were, an ongoing program of the kind of 'philosophical researches' that 'were given to us for the direction of our conduct in this life' (*TMS* III.5.5).

If there is any plausibility to this final and extremely tentative suggestion, then exploring it would properly belong to another treatise, as Plutarch says when he identifies philosophical issues arising from the details of a biography (such as, *Life of Pericles* 6 and 39). That exploration would examine in what ways Smith might entertain moral philosophy as one possible guide to real happiness in the world as he postulated it to be.[45] If that function of philosophy is at all conceivable, then one implication of a Diogenes allusion in *TMS* might be that Diogenes was an example of an individual who had made his life an answer to Smith's question,

> Are you in earnest resolved never to barter your liberty for the lordly servitude of a court, but to live free, fearless, and independent? There seems to be one way to continue in that virtuous resolution; and perhaps but one. Never enter the place from whence so few have been able to return; never come within the circle of ambition; nor ever bring yourself into comparison with those masters of the earth who have already engrossed the attention of half mankind before you.
>
> (*TMS* I.iii.2.7)

In the end, of course, my primary suggestion that, at *TMS* IV.1.10, Smith is making an allusion to the ancient story of the encounter between Diogenes the philosophic sunbathing beggar and Alexander the powerful king cannot more be than that, a suggestion. It is my hope, however, that if the hypothesis seems at least conceivable, that will be so because it aligns with the recognition that the depth of Smith's knowledge of classical texts made him capable of such a reference, and that the awareness of this capability on his part can help keep his readers alert to the possibility that their appreciation of his thought, especially in *TMS*, can at appropriate points be deepened through reflection on the ancient history and literature so well known to Smith.[46]

Notes

1   The fundamental studies are Vivenza 2001, 2004, and 2007. On ancient Greek sources in particular, see Scott 1940.
2   Rae 1895: 23.
3   See the lists in Bonar 1932 and Mizuta 2000. Smith's Greek and Latin texts specifically relevant to ancient Greek history and philosophy included editions of Aelian

Historical Miscellany, Aeschines, Aeschines Socraticus, Archimedes, Aristophanes, Aristotle, Arrian *Expedition of Alexander and Indica*, Athenaeus, Marcus Aurelius, Cicero, Quintus Curtius Rufus, Demosthenes, Diodorus Siculus, Diogenes Laertius, Epictetus, Eunapius, Herodotus, Isaeus, Isocrates, Justin, Juvenal, Lucian, Lucretius, Lysias, Pausanias, Plato, Pliny *Natural History*, Plutarch *Parallel Lives* and *Moralia*, Pollux, Polybius, Seneca, Sextus Empiricus, Strabo, Thucydides, Valerius Maximus *Memorable Doings and Sayings*, and Xenophon. According to Bonar, Latin and Greek classics made up a fifth of Smith's library.

4   On Smith's attitude toward Shaftesbury, see Ross 2010: 84–5.

5   For Locke's influence, see Cranston 1957: 193; Voitle 1984: 9–11. On Locke's extensive knowledge and use of Latin, see Cranston 1957: 31, 63, 78, 92; for Locke's views on learning the language by speaking it with a private tutor, See Cranston 1957: 25, 242. Shaftesbury was tutored privately by a Mrs. Birch, the daughter of a schoolmaster and proficient in Greek and Latin. See Brett 1951: 38. Is it possible that Smith's criticism of Shaftesbury reflected a tinge of jealousy at the earl's early, privileged, and extremely effective education in the Classics? At *LRBL* i.137–i.v.148, where Smith launches into a condemnation of Shaftesbury for a variety of failings in religion, thought, and 'a grand and pompous diction', Smith begins his jeremiad with an otherwise seemingly unmotivated comment about Shaftesbury 'having been educated under a tutor'. Smith did not enjoy that privilege in his youthful study of Greek and Latin.

6   On Smith's classical education, see Rae 1895: 5, 9–10, 23; Ross 2010: 18–20, 39–42; Phillipson 2010: 18, 40–1. For the influence of ancient Greek texts on Smith, see Scott 1940: 81. On Smith's education in general, see also Scott 1937 and Foley 1976: 80–99.

7   The topic of the invisible hand has of course received immense attention from Smith scholars. I will not attempt to cite any of this vast literature, as the topic itself does not affect my hypothesis.

8   Gray 1976: 161.

9   Boxill 2010: 541–2.

10 Sullivan 2009.

11 See p. 179, n. 1, for the passages in Hume of which Smith is primarily thinking as identified by the editors of the Glasgow edition of Smith.

12 While the phrase 'heaven in its anger' perhaps most plausibly refers to the Christian notion of the just anger of God, is it also possible that it could be an allusion to the *ira deorum* known from Greco-Roman religion as a source of punishment for human beings sent by the pagan gods to impose justice, despite accounts in ancient literature of the divinities' own often seemingly amoral behavior toward one another? Authors such as Plutarch (for example, in *Life of Pericles* 39) decisively rejected as malicious fiction all depictions of the gods that did not present the Greek and Roman deities as the authors only of good and never of evil, thereby arguing that the gods were in fact the source of cosmic justice. If Smith with his reference to the anger of heaven is alluding to this view of divine justice from classical antiquity, which aligns with that of Christian theology, an indirect reference of this kind would be in keeping with the suggestion being made in this paper that Smith meant the passage on a sunbathing beggar in *TMS* to evoke classical echoes. Smith surely knew of the topic of the anger of the gods as found throughout ancient literature, from (to cite authors well known to Smith) the epics of Homer to Plutarch's essay *On the Delays of Divine Vengeance*. For modern discussion of this topic in Greek and Roman thought, see, for example, Burkert 1985: 246–50; Muellner 1996: p. 8 (with a list of examples of divine anger from *The Iliad* and *The Odyssey*), and Fantham 2003.

13　For a recent discussion of Smith's treatment of poverty in terms of his economic thought (separate from his philosophic thought) and his views on what commercial society should and should not do about the poor, see Vaughan 2008: 81–93, who (p. 100, n. 140) includes copious references to earlier scholarly work on Smith and poverty. For a discussion of Smith's ideas concerning the moral character of the poor and, especially, whether the poor were benefited more by government intervention or *laissez-faire* in the real world, see Rimlinger 1976).

14　In fact, Smith says, the desire of the poor man to be thought rich can induce him to make expenditures that reduce him to 'beggary' (I.iii.3.7).

15　Although Providence is certainly a prominent feature of Christian theology, the likelihood of Smith's knowledge of ancient texts relevant to ancient philosophical ideas on providence such as Plato, *Laws*, Cicero's *On the Nature of the Gods*, and Plutarch, *On Stoic Self-Contradictions* perhaps makes it possible that this reference to Providence could (also?) allude to ancient philosophy in general and Stoicism in particular. For providence in Stoic thought, see, for example, Bobzien 1998: 45–7. For specific original texts, see de Vogel vol. III 1973: nos. 927–33. Scholarship on Smith and Stoicism is a vast subject far beyond the scope of this paper. For a nuanced discussion of the influence of Stoicism on Smith, see above all Vivenza 2001: 191–212, 239. It should be specially noted, however, that Vivenza (p. 209) argues against regarding ancient Stoicism as playing a part in what can be called 'providential reasonings' as seen in Smith. See Ross 2010: 41, 182–3. Waszek 1984 discusses original Greek terms that can be compared to Smith's ideas.

16　Smith in other works describes the beggar as engaging in 'truck and barter' to a certain extent because he cannot secure the necessities of life by relying solely on the 'benevolence of his fellow–citizens' (*WN* I.ii.2; cf. LJ 'Report of 1762–3' vi.46 and 'Report dated 1766' 220).

17　Sellars 2006) provides an overview of ancient Stoic concepts. For discussion of selected topics, see Inwood 2003.

18　I am indebted to one of the anonymous readers for this significant point.

19　On Epicurus in *TMS*, see Vivenza 2001: 79–80. For a survey of ancient Epicureanism, see O'Keefe 2010.

20　I.i.1.13, I.ii.2.3, I.iii.2.1, III.2.20, III.3.4, III.3.31, III.3.33, III.3.44, III.4.12, and IV.i.8.

21　I.iii.2.6, II.ii.1.4, and II.ii.1.8.

22　See, for example, Pliny *Natural History* 14.12. Plutarch *Pyrrhus* 20 explicitly connects Cineas to knowledge of Epicurus' ideas; Cicero *On Old Age* 43 (13) does so as well, without naming Epicurus.

23　For a different interpretation of happiness in Smith, see Rasmussen 2006: 314, who explains the beggar's real happiness as his being personally free and relatively secure in a commercial society. Den Uyl and Rasmussen 2010: 29–40 respond to Rasmussen's arguments regarding the contradiction that he posits between philosophy and commerce in Smith's work.

24　For a list of more than 20 references to the encounter between Diogenes and Alexander, including those making only a passing mention, see Berve vol. II 1926: p. 417, n. 3. For translations of passages collected as Diogenes' 'Confrontations with Alexander the Great', see Hard 2012: 53–7.

25　Following Schwartz vol. II 1910: 1–23, modern scholars usually regard the story of the encounter of Diogenes and Alexander at Corinth as fictional. See, for example, Heckel 2006: 113, s. v. Diogenes [1].

26　For the visit, see Diodorus 17.4.9, Plutarch Alexander 14, and Arrian Anabasis 1.1.1–2.

27   There is practically limitless disagreement today, as in antiquity, concerning the interpretation of Alexander's goals and the consequences of his actions. For the views to which I subscribe, see Martin and Blackwell 2012.

28   'Dog' in Greek (*kyōn*) is the source of the term 'cynic' ('like a dog'). For a survey of ancient Cynicism, see Desmond *Cynics* 2008.

29   Despite the prominence of Diogenes in the works of Dio Chrysostom (ca. AD40/50–after 110), excerpts from Dio are not included here because Smith did not have a copy of that author's works in his library and, in a letter to John Maclaurin, explicitly says, 'I am totally unacquainted with the writings of Dion Chrysostom' (Corr. Letter Appendix E.s to John Maclaurin, Lord Dreghorn, *Works* (Edinburgh, 1798), i. xxvii.). Dio is not cited in *TMS*. Dio in fact composed *Oration 4: On Kingship* as an extended (and of course largely invented) dialogue between Diogenes and Alexander on the occasion of the latter's visit to Corinth. Dio also made Diogenes a central figure in his *Orations* 6, 8, 9, and 10. According to Dio in *On Kingship*, Alexander wanted to see Diogenes because, despite looking down on him for his poverty and cheapness in his life, the king admired and envied the philosopher's reputation, recognizing that while he as an ambitious commander needed armies and riches to remain safe and to achieve fame, Diogenes in his disdain for possessions could go about without danger and do whatever he desired without having to have money (4.6–10). Dio then says (4.14) that when Alexander approached the seated Diogenes and greeted him, the latter looked up at him 'like a lion' and ordered him to stand aside a little because, Dio adds, Diogenes happened to be warming himself in the sun.

30   Laertius 6.23, 43 reports that Diogenes while in Athens lived in a *pithos*, a very large storage jar made of clay. Juvenal is the only source to report that Alexander saw Diogenes inside the jar and in Athens; most likely in doing so he is exercising a poet's freedom to reinvent a story to suit his own goals as a literary artist. Lucian, *How to Write History* 3, depicts Diogenes living in this sort of vessel in Corinth.

31   Epictetus, not long before (3.22.72) in this section on Cynicism in the *Discourses*, cited the same line from the Iliad quoted by Diogenes to contrast the onerous duties of a king with the freedom from responsibility that it was better for a Cynic to enjoy. For the topos that intimate knowledge of Homeric epic was the mark of a superbly educated man, see the interchange that Xenophon narrates (*Symposium* 3.5–6) between Socrates, Antisthenes, and Niceratus, the latter of whom claimed that his father, Nicias the fifth-century BC Athenian general, had compelled him to learn the *Iliad* and the *Odyssey* by heart. Alexander was well known for his love of the *Iliad*, a copy of which he kept under his pillow, as, for example, Plutarch *Alexander* 8 reports.

32   Craneion was a grove of cypresses near the fortification wall surrounding Corinth that was frequented for recreation by wealthy people, such as Diogenes' owner Xeniades (on whom see below). Diogenes Laertius 6.77 and Dio Chrysostom *Oration 8. 4* and 9.4 describe Diogenes spending time there; Dio also says (4.14) that Alexander met Diogenes in that location. On Craneion, see Xenophon, *Hellenica* 4.4.4; Pausanias 2.2.4; Plutarch, *On Exile* 601B.

33   Diogenes Laertius 6.38 gives (with some minor differences) the same quotation as does Aelian. It is not possible to say whether one author was using the other, as we are not sure of the precise chronology of their careers as authors.

34   *TMS* includes other references that could possibly be taken from Plutarch's biographies, as noted by Raphael and Macfie in the Glasgow edition, *ad locc*: I.iii.2.6, II.iii.2.3, II.iii.2.6, III.3.31, VI.ii.2.3, and VI.ii.2.16. There are other possible references to Plutarch's *Moralia* at VI.iii.32. The only place in Smith's works in which he makes

reference to a specific work of Plutarch, so far as I can determine, is in the *History of Astronomy* (EPS IV.18). There, Smith mentions '[Plutarch's] second book, concerning the opinions of philosophers, all the ancient systems of Astronomy'. This is a reference to the essay *On the Opinions of Philosophers* found in Plutarch's *Moralia* 874D–911B. Smith explicitly refers to Alexander elsewhere six times in *TMS* at I.iii.2.9, II.iii.2.3, VI.i.10, VI.iii.28, VI.iii.30, and VI.iii.32. In fact, one of Smith's first textbooks in school had been the Latin author Justin's epitome of the *Philippic History of Pompeius Trogus*. See Ross 2010: 19. Justin's account covers the career of Alexander in Books 11 and 12. Smith does not mention Diogenes of Sinope in *TMS*, though at *LRBL* Lecture 9.i.124 he does refer to Lucian's comparison between himself and Diogenes in the latter's essay *How to Write History* 3. It is perhaps worth mentioning that Epictetus, to whose thought Smith refers multiple times in *TMS*, refers in his *Discourses* to Diogenes more often than to any other philosopher except Socrates. See Long 2002: 58. Smith cites passages from the *Discourses* (without, however, mentioning the title) at *TMS* VII.ii.1.19, 25, and 26. He had Epictetus' *Encheiridion* in his library.

35 Whether Diogenes was situated literally 'at the side of the highway' is a question with which the sources do not concern themselves, though my interpretation of the text of Valerius Maximus is that it suggests that Diogenes was in fact sitting down on a sidewalk. The text says that Diogenes was sitting in *crepidine*. Glare 1982: 457 defines the noun *crepido* as, among other things, 'a raised causeway in a street, sidewalk'. Shackleton Bailey vol. I 2000: 385, however, translates this phrase as 'on a step'.

36 On Diogenes and Cynicism in eighteenth-century thought, see Niehues-Pröbsting 1996; Shea 2010: 23–127, especially on D'Alembert and Diderot. (Smith had copies of their works in his library; see Mizuta 2000: nos. 23–7 and 500–3.)

37 Fielding 1998: 122–123.

38 For the text of Fielding's *Dialogue*, see Fielding vol. 1 1972: 226–262; Fielding 2003: 208–209. See also the discussion of the *Dialogue* in Mazella 2007: 97–104.

39 See Johnson vol. 7 1811: 48–51. Smith owned a two–volume edition of *The Idler* published in 1767 (Mizuta 2000: no. 879).

40 Although written in probably 1751, the essay was not published until 1768, without Rousseau's permission. See Kelly 2003: 83. Smith had several volumes of Rousseau's works in his library (Mizuta 2000: nos. 1446–1453), but it is not possible to determine if this essay was in his collection.

41 It is unclear whether this charge was literal, in the sense of the prosecution of a mint official for peculation through reducing the amount of precious metal in Sinope's silver coins to his own profit, or whether perhaps the phrase had some sort of metaphorical reference, such as some other sort of public fraud or even politically–motivated factional plotting against the regime in power. See Diogenes Laertius 6.71 for an interpretation of this phrase as meaning the defying of social convention in favor of living in accordance with nature. In the standard English lexicon of ancient Greek, the metaphorical meaning is cited (without specifying its actual content): Liddell, Scott, and Jones 1996: 1330, s. v. *paracharassō* I.

42 Aelian *Historical Miscellany* 8.14 appears to put Diogenes' death in Athens, perhaps from a misinterpretation of his remark reported in Diogenes Laertius 6.79 that he said he wanted his body to be thrown out into the Ilissus River instead of being buried. It seems decisive, however, that Demetrius of Magnesia (cited in Diogenes Laertius 6.79) says that Diogenes died in Corinth and that Pausanias says he was buried there.

43 Dio Chrysostom *Oration* 8.1 also affirms that Diogenes came to Athens already 'differing from none of the very common people', meaning he was at a low socio-economic status.

44   Alexander's admiration for Diogenes perhaps reflected his own feelings – he was famed for his lack of interest in money and other conventional riches for their own sake. See, for example, Plutarch, *Life of Alexander* 5, 15, and 40.
45   At *TMS* VII.ii.4.14, for example, Smith briefly discusses the merits of moral vs. (wrongly conceived) natural philosophy 'to account for the origin of our moral sentiments'.
46   I am grateful to the anonymous reviewers for their critical and penetrating comments, which greatly sharpened my arguments and saved me from errors. I of course am solely responsible for all the essay's remaining shortcomings and mistakes. Fonna Forman deserves especially warm appreciation for her patient and perceptive guidance as editor of *Adam Smith Review*. I also want to thank Douglas J. Den Uyl for his expert advice and encouragement, Henry C. Clark for bibliographic help, Daniel B. Klein for corrections, and Liberty Fund for the opportunity to read and discuss all of Smith's works in learned and cordial company.

Bibliography

Berve, H. (1926) *Das Alexanderreich auf prosopographischer Grundlage*, Munich: C. H. Beck'sche Verlagsbuchhandlung.
Bobzien, S. (1998) *Determinism and Freedom in Stoic Philosophy*, Oxford: Oxford University Press.
Bonar, J. (1932) *A Catalogue of the Library of Adam Smith*, 2nd edn, London: Macmillan and Co.
Boxill, B. (2010) 'Discrimination, affirmative action, and diversity in business', in G.G. Brenkert and T.L. Beauchamp (eds), *The Oxford Handbook of Business Ethics*, Oxford: Oxford University Press, pp. 535–62.
Brett, R.L. (1951) *The Third Earl of Shaftesbury: A Study in Eighteenth-Century Literary Theory*, London: Hutchinson's University Library.
Burkert, W. (1985) *Greek Religion: Archaic and Classical*, trans. J. Raffan, Oxford: Blackwell.
Cranston, M. (1957) *John Locke. A Biography*, London: Longmans.
de Vogel, C.J. (1963–1973) *Greek Philosophy. A Collection of Texts. With Notes and Explanations*, 3rd edn, Leiden: E. J. Brill.
Den Uyl, D.J. and Rasmussen, D.B. (2010) 'Adam Smith on economic happiness', *Reason Papers* 32: 29–40.
Desmond, W.D. (2008) *Cynics*, Berkeley and Los Angeles, CA: University of California Press.
Fantham, E. (2003) 'The angry poet and the angry gods: problems of theodicy in Lucan's epic of defeat', in S. Braund and G.W. Most (eds), *Ancient Anger: Perspectives from Homer to Galen*, Cambridge: Cambridge University Press, pp. 229–49.
Fielding, H. (1972–1997) *Miscellanies by Henry Fielding, Esq.*, H. K. Miller (ed.), Oxford: Clarendon Press.
Fielding, H. (2003) *Contributions to the Champion and Related Writings*, W.B. Coley (ed.), Oxford: Clarendon Press.
Foley, V. (1976) *The Social Physics of Adam Smith*, West Lafayette, IN: Purdue University Press.
Glare, P.G.W. (ed.) (1982) *Oxford Latin Dictionary*, Oxford: Clarendon Press.
Gray, A. (1976) 'Adam Smith', *Scottish Journal of Political Economy* 23: 153–69.
Hard, R. (2012) *Diogenes the Cynic: Sayings and Anecdotes with Other Popular Moralists*, Oxford: Oxford University Press.

Heckel, W. (2006) *Who's Who in the Age of Alexander the Great: Prosopography of Alexander's Empire*, Oxford: Blackwell.

Hume, D. (1998) *An Enquiry Concerning the Principles of Morals. A Critical Edition*, T. L. Beauchamp (ed.), Oxford: Clarendon Press.

Inwood, B. (ed.) (2003) *The Cambridge Companion to the Stoics*, Cambridge: Cambridge University Press.

Johnson, S. (1809–1812) *The Works of Samuel Johnson, L.L.D.: In Twelve Volumes*, A. Murphy (ed.), Boston, MA: Hastings, Etheridge, and Bliss.

Kelly, C. (2003) *Rousseau as Author: Consecrating One's Life to the Truth*, Chicago: University of Chicago Press.

Liddell, H.G., Scott, R., and Jones, J.S. (1996) *A Greek–English Lexicon*, 9th edn, Oxford: Clarendon Press.

Long, A.A. (2002) *Epictetus: A Stoic and Socratic Guide to Life*, Oxford: Oxford University Press.

Martin, T.R. and Blackwell, C.W. (2012) *Alexander the Great: The Story of An Ancient Life*, New York: Cambridge University Press.

Mazella, D. (2007) *The Making of Modern Cynicism*, Charlottesville, VA: University of Virginia Press.

Mizuta, H. (2000) *Adam Smith's Library: A Catalogue*, Oxford: Oxford University Press.

Muellner, L. (1996) *The Anger of Achilles: Mēnis in Greek Epic*, Ithaca, NY: Cornell University Press.

Niehues-Pröbsting, H. (1996) 'The modern reception of cynicism: Diogenes in the Enlightenment', trans. P. Gilgen, in R.B. Branham and M.-O. Goulet-Cazé (eds), *The Cynics: The Cynic Movement in Antiquity and its Legacy*, Berkeley, CA: University of California Press, pp. 329–65.

O'Keefe, T. (2010) *Epicureanism*, Berkeley, CA: University of California Press.

Phillipson, N.T. (2010) *Adam Smith: An Enlightened Life*, New Haven, CT: Yale University Press.

Rae, J. (1895) *Life of Adam Smith*, London: Macmillan and Co.

Rasmussen, D.C. (2006) 'Does "bettering our condition" really make us better off?' *American Political Science Review*, 100: 309–318.

Rimlinger, G. V. (1976) 'Smith and the merits of the poor', *Review of Social Economy*, 34: 333–44.

Ross, I.S. (2010) *The Life of Adam Smith*, 2nd edn, Oxford: Oxford University Press.

Schwartz, E. (1910) *Charakterköpfe aus der antiken Literatur*, 1st series, 3rd edn, Leipzig: B.G. Teubner.

Shackleton Baily, D.R. (2000) *Valerius Maximus. Memorable Doings and Sayings*, Cambridge, MA: Harvard University Press.

Shea, L. (2010) *The Cynic Enlightenment: Diogenes in the Salon*, Baltimore, MD: Johns Hopkins University Press.

Scott, W.R. (1937) *Adam Smith as Student and Professor, with Unpublished Documents, Including Parts of the 'Edinburgh Lectures', a Draft of the Wealth of Nations, Extracts from the Muniments of the University Of Glasgow and Correspondence*, Glasgow: Jackson, Son and Co.

Scott, W.R. (1940) 'Greek influence on Adam Smith', in K. Varvaressos (ed.), *Études dédiées à la mémoire d'André M. Andréadès*, Athens: Pyrsos: 79–100.

Sellars, J. (2006) *Stoicism*, Berkeley, CA: University of California Press.

Smith, A. (1976a) *The Theory of Moral Sentiments*, D.D. Raphael and A.L. Macfie (eds), Oxford: Oxford University Press; Glasgow edn. Reprinted, Liberty Fund (1982).

Smith, A. (1976b) *An Inquiry into the Nature and Causes of Wealth of Nations*, R.H. Campbell and A.S. Skinner (eds), Oxford: Oxford University Press; Glasgow edn. Reprinted, Liberty Fund (1982).

Smith, A. (1978) *Lectures on Jurisprudence*, R.L. Meek, D.D. Raphael and P.G. Stein (eds), Oxford: Oxford University Press; Glasgow edn. Reprinted, Liberty Fund (1982).

Smith, A. (1980) *Essays on Philosophical Subjects*, W. P. D. Wightman (ed.), Oxford: Oxford University Press; Glasgow edn. Reprinted, Liberty Fund (1982).

Smith, A. (1983) *Lectures on Rhetoric and Belles Lettres*, J.C. Bryce (ed.), Oxford: Oxford University Press; Glasgow edn. Reprinted, Liberty Fund (1982).

Smith, A. (1987) *Correspondence of Adam Smith*, 2nd edn, E.C. Mossner and I.S. Ross (eds), Oxford: Oxford University Press; Glasgow edn. Reprinted, Liberty Fund (1982).

Sullivan, T. (2009) Christian economy versus capitalism and versus socialism. Denver, CO: Radical Christian Press. Available online at: www.radicalchristianpress.org/Pages/ChristianEconomy.aspx (last accessed 18 July 2014).

Vaughan, S.K. (2008) *Poverty, Justice, and Western Political Thought*, Lanham, MD: Lexington Books.

Vivenza, G. (2001) *Adam Smith and the Classics: The Classical Heritage in Adam Smith's Thought*, Oxford: Oxford University Press.

Vivenza, G. (2004) 'Reading Adam Smith in the light of the classics', *Adam Smith Review*, 1: 107–24.

Vivenza, G. (2007) 'Adam Smith as a teacher on classical subjects', *Adam Smith Review*, 3: 98–118.

Voitle, R. (1984) *The Third Earl of Shaftesbury 1671–1713*, Baton Rouge, LA: Louisiana State University Press.

Waszek, N. (1984) 'Two concepts of morality: a distinction of Adam Smith's ethics and its stoic origins', *Journal of the History of Ideas* 45: 591–606.

Perception by sympathy

Connecting Smith's *External Senses* to his *Sentiments*

Brian Glenney

In his early essay, *Of the External Senses* (hereafter *ES*), Adam Smith argues that we see, hear, and smell objects by simulating their tactile effects were they to make contact with our body.[1] Perception then allows us to anticipate the most beneficial way to react to objects that we observe from a distance:

> The benevolent purpose of nature in bestowing upon us the sense of seeing, is evidently to inform us concerning the situation and distance of the tangible objects which surround us. Upon the knowledge of this distance and situation depends the whole conduct of human life, in the most trifling as well as in the most important transactions.
>
> (*ES* 60)

Given the importance of simulation for, "the whole conduct of human life," we should not be surprised to see it play a significant role in Smith's more developed thought. In *The Theory of Moral Sentiments* (hereafter *TMS*), simulation is fundamental to how we understand the moral and social significance of another's actions by feeling something approximate to their experience:[2]

> By the imagination, we place ourselves in his situation…we enter as it were into his body, and become in some measure the same person with him, and thence form some idea of his sensations, and even feel something which, though weaker to a degree, is not altogether unlike them.
>
> (*TMS* I.i.1.2)

According to Smith, when we simulate the actions of others we also *evaluate* their actions, and thereby sympathize with their condition.[3] As Charles Griswald writes:

> [T]hrough sympathy the emotions communicate evaluations as well as information to other agents. Crucially, the sentiments are "cognitive", in the sense that judgments form part of them…and Smith therefore speaks of emotions as judging (VII.iv.33) as well as being judged.
>
> (Griswald 1999: 137)

By sympathy, we spontaneously feel resentment and contempt of a criminal, or inspiration and praise for a hero (*TMS* I.ii.22), "discerning worth (or lack thereof) in their objects" (Griswald 1999: 137). The point, Griswald continues, is that sympathy is itself a *guide* to the moral and social life, "by informing it as to what matters and what does not". In sum, it appears that for Smith when we simulate other people like ourselves we also *judge* their actions, and when we simulate objects unlike us we do not judge, but only approximate their affects to our body.[4] However, if the goal of sympathy and simulation are the same, to guide "the whole conduct of human life", how is it that judgment is not necessary for both? I argue that the "practical" simulations of perception *do* have an evaluative component for Smith: guiding the body's interaction with objects in a way that support its health and avoid its harm. Not only does such a discussion help elucidate Smith's early thoughts about perception in *ES*, but how *ES* pre-figures and connects with his later, more developed views of morality and social interaction. It also provides a basis for connecting Smith's account of perception with recent research in neuroscience, as I argue in this paper's conclusion.

Sympathy and moral evaluation

In *TMS*, Smith argues that the basis of our understanding of other people is our capacity to project our behavioral propensities into the situation of others. This capacity arises whenever we observe others. As Robert M. Gordon describes, "we find ourselves turning our attention to the *cause* of the other's emotion. We imagine ourselves being in the other's situation, ourselves faced with whatever is causing the other's emotion" (1995: 741). We also instinctually feel praise for those whose actions involve behavior caused by sentiments similar to our own. Such an evaluation is not conscious or deliberative, but immediate (*TMS* I.i.4.9). As Smith observes, "To the man who first saw an inhuman murder, committed from avarice, envy, or unjust resentment...[h]is detestation of this crime, it is evident, would arise instantaneously" (*TMS* III.iv.8). The blame we spontaneously feel in this case is due to a dissimilarity between the actions we see and the sentiments we ourselves feel when we imagine what it would be like to exist in their body. As "avarice, envy, or unjust resentment" are not sentiments we find within ourselves upon witnessing a murder, we immediately disapprove. "We either approve or disapprove of the conduct of another man according as we feel that, when we bring his case home to ourselves, we either can or cannot entirely sympathize with the sentiments and motives which directed it" (*TMS* III.i.2).[5] By contrast, we may feel approving emotions of this action were we to attribute self-defense as the cause of an observed killing *and* have parallel self-defensive feelings, such as fear and self-preservation, when approximating the conditions of the killing.

On this analysis of sympathy, allowing also for the diversity of sympathy's structure and use (see note 5), sympathy is a process that involves several sub-stages of simulation and evaluation:[6]

- *Attribution*: We instinctually attribute an emotional state as the cause of the observed activity of the person whose actions we are observing.

- *Projection*: We project ourselves into the environment of the person whose actions we are observing.
- *Approximation*: We feel the emotional experiences approximate to what we would feel in the projected environment.

Sympathy includes an additional evaluative stage:[7]

- *Evaluation*: We praise or blame the actions of the person we are observing.

In sum, the "moral judgment" we feel in response to watching the actions of others is grounded on comparing the sentiments one attributes to them, and the emotions or sentiments felt when approximating our own experiences when projected into their environment: if the comparison generates similarity of sentiments, the judgment is praise, if there is a difference of sentiments, the judgment is blame.[8]

These evaluations lend themselves to our own behavioral propensities and act as a guide for how to interact with others in a way that we would like others to judge us.[9] The perspective of our evaluations is not our own self, but rather a virtual self, what Smith calls the "impartial spectator" (*TMS* I.i.5.4), "impartial judge", "reason, principle, conscience, the inhabitant of the breast, the man within, the great judge and arbiter of our conduct" (*TMS* III.3.4). As Smith goes on to describe, "It is from him only that we learn the real littleness of ourselves, and of whatever relates to ourselves, and the natural misrepresentations of self-love can be corrected only by the eye of this impartial spectator" (*TMS* III.3.4). Thus, it is not we who compare the motivations of others with our own sentiments, but our conscience – our better half.

The point to be taken from this analysis is that without this evaluative component we could not employ our simulations as guides for a better life – for the kind of life we desire to desire.[10] For, simulation only generates attributions, projections, and emotions, which fail to modify our conduct or that of others. So, for simulation to have value to the general conduct of life, it must be subjected to some kind of evaluation. Hence, we should expect that the practical simulations of perception featured in *ES* have an evaluative stage for Smith, if in fact Smith sees them as a benefit to human conduct. But what part of human conduct would benefit from this evaluative stage if perception made use of sympathy – of both simulation and its evaluation? Might perception by sympathy moderate our fight or flight reflex? Would it keep our instinctual feelings in check. How exactly might our bodies benefit?

The external senses: simulation and evaluation

Smith's own discussion of perception simulating external features of internal sensations in *ES* includes no mention of the term "sympathy". However, there are several suggestive passages in *ES* and *TMS* where simulating tactile properties of objects provides a basis for evaluating whether a distant object will benefit or harm one's body. Such a proposal allows us to explicitly connect two of Smith's theories:

his account of perception and his account of sympathy, to form a Smithean account of perception by sympathy.

Smith's central concern in *ES* is Berkeley's problem of how it is that we attribute external causes to our internal sensations. Smith's answer, that inborn mechanisms simulate external or tactile properties from internal sensations of sight, audition, or olfaction is exemplified by several cases.[11] Warmth, "felt, not as pressing upon the body, but as in the body" (*ES* 20), is automatically attributed to an external object, a fire or the summer sun (*ES* 21). Distant objects are endowed with a large size – approximately the size were we within touching distance of the object – when they take up only a small amount of space in our visual field, "because almost our whole attention is employed, not upon the visible and representing, but upon the tangible and represented objects" (*ES* 54). Bodily harm is an immediate anxiety at the sound of an alarming noise making us, "roused and rendered circumspect and attentive to what we *think* is cause of the sound" (*ES* 87). In sum, Smith's answer to Berkeley's problem of external attribution is that we simulate tactile environments suggested by certain features of our internal visual or as the case may be, auditory, or olfactory sensations.

Smith appears to argue that perceiving objects involves simulating their tactile significance in three sub-stages, not unlike sympathy:[12]

- *Attribution*: We attribute distant external objects as the cause of internally felt visual, auditory, and olfactory/flavor sensations.
- *Projection*: We project ourselves into the virtual world of tactile objects we perceive from a distance.
- *Approximation*: We approximate the tactile experiences that would be felt in a projected tactile world.

These substages of simulation, owing to the diversity of its structure and use, are not always present in perception; we may attribute warmth to other human bodies, but not have regard for the significance this warmth has to our own body. However, cases that include the final substage of approximation, known today as "tactile empathy" (Keysers 2004), are indeed common.[13] (I argue in the conclusion that Smith anticipates some surprising findings in neuroscience that support his contention that we simulate the tactile significance of objects we see, hear, and smell.) But does tactile empathy or simulation employ an evaluative component, as is found Smith's more developed notion of sympathy, which might be crucial for simulation to benefit "the whole conduct of human life?".

Smith alludes to evaluative features of the benefit objects might bring to our body when related to the gratification of sexual, gustatory and other appetites. "But all the appetites which take their origin form a certain state of the body, seem to suggest the means of their own gratification" (*ES* 79). Some objects are instinctually known to have some value to our body and our judgment of their benefit is in our reactions to seeing, hearing, or smelling them.[14] "The appetite for food suggests to the new-born infant the operation of sucking, the only means by which it can possibly gratify that appetite" (*ES* 79). Other examples include the basic need of warmth, but, here, Smith is more explicit about an evaluative component to our perception of it and its benefit to our body:

> The degrees of Heat and Cold which are agreeable...are likewise healthful; and those which are disagreeable, unwholesome. The degree of their unwholesomeness, too, seems to be pretty much in proportion to that of their disagreeableness. ...Those sensations appear to have been given us for the preservation of our own bodies.
>
> (*ES* 86)

Smith may have thus assumed an evaluative substage as part of our perception of distant objects, which may be rendered as follows:

• *Evaluation*: We judge the benefit or harm of a distant external object we are perceiving.

If Smith thought that perception had an evaluative component, why did he fail to make this explicit? Furthermore, how might the evaluative substage function? Does the judgment of perception compare the substages of attribution and approximation as it does in his account of sympathy?

Smith's explicit interest in *ES* was to demonstrate that internal sensations are of external objects. And one of Smith's central arguments was that we must assume that objects are in fact external if the objects we perceive at a distance are judged as either harmful or beneficial to our bodies (*ES* 86). It has been argued that Smith also claims the inverse view in *ES*, that if we assume an externality to our internal sensations, we must attribute benefit or harm to these distant bodies (Cf. Glenney 2011: 217–18). Smith, in fact, appears to conclude *ES* with this inverse claim:

> The three senses of Seeing, Hearing, and Smelling, seem to be given to us by Nature, not so much in order to inform us concerning the actual situation of our bodies, as concerning that of those other external bodies, which, though at some distance from us, may sooner or later affect that actual situation, and eventually either benefit or hurt us.
>
> (*ES* 88; Cf. *ES* 60)

The benefit that perception brings to our bodies assumes that perception includes an evaluative step to judge whether a distant object will be beneficial or harmful.

Further support comes from comparing Smith's account of perception to Hume's, the latter of which seems to be lacking any evaluative stage. Hume argued that our perception of objects includes a projection feature, "The mind has a great propensity to spread itself on external objects, and to conjoin with them any internal impressions, which they occasion" (*Treatise* 1.3.14). This projection includes attributions of external objects such as the idea of their external existence, which, according to Hume, is "conjoin'd with every perception of object of our thought" (*Treatise* 1.2.6). Smith's view of perception, as argued above, employs both attribution and projection stages, which includes the idiosyncratic features of a perceiver that add to the "gilding and staining" (*Enquiry* 88) of objects perceived. Smith exemplifies this more eccentric perception with sailors who, from a great distance, distinguish in a ship, "the number of her masts, the direction of her course, and the rate of her sailing" (*ES* 52).

However, Smith's account of sympathy parts ways with Hume's view because of its acknowledged goal of aiding human conduct. For this goal to be realized, Smith's theory of perception requires a kind of response-dependent mechanism built to track the tactile properties of the external world, i.e. the properties which cause harm or help to the body.[15] For instance, Hume's own account of perception by projection cannot explain Smith's example of the new-born animal's interaction with a source of heat:

> A new-born animal, which had the power of self-motion, and which felt its body, either agreeably or disagreeably, more heated or more cooled on the one side than on the other, would...endeavor to move towards the side in which it felt the agreeable, and to withdraw from that in which it felt the disagreeable sensation.
>
> (*ES* 85)

Such cases require appreciation of judging how the heat might benefit the body if felt at a distance availing warmth. In addition, the perception of warmth by new-born animals appears to require a comparison of one's projected sensations of heat and the attributed cause of the heat source in their process of judgment. I turn now to consider if Smith considered this possibility. If so, it suggests that *ES* pre-figures not only the evaluative component of sympathy, but the manner by which it functions.

Evaluation by comparison

It is possible to interpret Smith as arguing that the practical judgment of perception functions by comparing causal effects one attributes to an object, like heat, and the feelings one has regarding their tactile significance when projected into their environment. This describes the process from Smith's example by which a new-born animal moves away or towards a source of heat in approximation to what would be an "agreeable" sensation, which in turn provides benefit to our bodies (*ES* 85). We see Smith draw on such comparative terms as "proportion" when accounting for this evaluative process (see *ES* 86 quoted above). I take Smith to be attempting to explicitly account for the connection between attributing external bodies as the cause of our internal sensations and the "proportional" benefit this attribution brings to our bodies, like connecting agreeable sensations with health. However, this analysis of Smith's example remains speculative given what little Smith contributes in exploring the evaluative component of perception in *ES*.

Further evidence for both an evaluative feature and its comparative function comes from his more developed thought in *TMS*, where Smith exemplifies the evaluative feature and the comparative function of sympathy by alluding to his account of perception in *ES* 54:

> In my present situation an immense landscape of lawns, and wood, and distant mountains, seems to do no more than cover the little window which I write by and to be out of all proportion less than the chamber in which I am sitting. *I can form a just comparison between those great objects and the little objects around me*, in no other way than by transporting myself, at least in fancy, to a different station, from whence I can survey both at nearly equal distances, and thereby *form some judgment of their real proportions.*
>
> (*TMS* III.iii.2; my emphasis)

Smith's utilization of the imagination in perception to, "form some judgment," helps substantiate interpreting Smith as holding to a conception of perception by sympathy. Furthermore, the mechanism by which this evaluation works is, "a just comparison between those great objects and the little objects around me". We judge the "real" size of these large objects by comparing the close large objects in one's visual field, in the room where we sit so to speak, with the distant and small objects in our visual field, outside the "little window". Given Smith's allusions to comparison in *ES* and this explicit discussion in *TMS*, judgment by comparison is a reasonable interpretation for how the evaluative feature of perception functions for Smith. On this interpretation, it remains unclear how such an analysis would translate for the perception of object properties other than size. It is also unclear, given what little Smith contributes on this point, whether the features of this process: attribution, projection, and approximation, are actually compared and if so, how.

What is important to note is Smith's claim to the accuracy of perception – the accuracy of our ability to simulate and evaluate the tactile significance of objects seen from a distance. "There is evidently, therefore, a certain affinity and correspondence between each visible object and the precise tangible object represented by it, much superior to what takes place either between written and spoken language" (*ES* 62). The correlations between visual and real tactile properties of objects are, according to Smith's description, of "exact size" (*ES* 67), "acute and distinct perception" (*ES* 70), and "precise shape and proportion" (*ES* 72). But, is Smith's account of sympathy really able to account for the accuracy of these evaluative features of perception? Smith himself recognizes the cognitive distance felt in one's simulations of other people's actions:

> As we have no immediate experience of what other men feel, we can form no idea of the manner in which they are affected, but by conceiving what we ourselves should feel in the like situation.
>
> (*TMS* I.i.1.2)

This distance leads to a failure to correctly ascertain the true causes of human actions. This problem generalizes to a failure to correctly judge perceptual simulations and practical judgments of the health benefits of certain objects. And, as I now turn to discuss, Smith noted in his *History of Astronomy* (hereafter *HA*) how this failure leads to significant misattributions of the causes of natural events and even misattributed moral status to natural objects.

Misjudged sympathy with natural events and objects

According to the present analysis of perception by sympathy, when we hear an alarming sound, we *project* ourselves into a hostile external environment, *attribute* a hostile external cause to our internal feelings, and feel an amount of pain approximate to these external environments, fleeing or fighting the attributed cause in accordance with our *evaluations* of the harm the object might bring about, an evaluation achieved by comparing the attributed cause with our approximated feelings of pain. Such an analysis avails itself to many occasions in life, but what of cases where the alarming sound was profoundly unique in appearance and origin? We will attribute *some* cause to these events, according to Smith, no matter how speculative.[16] Thunderclaps, for instance, inspire unique emotions of fear and reverence and an attributed existence of divine beings worthy of such status and an evaluation of the harm or benefit such beings pose:

> Comets, eclipses, thunder, lightning, and other meteors, by their greatness, naturally overawe him, and he views them with a reverence that approaches to fear. (...) [H]e is disposed to believe every thing about them which can render them still more the objects of his terror. That they proceed from some intelligent, though invisible causes, of whose vengeance and displeasure they are either the signs or the effects.
>
> (*HA* III.1)

While this passage further suggests that Smith appropriated an evaluative component to our perception of novel and surprising distant objects, anticipating Freud's own genealogy of religious belief,[17] it also shows that simulation is an unreliable process, misattributing causes of our perception of objects at a distance.

In addition to thunderous sounds attributed to supernatural beings desirous of humanity's humility and fear, there are less violent events to which one attributes a temperate spirit: "the good pleasure of Neptune...the indulgence of Ceres...the bounty of Bacchus (*HA* III.2). As Smith continues:

> With [the savage], therefore, every object of nature, which by its beauty or greatness, its utility or hurtfulness, is considerable enough to attract his attention, and whose operations are not perfectly regular, is supposed to act by the direction of some invisible and designing power.
>
> (*HA* III.2)

The perception of natural events, for Smith, inspires religious sentiments which include sympathy's evaluative feature to judge the "utility or hurtfulness" of the attributed objects, but these are still based on misattributed causes. We not only misattribute causes of natural events, but our evaluation of their health or harm is flawed.

Smith observes that our perception of natural objects can themselves elicit sympathy and moral evaluation:

> A child caresses the fruit that is agreeable to it, as it beats the stone that hurts it. The notions of a savage are not very different. The ancient Athenians, who solemnly punished the axe which had accidently been the cause of the death of a man, erected altars, and offered sacrifices to the rainbow.
>
> (*HA* III.2)

We also find Smith alluding to this flawed moral evaluation of objects in *TMS*, "we are angry, for a moment, even at the stone that hurts us. A child beats it, a dog barks at it, a choleric man is apt to curse it" (*TMS* II.iii.1.1) While, as Smith notes, these moral sentiments, "are presently checked by the reflection, that the things are not their proper objects" (*HA* III.2), these sentiments still, "begin to be felt even in the breasts of the most civilized" (*HA* III.2). So, the felt moral evaluation of the objects of perception in terms of the harm or benefit they bring to the body is unreliable. All this suggests that Smith proposes a mechanism of perception by sympathy that may fail as a viable means of attaining benefit and avoiding harm to our bodies given its misattribution of causes and faulty evaluation of its effects.

Sympathy also inaccurately tracks social evaluations of other people. For though sympathy recalibrates its emotional and behavioral responses with experience: "the ordinary commerce of the world is capable of adjusting our active principles to some degree of propriety" (*TMS* III.3.7), these recalibrations still fail to result in accurate projections. For instance, Smith accounts for our abhorrence of death by our imagining what horrors occur to the dead and, somewhat paradoxically, what it would be like to experience them as a conscious living being:

> It is miserable, we think, to be deprived of the light of the sun; to be shut out from life and conversation; to be laid in the cold grave, a prey to corruption and the reptiles of the earth; to be no more thought of in this world, but to be obliterated, in a little time, from the affections, and almost from the memory, of their dearest friends and relations.
>
> (*TMS* I.i.1.13)

These inaccuracies may partially explain why Smith himself never wholeheartedly aspired to employ the services of an evaluative component in his account of perception.[18] The unreliable feedback is due to observer-dependent anticipations and likely cannot account for the remarkable ability that humans have for anticipating seemingly observer-independent features of the external world suggested in *ES*.

As it stands, however, perception by sympathy does accurately account for the *immediacy* and *strength* of tactile simulation of seen objects – it accounts for the fact that we cannot help but feel anxiety at a loud unexpected noise (*ES* 87), or see movement of the sun even though we know better (*ES* 12; *HA* IV.38).[19] Smith, recognizing this explanatory feature of his account, writes that sympathy *can* account for tactile simulation that is "checked by reflection". However, we cannot interpret this as a kind of deliberative and conscious reflection as it would undercut the immediacy and strength that gives sympathy its value as a description. The inaccurate view of the external world generated by an observer-dependent sympathy, one recognized by Smith, makes such an account unfeasible when we are so pre-reflectively accurate about the tactile significance in our everyday perception as described by Smith himself and as demonstrated by our ability to survive in otherwise hostile environments.

Impartial perception?

Smith's account of moral sentiments by sympathy was also beleaguered by worries of observer dependence. As discussed above, he employed the notion of an "impartial spectator", a basis for judging our moral sentiments that corrects, "the natural misrepresentations of self-love" (*TMS* III.3.4). When we observe the actions of another, we evaluate them "impartially," as a spectator rather than another actor. "We evaluate ourselves", writes Griswold, "as we imagine that others evaluate us" (1999: 107). This allows for a perspective that generates selfless actions, the kind that we ourselves might find praiseworthy were we observing our own actions impartially, that does not require adding a conscious deliberative reflection to the process.

For Smith, the impartial spectator is analogous to the very process by which we attribute large tactile size to distant and small objects in our visual field (Cf. Griswold 1999: 138–9). In *TMS*, Smith proposes that a perceptual impartiality exists in the "natural eye of the mind," that corrects the eye of the body:

> [I]t is only by consulting this judge within [the impartial spectator], that we can ever see what relates to ourselves in its proper shape and dimensions; or that we can ever make any proper comparison between our own interests and those of other people. As to the eye of the body, objects appear great or small, not so much according to their real dimensions, as according to the nearness or distance of their situation; so do they likewise to what may be called the natural eye of the mind: and we remedy the defects of both these organs pretty much in the same manner.
>
> (*TMS* III.iii.2)

Just as the impartial judge provides moral subjects with a supposed "unbiased" judgment of behavior that recalibrates their sense of right and wrong, so, too, our "mental eye" attempts to provide knowledge that is perspective-independent and recalibrates our ability to project accurate evaluations of objects. Consider, for instance, Smith's claim of "how little those distant objects would appear to the eye, if the imagination, from a knowledge of their real magnitudes, did not swell and dilate them" (*TMS* III.iii.2). For Smith, both the impartial spectator and the mental eye purport to provide knowledge of "real" circumstances by employing the imagination to take on a perspective that is not dependent on the observer's visual judgment alone. Let us then reconsider the evaluative component in perception by sympathy as:

• *Evaluation*: We judge *from the perspective of our tactile sense* the benefit or harm of a distant external object.

This reading of Smith's analogy accounts for accuracy conditions for simulations of touch. For example, we never feel an obliquely presented coin as elliptical but rather as circular, though it can appear elliptical to sight. Touch is, however, perspective dependent – touch is not objective or omnipercipient – for only one surface of an object is presented to touch at a time.[20] On this view, the mental eye is just the simulated tactile representations that present objects to the mind as tactilely perspective dependent, capable of producing both pain and pleasure and thereby health or harm to the perceiving subject. But is this tactile perspective sufficient for Smith's claim of "exact" accuracy? No doubt, the mental eye can be educated for the sailor (*ES* 52), but as Smith notes in *HA* regarding the difficulty of perceiving the movement of our planet when observing a sunset, cognitive illusions persist. This inaccuracy, however, should not detract from Smith's account of perception but rather suggests its sagacity, anticipating not only the strength of these cognitive illusions (see endnote 19), but as I discuss in conclusion, recent work in neuroscience on mirror neurons.

This sketch of how Smith could have employed sympathy to account for external attribution includes the claim that when we perceive objects by senses other than touch, we simulate these objects as if they were the proper objects of touch and evaluate their significance to our body's health or harm. An attempt was also made to forestall an objection motivated by the inaccuracy of sympathetic evaluations based on a "mental eye" that is touch dependent – that uses imagination to transport one's body to within tactile distance of an object. In sum, it has been argued that we implicitly bring to mind all of the resisting experiences and their accompanying pain and pleasure when we have non-tactile experiences of objects at a distance.

Conclusion: sympathy and mirror neurons – a fourth point of correspondence

L. Lynne Kiesling's recent paper, "Mirror Neuron Research and Adam Smith's Concept of Sympathy: Three Points of Correspondence", proposes that the mirror neuron system predisposes humans towards several of the moral and social connections observed by Smith in *TMS*, "suggesting that humans have an innate capability to understand the mental states of others at the neural level" (2012: 300). I conclude with a further point of correspondence that concerns perceptual rather than social connections: Smith's theory of perception by sympathy, known today as tactile empathy, is also dependent on the mirror neuron system.

The above discussion presented several cases of tactile empathy from *ES* and *HA*. *TMS* also presents an intriguing case: The thought of a needle and the look of one should equally stimulate the displeasing feeling of a pin-prick, "as the immediate effect of them is pain and suffering, the sight of them always displeases us" (*TMS* I.ii.3.5). Smith's observations of how just seeing, hearing, or even thinking of objects that can bring about pain generates feelings of displeasure are supported by current work in neuroscience: when we perceive objects by senses other than touch, we simulate the object's contact with our body. This tactile empathy depends on "mirror neurons" – neurons that are active when a subject both performs a certain action and when they observe that same action (Gallese et. al., 2011). Mirror neurons are also active when we both feel the pain or pleasure of an object's contact with our body *and* see or hear that object in action. For instance, direct neuronal readings from macaques seeing, hearing, and feeling the same event exhibit similar levels of activation in the same area (known as F5) of the pre-motor cortex (Keysers *et al.* 2003). As Gallese notes, this shows not only the multimodal nature of simulation, but its significance for behavior: "Such neural mechanism enables to represent the endstate of the interaction, the content of the representation, independently from its different modes of presentation: sounds, images, or willed effortful acts of the body" (Gallese 2003: 174). This is evidence that when perceiving the action of an object by either audition or sight, macaques simulate the tactile significance of the object in the pre-motor cortex. And since the pre-motor cortex is dedicated to one's behavioral interaction with their environment, and hence is dedicated to the tactile significance of objects, the content of these simulations is tactile though it is triggered by the movement of visual and auditory stimuli. This suggests that macaques, at least, perceive by sympathy.

Human subjects exhibit similar neural patterns of activation in the pre-motor cortex when tickled on the left leg with a feather and when watching another leg being tickled by a feather (Keysers et. al. 2004). However, it remains unclear as to whether the motion of the object is activating the mirror neurons, or the object's tactile significance. The latter tactile significance seems to be the primary cause as the mental imagery of touch is known to be involved in this process:

> Therefore, it appears more reasonable to submit that our activation reflects a systematic tendency of our brain to transform the visual stimulus of touch into an activation of brain areas involved in the processing of our own experience of touch. (…) It should be noted, though, that the automatic activation we observe may share some mechanisms with the mental imagery of touch, in that both involve a "simulation" of touch…in the absence of a *real* tactile stimulus.

> (Keysers 2004: 342)

Both the single neuron readings of macaques and the functional magnetic resonance imaging readings of human subjects indicate that tactile empathy – that perception by sympathy – is a real feature of human perception.

Notes

1 There appears to be only one scholarly paper that discusses *ES* in any detail. Cf. Glenney 2011.

2 Forman-Barzilai nicely summarizes sympathy in terms of virtual proximity, "imaginary closeness produces understanding" (2005: 193).

3 Some commentators, including Griswold (1999: 83–103; 2006: 27–38), explore the possibility that some occasions of sympathy are non-evaluative for Smith, concerned with, perhaps, identifying the motivating features in another's actions. (*TMS* VII.iii.1.4; cf. McHugh 2011) This should not, however, detract from the focus of this paper, which is to situate practical simulations of perception on the end of sympathy's evaluative spectrum.

4 Smith also describes many situations in which we *do* judge the moral status of objects. These judgments are often in accordance with the benefit or harm they could bring to our bodies, but include blame or praise. I discuss this below.

5 See also *TMS* I.i.3.1.

6 Forman-Barzilai also presents Smith's account of sympathy in stages, but focuses on a latter stage concerned with how sympathy allows one to gain membership in society. By contrast, this paper attempts to understand the first "substage" of how one observes and judges others in society. Like Forman-Barzilai, I do not mean to suggest that these are temporally structured substages. Rather, they are *functionally* distinct facets of sympathy that may run in parallel.

7 McHugh, 2012 considers the evaluative feature of sympathy and whether it is in tension with the non-evaluative imaginative elements.

8 This follows how Gordon describes the evaluative mechanism of sympathy. "If we find the same sentiments and motives evoked in ourselves, we approve of the conduct; if not, we disapprove" (1995: 741).

9 As Griswold notes, "[Smith] attempts to show that we are naturally inclined to view ourselves in the light in which others see us or would see us if they were well informed" (1999:128–9).

10 I follow Griswold in connecting Smith and with H. G. Frankfurt's description of second-order desires (1999: 105).

11 This interpretation of *ES* follows Glenney, 2011.

12 Given that *ES* was written prior to *TMS* and that the present analysis, which demonstrates a structural similarity in Smith's accounts of perception and morality, is correct, it appears that Smith's famous account of sympathy has its origin in his account of perception.

13 Common examples from the literature of tactile empathy include: our stomach nervously dropping when gazing over the edge of a cliff, our body painfully twinging at a loud sound heard behind us, and feeling anxiety about our fate at the sight of a harmful insect on another's body.

14 Smith's claim appears to anticipate J. J. Gibson's (1979) theory of affordances, a view that notoriously claims an apple is perceived *as* edible.

15 These behaviors can be categorized by what kind of external existence is being attributed, whether merely "interactive" or actually "spatial". For an intriguing experiment that demonstrates these differences see Auvray et. al. (2005: 508).

16 Smith suggests that the demand to attribute causes to all actions and events is in some sense irresistible, "But our passions, as Father Malbranche (sic) observes, all justify themselves; that is, suggest to us opinions which justify them" (*HA* III.1). A similar reference is made in *TMS* III.4.3, but this is instead describing the "reasonable and proportioned" characteristics of the impartial spectator.

17   Freud argues that the first step of religious belief is our instinct towards the "humani-
      zation of nature". He describes this as follows: "Impersonal forces and destinies cannot
      be approached; they remain eternally remote. But if the elements have passions that
      rage as they do in our own souls, if death itself is not something spontaneous but the
      violent act of an evil Will, if everywhere in nature there are Beings around us of a kind
      that we know in our society, then we can breathe freely, can feel at home in the uncanny
      and can deal by psychical means with our senseless anxiety" (1961, 20).
18   Another possible explanation is that Smith's account of vision was likely conceived
      and set down in writing previous to the development of his thought on sympathy and
      the work wherein he employed this mechanism explicitly, *TMS*.
19   Smith's description suggests a very strong form of cognitive illusion regarding some
      misattributed causes, like the immobility of large bodies like our planet, that is not
      unlike Pylyshyn's (1999) own theory of cognitive impenetrability, where certain
      illusions such as the Muller-Lyer illusion cannot be experienced as veridical even
      though we can have veridical beliefs about them.
20   Smith may be reaching for a stronger understanding of the "mental eye" given his use
      of the imagination. But I take Smith to be attempting to employ the imagination toward
      a specific purpose of sympathy, and thus serving a role of perspective dependence on
      touch as opposed to omniperceipience or independence.

Bibliography

Brown, K. (1992) "Dating Adam Smith's essay 'of the external senses'", *Journal of the History of Ideas*, 53: 333–7.

Forman-Barzilai, F. (2005) "Sympathy in space(s): Adam Smith on proximity", *Political Theory*, 33 (2): 189–217.

Gallese, V., Gernsbacher, M.A., Heyes, C., Hickok, G. and Iacoboni, M. (2011) "Mirror neuron forum", *Perspectives on Psychological Science*, 6 (4): 369–407.

Gibson, J.J. (1979) *The Ecological Approach to Visual Perception*, Boston, MA: Houghton Mifflin.

Glenney, B. (2011) "Adam Smith and the problem of the external world", *Journal of Scottish Philosophy*, 9 (2): 205–23.

Griswold, C.R. (1999) *Adam Smith and the Virtues of Enlightenment*, Cambridge: Cambridge University Press.

Griswold, C.R. (2006) "Imagination: morals, science, and arts", K. Haakonssen (ed.), *The Cambridge Companion to Adam Smith*, Cambridge: Cambridge University Press, pp. 22–55.

Gordon, R. (1995) "Sympathy, simulation, and the impartial spectator", *Ethics*, 105 (4): 727–42.

Hume, D. (1978) *A Treatise of Human Nature*, P. Nidditch (ed.), Oxford: Clarendon Press.

Hume, D. (1975) *Enquiries Concerning Human Understanding and Concerning the Principles of Morals*, P. Nidditch (ed.), Oxford: Clarendon Press.

Keysers, C., Wicker, B., Gazzalo, B., Anton, J., Fogassi, L. and Gallese, V. (2004) "A touching sight: SII/PV activation during the observation and experience of touch", *Neuron*, 42: 335–46.

Keysers, C., Kohler, E., Umilta, M.A., Nanetti, L., Fogassi, L. and Gallese, V. (2003) "Audio-visual mirror neurons and action recognition", *Experimental Brain Research*, 153: 628–36.

Kiesling, L.L. (2012) "Mirror neuron research and Adam Smith's concept of sympathy: three points of correspondence", *Review of Austrian Economics*, 25: 299–313.

McHugh, J.W. (2011) "Relaxing a tension in Adam Smith's account of sympathy", *Journal of Scottish Philosophy*, 9 (2): 189–204.

Pylyshyn, Z.W. (1999) "Is vision continuous with cognition? The case for cognitive impenetrability of visual perception", *Behavioral and Brain Sciences*, 22 (3): 341–423

Smith, A. (1976) *The Theory of Moral Sentiments*, D.D. Raphael and A.L. Macfie (eds), Oxford: Oxford Universtiy Press; Glasgow edn. Reprinted, Liberty Press (1982).

Smith, A. (1980a) "On the external senses", *Essays on Philosophical Subjects*, W.P.D. Wightman and J.C. Bryce (eds), Oxford: Oxford Universtiy Press; Glasgow edn. Reprinted, Liberty Press (1982).

Smith, A. (1980b) "History of astronomy", *Essays on Philosophical Subjects*, W.P.D. Wightman and J.C. Bryce (eds), Oxford: Oxford Universtiy Press; Glasgow edn. Reprinted, Liberty Press (1982).

A known world

An analysis of defenses in Adam Smith's
The Theory of Moral Sentiments

Şule Özler and Paul A. Gabrinetti

Introduction

This chapter examines Adam Smith's path-breaking work in moral philosophy, *The Theory of Moral Sentiments* (hereafter referred to as *TMS*). Adam Smith's legacy was tied to the Scottish Enlightenment and the French and American Enlightenments. Adam Smith's *TMS* created a bedrock for a moral and ethical structure. The *TMS* won him high praise from Hume, Burke and Kant. Smith's system was seen as a giant step forward and was the product of the age of enlightenment in the eighteenth-century Scotland (Griswold 1999). Smith's work is a promulgation of the great themes of the Enlightenment. The *TMS* puts forward ideas that attempt to free us from war and faction, repressive institutions and especially religious institutions. His moral philosophy was very explicit about the correct attitudes of human behavior, took to task what was seen as the prejudicial and dogmatic assumptions about culture, social hierarchy, freedom and religion. He contended that modern liberty requires moral virtue not wisdom. Thus, it is not built upon philosophical reason, but on a doctrine of moral emotions. The *TMS*

> is a book that seeks to show that 'sentiments' (also termed "passions of emotions") can suffice for morality, virtue, liberty and in general for a harmonious social order. We are creatures of these passions. Smith seeks to understand and justify the passions as a basis for decent ethical life. The passions are not exclusive of reason, but as a basis for human life they displace "theoretical pursuits such as philosophy.
>
> (Griswold 1999, 14)

> In his *TMS*, Smith explores the social, economical and political conditions of a moral society and its historical development as part of the process of civilization, laying out a blueprint for the moral foundations of modernity. Based on observations of human behaviour, he argues that human beings are by nature disposed to take an interest in other people's well-being even if their own utility is not affected by it.
>
> (Fricke, 2011, p. 3–4)

The development of Adam Smith's system of ethics and moral structure is based on what he calls "sympathy". In modern lexicon, probably a better way of understanding his use of the word is to substitute the word "empathy". According to Smith, sympathy is "our fellow feeling with any passion whatever" (p. 13). Sympathy is considered as one of the principles of human nature that interests people "in the fortune of others". Even the greatest "ruffian" is not without it. Smith's argument is that "sympathy" is the process that allows us to build morality.

Smith begins to develop his idea of sympathy by employing the characters of the actor and the spectator. In the *TMS*, an actor and the spectator seek harmony because they get pleasure from the correspondence of their sentiments. In other words, the actor and the spectator seek harmony with each other's emotions owing to mutual sympathy. Smith prescribes actions that merit the impartial spectator's approval. The desire for approval leads the actor to adopt those actions. The actor also acts with a sense duty by applying the same rules to himself. What is virtuous in this system is clearly defined. Actors aim to have the "temper, tone and tenor" of conduct that would be approved by the impartial spectator. The presence and interaction of the spectator with the actor, which approves or disapproves the actor's passions, creates the behaviors that become the moral structure.

We argue that, for a person to go from an unconscious unreflective state that seeks sympathetic interactions and approval from others to a more deliberate consensual morality, it is necessary to employ psychological defenses. Carrasco (2011) states quoting Griswold (1999) "[the] desire for mutual sympathy is the first motivation for moral conduct or as Griswold says 'the mid-wife of virtues'". Analogously, we argue that to go from what Carrasco refers to, as "psychological sympathy" to "moral sympathy" necessitates a defensive structure. One of the essential elements to any social and moral structure is a psychological defense system that supports it. We often take it for granted. However, it is a necessary part of human interactions.

It is important to be clear what we mean by a "defense system" for the purpose of this chapter. For this, we need to refer back to the development of this concept in psychoanalysis and take it forward to our current use of the term for this chapter. Within the original context of psychoanalysis, "defenses" were used interchangeably with the term "resistances", and were seen as a negative force. In this context, "defenses" were employed by one's conscious attitude or ego, to use the psychoanalytic term, to resist psychoanalytic interpretations, and were seen as a negative force for resisting treatment (Freud, 1921). By the mid to later part of the 1930s, the work of Anna Freud (1936) and Heinz Hartman (1939) looked to free the ego from an impossibly subordinate role relative to the instincts. Thus, they and others began to look at defenses from the perspective of their necessity for adaptation. Barrett and Yankelovich (1969) described this evolution starting with Anna Freud by saying that she,

> showed the ego and its workings in a new light. Where previously the ego's defenses had been regarded as obstacles to successful therapy (the defenses were technically regarded as "resistances") she showed that these resistances

were, in fact, highly adaptive at least in their origins. She further demonstrated that…each individual's defenses (intellectualization, reaction formation, ego restriction, etc.) were characteristic to his total adaptation to life, forming a distinctive part of his personality.

(Barrett and Yankelovich, 1970, p. 96)

This began an evolution within psychoanalysis that included Ernst Kris (1952), and Erik Erikson (1950), among others, who viewed the "defenses" as an important structural component that facilitated human adaptation for human development. These defensive adaptations cover the spectrum from managing the daily life struggles of anxiety and ambiguity on the one hand, to managing deep emotional affect on the other. As a result of this defensive structure, life becomes more manageable and less unpredictable. Depending on the nature of our defensive structure, which becomes a component part of our character structure, we have the advantage of a more manageable life and the limitation that any protective structure brings because it excludes certain experiences. Therefore it can be said that one's defensive structure is a "compromise" (Freud, 1923).

It is in this light that we use the term "defenses" as a necessary and important structural component to forming an attitude towards life. So, when we speak of Smith's use of defenses in his moral philosophy, we are attempting to analyze the strengths and limitations that are the natural extension of any defensive system. We view defenses as adaptive to a social and moral world.

The content of Smith's work points to ego (adaptive) defenses that are in the service of ego ideals, what Freud (1923) came to term the super-ego. These super-ego ideals, we argue, are synonymous with Smith's moral structure. We are applying basic psychoanalytic understanding of defenses to Smith's elaborate eighteenth-century theory to bring to light the defensive structure that is needed to go from a natural unreflective state to a more ego-ideal-based moral structure that Smith advocates.

On that basis we analyze the psychological defensive system that Smith employs in the *TMS*, his need for a known world; what this known world includes, what it excludes, and what are its consequences. By a known world, we mean a world in which consensual rules are implemented and followed by all people creating a stable system. Thus the known world is a system that allows the implementation of a moral structure.

In addition, Smith saw the need for larger social forms to accommodate interactions among individuals. The capacity of individuals to contain the more chaotic aspects of human passion become more and more necessary as their interactions become more complex; particularly the capacity to delay the gratification of instinctual needs and impulses (Freud, 1920). It is therefore necessary to employ defenses that allow us to protect ourselves against the intrusion of inner impulses that would disrupt the social order and defenses which would protect us from the overwhelming influence of others that would also disrupt social order.

Smith's primary defensive structure is composed of the rationalization of his positions, the moralization of the rightness of his positions and the rational intellectualization of his positions. These are all methods that allow for the separation (or splitting) of thought from affect (Freud, 1936; McWilliams, 1994). In addition, he carefully and exactingly displaces anger according to his moral structure on to the proper objects of resentment. This type of displacement also requires both repression and suppression of affective impulses in order to accomplish its purpose. All of these strategic defensive arrangements make possible the structure of his known world.

In this chapter, we argue that a system of defenses is necessary for the creation of Smith's moral structure. This system of defenses in the *TMS* like any other defensive system has both strengths and limitations. Its strengths facilitate the structure of the moral system that Smith promotes, and within that structure it limits individual creativity, change, dynamism and spontaneity.

Analysis of defenses in the *TMS*

Before presenting our analysis, we provide an overview of the four fundamental parts in the *TMS*: propriety of action, merit and de-merit, duty and virtues. We choose these parts because of their fundamental roles in creating a known world.

Sympathy, which is described in the part entitled "of the propriety of action", is the foundation of the entire book. According to Smith sympathy is "our fellow feeling with any passion whatever" (p. 13). In this system where there is a "spectator" and an "agent" (or actor) sympathy occurs through spectator's imaginative process. Spectator by putting himself in the actor's situation forms an idea of how the actor is affected in that situation.

Fellow feeling is closely linked to approval and disapproval, and approval and disapproval form the basis of our sense of morality. We approve of other people's sentiments to the extent we go along with them. Spectatorship is a crucial component of Smith's system of sympathy because it is spectators who sympathize. Yet, we might sympathize with someone but not approve of him or her since we can sympathize with almost any passion. Equating sympathy with approval would destroy the possibility of ethical evaluation.

For Smith, all forms of fellow feeling give pleasure. The agent's consciousness of the spectator's fellow feeling for him is a source of pleasure for the agent. Similarly, the spectator's consciousness of his own fellow feeling for the agent is a source of pleasure for him. Correspondence of sentiments is what gives "another source of satisfaction". Furthermore, any pains we feel by sympathy is usually outweighed by the pleasure of the correspondence of sentiments. Mutual sympathy, thus, is the source of the actor and the spectator's search for harmony. Because of the pleasure of fellow feeling both the actor and the spectator work hard to reach harmony of sentiments.

In his discussion in the part entitled "of merit and demerit: or, of the objects of reward and punishment", Smith tells us that an action deserves reward if it is proper and approved of object of that sentiment. Similarly and action deserves punishment if it is the proper and approved of object of that sentiment. It is gratitude that prompts us to reward and resentment prompts us to punish, and that we would like to be instrumental in rewarding and punishing. The passions of gratitude and resentment are seen as proper if they are approved of. As before, these passions are approved of "when the heart of every impartial spectator entirely sympathizes with them" (p. 81). To sympathize with the gratitude of the person who receives the benefit from the actions of the agent there must be propriety in the motives of the agent. A similar argument holds for resentment.

In the part entitled "of the foundation of our judgments concerning our own sentiments and conduct, and of the sense of duty" Smith discusses duty. Duty is our application of judgments of propriety and merit to ourselves, rather than to others. We approve or disapprove of our conduct in the same manner we do of others' conduct. We wish to examine our own conduct through the eyes of the impartial spectator. In order to attain the satisfaction of gaining the admiration of others we must again be the impartial spectators of our character and conduct. Approbation of others confirms our self-approbation and their praise increases our sense of praise-worthiness. For Smith, the sole principle of our conduct should be our sense of duty.

In the part entitled "of the character of virtue", Smith addresses what is virtuous. He says that virtue consists in "the tone of temper, and tenour of conduct, which constitutes the excellent and praise-worthy character, the character which is the natural object of esteem, honour, and approbation." (p. 313). The fundamental virtues for are prudence, benevolence and self-command. "The care of health, of the fortune, of the rank and reputation of the individual, the objects upon which his comfort and happiness in this life are supposed principally to depend, is considered as the proper business of virtue which is commonly called Prudence" (p. 249).

Of benevolence, Smith tells us that "our good-will is circumscribed by no boundary, but may embrace the immensity of the universe". Even the "meanest" as well as the "greatest" man are cared and protected by "that great, benevolent, and all-wise Being, who directs all the movements of nature; and who is determined… to maintain…the greatest possible quantity of happiness" (p. 277).

Self-command is "not only itself a great virtue, but from it all the other virtues seem to derive their principle luster" (p. 284). Self-command is bringing down our emotions to what others (especially the impartial spectator) can enter into. Self-command is a part of every virtue. However, it is not a sufficient condition for the entirety of virtue. One could have great command over the fear of death. When they are combined with justice and benevolence they are great virtues and increase the glory of other virtues. However, they may sometimes be "dangerous". "The most intrepid valour may be employed in the cause of the greatest injustice." (p. 284).

These structural components, sympathy, merit, duty and virtue are the corner stones of creating Smith's known world. Sympathy is the structural mechanism by which we connect to the other. Because we have mutual sympathy we have the basis for morality. This is the basis for reflection about how we want to be treated and how we want to treat others. The remainder of the sections, duty, merit and virtue, are the rules and character traits that systematically carry out this morality based on sympathy.

Part I: Of the propriety of action

Throughout this section, we discuss the necessary defensive attitudes that are essential to develop the moral structure that are integral to his "know world". Adam Smith's system of ethics and moral structure is based on what he calls sympathy. According to Smith, sympathy is "our fellow feeling with any passion whatever" (p. 13). Sympathy is considered as one of the principles of human nature which interest people "in the fortune of others". Even the greatest "ruffian" is not without it. Smith's argument is that "sympathy" is the process that allows us to build morality.

His conceptualizes the argument by using the characters of the "spectator" and "agent" or actor. The spectator puts himself in the actor's situation and forms an idea of how the actor is affected in that situation. The dynamic of this interaction between spectator and agent is used throughout the book to illustrate the development of his moral structure. Smith says we put ourselves in the other's situation because we do not have any immediate experience of what others feel:[1]

> Though our brother is on the rack, as long as we ourselves are at our ease, our senses will never inform us of what he suffers. It is by *imagination* only that we can form any conception of what are his sensations…by imagination we place ourselves in his *situation*, we conceive ourselves enduring all the same torments, we enter as it were into his body, and become in some measure *the same person with him*, and thence form some idea of his sensations, and even feel something which, though *weaker in degree*, is not altogether unlike them.
>
> (pp. 11–12; emphasis added)[2]

This quote is an example of how Smith employs splitting as a defense maneuver. Smith splits the extreme affect of torture from the intellectual analysis of the process of sympathy. In so doing, he establishes how important splitting is to this human experience. His objectified attitude allows Smith to speculate about morality because he is split off from the dominating affect that torture evokes.

It follows that Smith insists on entering into another person's situation rather than entering to another person's feelings. As Griswold (1999) summarizes, it introduces an element of objectivity, demands a measure of understanding and allows for the explanation of cases where "the spectator sympathizes with the actor even though the actor does not feel the emotions that the spectator thinks he does" (Griswold, 1999, pp. 88–89).

In this context, it is also important to point out vision or seeing of oneself and others is important in the *TMS* (Brown 1994). Rothschild (2010) states that

> The experience of moral judgment consists of looking at the inner life; of seeing inside, or seeing which cannot be seen…To have moral sentiments is to have looked at, in as clear a light as possible, at the outside events of life, and to have imagined the life within.
>
> (p. 27)

Smith then expands sympathy, saying that it may seem to arise from a view of certain *emotion* in another person. "The passions, upon some occasions may seem to be transfused" (p. 13). He then softens his stance on this matter by saying that this use of sympathy does not hold universally true because we need to know the situation that led to the feelings of the agent. He uses the example of an angry man, saying that such emotion may upset us against him and that anger does not generate immediate sympathy.

Smith gives credence to the emotional experience and, at the same time, he exclusively evaluates it intellectually. He creates a linear and logical structure that we are terming a known world by splitting the emotional experience from the cognitive structure of morality that he is creating.

Spectatorship is a crucial component of Smith's system of sympathy because spectators sympathize. The spectator is not a real person, but a product of the imagination of the actor. The imagined spectator is another who observes the actor at a *distance*. The existence of an impartial spectator, however, is due to existence of real spectators. Outer people are internalized to construct the inner man. As such the impartial spectator is not a specific member of society. Smith considers the impartial spectator as an inner man. (Broadie, 182) Since the agent is imagining how he would be judged, the judgments he is imagining are his own. The spectator is an introject of the approval and disapproval that occurs as the result of human interaction. It is similar to the Freudian notion of "super-ego" (Freud, 1930).[3]

"Mutual sympathy" refers to the experience of two people feeling for each other's experience. It is this correspondence of sentiments that gives "another source of satisfaction". Even in the face of painful feelings of others we are pleased when we are able to feel sympathy for them. In modern psychoanalytic parlance, we might call Smith's mutual sympathy an elaboration of the mirroring process between two people, which affirms mutual experiences. Smith saw this type of interaction as bringing pleasure and later on elaborates on this "mutual sympathy" as a further building block of his moral structure.

Fellow feeling is closely linked to approval and disapproval, and approval and disapproval form the basis of our sense of morality. He is elaborating on the use of "fellow feeling" in the development of moral structure. Because we find pleasure in such fellow feeling and its lack brings pain, approval and disapproval are great but not exclusive sources of motivation. He indicates that even if we sympathize we can disapprove, thus he does not give a sympathetic view of all passions. We approve of other people's sentiments to the extent we go along with them. Sympathy is not to be equated with approval. Because equating sympathy with approval would destroy the possibility of ethical evaluation and "entail that disapproval amounted to no more than the inability of a spectator enter into the situation of an actor" (Griswold, 2006, p. 25). Sugden (2002) also rightfully argues that approval that the imaginative identification constitutes is only partial because it is only in this case disapproval is possible.

The actor is continuously interacting with the spectator putting himself in the spectators' perspective. In this dynamic the actor is seeking the relief, which can be experienced when his affections and the spectators' are in concordance. This can often result in the actor lowering the pitch of his emotions. As Smith puts it, "we…endeavor to bring down our passions to that pitch, which the particular company we are in may be expected to go along with them" (p. 28). As such, there is a premium put on the containment of one's emotional pitch for the sake of social order. This once again reflects Smith's bias of reason over passion, which is accomplished by the splitting of, thought and affect. This allows the intellectual rational of bringing down "our passions…to go along with them" (p. 28).

Actor and spectator seek harmony with each other's emotions, thus replacing the power of the individual by the power of the community.[5] This is due to mutual sympathy. Mutual sympathy, thus, is the source of the actor and the spectator's search for harmony. Because of the pleasure of fellow feeling the actor works hard to gain the approval of the spectator. Furthermore the actor desires to avoid the pain of solitude that would come from disapproval. The spectator in turn works hard to approve the actor because of his longing for pleasure of sympathy. The actor works harder than the spectator because the actor's emotions are related to a real situation, whereas the spectator's emotions are imaginary. The actor is more invested in the situation and has more at stake than the spectator. Smith goes on to say that it is nature that teaches spectators and actors to reach harmony. This harmonious world is the moral world, the known world.

Smith's perspective on the passions goes from the personal level from the interplay of the agent and spectator and move on to the development of a larger social structure. When this social structure reaches a critical mass, it then becomes the basis for his social order, and the structure of what in this chapter we have deemed the known world.

Smith outlines his elaborate understanding of the human passions that are in need of self-command. Indeed self-command becomes the basis for self-govern-ment, and the usefulness of those virtues that support the social order. It can be seen once again how necessary it is for a clear defensive system is to enable the action of self-command. The chaos of unbridled passion threatens the self-command that is essential to the personal and collective moral system. Smith clearly discriminates among the expression of certain feelings states. On the one hand, he is very open to the acknowledgement of most all aspects of human emotion and feeling states. On the other hand, however, particularly to the modern reader, he is quite unrestrained with his level of discrimination between what is acceptable and what is not acceptable, and is very exacting in his preferences. For example Smith tells us that "We are disgusted with that clamorous grief, which without and delicacy, calls upon our compassion with sighs and tears and impor-tunate lamentations" (p. 29). Similarly, he tells us "The insolence and brutality of anger, in the same manner, when we indulge its fury without check or restraint, is, of all objects, the most detestable" (p. 30). On the other hand, according to Smith, "to feel much for others and little for ourselves…constitutes the perfection of human nature" (p. 30).

Smith goes on to demonstrate his differentiation relative to the passions. He defines: passions which take their origin from the body; passions that take their origin from the imagination, such as love; unsocial passions such as hatred and resentment; social passions, such as generosity, humanity, kindness, compassion, mutual friendship and esteem, all the social and benevolent affections; and the selfish passions such as grief and joy.

These passions are discriminated on the basis of his sense of propriety and virtue as they relate to the social structure. Smith argues against what he refers to as the bodily passions such as sex and hunger. Bodily passions are beneath dignity in their expression and he advocates for a strong level of repression. In his discussion of bodily passions, he employs both moralization and compartmentalization to rationalize his known world. Smith goes as far as to say that, while on the one hand we have sympathy with bodily pain, on the other hand if a violent outcry is made from pain he states that the spectator would never fail to despise him. This is typical of Smith's attitude towards all passions that take their origin from the body. He acknowledges it but is against its expression. This is literally repression. In this case he distinguishes what is not acceptable, then he advocates for repression.

He moves on and talks about the passions that derive their origin from the imagination and speaks of love between the two sexes. Even though he acknowledges that love is an important human emotion on the one hand, he takes a strong stand against its expression on the other. Smith further declares that although love's expression might be "ridiculous" and though it might have dreadful consequences, its intensions are not mischievous.

The unsocial passions of hatred and resentment are also derived from the imagination and as with love, he advocates strongly against their expression, seeing them as not being graceful or becoming. He next turns to the social passions of generosity, humanity, kindness, compassion, mutual friendship and esteem, "all the social passions of benevolent affections". These passions please the impartial spectator in almost every occasion. Smith goes on to talk about what he calls the selfish passions of grief and joy. He sees them as neither amenable nor terrible.

Smith acknowledges that we have a desire to be respected and respectable. On the one hand he acknowledges that one way to achieve that is to become rich and powerful, however he also says that "This disposition to admire the rich and powerful and to despise to neglect persons of poor and mean condition though necessary to establish and maintain the distinction of ranks and the order of society is the great and most universal cause of the corruption of our moral sentiments" (p. 72). Here, Smith is both rationalizing and moralizing the need for distinction of rank and wealth. On the other hand the other way to become respected and respectable is through the practice of virtue. Smith states that only a select group of people admires others for their virtue, while the mob generally admires people for their wealth and power.

This final section of sympathy continues to shape the creation of the "known world" through its rationalization for a stable social order. He creates this "know world" through the splitting of thought from affect, moralization of the rightness of his positions, the rationalization of his position, and then intellectualizing his overall structure. Starting here with "sympathy," Smith shows the development of a meticulously constructed, rational structure. Implicit in his system is a desire for social order, stability, propriety and consistency. These are the hallmarks of what we are postulating as a known world. Psychological defenses are necessary to make this structure possible in the face of the fundamental human condition, which includes emotion and irrationality.

From a defensive perspective it is first necessary to separate affect from cognition. This separation is accomplished through rationalization, moralization, and intellectualization. Briefly, he rationalizes the need for the separation of affect from cognition. He then uses extensive moralization to bolster the need to exalt certain passions as virtuous while others are not. He accomplishes his discriminations through a rigorous application of purely intellectual reason. His structure requires (as he in fact indicates) the selective repression of certain emotions such as pain. Smith also uses the displacement of emotion (particularly anger) from one source to a legitimate target. The legitimate target of anger is based on the spectator's evaluation. Finally as was indicated in the previous text, Smith consigns certain feeling states to a devalued position and associates them with weakness.

Psychological defenses enable the building of his structure. Smith's defensive system necessarily includes and excludes certain life experience. This exclusion of experience both facilitates his structure and limits its flexibility and application because it eliminates certain aspects of human experience. This also includes the development of a systematic method for a collective morality and structure. In so doing it excludes uniqueness and individual development that fall outside of his known parameters.

Part II: Merit and demerit: objects of reward and punishment

In this section, Smith is rationalizing the use of merit and demerit as a means of shaping social behavior. This is the implementation of his rationalized hierarchical values from which reward and punishment are deemed appropriate. He is concerned with "the beneficial or hurtful nature of the effects which aims at, or tends to produce consists of the merit and demerit of the action, the qualities by which it is entitled to reward or is deserving of punishment" (22). Merit and demerit are the active mechanisms that govern behavior. In this section Smith provides us the rules of his " known world" by stating what deserves reward and what deserves punishment. It is gratitude that prompts us to reward and resentment that prompts us to punish, and that we like to be instrumental in rewarding and punishing. The net effect of the ongoing practice of these rewards and punishments is to create a consensual morality practiced by the collective culture and reinforced by the active use of merit and demerit or rewards and punishments.

The objects of gratitude and resentment are seen as proper if they are approved of. As with sympathy, these passions are approved of "when the heart of every impartial spectator entirely sympathizes with them, when every impartial spectator entirely enters into, and goes along with them" (p. 81). The impartial spectator represents the moral structure that constitutes the proper objects of gratitude or resentment. In Smith's reassertion of the importance of the impartial spectator, we are again seeing the uniformity of his thought across every aspect of his theorizing. He rationalizes the use of punishment and reward to implement this position.

He then compares the virtues of benefice and justice. On benefice he tells us the following: "Actions of beneficent tendency, which proceed from proper motives, seem alone to require reward; because such alone are the approved objects of gratitude" (p. 91). Along this same line, the man who does not reward his benefactor when he has the power to do so is also "is guilty of the blackest ingratitude" (pp. 91–92). Also, hurtful actions that proceed from improper motives deserve punishment. The motivation for such resentment and punishment is given to us by nature for defense only. Resentment is seen as a safeguard of justice and the security of innocence. Smith is speaking about resentment as a philosophical and societal defense against hurtful actions and injustice on the part of the agent.

The text goes on to address another important virtue in this section, which is justice. Justice is unique from the other virtues. Griswold (1999, p. 228) tells us that justice, for Smith, is first a social and political virtue, and that it may be extracted by force. The rules of justice are precise; Smith compares them to the rules of grammar. Justice is a "negative virtue" (p. 95) and "only hinders us from hurting our neighbor" (p. 95). He asserts that retaliation is an important instrument to bring about justice:

> Every man doth, so shall it be done to him, and retaliation seems to be the great law which is dictated to us by nature...The violator of laws of justice ought to be made himself that evil which he has done to another; and since no regard to the sufferings of his brethren is capable of restraining him, he ought to be over–awed by the fear of his own.
>
> (p. 96)

Here, Smith rationalizes the use of retaliation as a basis for social control. By the use of retaliation Smith endeavors to create guilt and remorse. He points out that remorse plays an important role in adhering to justice:

> it is made up of shame from which the sense of impropriety of past conduct; of grief of the effects of it; of pity for those who suffer by it; and of the dread and terror of punishment from the conscious of the justly provoked resentment of rational creatures.
>
> (p. 99)

The violator of justice feels "all the agonies of shame, and horror, and consternation" (p.98). It should be noted that shame is the signal that lets the agent know that he has deviated from a particular moral structure, or the known world that compels the agent to follow the rules of the structure. When looked at this way, Smith is building on what from a psychoanalytic perspective are the component parts of the super-ego structure.

Smith assumes, as one of the bases for his moral/super-ego structures, that one finds indefinite solitude horrifying. This is what keeps someone who has violated some aspect of this structure from fleeing justice by flying away from the social group. "But solitude is still more dreadful than society…the horror of solitude drives him back to society" (p. 99). In order not to be left in this situation the agent is compelled to adhere to the rules of the known world.

In contrast to shame and punishment, feelings of being the natural object of love and gratitude, esteem and approbation arise in a man who has performed generous actions. He finds himself applauding himself as the impartial judge would, which is a very agreeable state. There is harmony and friendship that such a person experiences with mankind. All of these sentiments constitute the conscious incorporation of merit. This is also illustrative of how the reinforcement and rationalization of proper behavior is facilitated within the moral structure. Human consciousness and awareness of both the merits and demerits of our actions speak to the internalization of Smith's known world. From a psychoanalytic perspective, this constitutes the internalization of a consensual super-ego structure.

Smith says, "All members of human society stand in need of each other's assistance…Where the necessary assistance is reciprocally afforded from love, from gratitude, from friendship, and esteem, the society flourishes and is happy" (p. 100). There is great value in such harmonious assistance with one another. According to Smith. society cannot subsist when members hurt and injure one another. Here he makes a strong case for the self-perpetuating nature of his known world based on the conscious awareness of idealized potential for happiness and social harmony.

He reasserts the necessity and importance of justice to reinforce this harmony and the warning that injustice threatens it:

> in order to enforce the observation of justice, therefore, Nature has implanted in the human breast that consciousness of ill-desert, those terrors of merited punishment which attend upon its violation, as the great safe-guards of the association of mankind, to protect the weak, to curb the violent, and chastise the guilty.
>
> (p. 101)

In so saying, he indeed personifies what Freud (1923) came to refer to as the super-ego. In this section, Smith is solidifying his moral structure by adding the governing components of merit and demerit. As we indicated in this section, the accomplishment of merit and demerit requires the exercise of both moralization and rationalization to justify the use of punishment and reward to reinforce his views on social justice.

Part III: Of the foundation of our judgments concerning our own sentiments and conduct, and of the sense of duty

In this section, Smith goes into what he refers to as duty, which he sees as the applications of judgments of propriety and merit to ourselves. We approve or disapprove of our own conduct in the same way that we of others. We examine our conduct through the eyes of the impartial spectator. This observation is accomplished by removing ourselves from our immediate situation, viewing our sentiments and motives, and then making judgments about them.

Modern psychoanalytic Kohut (1968, 1971), Winnicott (1971) thinking supports Smith's assertion that interpersonal object relations which bring about "mirroring" are integral to human development. The mirroring of significant others, particularly the mother in early development, is fundamental to how we come to know our genuine or "true" selves. These experiences of ourselves through the eyes of those who are significant to us also help in development of our sense of morality, cultural identity and consensual norms. This mirroring from significant others also conveys a defensive structure that is integral to the personal and cultural norms that are conveyed in these interactions.

Smith talks about the human need for communication with other members of our own species and how as a result such societal interactions shape our perceptions about ourselves. He tells us:

> Were it possible that a human creature could grow up to manhood in some solitary place, with any communication with his own species, he could no more think of his own character, of the propriety or demerit of his own sentiments and conduct, than of the beauty or deformity of his own mind, than of the beauty or deformity of his own face. All these are objects that he cannot easily see, which naturally he does not look at, and with regard to which he is provided with no mirror that can present them to his view. Bring him into society, and he is immediately provided with the mirror which he wanted before.
>
> (p. 129)

Smith sees each human being as inextricably intertwined with others; indeed we are social beings and are only at home in relation to others. We have moral criticism of others and others have it of us. "This is the only looking-glass by which we can, in some measure, with the eyes of other people, scrutinize the propriety of our own conduct" (p. 131). The spectator is an analogue of what Freud (1923) refers to as a super-ego function. Smith focuses on what would be termed the development of the "super-ego" functions of morality. Thus the known world is created through these interactions, which includes the development of propriety, merit and demerit.

This super-ego development evolves through the observation and mirroring of significant others. Smith goes on to further assert that not only do we want praise, but also we want to be praise worthy. The approbation of others confirms our self-approbation and their praise increases our sense of praise-worthiness. Smith makes a very strong argument that one of the great motivators is what Freud (1920) later saw in a similar light and termed the "pleasure principal".

Smith goes on to express strong views about nature:

> The all-wise Author of Nature has…taught man to respect the sentiments and judgments of his brethren; to be more or less pleased when they approve of his conduct, and to be more or less hurt when they disapprove of it. He has made

man, if I may say so, the immediate judge of mankind; and has in this respect,…created him after his own image, and appointed him his vicegerent up on earth, to superintend the behavior of his brethren.

(p. 149)

He clearly advocates that nature gives the impartial spectator the authority to determine where we ought to go.

A strong emphasis is placed on self-command. Self-command is acquired from the great discipline of nature and gains the regard of the real spectator of our conduct. Smith equates the level of self-approbation that one has with the level of self-command. Nature rewards proportionally to the level of self-command and good behavior that one has mastered. He further rationalizes that those who are best able to acquire complete control of their joys or sorrows are those who feel the most for the joys and sorrows of others. Those who have the most exquisite humanity are those who are most capable of acquiring the highest degree of self-command. Smith's statements about nature indicate a defensive grandiosity, as he seems to be arbitrating for God which is the basis for his moral/super-ego development. His rationalization of moral/super-ego development as being based on Nature/God anchors his defensive structure in the deity.

For Smith, half of the human disorders are seen as the result of self-deceit.

Our continual observation upon the conduct of others, insensibly lead us to form to ourselves certain general rules concerning what is fit and proper whether to be done or to be avoided. It is thus that the general rules of morality are formed. They are ultimately founded upon experience of what, in particular instances, our moral faculties, our natural sense of merit and propriety, approve, and disapprove of.

(p. 185)

This leads to the point that Smith is making in this section, these general rules are referred to as a sense of duty, "a principle of the greatest consequence in human life, and the only principle by which the bulk of mankind are capable of…directing their actions" (p. 188). He views these rules as sacred and necessary.

Smith becomes obsessively redundant on this matter when he restates that our moral facilities were intended to be governing principles of human nature. These rules are to be regarded as the "commands and laws of the Deity, promulgated by those vicegerents which he has thus set up within us" (p. 193). He sees this as the gesture of a beneficent God that set all of these rules up for the happiness of mankind:

When the general rules which determine the merit and demerit of actions, come to be regarded as the laws of an All-powerful being, who watches over our conduct, and who, in a life to come, will reward the observance, and punish the breach of them; they necessarily acquire a new sacredness from this consideration.

(pp. 197–8)

Smith finally declares directly; that the sole principle of our conduct should be our sense of duty. When our actions arise from a sense of duty and with regard to general rules then all questions are answered. He then allows that these rules are generally loose and inaccurate and that they can scarcely conduct our lives entirely by them. The only exception is the virtue of justice. The rules of justice are compared to the rules of grammar.

The general rules appear to be circular. God created these rules and the right-minded approve of what is virtuous, then they become general rules. It is our duty to follow the general rules. Greater good comes from virtue. If we agree to be virtuous then we are in a much better social cultural environment. If we do this it will create the greatest freedom for the greatest number of people. The ordering is as follows: virtues, accomplishment, social system with greater commerce, and greater freedom.

Smith accomplishes this large linear system of thought by the enormous use of rationalization. This system is supported by his deference to the higher wishes of the deity. He seems to have made a grandiose identification with the deity in order to accomplish this large task. In short, he attempts to subdue the instincts and put them in the control of his rational morality under the authority of God.

Part IV: Of the character of virtue

Virtue is a cornerstone that is present throughout *TMS*. In this section, Smith describes and defines the traits that are necessary for his moral structure and moral world. For Smith, virtue shapes the "tone and temper, and tenor of conduct, which constitutes the excellent and praise-worthy character, the character which is the natural object of esteem, honor, and approbation" (p. 313). In short, virtue for Smith is the ideal attitude by which we approach our life and that of others, and virtue shapes the attitude that we exercise when carrying out our lives, and manifest in relation to our "own happiness and secondly, as it may affect that of other people" (p. 248). As can be seen, virtue then interacts with all of the other principles that he so meticulously articulates in *TMS*. He presents an intellectually articulate and linearly rational argument for the integral use of virtue in his moral structure. In his idealization of virtue, there is a defensive perfectionism that postulates an ideal attitude. This aspect of his defensive structure sets out a perfectionistic ideal that does not include the human reality which often falls short.

Virtue is discussed though out the *TMS*. For example, when Smith discusses sympathy early in *TMS*, he describes the efforts of the spectator to enter into the emotions of the agent. And for the agent to bring down his emotions to what the spectator can go along with. This is founded on two different sets of virtues: self-command and propriety. It also allows the spectator and agent to find the appropriate pitch for a given emotion. Another example comes in his section on merit and demerit where he talks about the virtue of justice. Justice is a social virtue that is required for the existence of society. Justice bears the distinction of being the one virtue that may be enforced by force and have a greater precision than other virtues. Smith compares the rules of justice to the rules of grammar.

Justice is primarily a "negative virtue, in that it's abstention from wrongdoing" (p. 95).

Smith's fundamental virtues from which others are derived are: prudence, benevolence and self-command.

> The care of health, of the fortune, of the rank and reputation of the individual, the objects upon which his comfort and happiness in this life are supposed principally to depend, is considered as the proper business of virtue which is commonly called Prudence.
>
> (p. 249)

Security is identified as the first object of prudence; and a prudent man is serious in his studies, is sincere, is always capable of friendship, and is not offensive in his conversations. In addition a prudent man is industrious, frugal and sacrifices the present for the future enjoyments. Following from this attitude, a prudent man lives within his income, is contented with his situation, and does not subject himself to any responsibility that is not imposed by duty. The prudent man is also just. He does not harm others, cheat, or steal. He does not have ambition to dominate others. Smith sums up the acts of a prudent man by declaring that he has the entire approbation of the impartial spectator. Prudence is a very important virtue for Smith; he demonstrates this by writing a long paragraph about each of the attributes of a prudent man, and he exactingly describes each attribute. In this discussion Smith describes in hierarchical detail the idealization of virtue in all of its manifestations. In order to accomplish the idealization of the virtues of prudence, benevolence and self-command he uses intellectualization, rationalization, moralization and compartmentalization of virtues into specific categories of behavior and motives. As a result of such perfectionistic attitude, and such rational defenses, human feelings (particularly those that do not fit into preformed rational forms) are put in a devalued realm.

It follows that Smith also places a great deal of importance on exercising self-command in relation to others and sees no good reason to hurt the happiness of our neighbors unless there is a proper resentment for an injustice that has been attempted or actually committed.

On how the character of the individual affects the happiness of other people Smith tells us that every man is first recommended to his own care. Then there is an expanding circle of individuals that we are to care for: our immediate family; our extended family. There is a partiality towards members of our own circle.

> The general rule is established, that persons related to one another in a certain degree, ought always be affected towards one another in a certain manner, and that there is always the highest impropriety, and sometimes even a sort of impiety, in their being affected in a different manner.
>
> (p. 258)

He considers what he calls natural affection the "effect of the moral than of the supposed physical connection" (p. 262).

He then turns to friendships. The necessity and convenience of mutual accommodation among well-disposed people generates a friendship similar to what takes place in those who are born in the same family. He considers attachments that are founded upon "esteem and approbation of his conduct and behavior...the most respectable" (p.264). The attachment based on "the love of virtue" is the most virtuous. After those people come those who are rich and powerful, the poor and the wretched. The former, however determine the peace and order in society, which is more important than the relief of the miserable. Once again, we see a rationalization of rank, distinction and class difference. This rigidly defined hierarchy idealizes certain attachments and social rankings and necessarily devalues others. This defensive idealization serves to include those attitudes and behavior that perpetuate his moral structure and exclude those that do not.

As an extension of the love of virtue, Smith declares that Nature has formed men for mutual kindness, and that "kindness is the parent of kindness" (p. 265). He makes it clear that the evolution of virtue comes from a universal benevolence that knows no bounds, and is interwoven with a Divine Creator.

> The idea of that divine Being whose benevolence and wisdom have form all eternity contrived and conducted the immense machine of the universe so as at all times to produce the greatest possible quality of happiness is certainly of all the objects of human contemplation by far the most sublime.
>
> (p. 278)

Here, Smith gives the impartial spectator the authority of God. This grandiose identification with the deity supports the perfectionistic idealization of his hierarchy, and is the fundamental defensive position to his moral structure. Without his appeal to an absolute authority as the rational to his system, the defensive justification of his structure would not work.

Of self-command, Smith says:

> The man who, in danger, in torture, upon the approach of death, preserves his tranquility unaltered, and suffers no word, no gesture to escape him which does not perfectly accord with the feelings of the most indifferent spectator, necessarily commands a very high degree of admiration.
>
> (p. 280)

Similarly, he sees the command of anger as a great and noble power. According to Smith, the disposition to anger, hatred, envy, revenge, and malice, the passions that drive men from one another would offend the impartial spectator. Here Smith idealizes an extreme view of self-command even in the face of self-destruction, and then moralizes the virtuousness of such a defensive position.

Acting according to the rules of perfect prudence, justice and benevolence may be considered perfectly virtuous. However, he says, a man's own passions are likely to mislead him. These other virtues then must be supported by self-command. Self-command is emphasized throughout the *TMS* as "not only itself a great virtue, but from it all the other virtues seem to derive their principle luster" (p. 284). One of the principle acts of self-command is bringing down our emotional expressions to what others (that is, the impartial spectator) can enter into.

Throughout this section, Smith makes the argument for self-command in relation to one's life. In particular, he focuses on the emotions of fear and anger which require the greatest exercise of virtue. Indeed, he sees the spontaneous indulgence of these and of other such emotions as vanity. Consistent with his meticulous observations and exacting prescriptions, he also orders the passions in terms of their difficulty to contain. On the one hand, there is anger and fear that require the highest degree of virtuous self-command to the restraint of affection that requires less. On the other hand, the exercise of virtue is intended to provide harmony within the individual and harmony within the greater society. Smith puts it clearly:

> The virtues of prudence, justice and beneficence have no tendency to produce any but the most agreeable effects. Regard to those effects as in originally recommends them to the actor so does it afterwards to the impartial spectator. In our approbation of all those virtues our sense of the agreeable effects of their utility either to the person who exercises them or to some other persons joins with our sense of their propriety and constitutes always a considerable frequently the greater part of that approbation.
>
> (p. 309)

This section points out Smith's diligent exercise of a defensive structure to create and maintain a known world. He has skillfully intellectualized the exercise of virtue and has moralized the hierarchy of virtuous acts. This structure is rationalized through the appeal to, and grandiose identification with a deity to support his structure. Self-command is an important structural component of virtue and dictates the most obsessive compartmentalizing of human impulse and interactions. As such, spontaneous and intuitive human actions are put in a devalued position. In addition individual feeling states are devalued in favor of collectively approved attitudes and actions.

Discussion

This chapter attempts to look at Adam Smith's *TMS* and the essential psychological defensive arrangements that he employs to implement his theory of moral structure. In particular, we are arguing that the transition from the initial condition of sympathy that Smith postulates, to the implementation to his moral structure requires a psychological defense system to facilitate that transition. As such, this chapter attempts to address this gap in the literature.

We have presented the fundamentals of his elaborate and elegantly structured theory that results in what has been referred in this paper as a known world. Smith's work is dependent upon the use of psychological defenses to: 1) implement his moral theory in the face of the natural human unreflective and instinctual human condition; and 2) to facilitate its necessary internal consistency. As stated earlier in this chapter, defenses are necessary operational components to any system that is applied to human behavior, and as such has both strengths and deficits. We often take for granted the need for defenses because they are so much a part of our particular social structure. Indeed, the human need for defenses allow us to come to terms with and make sense of the otherwise chaotic nature of internal need and external reality, and cannot be overstated. A further example of this has been discussed in Ozler (2012). Smith's theory creates a social and moral structure that prescribes a set of priorities and behaviors. In order to implement these priorities and behaviors, there is a need to manage the instinctual affective life within an individual that interacts with these priorities. Indeed this is where a defensive structure becomes necessary.

Smith's reliance on sympathy as a foundational part of his work also creates the need for defenses to limit the overwhelming affects that sympathy creates in our interactions with others. Our capacity for sympathy also reveals the need to limit the influence of others experience upon us.

In the broadest perspective, Smith's theory is defending against the fundamental instincts of aggression, and sexuality. In particular it defends against the affects that are the result of the dynamic conflict of these instincts both within an individual and in relation to others. Further, his system evolves into the prescription of an elaborate arrangement of social interactions where he defends against the potential of losing his relationship to others. He adopts an exclusively rational perspective that makes his system is vulnerable (as any individual would be) to the eruption of irrational affect, unforeseen circumstances, or the spontaneous expressions of feeling that do not fall into the prescribed category of feeling values that his structure dictates. In particular, he defends against the *expression* of affective states such as rage, anger, hate, frustration, sexual desire, and affection, in a spontaneous way that falls outside his structure.

In Smith's view, we are saddled with opposing forces of an inner human condition, which includes instinctual impulses on the one hand, and on the other hand are also endowed by God with "all-seeing...powers of judgment" (Roths-child, 2010 p. 27). In order to resolve these discrepancies within the human being we argue that a defensive system is necessary to bring about this "all-seeing" ego ideal.

One of the most dominant defenses employed by Smith is that of splitting: the turning of emotional states into good and bad, black and white, or right and wrong. In particular, his system has little room for the subtleties of context or uniqueness. His theory defends against the expression of affect by evaluating such expression with the "disapprobation of the spectator". He further reinforces this split by rationalizing and moralizing about the "virtue" of the suppression of affective states.

All of Smith's structures (virtue, propriety, merit, duty) are applications of his foundational defense system that we have outlined. In his thoughtful and meticulous way he has masterfully woven together these structures to create a logic tight system of morality and behavior. The strength of Smith's purely rational approach is that it can be internally consistent, linear, follow logical rules, and can conceptually account for a large portion of behavior and details. It further supports a majority collective view of human action based on the external need for relationship with others which is mediated by the "approbation" of others. On the other hand, this rational approach leaves little room for individual differences, creativity, change, dynamism, and spontaneity within it's system. Because of it's exclusive focus on the dependency of the individual on the approbation of others, it also leaves out people who "march to their own drummer" such as: Martin Luther, Martin Luther King, Gandhi, and Einstein, all of whom were able to go in their own direction, sometimes at great peril and at the risk of great disapprobation by the dominate culture. The attributes and personal styles that are left out of Smith's "known world" would easily be the subject of yet another study.

Acknowledgements

We thank Joyce O. Appleby, D. James Fisher and Charles L. Griswold for their helpful comments.

Notes

1   Freud (1930) makes an analogous statement: "We shall always consider other people's distress objectively; that is, to place ourselves, with our own wants and sensibilities, in their conditions, and then to examine what occasions we should find in them for experiencing happiness or unhappiness" (p. 89).

2   The phrase "become in measure the same person with him", or identification with the sufferer, is somewhat ambiguous. Do I suffer what I would suffer if I were in your situation, or do I suffer what you suffer if I were you? Smith initially suggests that I put myself in your situation, taking my characteristics and person. (p. 12). Yet later on Smith states that it is not I, who suffers on my account, but "I consider what I should suffer if I was really you" (p. 374).

3   Freud (1930) asserts that "the community, too, evolves a super-ego under whose influence cultural development proceeds" (p. 141). "The cultural super-ego has developed its ideals and set up its demands. Among the latter, those which deal with the relations of human beings to one another are comprised under the heading of ethics" (p. 142).

4   Freud (1930) makes an analogous statement. "The replacement of the power of the individual by the power of a community constitutes the decisive step of civilization" (p. 95); "the characteristic features of civilization remains to be assessed: the manner in which the relations of men to one another, their social relationships, are regulated" (pp. 94–5).

Bibliography

Barret, W. and Yankelovich D. (1970) *Ego and Instinct: The Psychoanalytic View of Human Nature – Revised*. New York: Random House.

Brodie, A. (2006) 'Sympathy and the impartial spectator,' in K. Haakonssen (ed.), *The Cambridge Companion to Adam Smith*. Cambridge: Cambridge University Press.

Bromberg, P.M. (2007) 'Reply to review of awakening of the dreamer: clinical journeys by Philip M. Bromberg,' *Psychoanalytic Dialogues*, 17: 769–87.

Brown, V. (1994) *Adam Smith's Discourse: Canonicity, Commerce and Conscience.* London: Routledge.

Campbell, J. (1972) *The Hero With a Thousand Faces.* Princeton, NJ: Princeton University Press.

Carrasco, M.A. (2011) 'From psychology to moral normativity,' *Adam Smith Review*, 6: 9–29.

Erikson, E.H. (1950) *Childhood and Society.* New York: Norton.

Freud, A. (1936) *The Writings of Anna Freud*, vol. II. New York: International University Press.

Freud, S. (1961) 'Beyond the pleasure principle,' in *The Standard Edition of the Complete Psychological Works by Sigmund Freud*, vol. XVIII. J. Strachey (trans.), in collaboration with A. Freud and assisted by A. Tyson, (pp. 7–66). London: Hogarth Press. (Original work published in 1921.)

Freud, S. (1961) 'Civilization and its discontents,' in *The Standard Edition of the Complete Psychological Works by Sigmund Freud*, vol. XVIII. J. Strachey (trans.), in collaboration with A. Freud and assisted by A. Tyson, (pp. 59–148). London: Hogarth Press. (Original work published in 1930.)

Fricke, C. (2011) 'Introduction: Adam Smith and the conditions of a moral society,' *Adam Smith Review*, 6: 3–8.

Griswold, C.L. (1999) *Adam Smith and the Virtues of Enlightenment.* Cambridge: Cambridge University Press.

Griswold, C.L. (2006) 'Imagination: morals, science, and arts,' in K. Haakonssen (ed.). *The Cambridge Companion to Adam Smith.* Cambridge: Cambridge University Press.

Hartman, H. (1939) *Ego Psychology and the Problem of Adaptation.* New York: International University Press.

Kohut, H. (1968) 'The psychoanalytic treatment of narcissistic personality disorders,' *Psychoanalytic Study of the Child*, 23: 86–113.

Kohut, H. (1971) *The Analysis of the Self: A Systematic Approach to the Psychoanalytic Treatment of Narcissistic Personality Disorders.* New York: International Universities Press.

Kris, E. (1952) 'The development of ego psychology,' *Samiksa: the Indian Journal of Psychoanalysis*, 5: 153–68.

McWilliams, N. (1994) *Psychoanalytic Diagnosis: Understanding Personality Structure in the Clinical Process.* New York: Guildford.

Ozler, S. (2012) 'Adam Smith and dependency,' *Psychoanalytic Review*, 99 (3): 333–58.

Rotshchild, E. (2010) 'The theory of moral sentiment and the inner life,' *Adam Smith Review*, 5: 25–36.

Schore, A.N. (2007) 'Review of the dreamer: clinical journeys by Philip M. Bromberg,' *Psychoanalytic Dialogues*, 17: 753–67.

Smith, A. (2007) *The Theory of Moral Sentiments*, edited by K. Haakonssen. Cambridge: Cambridge University Press. (Original work published in 1759.)

Sugden, R. (2002) 'Beyond sympathy and empathy: Adam Smith's concept of fellow-feelings,' *Economics and Philosophy*, 18: 63–87.

Sullivan, H.S. (1953) *The Interpersonal Theory of Psychiatry.* New York: W.W. Norton.

Winnicott (1967) 'Mirror-role of the mother and family in child development,' in *Playing and Reality* (pp. 111–18). New York: Basic Books.

Adam Smith's views on consumption and happiness

Paul D. Mueller

Introduction

> Consumption is the sole end and purpose of all production.
>
> (*WN* 660.49)

One of the most important contributions of *An Inquiry into the Nature and Causes of the Wealth of Nations* (*WN*) was the discrediting of the mercantile system. The advocates of that system claimed that the wealth of a nation was to be found in its stores of gold and silver (*WN* 450.35). The nation became wealthier when it had a favorable balance of trade – which meant exporting as many goods as possible in exchange for gold and silver while limiting imports. Smith's most important critique of mercantilism was that gold and silver are only proxies for wealth: "Every man is rich or poor according to the degree in which he can afford and enjoy the necessaries, conveniencies, and amusements of human life" (*WN* 47.1). The man with a vault full of gold is considered rich, but only because of what he can buy with his gold. If he were prohibited from spending any of the gold in his vault, he would be little more than a pauper. So it is with nations.

Goods and services are the real wealth of a nation; not gold coins, but chairs, clothing, books, and bread. Mercantilism was particularly pernicious because it deliberately sacrificed real wealth (goods) to stockpile idle metals. Despite demolishing the mercantilist fallacy that gold and silver are wealth, Smith runs into his own conundrum between how to value the "nature" of wealth (consumption) and its "causes" (production). The reason that goods and services constitute wealth is because people's lives are made better by consuming them. Yet Smith does not condone all consumption as contributing to one's wellbeing. He thinks that consumption can be wasteful, extravagant, ill-conceived, and socially damaging. This chapter addresses the following question: How is it that Smith could think that consumption is the true measure of wealth, the sole end of production, and yet sometimes be a bad thing?

For the past century economists have shied away from passing any judgment on consumption decisions. Ludwig von Mises (1949) argues stridently in *Human Action* that the economist only evaluates the means to accomplish some end, not the end itself. The consumer is king and his consumption choices cannot be disputed or criticized except within a means–ends framework:

> economics deal[s] with the means for the attainment of ends chosen by the acting individuals. They do not express any opinion with regard to such problems as whether or not sybaritism is better than asceticism. ...Any examination of ultimate ends turns out to be purely subjective and therefore arbitrary.
>
> (Mises 1949: 95–6)

Gary Becker and George Stigler (1977) argue that people's preferences should be taken as given so that the economist can focus on evaluating their means, not their ends. Normative judgments have no place in the "science" of economics and explanations of economic phenomena by preferences are no explanations at all. Stringham (2010) follows a similar line of reasoning when he argues that subjectivism not only prohibits judgments of what people value, it also prohibits any judgment about cost/benefit comparisons in society. Although many economists will call people's choices imprudent or even foolish in private, the official mantra is that people's ends relate to psychology and should not, or cannot, be evaluated using economics.

Deirdre McCloskey (2008, 2010) battles against the tradition that subjective consumption is the sole standard of economic analysis. Her condemnation of "Max U" theorizing and her promotion of the "bourgeois virtues" offer a window into how we can see consumption as good and important but not ultimately or absolutely so. She claims that Smith himself was more concerned about virtue than he was about consumption. If McCloskey is right, then considering how Smith thought about virtue will shed light on why he alternates between viewing consumption favorably and unfavorably in both the *Wealth of Nations* (*WN*) and in *The Theory of Moral Sentiments* (*TMS*). But human wellbeing is not just about virtue either. Modern research suggests that there is a significant correlation between wealth and happiness in country by country comparisons (Headey, Muffels and Wooden 2004; Stevenson and Wolfers 2008).

Smith's characterization of consumption in the *Wealth of Nations* is informed by his moral philosophy in *TMS*. The key to understanding Smith's contrasting comments about consumption is realizing that he viewed happiness as every individual's final and most important goal. He thought consumption to be a necessary, but not sufficient, condition of human happiness. Other conditions include the practice of virtue and conformity to standards of propriety. The rest of this paper explains Smith's comments on consumption in light of his goal of promoting human happiness.

We should dwell for a moment on how Smith defines happiness in *TMS*: "Happiness consists in tranquillity and enjoyment. Without tranquillity there can be no enjoyment; and where there is perfect tranquillity there is scarce any thing which is not capable of amusing" (*TMS* 149.30). By "tranquillity", Smith does not mean a peaceful state of the world but a peaceful state of mind and conscience. Without that inner peace, he argues, it is nearly impossible to enjoy anything, even consumption. So his praise or criticism of consumption works off of the foundation that happiness requires internal "tranquillity".

Ultimately, Smith favors consumption on the whole as contributing to people's happiness with a few exceptions, *not* vice versa. The following section develops the tensions and conflicts in Smith's discussions of consumption in the *WN* and in *TMS*. The next section develops Smith's standards, such as virtue, propriety, and morality, for evaluating whether consumption promotes happiness. The final section concludes with thoughts about how Smith's various standards affected his views of consumption *and* how his views of consumption affected his economics.

Smith's comments about consumption

As a general rule, Smith favored consumption. He was no aesthetic. As the opening quote of this paper pointed out, he claims that consumption is the *sole* purpose of production. Consumption is the end, production the means. There are several other examples of Smith's favorable view of consumption in both *WN* and *TMS*. Most importantly, Smith argues that a reasonable amount of consumption is necessary for happiness. His criticisms of consumption, therefore, should be seen as exceptions, not the rule. This section highlights where Smith favors consumption. After that, it considers many of the exceptions to that rule where he criticizes consumption.

Consumption recommends itself to us by nature when we are children. As Smith says:

> The preservation and healthful state of the body seem to be the objects which Nature first recommends to the care of every individual. The appetites of hunger and thirst, the agreeable or disagreeable sensations of pleasure and pain, of heat and cold, etc. may be considered as lessons delivered by the voice of Nature herself, directing him what he ought to chuse, and what he ought to avoid.
>
> (*TMS* 212.1)

Here, Smith seems to recommend that we should care about our physical utility; that is, that we should consume. Nature plays a prominent role in his arguments about virtue and happiness. There should be harmony between our natural senti-ments and our happiness. Not that whatever passing feeling we have "naturally" is right, but that, upon reflection, we can see how virtue recommends itself to us through the natural order of the world.

Smith argues that prudence is the most natural virtue, the one that recommends itself to us first. It recognizes that:

> some care and foresight are necessary for providing the means of gratifying those natural appetites, of procuring pleasure and avoiding pain, of procuring the agreeable and avoiding the disagreeable....this care and foresight consists the art of preserving and increasing what is called his external fortune.
>
> (*TMS* 212.2)

Being prudent requires men to provide for their future consumption. The prudent man achieves his goals of satisfaction, ease, and contentment when he

> lives within his income, is naturally contented with his situation, which, by continual, though small accumulations, is growing better and better every day. He is enabled gradually to relax, both in the rigour of his parsimony and in the severity of his application; and he feels with double satisfaction this gradual increase of ease and enjoyment.
>
> (*TMS* 215)

This is not merely positive description, Smith holds out the rewards of prudence as *the* means of achieving happiness. He believes that it is what everyone *should* pursue.

Smith's approval of consumption can also be seen in his discussion of wealth. Although he often makes the mistake of calling wealth the ability to command labor, the reason one wants to command labor is to receive its produce. Control and use of goods and services are what make people wealthy. From the first sentence of *WN*, Smith talks repeatedly about the wealth of nations consisting in the "necessaries and conveniencies" of life (*WN* 10.1, 10.2, 23.11, 47.1, 51.9, 181.7). A major benefit of the division of labor, according to Smith, is that it increases the quality and variety of goods *that people can enjoy*. That is why he can say that the frugal peasant in Britain is wealthier than the African king who rules over thousands of savages yet has fewer of these "necessaries and conveniencies" (*WN* 24.11). Although that claim may have been a stretch 250 years ago, it is undeniable today. The average, or even the poor, citizen of the United States has access to better food, clothing, entertainment, sanitation, etc. than even the royalty in Britain had during Smith's time!

Smith describes the enjoyments of ordinary laborers in great detail and in a positive light. Common laborers generally had a large assortment of goods including clothing, furniture, silverware, shelter, and food (*WN* 22–23.11); all courtesy of the division of labor. When discussing the ale house and the brewer, Smith suggests that they serve a reasonable interest of the workingman and the wealthy in consuming alcohol (*WN* 491–493.8). He does say that the freedom to consume alcohol may be abused and bring some people to ruin, but, on the whole, such behavior is uncommon. For the responsible majority, alcohol is a reasonable good that promotes human happiness and wellbeing.

Another clear example of Smith favoring consumption comes from a passage in the *WN* where he points out the superiority of goods over money:

> Goods can serve many other purposes besides purchasing money, but money can serve no other purpose besides purchasing goods....The man who buys, does not always mean to sell again, but frequently to use or to consume; whereas he who sells, always means to buy again. ...It is not for its own sake that men desire money, but for the sake of what they can purchase with it.
>
> (*WN* 439.18)

Consumption, not hoarding gold or apathetic indifference to the world, ultimately gives meaning to production and money. Mises makes a similar point saying: "All other things are valued according to the part they play in the production of consumers' goods" (1945: 94). Smith understands why people labor and produce. It is not because they like doing it, but because of what they can get from it.

Another important aspect of having enough wealth to live in relative comfort is that it allows people to exercise care for others. Smith praises material wealth as a conduit to human well-being. He writes: "Before we can feel much for others, we must in some measure be at ease ourselves. If our own misery pinches us very severely, we have no leisure to attend to that of our neighbour" (*TMS* 205.9). And when speaking of the virtue of humanity, he says "The man who is himself at ease can best attend to the distress of others" (*TMS* 153.37). Wealth and consumption are important, not only for our own enjoyment, but also because they allow us to exercise virtue and improve the well-being of others.

Now we should turn to consider some of Smith's caveats and condemnations of consumption. His primary scorn is reserved for the spendthrift – for the man who slowly (or quickly) dissipates his wealth or capital or stock. Smith has scathing criticism for landlords who have lost the ownership of their land through prodigality:

> Having sold their birth-right, not like Esau for a mess of pottage in time of hunger and necessity, but in the wantonness of plenty, for trinkets and baubles, fitter to be the play-things of children than the serious pursuits of men, they became as insignificant as any substantial burgher or tradesman in a city.
>
> (*WN* 421.15)

These landlords wasted their wealth on vanity and impoverished themselves for no good reason. Notice how Smith is critical of the "trinkets and baubles" that were purchased with the land, regardless of how much the landlords subjectively enjoyed them. These landlords are violating the *should* of providing for the future mentioned earlier. Elsewhere Smith notes that "many people ruin themselves by laying out money on trinkets of frivolous utility" (*TMS* 180.6). These acts of consumption violate the virtues of prudence, moderation, and self-control; making those individuals worse off and, in Smith's opinion, less happy over time. Here consumption has usurped virtue, with unpleasant consequences.

Continuing on the themes of frivolity and waste, Smith also writes that "the man who borrows in order to spend will soon be ruined" (*WN* 350.2). In a longer condemnation of wasteful consumption he writes of the prodigal:

> By not confining his expence within his income, he encroaches upon his capital...he pays the wages of idleness. ...diminishing the funds destined for the employment of productive labour, he necessarily diminishes...the real wealth and revenue of [his country's] inhabitants. If the prodigality of some was not compensated by the frugality of others, the conduct of every prodigal,

by feeding the idle with the bread of the industrious, tends not only to beggar himself, but to impoverish his country.

(*WN* 339.20)

Not only does he condemn the prodigal for wasting his money and impoverishing himself, Smith argues that the prodigal's behavior is bad for society too because it uses up stock. The spendthrift does not promote future consumption because he is using up capital to fund his consumption and not replacing it. The rich man who hires servants to wait upon him or entertainers to perform for him is dissipating his wealth and the accumulated stock of the country. After paying the servants and entertainers, he is not left with any greater stock than before and so is less likely to be able to employ them in the future.

Smith's concern about the prodigal using up capital and impoverishing himself and his country helps us understand why Smith distinguishes between productive and unproductive labor. His major concern is whether people's behavior, either producing or consuming, will promote economic growth and future consumption; which is necessary for human happiness and wellbeing. The servants and entertainers may have provided a valued service but their actions do not contribute to more food or houses or machines in the future. As he puts it, they have contributed "to the value of nothing" (*WN* 330–332).

Smith's criticism is not limited to people who spend more than they make – it also includes particular types of consumption. In his discussion of using precious metals as money he says that the value of gold and silver fluctuates because of, among other reasons, "the continual waste of them in gilding and plating, in lace and embroidery" requiring "a continual importation, in order to repair this loss and this waste" (*WN* 62–63.40). Gold is valued for its scarcity, and therefore for the status of those who own it. In *TMS*, Smith argues that many people value wealth because of the admiration they receive from others for it, not because they actually consume or use the wealth itself. But that sort of valuation, Smith argues, is not conducive to happiness. Therefore taking gold and silver out of the useful role of money and using it for decoration to suit people's vain fancies appears wasteful to Smith.

Smith takes several pages to explain the difference between whether a wealthy man spends his money on food, drink, hospitality, and menial servants or on physical objects (*WN* 346–9). The first set of expenses are enjoyed and disappear forever. The second set, however, can be enjoyed now and in the future. They can also be resold or inherited. One type of consumption promotes wealth, and thereby human wellbeing, more than the other does.

Smith concludes that "every prodigal appears to be a publick enemy, and every frugal man a publick benefactor" (*WN* 340.25). Consumption can promote long-term prosperity or produce ruin. It is worth noting, however, that Smith does not worry about too many prodigals ruining a country. He says that the tendency towards prudence and industry is far too strong for more than a handful of people to ignore. What he is concerned about, however, is long-run consumption. Therefore he places a normative weight on actions affecting it. This is not surprising in light of how he thinks about happiness, virtue, and morality in *The Theory of Moral Sentiments*, to which we now turn.

Standards for evaluating consumption

For Smith, consumption is important only inasmuch as it contributes to human happiness. Most economists assume that consumption and happiness are basically the same. Therefore, since utility is subjective and varies by individual, happiness must as well. Unlike modern economists who claim that whatever people choose in the moment (their revealed preference if you will) must give them the highest utility, and therefore happiness, Smith thinks that people can choose to consume in ways that make them less happy in the long run. In this he rejects basic utilitarianism. For example, when individuals puff up their vanity and pride in the moment, they are actually reducing their ability to be happy and contented in the long run. Certain types of consumption can be wasteful, or even destructive. The stoics, on the other hand, argued that happiness and consumption are unrelated, or even inversely related. Smith tries to take a middle position between utilitarianism and stoicism.

Smith rejects both positions as being too extreme and contrary to nature. Morality cannot be boiled down to a single principle like utility or asceticism (*TMS* 299). The ways in which Smith criticizes both of these philosophies and contrasts them with his own will highlight how he thinks about consumption. This section outlines Smith's views of consumption by looking at how he contrasts his own views of virtue and morality with the extreme self-interested utilitarianism of Mandeville and the extreme aestheticism of the stoics.

According to Smith, Mandeville argues that the gratification of any desire beyond the bare necessity of maintaining life should be considered luxury and vice. Unlike the stoics, however, Mandeville uses this claim to argue that the categories of virtue and vice are meaningless because they have such extreme implications for human behavior and society. Hence, Mandeville argues in *The Fable of the Bees* (1714) that "private vices are public benefits" (*TMS* 313.12). As Smith puts it:

> Wherever our reserve with regard to pleasure falls short of the most ascetic abstinence, he treats it as gross luxury and sensuality. Every thing, according to him, is luxury which exceeds what is absolutely necessary for the support of human nature, so that there is vice even in the use of a clean shirt, or of a convenient habitation.
>
> (*TMS* 312.11)

Mandeville's fable derides ordinary views of virtue and vice, claiming both playfully and seriously that the distinction between the two is blurry or even nonexistent. That is why Smith calls Mandeville's system "wholly pernicious" and finds it to be full of vice and error (*TMS* 308). He thinks that Mandeville wrongly condemns certain amenities of life, like a clean shirt or a pleasant home, as vice. Smith certainly did not consider them to be so.

An important passage about Mandeville's system of philosophy reveals what Smith thinks about the use, or consumption, of luxuries or otherwise unnecessary goods. He writes:

> If the love of magnificence, a taste for the elegant arts and improvements of human life, for whatever is agreeable in dress, furniture, or equipage, for architecture, statuary, painting, and music, is to be regarded as luxury, sensuality, and ostentation, even in those whose situation allows, without any inconveniency, the indulgence of those passions, it is certain that luxury, sensuality, and ostentation are public benefits: since without the qualities upon which he thinks proper to bestow such opprobrious names, the arts of refinement could never find encouragement, and must languish for want of employment.
>
> (*TMS* 313.12)

There are several things to note in this passage. First, Smith describes the "luxuries" in praiseworthy, rather than belittling, terms. We have the "elegant" arts when he could have said "frivolous". He talks about what is "agreeable" rather than what is "superfluous," "extraneous," or "vain". He also calls these various conveniencies "improvements" in human life, not "distractions". Though Smith's word choice may seem like a minor point in the context of this passage, when viewed with respect to the whole book, where he uses words like "frivolous" and "vain" to condemn various practices and objects, it is worth noting that he seems to view the luxuries in the previous passage as good and proper for people to enjoy.

Smith also argues in the passage that the elegant arts and nice furniture or architecture should be enjoyed by: "those whose situation allows, *without any inconveniency*, the indulgence of those passions". What exactly does Smith mean by "inconveniency"? Although he does not tell us directly, it seems quite likely that he is referring to physical provision – hence his comment on the "situation" allowing indulgence. His prior discussion of prudence also suggests that consumption can only be proper if it takes place within one's means. That brief exegesis provides more evidence that Smith favored consumption generally, even in fine dress or furniture, as long as the individual took responsible care for his future provision.

But Smith does qualify his praise of consumption by saying that it is only right under some conditions, not others. Virtue, for example, must be present with consumption. Neither one without the other. He says that: "virtues, however, do not require an entire insensibility to the objects of the passions which they mean to govern. They only aim at restraining the violence of those passions so far as not to hurt the individual, and neither disturb nor offend the society" (312.12). Although Smith disagrees with Mandeville's claim that everything beyond survival is vice, he still considers the "violence" of some types of consumption or behavior to be vice – particularly, but not solely, because such behavior harms the individual himself or those around him.

He uses the mechanism of the impartial spectator to argue that providing for future consumption is a moral matter. In *TMS*, Smith uses the views of an impartial spectator as a benchmark for propriety. Men who do not save for their future consumption are blameworthy *in a moral sense* because they are disregarding the views of an impartial spectator:

> In the steadiness of his industry and frugality, in his steadily sacrificing the ease and enjoyment of the present moment for the probable expectation of the still greater ease and enjoyment of a more distant but more lasting period of time, the prudent man is always both supported and rewarded by the entire approbation of the impartial spectator. …The impartial spectator does not feel himself worn out by the present labour of those whose conduct he surveys; nor does he feel himself solicited by the importunate calls of their present appetites. To him their present, and what is likely to be their future situation, are very nearly the same…and is affected by them very nearly in the same manner. He knows, however, that to the persons principally concerned…they naturally affect *them* in a very different manner. He cannot therefore but approve, and even applaud, that proper exertion of self-command, which enables them to act as if their present and their future situation affected them nearly in the same manner in which they affect him.
>
> (TMS 215.11; emphasis in original)

The impartial spectator is an important check upon our natural passions and appetites. The virtuous man, Smith argues, is the one who can most closely view his situation, passions, and actions as an impartial spectator would because when he does so, he can truly act justly and virtuously, rather than out of excessive selfishness. In the passage above, Smith brings the impartial spectator (morality if you will) into the decision of present versus future consumption. The impartial spectator does not have a clear time preference for other people's consumption – therefore the moral person, adopting as best he can the views of the impartial spectator, should exercise restraint and maintain or increase his consumption over time. That moral claim informs most of Smith's criticisms of profligacy, waste, and imprudent or impulsive spending beyond one's means.

We cannot fully appreciate why Smith alternates between praising and criticizing consumption unless we understand why he thought that individuals could actually harm themselves through their consumption choices out of ignorance or weakness. Smith argues that the ambitious man who pursues a fortune causes himself a great deal of trouble because:

> To obtain the conveniencies which these [riches] afford, he submits in the first year, nay in the first month of his application, to more fatigue of body and more uneasiness of mind than he could have suffered through the whole of his life from the want of them.
>
> (TMS 181.8)

To put it simply, the ambitious man values the future conveniencies of wealth too highly and under appreciates how much unease he will have in pursuing them. With characteristic flair, Smith writes: "The poor man's son, whom heaven in its anger has visited with ambition, when he begins to look around him, admires the condition of the rich" (*TMS* 181.8). The ambitious man pursues the vanity and ostentation of the rich because he wrongly believes that it will bring him happiness. There is a tension here between subjective utility and happiness. Smith is claiming that, based upon human nature, he, Adam Smith, can argue that another man will not find some particular situation or pursuit conducive to his happiness; even if the man gets subjective utility from that activity in the moment.

Flattering his vanity will not bring any happiness greater than what the man could already obtain without it. That man will find his riches

> to be in no respect preferable to that humble security and contentment which he had abandoned for it...he begins at last to find that wealth and greatness are mere trinkets of frivolous utility, no more adapted for procuring ease of body or tranquillity of mind than the tweezer-cases of the lover of toys; and like them too, more troublesome...than all the advantages they can afford him.
>
> (*TMS* 181.8)

What is more, the necessary level of work to gain a fortune will substantially impinge on the man's current happiness. Smith does not advocate workaholism in the name of increasing production as much as possible. Indeed, man's natural goal, according to Smith, is to worry less and less about his physical provision over time so that he has more leisure to exercise his mind and his virtue.

When addressing the stoics, Smith has to shift gears and argue that enjoying consumption is important. His treatment of the stoic philosophy is the best example of his thinking on the topic. The stoics argued that happiness, fulfillment, and virtue can, and should, be obtained independently of wealth or other worldly circumstances. The focus is upon what one can control unhindered – one's own mind, belief, and actions. To achieve that control, however, one needs to recant the world and live in stony apathy. The fact that in *TMS* Smith devoted nearly as many pages to discussing stoicism as he did to the philosophies of Plato, Aristotle, Epicurus, Hutcheson, and Mandeville combined demonstrates that he clearly admired elements of stoicism.

We can see his admiration in almost every discussion of the impartial spectator where considering the views of others shows us that generally the proper course of action is to dampen our natural passions and emotions. That dampening of emotions clearly follows in the stoics' footsteps. We can also see his admiration of stoicism in his reference to the sunbathing beggar who has the internal security and tranquility that "kings are searching for" (*TMS* 185.10). Thomas Martin has written (in this volume, p. 217) an illuminating paper arguing that Smith was referencing a story about Diogenes the Cynic (akin to stoicism) and Alexander the Great. Alexander admires Diogenes' stoicism and offers him whatever he wants. Diogenes replies that all he wants is for Alexander to move aside so that he is not blocking the sun. The point of the story is that riches and power cannot deliver contentment or virtue.

Consumption promotes happiness because people, by their very nature, are made to enjoy it. The stoics, on the other hand, argued that people should focus on their internal state of mind and ignore their external circumstances. To do that, they argued, one must give up worldly pursuits and extraneous consumption in order to pursue internal peace and virtue. Smith criticizes these goals for being unnatural:

> The plan and system which Nature has sketched out for our conduct, seems to be altogether different from that of the Stoical philosophy....By the perfect apathy which it prescribes to us, by endeavouring, not merely to moderate, but to eradicate all our private, partial, and selfish affections...it endeavours to render us altogether indifferent and unconcerned in the success or miscarriage of every thing which Nature has prescribed to us as the proper business and occupation of our lives.
>
> (*TMS* 292–3)

Not only would the widespread practice of stoicism reduce the wealth of nations, it would also cut against most of Smith's moral theory that encouraged people to consider how others (that is, the impartial spectator) view their behavior. Smith argued that rather than being apathetic and inward-focused, people should actively produce and consume. Free enterprise, invention, skillful labor, all of these are good and right for men to pursue. Likewise their various pleasures and enjoyments, within moderation and prudence, promote contentment and happiness.

Smith criticizes what he sees to be frivolous consumption. Not frivolous solely in the sense of being unnecessary, but frivolous in terms of not promoting virtue or happiness. He argues repeatedly that the reason people pursue wealth (as in a fortune, not modest profit) is to improve their social status and flatter their vanity with others' praise: "it is chiefly from this regard to the sentiments of mankind, that we pursue riches and avoid poverty...Do [the rich] imagine that their stomach is better, or their sleep sounder in a palace than in a cottage?" (*TMS* 50.1). In Smith's mind there is little physical pleasure to be gained by amassing a fortune. The food, drink, and shelter that the wealthy enjoy is not substantially different from that of the poor: "The rich only select from the heap what is most precious and agreeable. They consume little more than the poor" (*TMS* 184.10). Therefore, there must be some other source of utility for the rich. Smith thinks it is in vanity and others' regard for him that the rich man enjoys his wealth.

He criticizes the consumption of the wealthy that promotes the "pleasures of vanity and superiority" rather than "tranquillity and enjoyment". He argues that such pleasures are unnecessary, and even detrimental, to happiness:

> In the most glittering and exalted situation that our idle fancy can hold out to us, the pleasures from which we propose to derive our real happiness, are almost always the same with those which, in our actual, though humble station, we have at all times at hand, and in our power. Except the frivolous pleasures of vanity and superiority, we may find, in the most humble station, where there

is only personal liberty, every other which the most exalted can afford; and the pleasures of vanity and superiority are seldom consistent with perfect tranquillity, the principle and foundation of all real satisfactory enjoyment.

(*TMS* 150.31)

That passage explains how he thinks that the foundation of enjoying consumption comes from perfect tranquility, which is just as available to the poor man from "humble station" as to the rich man. Furthermore, he makes the point that "our real happiness" comes from the simple "pleasures" available to rich and poor alike. He also slips "personal liberty" into this discussion in a way that suggests that it too has an important contribution to human happiness. Perhaps the best way to end this section is with Smith's own words about why he thought power and riches, leading to excessive and frivolous consumption, make their owners miserable rather than happy:

Power and riches appear then to be...enormous and operose machines contrived to produce a few trifling conveniencies to the body...which must be kept in order with the most anxious attention, and which in spite of all our care are ready every moment to burst into pieces, and to crush in their ruins their unfortunate possessor.

(*TMS* 182–183.8)

Conclusion

Smith's works concern themselves with promoting the well-being and prosperity of people in England and Scotland. Yet he clearly thought most of his ideas would apply in other places and other times. Even in the *WN*, he does not limit his concerns to solely the economic and material. Justice, peace, contentment, enjoyment, and even virtue are important sub-themes throughout the work. But seeing his overall goal in a normative sense should also cause us to realize that political economy is not purely a dry, abstract, positive science. It is intertwined with questions of justice, morality, and human happiness.

Unlike modern "Max U" theorists who equate happiness with utility gained through consumption, however broadly defined, Smith clearly separates the two. He argued that virtue and vice exist and that people's behavior can be praiseworthy or blameworthy. In *TMS*, he outlines what behavior constitutes the good life and is most conducive to happiness. Although he thought that consumption was good and important, he did not consider it to be the sole measure of wellbeing. Happiness requires more than high levels of consumption. It requires internal tranquility, which some forms of consumption can actually disrupt. This inner tranquility comes by exercising virtue. Prudence requires that men concern themselves with sustaining their wealth over time because that is what the impartial spectator applauds. Therefore for Smith, saving, investing, or consuming are moral decisions.

In some ways Smith seems amenable to the stoic idea that happiness and virtue are completely independent of wealth. That certainly fits his indifference, or even hostility, towards ostentatious displays of wealth or ambitiously pursuing wealth believing it to be a means to happiness. Yet at the same time, Smith distances himself from the stoics. He says the indifferent apathy they preach is contrary to nature. And even though he admires Diogenes for his contentment even as a beggar, he also suggests that such a mindset and circumstances are unusual and should not be pursued. Some basic level of wealth, security, and comfort are both consistent with, and even supportive of, contentment, virtue, and happiness. Knowing how Smith defined happiness helps us reconcile his conflicting descriptions of consumption in the *WN*.

Bibliography

Hayek, F.A. (1945) 'The use of knowledge in society,' *American Economic Review*, pp. 519–30.

Hayek, F.A. (1978) 'Competition as a discovery procedure,' in F.A. Hayek (ed.) *New Studies in Philosophy, Politics, Economics, and the History of Ideas*. Chicago, IL: University of Chicago Press, pp. 179–90.

Headey, B., Muffels, R. and Wooden, M. (2004) *Money Doesn't Buy Happiness…Or Does It? A Reconsideration Based on the Combined Effects of Wealth, Income and Consumption*. IZA Discussion Paper Series, no. 1218. Bonn: Institute for the Study of Labor.

Klein, D.B. (2012) *Knowledge and Coordination: A Liberal Interpretation*. New York: Oxford University Press.

Mandeville, B. (1714) *The Fable of the Bees: Or, Private Vices, Publick Benefits*. Oxford: Clarendon Press. 2 vols.

McCloskey, D. (2008) 'Adam Smith, the last of the former virtue ethicists,' *History of Political Economy*, 40 (1): 43–71.

McCloskey, D.N. (2010) *The Bourgeois Virtues: Ethics for an Age of Commerce*. Chicago, IL: University of Chicago Press.

Mises, L.V. (1949) *Human Action*. Indianapolis, IN: Liberty Fund.

Smith, A. ([1776] 1981) *An Inquiry Into the Nature and Causes of the Wealth of Nations*. R.H. Campbell and A.S. Skinner (eds), vol. II of the *Glasgow Edition of the Works and Correspondence of Adam Smith*. Indianapolis, IN: Liberty Fund.

Smith, A. ([1759, 1790] 1982) *The Theory of Moral Sentiments*. D.D. Raphael and A.L. Macfie (eds), vol. I of the *Glasgow Edition of the Works and Correspondence of Adam Smith*. Indianapolis, IN: Liberty Fund.

Stevenson, B. and Wolfers, J. (2008) *Economic Growth and Subjective Well-being: Reassessing the Easterlin Paradox*, no. 14282. Cambridge, MA: National Bureau of Economic Research.

Stigler, G.J. and Becker, G.S. (1977) 'De gustibus non est disputandum,' *American Economic Review*, 67(2): 76–90.

Stringham, E.P. (2010) 'Economic value and costs are subjective,' in P.J. Boettke (ed.) *Handbook on Contemporary Austrian Economics*. Cheltenham: Edward Elgar.

Book reviews

Guest editor: Craig Smith

Michael L. Frazer, *The enlightenment of sympathy: Justice and the moral sentiments in the eighteenth century and today*

Oxford: Oxford University Press, 2010, 237pp.

ISBN: 978-0-19-539066-7; ISBN-13: 978-0199920235

Reviewed by Michelle A. Schwarze

Research within and across the social sciences has been characterized recently by a renewed interest in sentimentalism, driven in part by calls for impassioned moral and political deliberation (e.g., Hall 2002; Kingston and Ferry 2008). From neuroscientists (Damasio 2000) to economists (Bowles 2011; Zak 2008) to political theorists (Krause 2008), sentimentalism's supporters have sought to show how affect engages individuals and connects them to one another through mediating faculties like sympathy. Yet rationalism and a focus on deriving deliberative standards from reasoned consensus still dominates contemporary debate about deliberation. While the title of his book might suggest a stronger preference for the former, Michael Frazer in fact defends a more moderate position, which he deems 'reflective sentimentalism', in which passionate and informed moral judgment results from the 'reflective self-correction of our moral sentiments' (p. 73). His book focuses on the positive project of sentimentalist thinkers like Hume and Smith, who proposed egalitarian systems of moral development in which authoritative norms are endogenously generated through reflective sympathy with oneself and others, complementing and expanding our natural passions. By highlighting its liberal egalitarian features, Frazer hopes to encourage contemporary normative theory, empirical social science and modern political practice to look to reflective sentimentalism as a valuable resource for research in moral and political psychology.

The book proceeds by detailing the development of sentimentalist moral psychology alongside the shifts of authority of conscience away from hierarchical sources and toward individually generated and approved ones. After briefly discussing the contributions of pre-Humean thinkers on questions of moral authority and human nature, Frazer spends a significant amount of time expounding Hume's sentimentalism and theory of justice, the latter of which he goes on to critique on individualist grounds. This critique makes way for Frazer's fourth chapter on Smith, whom he lauds for building on the autonomous aspects of Hume's sentimentalism while moving away from Hume's 'public-interest-based' (p. 90) approach to justice. For Frazer, only something resembling Smith's 'liberal sentimentalism' can be justified by the enlightened self-reflection the book advocates. The final two theoretical chapters first digress to explain Kant's reaction to sentimentalism and then culminate by noting Herder's important theoretical contributions to reflective sentimentalism on diversity. Frazer closes the book by discussing how reflective sentimentalism might inform empirical research in the social sciences and our approach to civic education.

Before moving to the description of Hume's sentimentalism that serves as a focal point for the book, Frazer explains how three heralds – Butler, Shaftesbury and Hutcheson – shift the focus of eighteenth-century moral philosophy toward a benevolence grounded in human psychology and the problem of the authority of conscience, despite remaining committed to the latter's divine origins themselves. Frazer begins the book beautifully by ensuring his readers avoid the common misconception that sentimentalism advocates *any* expression of *any* passion whatsoever; a feat he achieves by showing the Stoic roots of sentimentalist thought, especially evident in their joint understanding of happiness as the 'harmony of the mind' (p. 19). Rather these pre-Humeans were innovative because they combined a Hobbesian approach to grounding morality in psychological principles with a distinctly non-Hobbesian psychology. As Frazer explains, Hutcheson and others proposed a moral theory based on a moral sense and the disinterested benevolence it naturally approved, which inevitably allowed for greater individual autonomy and greater distance from religion in moral matters. They also brought the problem of the authority of conscience to the forefront, though most believed conscience's authority to be divine in origin themselves. While Hume and contemporary secular philosophers find early sentimentalism's religious foundations unsatisfying, Frazer rightly suggests a possible practical advantage to be derived from it: for reflective sentimentalism to 'provide a widely shared basis for our moral and political commitments in religiously and philosophically pluralistic societies, then it must be presented in a way attractive to those who insist that their convictions have an ultimately religious or metaphysical foundation' (p. 30).

The two chapters of the *Enlightenment of Sympathy* devoted to Hume are perhaps the most detailed and critical, as there Frazer provides Hume's solution to the moral authority problem posed by the early sentimentalists but also takes issue with Hume's proto-utilitarianism. According to Frazer, Hume's key contributions to the sentimentalist project lie in the positive nature of his theory and its insistence on the legitimate moral authority of sentiments produced through 'harmonious reflective equilibrium' (p. 40). In one of the most creative and compelling sections of the book, Frazer argues that standards Hume provides for aesthetic judgment can be applied to moral judgment to render it more authoritative, avoiding skeptical relativism which might emerge from the seemingly subjective nature of sentiment. By doing so, he shows yet another point in Hume's philosophy in which 'skeptical conclusions are undermined by common sense and the practices of everyday life' (p. 47).

But Frazer insists that Hume fails to consider common life experiences when he presents his theory of justice, as Hume bases the moral approval of justice on sympathy with the long-term public interest – a very uncommon affective experience. Furthermore, Frazer suggests that the absence of a 'liberal concern for fairness to individuals' (p. 88) must ultimately lead contemporary sentimentalists concerned with a Rawlsian respect for persons to reject Hume's notion of justice in favor of more individualistic accounts, such as the sentimentalist positions proffered by Smith and Herder that Frazer describes. We might wonder, however, whether Hume's account of justice might not reserve more space for revising repressive laws than Frazer allows, given his claim elsewhere that a constitution which cannot provide remedies against maladministration 'affords us an opportunity of erecting a better in its place' (Hume 1985: 18).

Frazer's treatment of Smith's 'liberal sentimentalism' in the fourth chapter illustrates how a revised understanding of sympathy allows Smith to incorporate individual respect and fairness into a Humean free-standing sentimentalist ethics. Unlike Hume, sympathy for Smith is decidedly cognitive and sympathizing with others is 'difficult imaginative work' (p. 97); individuals engaged in sympathetic interaction with others make moral judgments based on standards of propriety and thus may disapprove of actions they find blameworthy upon reflection. As a result of the refinement of sympathy, Smith is able to move away from a Humean theory of justice grounded in public utility toward a justice based on sympathetic resentment with individuals who suffer harm. This distinctly individualistic modification to sentimentalist accounts of justice is incredibly valuable according to Frazer, because spectators will consider individual circumstances rather than utility when judging acts as just or unjust. Nonetheless, as Frazer acknowledges, individuals sometimes *do* consider necessity (p. 109–11) when making decisions about justice (e.g., when deciding to put a criminal to death). Along with Smith's insistence on the laws of justice being 'sacred' and 'inviolable' and the great reliance of many people on general rules for moral decision making, this deviation might sometimes obscure individual need in Smith's sentimentalism as well.

Following a digression on Kant's rejection of sentimentalist principles that includes a developmental account of Kant's position on sympathy, Frazer ends his theoretical chapters with Herder's pluralist sentimentalism and embrace of cultural diversity. Herder encourages individuals to empathetically engage with history in order to develop humanity and tolerance, which Frazer argues makes him a link between his sentimentalist predecessors and contemporary liberals; he allows the 'sentimentalist account of moral and political reflection familiar from Hume and Smith to function successfully in a world characterized by a remarkable diversity of cultures and worldviews' (p. 167).

The book closes in a fitting way, given Frazer's claim that 'reliance on empirical psychology is one of the distinctive features of reflective sentimentalism' (p. 80), by briefly reviewing recent empirical work on the sentiments and suggesting some avenues for future research. Most notable is Frazer's entreaty to social psychologists to continue to study conscious, reflective behaviors alongside automatic processing. While he does not state it as such, focusing on automaticity restricts researchers to providing proof for a Humean instinctive sympathy while foreclosing on the potential of empirically grounding the more desirable Smithean reflective type. Given the book's interdisciplinary approach, myriad insights on individual political philosophers and skilled weaving of disparate sentimentalist accounts into a cohesive narrative, *The Enlightenment of Sympathy* is an important resource for those interested in the study of moral psychology and its role in political life.

Biblography

Bowles, S. (2011) *A Cooperative Species: Human Reciprocity and Its Evolution*, Princeton, NJ: Princeton University Press.

Damasio, A. (2000) *Descartes' Error: Emotion, Reason, and the Human Brain*, New York: HarperCollins.

Hall, C. (2002) *The Trouble with Passion: Political Theory Beyond the Reign of Reason*, New York: Routledge.

Hume, D. (1985) 'That politics may be reduced to a science,' in Eugene F. Miller (eds) *Essays Moral, Political, and Literary*, Indianapolis: Liberty Fund, pp. 14–31.

Kingston, R. and Ferry, L. (2008) *Bringing the Passions Back In: The Emotions in Political Philosophy*, Vancouver, BC: University of British Columbia Press.

Krause, S. (2008) *Civil Passions: Moral Sentiment and Democratic Deliberation*, Princeton, NJ: Princeton University Press.

Zak, P. (2008) *Moral Markets: The Critical Role of Values in the Economics*, Princeton, NJ: Princeton University Press.

Andrew Hamilton, *Trade and empire in the eighteenth century Atlantic world*

Newcastle upon Tyne: Cambridge Scholars Publishing, 2008, 168pp.

ISBN HARDBACK: 1-84718-837-0

Reviewed by Edwin van de Haar

Focusing on Anglo-American relations in the late eighteenth century, the purpose of this book is to 'reveal the practical application of Adam Smith's theories to political settlements during a time of considerable change and upheaval, when the definition of empire was shifting from military conquest to commercial domination' (p. viii). The author was motivated by Vincent Harlow's commendable remark that much research needs to be done on the influence of Smith's doctrines on the economic policy of British political leaders during the late eighteenth century. Hamilton attempts to achieve this through a study of the ideas of some thinkers who have thus far received scarce academic attention, and their influence on some of the pivotal political figures in the early American republic. He embraces Bailyn's argument that early American culture was mostly the result of further developing metropolitan Western European culture, not least in economic thought. Hume's, Smith's and Tucker's ideas on political economy have remained under-analysed in recent biographies of John Adams and Benjamin Franklin. Still, the author posits, 'the dialogue of ideas that the British thinkers exchanged with their American counterparts is imperative to understand how the new country positioned itself in relation to other nation-states' (p. xvi). The pivotal figure in the book is Benjamin Vaughan (1751–1835), the influential private secretary of Lord Shelburne, while both men are singled out as major proponents of Smith's ideas.

By way of context, the book commences with an overview of the debate on trade in the eighteenth century, particularly the alleged dichotomy between *laizzez-faire* and mercantilist 'reason of state'. It must be noted that, throughout the entire book, the author proceeds in a very fragmented way, apparently more informed by the content of his secondary literature, than the specific purpose of the book. So here, in just a few pages, he analyses Stewart's biography of Smith, follows up with three French thinkers (Turgot, Gournay and d'Argenson) and continues with Jacob Viner and the role of the Christian tradition in the trade debate going back to the fourth-century pagan Libanius. Then, two German thinkers, Oberfohren and Rothkrug, are briefly introduced, before the argument returns to France with a focus on Belesbat and Boisguilbert. While all this is interesting, it fails to provide convincing evidence for the claim that 'a genealogy of Smith's *Wealth of Nations* must necessarily include these French influences' (p. 17). The reader longs for a more analytical approach, as for example provided by Douglas Irwin (1996), while it remains unclear why other participants in the trade debate in that period are excluded (for example those presented in Clark, 2003).

From the second chapter onwards, Hamilton turns to Vaughan; in his words, 'the essential yet overlooked figure' in free-trade theories in the context of British colonial relations (p.23) and the 'cosmopolitan staunch defender of the liberal system' who kept his back straight, while Smith and John Adams were 'eventually pressed to reverse their free trade stances in the face of international trade sanctions' (p. 24). The author starts with an account of the life of the second Lord Shelburne (William Petty). Petty's brother was a lodger of Smith and he and Shelburne were lifelong friends, In Shelburne's own words, Smith's principles 'constituted the happiness of my life' (p. 31). Vaughan, as his confidential secretary, was a key figure in Shelburne's circle from the 1770s onwards, while he was also a friend of Benjamin Franklin. Consequently, Vaughan acted as trusted friend of both sides during the Paris peace negotiations between America and Britain in 1782–1783. He tried hard to include articles guaranteeing free trade in the peace agreement, but failed. Shortly afterwards, he helped to prepare Shelburne's speaking notes for his defence of the peace treaty in parliament but this also failed, leading to the latter's fall as a prime minister. Vaughan then followed in his father's footsteps as a politically active merchant. He continued to object to moves to limit trade; for example, the initiative to exclude the Americans from commerce with the British West Indies. Vaughan kept friendly relations with many important thinkers and activists in many countries, particularly in France. After the French revolution had escalated, Vaughan left Britain because he feared imprisonment in the wake of investigations into 'revolutionary enthusiasts'. He ended up in Maine, USA, where he spend the last 35 years of his life as a politically influential land owner.

Vaughan was the editor of Franklin's collected writings and had a hand in the translation of Condorcet's *Vie de M. Turgot* into English. His own writings mainly consisted of essays and letters; for example, advising Shelburne on the American question. In line with Turgot, he consistently emphasised the importance of free trade between Britain and the Americans. Although published anonymously, *New and Old Principles of Trade* (1788) was almost certainly written by Vaughan (p. 119–120). The essay was republished in 1859 in the collection, *New and Old Principles of Trade*, edited by the influential free trade supporter John Ramsay McCulloch. Vaughan's brief treatise was, in the words of Hamilton, 'not the earliest, yet the most perfect expression of *laissez-faire*, cosmopolitanism and benevolence before the French Revolution' (p. 124). In it, Vaughan attacked mercantilism with the help of four conceptual tools. He attempted to show that all participating countries benefited from free trade (the rich country–poor country question) and that free trade fostered peace. He even believed in the beneficial effects of trade between belligerent neighbours. He provided arguments and examples to show that trade theory would work in practise, while he also used 'providential arguments', as Viner has called it, or the idea that God has purposely scattered the resources across the Earth to compel humans to cooperate through commerce. Together the treatise provided a fully cosmopolitan vision of the world.

Hamilton follows Hirschmann in the argument that the eighteenth century witnessed a shift in thinking about colonial relations, from passion and power-based *raison d'état*, to an interest-based *doux commerce*, as Montesquieu has coined it. Here, the peace enhancing effects of international commercial relations were central. Hamilton also places Hume and Smith (p. 95) in this category. That is simply erroneous. Of course, both Hume and Smith highly valued trade for numerous reasons, not least economic and cultural. Yet they did not expect that increased commercial ties between nations would ensure or even just foster peace. Indeed, they pointed out that the increased wealth of nations as a result of free trade would go together with increased military capacity and that many causes of war remained (see Van de Haar 2009, 2010, 2013).

While the author is not unique in making this mistake, it is symptomatic for the whole book. It lacks a yardstick for the selection of the numerous thinkers presented. It is only a short book, so there is no room for a sufficiently detailed analysis of their thought. This leads to a very scattered information flow. The author's choice has clearly been to use a broad-brush approach to the history of ideas. That choice in itself is of course valid, yet becomes troublesome if the main questions of the book remain unanswered. To give the most prominent example: the author set out to analyse the practical influence of Adam Smith's theories. Of course this demands a thorough knowledge of those theories, for which the author does not provide much evidence. The bibliography just lists the Hackett and Cannan versions of the *Wealth of Nations* as primary sources, no other works of Smith are mentioned.

Hence, the book does not qualify as a solid piece of Smith-related scholarship. This said, it is still of some interest to Smith scholars, as the author does succeed to draw attention to the interesting figure of Benjamin Vaughan. Vaughan was one of those almost forgotten yet influential contemporaries of Smith. The two men knew each other and like Shelburne, Vaughan attempted to bring Smith's principles into practical policy making, particularly in the transatlantic context. His close ties with Franklin and his role during the peace negotiations make it worthwhile to get (re)acquainted with his life story and his writings on trade. The book offers an opportunity for this.

Bibliography

Clark, H.C. (ed.) (2003) *Commerce, Culture, and Liberty. Readings on Capitalism Before Adam Smith*, Indianapolis, IN: Liberty Fund.

Irwin, D. (1996) *Against the Tide. An Intellectual History of Free Trade*, Princeton, NJ: Princeton University Press.

Van de Haar, E. (2009) *Classical Liberalism and International Relations Theory. Hume, Smith, Mises, and Hayek*, New York: Palgrave Macmillan.

Van de Haar, E. (2010) 'The liberal divide over trade, peace and war,' *International Relations*, 24 (2): 132–54.

Van de Haar, E. (2013) 'Adam Smith on empire and international relations,' in C. Berry, C. Smith and M. Paganelli (eds), *The Oxford Handbook of Adam Smith*, Oxford: Oxford University Press, pp. 417–39.

Daniel B. Klein, *Knowledge and coordination: A liberal interpretation*

New York: Cambridge University Press, 2013, 384pp.

ISBN 978-0199355327

Reviewed by Gavin Kennedy

In his new book, Daniel Klein demonstrates the originality of his thinking. He ranges well beyond the confines of neoclassical economics and links his themes to the tradition of (British) classical liberalism, which he defines as 'best represented by Adam Smith, and politically by Liberal Party politicians Richard Cobden, John Bright, and William Gladstone' (p. 320).

Klein insists that readers understand the differences between 'concatenate coordination', in which its 'components or elements find an order more pleasing or desirable according to some relevant standard' (p. 317), and 'mutual coordination', in which actions 'mesh according to a situational coincidence of interest' (p. 321). Concatenate coordination was what economists meant by 'coordination' from around 1890 to the 1960s, and it often referred to 'social order' where employee coordination is imposed not by the price mechanism but by an entrepreneur's commands. Mutual coordination, explains Klein, emerged in the 1960s with Thomas Schelling and game theory. At the same time, concatenate coordination receded, losing ground to 'efficiency', 'social welfare function' and 'optimality.' He implies economics is the poorer since concatenate coordination lost ground.

These distinct coordinations are explored in greater detail using Smith's example of the labourer's woolen coat from *Wealth of Nations* (*WN* I.ii.12:22–24), which Klein says (p. 55–6), and I agree, is of special concatenate significance compared with Smith's more famous example of pin-making, which he took from Diderot's *Encyclopédie* (Peaucelle 2006). Klein links the woolen coat example to Hayek's 'spontaneous order', supported with a literature survey. He criticises 'general equilibrium' models for ignoring the process of 'concatenation of market activities that makes a woolen coat'. Klein (p. 73–5) explores 'co-operation', helpfully supported by formal discussions of concatenate and mutual coordination that turn on the ambiguity of cooperation when either concatenate coordination or mutual coordination are present.

Knowledge is the other pole of Klein's book. He turns his attention to what D. N. McCloskey dubbed as 'Max-U' theorizing and the logic of choice optimising among multiple ends with limited means. He discusses Israel M. Kirzner's work in detail, particularly on 'entrepreneurship', which also involves discovering new ends and means by transcending what is currently available. Klein (p. 13–15) quotes Somerset Maugham's short story of a verger discovering an opportunity for opening a tobacco shop. He does so and makes his fortune. He was not seeking a business opportunity; he need not have acted having found one; he could just as easily have grumbled and looked elsewhere for cigarettes. That he followed through illustrates entrepreneurial qualities.

Entrepreneurial interventions are not accommodated in neoclassical optimising models, nor are they common among central planners, despite feeble efforts by some social democrats to proselytise for 'salaried entrepreneurs.' However, entrepreneurs are endemic in the real world. By removing entrepreneurs because of an inability to model them, the key difference between markets (with entrepreneurs who risk their own capital) and state functionaries (who spend compulsory taxation) is eliminated, along with our understanding of the real world. Klein rightly is suspicious of the neglect of the entrepreneurial role.

He reports on what Mises, Hayek and Kirzner said about the entrepreneurial function, together with a detailed critique of their conflicting nuances (p. 139–41; 81–118; 261–304). He dehomogenises Mises and Hayek and exalts Smith-Hayek over Mises-Rothbard, thereby challenging the Kirzner-Boettke wing of the Austrian project. He summarises an entrepreneur's roles as: 'discovering' betterment opportunities; 'creating' new products or methods; improving products; 'bearing' uncertainty; 'owning' capital; 'owning or managing' business enterprise'; and 'organizing' through speech, rhetoric and persuasion (p. 142).

Controversially, he introduces the alleged links of Smith's use of the 'invisible-hand' metaphor to an allegorical 'Joy', who is an invisible, 'humanitarian' and 'liberal', and who generates a dynamic, complex spontaneous order which, because it is generally decentralised and spontaneous, is 'more pleasing than the order generated by the rather more controlled or centrally directed economic system', which inevitably is coercive (p. 61–2; 221–3; 229–30). But much of Klein's worthwhile critique is compromised by his allegorical fiction. He believes his allegory of the role of entrepreneurs in market economies supports what he claims is Adam Smith's 'presumption of liberty'. This argument extends his defence of the significance of Smith's use of the invisible hand metaphor over which he and I have politely disagreed since 2009 (Klein 2009; Klein and Lucas 2011a,b; Kennedy 2009, 2011).

Klein's admirable attempt to reintroduce the absent entrepreneur to explain why voluntary markets are more successful than compulsory state-managed interventions is welcome. However, his use of 'Joy' is unconvincing because allegories are only 'extended' metaphors (Smith 1762: 30) that have potential beauty, but also, along with 'Metonymies, Similies…and Hyperbolls', they have the grammatical limitations 'equally applicable' to 'the justness and propriety of metaphors' (Smith 1762: 30). Smith taught that metaphors 'give due strength of expression to the object to be described' and they do this in 'a more striking and interesting manner' (Smith 1762: 29). Smith, of course, became even more famous from the 1950s (Kennedy 2010), inside and outside the academy, for his misunderstood use of the popular eighteenth-century metaphor of the invisible hand (Harrison 2010).

Now Smith was perfectly clear as to the significance of an 'invisible hand' metaphor's objects on the two occasions he used it. In *Moral Sentiments* (*TMS* IV.1.10: 184) its 'object' was the obvious inescapable necessity that led a 'proud and unfeeling landlord' to feed his labourers from his crops. Obviously, without food they could not produce crops to feed anyone. In *Wealth of Nations*, the 'invisible-hand' metaphor's 'object' referred to those merchants whose sense of insecurity, if they sent their capital abroad, led them to invest solely in 'domestic industry', thus arithmetically increasing 'domestick revenue and employment' (*WN* IV.ii.9: 456).

The 'invisible hand' metaphor was intended to catch the reader's attention, although, interestingly, only about a dozen or more readers remarked on its presence between 1759 through to the 1930s (Samuels 2011; Kennedy 2010). Clearly, not all metaphors that have 'beauty' are appreciated, nor are their 'objects' widely identified. Specifically in *Moral Sentiments*, the necessity of feeding dependent labourers and their families unintentionally 'advance[d] the interests of society, which afford[ed] the multiplication of the species' (Smith 1759: IV.1.10: 185). In *Wealth of Nations*, the avoidance of foreign trade from the insecurity felt by some merchants, led in turn unintentionally to their domestic investment promoting 'the publick interest' (Smith 1776: IV.ii.9: 456).

Not all metaphors have 'beauty'. In neither case did Smith suggest, as is widely believed today, that an actual invisible hand existed. It was purely a metaphor for the hidden (thereby invisible) motives of those individuals whose resulting behaviour led to the unintended outcomes he described as being in the 'public interest.' He specifically denied that acting in the 'public interest' was 'very common among' merchants (Smith 1776: IV.ii. 9: 456).

Klein took the idea for his 'Joy' allegory from Edwin Canaan (1902: 461), an 'ardent Smithian' (p. 221), who wrote: 'The reason why it pays to do the right thing – to do nearly what an omniscient and omnipotent benevolent Inca would order to be done', led Canaan to suggest, as Klein puts it, that 'the free-enterprise system… leads to patterns of activities that please a benevolent being' (p. 27). Klein's benevolent 'Joy' 'tells Bridget the baker that perhaps she should buy new ovens, lookout for better deals in flour, and advertise her confections. Within the allegory, Joy communicates these instructions to Bridget. …Within the allegory, Bridget, who is sensible to Joy's benevolence and ethical wisdom, follows not market signals, but Joy's communications, embraced voluntarily by Bridget from what Smith calls her sense of duty'. Quoting Smith, Klein suggests that, within the allegory, Bridget 'enters, if I may say so, into the sentiments of that divine Being' (*TMS*: 276) (p. 222). Though, to be clear, Smith never said anything about a divine being conveying benevolence and ethical wisdom to entrepreneurs by inviting them to ignore visible market signals or to consciously act as if they knew that what they were doing was ethically good, nor that they were motivated by 'divine benevolence' rather than by their self interest.

Absurdly, Klein's fictional 'Joy' (no less than Canaan's 'Inca') tells Bridget 'to take actions rather like the actions that the market signals would lead her to take' (p. 222)! So why doesn't Klein stick to explaining why Bridget and other entrepreneurs follow the visible signals of market prices and the consequences for them and others of so doing without inventing a benevolent gloss? 'Joy' adds nothing to our understanding of the role of visible market prices, and serves no useful purpose other than legitimising Klein's allegory, and his blessing of markets for their divine-like 'benevolence'. Smith pointedly makes very clear the non-role of benevolence in markets because markets work under different imperatives. Specifically, persuasion and offers of exchanges by bargaining ('Give me that which I want, and you shall have this which you want.') are not about benevolence, but about addressing each other's self-interests and, crucially, not our own (*WN* I.ii.1.26–7).

Klein's circumlocution goes a long way trying to explain that those entrepreneurs who follow visible market prices, attempt to weigh up the respective benefits and costs against their business opportunities, and who add their spark of that scarcest of all entrepreneurial qualities, their judgement, who are more likely to benefit than those would-be entrepreneurs who ignore price signals and press on regardless, based on decisions deficient in some respect against the available evidence of price signals (p. 261–304). With respect, Klein's 'Joy' adds nothing to the entrepreneurial role.

Klein's discussion of the works of Hayek is excellent and informative. Interestingly, he quotes from Hayek's 'The Trend of Economic Thinking' (1933) lamenting the absence of an 'adequate and permanent place in our thinking' of 'spontaneous coordination', without 'using misleading metaphorical words' because 'as soon as we take such phrases in a literal sense, they become untrue... And as soon as we recognise this, we tend to fall into an opposite error...we deny the existence of what these terms are intended to describe' (p. 221). To which I say: precisely!

It is better to explain economics without using misleading metaphors or allegories, and, if we do use them, we should never do so without identifying their objects to check on our credibility. Using metaphors or allegories in place of understanding economics always ends up in ideological sloganising, which adds nothing to our knowledge. Wishful ideologues say: 'Leave markets to the invisible hand'; 'No', say statists, 'use the visible hand of the State, instead!'. Both are deficient in knowledge of the intricacies of entrepreneurial market coordination that Daniel Klein brings to our attention.

Bibliography

Canaan, E. (1902) 'The practical utility of economic science,' *Economic Journal* 12(48): 459–71.

Hayek, F.A. ([1991] 1933) 'The trend of economic thinking,' in *The Trend of Economic Thinking: Essays on Political Economists and Economic History*, W.W. Bartley III and S. Kresge (eds) Chicago, IL: Chicago University of Press.

Kennedy, G. (2009) 'Adam Smith and the invisible hand: from metaphor to myth,' *Econ Journal Watch* 6(2): 239–62.

Kennedy, G. (2010) 'Paul Samuelson and the invention of the modern economics of the invisible hand,' *History of Economic Ideas* 18(3): 105–19.

Kennedy, G. (2011) 'Adam Smith and the role of the invisible hand,' *Economic Affairs* 31(1): 53–7.

Klein, D.B. (2009) 'On Adam Smith's invisible hands: comment on Gavin Kennedy,' *Econ Journal Watch* 6(2): 264–79.

Klein, D.B. and Lucas, B. (2011a) 'In a word or two, placed in the middle: the invisible hand in Smith's Tomes,' *Economic Affairs* 31(1): 43–52.

Klein, D.B. and Lucas, B. (2011b) 'On the deliberate centrality of an invisible hand: a reply to Gavin Kennedy, Ryan Hanley, and Craig Smith,' *Economic Affairs* 31(2): 90–2.

Peaucelle, J.-L. (2006) 'Adam Smith's use of multiple references for his pin making examples,' *European Journal of the History of Economic Thought* 13(4): 480–512.

Samuels, W. (2011) *Erasing the Invisible Hand: Essays of an Elusive and Misunderstood Concept in Economics*. New York: Cambridge University Press.

Smith, A. ([1759] 1976) *The Theory of Moral Sentiments*. Oxford: Oxford University Press.

Smith, A ([1776] 1976) *An Inquiry into the Nature and Causes of the Wealth of Nations*. Oxford: Oxford University Press.

Smith, A. ([1762–63] 1983) *Lectures on Rhetoric and Belles Lettres*. Oxford: Oxford University Press.

AUTHOR'S RESPONSE

Daniel B. Klein's response to review by Gavin Kennedy

The kindness and generosity of Gavin Kennedy has touched me many times before, and now does so again. He delivers one chief criticism. He correctly notes that I see metaphor and allegory in Adam Smith, even in *WN*, and in economics generally. I elaborate and embrace allegory. Gavin says I do so 'absurdly.' He protests: 'It is better to explain economics without using misleading metaphors or allegories'.

In discussing market forces, Adam Smith employed simile and metaphor. He sketches an aspect of social coordination: 'It is the interest of the people that their daily, weekly, and monthly consumption should be proportioned as exactly as possible to the supply of the season' (Smith 1776, IV.v.b.3: 524–5). The grain dealer adjusts his prices and quantities in ways that conduce to such coordination:

> Without intending the interest of the people, he is necessarily led, by a regard to his own interest, to treat them, even in years of scarcity, pretty much in the same manner as the prudent master of a vessel is sometimes obliged to treat his crew. When he foresees that provisions are likely to run short, he puts them upon short allowance. Though from excess of caution he should sometimes do this without any real necessity, yet all the inconveniences which his crew can thereby suffer are inconsiderable in comparison of the danger, misery, and ruin to which they might sometimes be exposed by a less provident conduct.
> (Smith 1776, IV.v.b.3: 525)

Here, Smith ventures to teach by simile. Does the simile rumple Gavin's sensibilities? I'm not sure – maybe the prudent shipmaster is not a 'misleading' figure.

But it is clear enough that the simile of the prudent shipmaster is a miniature of the metaphor of the being whose hand is invisible. Is that metaphor 'misleading'?

How will we know whether it is unless we take the trouble to elaborate what the metaphor is? Gavin blasts me for exploring the matter. I mount a case for recognizing, declaring, elaborating, and affirming allegory (see Klein 2012a: 73–5, 217–37; for a short pitch online, see Klein 2012b). I discuss the allegorical nature of our talk of the price system as communication, of cooperation throughout the woolen-coat-making system, of market error and correction, of policy error and correction, and of other central tropes of our discourse. But Gavin's otherwise generous review does not treat that case; he does not engage it. He writes as though no such case is made.

That case challenges Gavin: Are you ready to reject talk of the price system as communication, etc.? If Gavin is ready to reject such talk, he should face up to it and say so.

I don't think he is ready to reject such talk. In the review, Gavin himself speaks of prices as 'signals.' Many of my readers may have frequently talked this talk, just as many of Adam Smith's readers may have danced the dance of the minuet:

> Even some of our dances, which are said to have been originally imitative, have, in the way in which we practice them, almost ceased to be so. The minuet, in which the woman, after passing and repassing the man several times, first gives him up one hand, then the other, and then both hands, is said to have been originally a Moorish dance, which emblematically represented the passion of love. Many of my readers may have frequently danced this dance, and, in the opinion of all who saw them, with great grace and propriety, though neither they nor their spectators once thought of the allegorical meaning which it originally intended to express.
>
> (Smith 1980: 207)

As I explain in the book, Safeway's price of $1.89 for a dozen eggs is, in literal terms, nothing more than a plain message saying, 'Yours for $1.89'. It is a signal – perhaps to buy eggs, perhaps to not buy eggs; perhaps to produce more eggs, perhaps to produce fewer eggs; perhaps to produce substitutes, etc. – only in an allegorical sense. Gavin's own 'signal' talk can be saved only by allegory.

Gavin treats the important 1933 Hayek quote about dual errors in relation to allegorical discourse, but, by mistaking what Hayek means by 'the existence of what these terms are intended to describe,' he falls into the second of the two errors.

Gavin speaks of 'Using metaphors or allegories in place of understanding,' as though understanding is one thing and metaphor is another. He misses the book's subsection, 'Unfolding the Allegory Makes It Innocuous,' in which I write: 'The more the allegory is spelled out – in particular, as Joy being knowing – the less it seems to correspond to any external being or institution' (Klein 2012, 224).

Allegory is everywhere. It is, for example, in the subtitle of my book: 'A Liberal Interpretation'. On the matter of divine providence, I am Humean. There is no expression from God that we interpret, in a literal sense. Yet we wisely speak of interpreting the world.

Aside from allegorical indigestion, Gavin's review is entirely fair and generous, and I am grateful. And even on the matter of allegory, perhaps Gavin promotes an end which was no part of his intention.

Bibliography

Klein, D.B. (2012a) *Knowledge and Coordination: A Liberal Interpretation*. Oxford: Oxford University Press.

Klein, D.B. (2012b) 'Allegory and political economy: communication and cooperation'. *The Freeman* 64(2): 3235. Available online at: www.fee.org/the_freeman/detail/allegory-and-political-economy-communication-and-cooperation (last accessed 18 July 2014).

Smith, A. ([1776] 1976) *An Inquiry into the Nature and Causes of the Wealth of Nations*. R.H. Campbell and A.S. Skinner (eds), Oxford: Oxford University Press. Indianapolis, IN: Liberty Fund, 1981.

Smith, A. (1980) *Essays on Philosophical Subjects*. W.P.D. Wightman and J.C. Bryce (eds), New York: Oxford University Press. Reprint: Indianapolis, IN: Liberty Fund, 1982.

Steven G. Medema, *The hesitant hand: Taming self-interest in the history of economic ideas*

Princeton, NJ: Princeton University Press, 2009, 230pp.

ISBN PAPERBACK: 978-0-691-15000-0

Reviewed by Farhad Rassekh

The British historian, Henry Thomas Buckle (1873, v. 1: 154) described the *Wealth of Nations* (*WN*) as 'probably the most important book that has ever been written, and is certainly the most valuable contribution ever made by a single man towards establishing the principles on which government should be based'. It may be puzzling that Buckle referred to Smith's tome as a political treatise. But this characterization of the *WN* reflects the fact that economics, at least since Adam Smith, has largely revolved around the role of the market versus the role of the state in a market economy. Economic textbooks teach that under certain conditions the market transforms self-interest into the public interest, but then quickly argue that such conditions are violated in the real world and call for government interventions to correct market failures. This presentation of economics, however, is incomplete and misleading, for 'failure' is not limited to the market; it encompasses the government as well. To understand the conception and evolution of the theories of market failure as well as of government failure, one must read Steven Medema's splendid book, *The Hesitant Hand*.

Medema's book is composed of seven chapters. Chapter one, entitled, 'Adam Smith and His Ancestors' provides a brief review of the ideas on the role of self-interest in society prior to Smith, as well as Smith's own analysis of the role of self-interest in the economy. The publication of *Leviathan* in 1650 ushered in a fascinating period in western thought as a number of thinkers set out to refute Hobbes's pessimistic and materialistic portrait of human nature. In particular, several thinkers saw a beneficial role for self-interest in the market. For example, in 1713, William Derham argued that we naturally pursue our 'genius' and gravitate towards the employment we enjoy. Since each person is endowed with a unique talent, division of labor ensues. In 1744, James Harris carried the argument further and showed that the division of labor connects the interests of individuals together and promotes the public interest (Myers 1983). In 1734, Alexander Pope expressed the idea that was gaining acceptance at the time:

> From sounds to things, from fancy to the heart:
> For Wit's false mirror held up Nature's light,
> Show'd erring pride, Whatever is, is right;
> That Reason, Passion answer one great aim;
> That true Self-love and Social are the same;
> That Virtue only makes our bliss below,
> And all our knowledge is, ourselves to know.

(1734/1931: 155)

By the time Smith began his scholarly life, the harmony of self-interest and social interest was no longer a novel idea. Quite influentially, Smith's teacher Francis Hutcheson had elevated self-love to the same level as benevolence. Smith cogently presented the ideas he had inherited from Derham, Harris and others, and raised them to a higher level by arguing that not only the public interest but also the market order itself arises from individuals attempting to better their lives. Thus, Medema states that in Smith's writings 'Self-interest, then, had finally found legitimacy' (p. 25). Smith, however, offered a rather long list of exceptions and qualifications to the beneficence of the market. Medema quotes Jacob Viner, who wrote that if Smith 'had been brought face to face with a list of the modifications to the principle of *laissez faire* to which he at one place or another had granted his approval, I have no doubt that he would have been astounded at his own moderation' (p. 24).

Chapter Two, which I believe is the most important part of the book, presents the views of John Stuart Mill and Henry Sidgwick on the economic role of government in the system of natural liberty. Both thinkers applied the utilitarian apparatus to the role of the state in the economy, but Sidgwick saw more failings in the system of natural liberty than did Mill. Mill operated on the principle that 'The only purpose for which power can be rightfully exercised over any member of a civilized community, against his will, is to prevent harm to others' (quoted in Medema, p. 35). Accordingly, power can be rightfully exercised over polluters. As Medema puts it, 'For Mill there was a universal rule for noninterference, but not for interference: utilitarianism comes in, and only comes in, in the presence of harmful spillover effects' (p. 51). Moreover, Mill did not think of government as the all benevolent and omnipotent entity that can always 'improve on market performance' (p. 51). The case for interference had to be strong. But Sidgwick exhibited more faith in government, and heavily influenced Arthur Pigou, the main architect of the modern theory of externality.

Chapter Three covers the views of Alfred Marshall and Pigou on the economic role of government, but it is Pigou who rightly dominates the chapter. Pigou applied the recently developed analytical tools of neoclassical economics and showed that 'self-interest and social interest will coincide – only when marginal private net products are equal to marginal social net products' (p. 61). Since in the presence of externality this condition does not hold, the market fails to deliver the optimal outcome. Pigou rejected the proposition that the pursuit of self-interest promotes social interest. He said that in the 'absolute and rigid form' even Adam Smith did not believe in it. Further, Pigou argued that the 'ideal' outcome may not be feasible, 'For we cannot expect that any public authority will attain, or will even wholeheartedly seek that ideal' (quoted in Medema, p. 69). The reason according to Pigou, Medema writes, is 'information problems faced by, and the pressure brought to bear on, government agents' (p. 69). Here Pigou seems to have recognized a mild version of what later on, under the influence of Friedrich Hayek, came to be known as the knowledge problem; namely, for the state to engage in economic actions it needs the relevant information which can be revealed only through the market process as economic agents interact with each other. Nonetheless, Pigou (and some other influential thinkers) argued for the expansion of the role of government in the economy. In the meantime, mathematical models strengthened the Pigovian stance, which along with the Keynesian revolution marginalized laissez-faire economics and turned it into an impossible dream of a small group of thinkers such Ayn Rand, Ludwig von Mises, and their followers.

But the Pigovian economics constitutes only a part of this intellectual odyssey. Chapter Four introduces the contributions of a group of Italian scholars whose work on government failure is unknown to the English-speaking economists. This chapter also introduces the theories of Knut Wicksell who influenced James Buchanan, the main architect of the social choice theory, the theme of Chapter Six. Public choice 'is the economic analysis of politics' which applies 'the self-interested rational actor' model 'to the analysis of politics' (p. 127). Medema notes that this approach 'led to a theory of government failure that parallels the theory of market failure' (p. 128). Although public choice opened a new chapter in economic and political literature, it has not gained nearly as much traction in mainstream economics as the theory of market failure.

Chapters five and seven focus on the Coase theorem, which exposed some fundamental problems with the Pigouvian analysis of externality. These two chapters are quite fascinating and very well-executed because the Coase theorem is the author's specialty. Medema (2011) chose the Coase theorem as the theme of his Presidential Address at the 2010 History of Economics Society. In the conventional analysis of negative externality, as Coase put it, if 'A inflicts harm on B' the question 'is: how should we restrain A?' (quoted in Medema, p. 105). Coase realized that the harm is reciprocal because if B forced A to curb pollution, a harm would befall A. Thus, the question is no longer how and how much pollution should be reduced; rather, as Coase put it, 'Should A be allowed to harm B or should B be allowed to harm A?'. This profound insight brought to light the centrality of property rights in the analysis of externality. Moreover, Coase showed that in the absence of transaction costs the efficient solution arises regardless of the initial assignment of property rights. Medema (2009) has noted that 'the implications here are stunning: If market transactions are costless, court decisions assigning liability for damages will have no effect on the allocation of resources' (p. 111). If A and B could negotiate with each other, then the role of government would be confined to the assignment and protection of property rights. These ideas have been more than a theoretical possibility. Coase's insights, as Medema points out, have led to the 'use of marketable pollution permits and the auctioning of licenses for the new portable telephone technologies' (p. 124). Nevertheless, Mark Blaug (2007), among others, has sharply criticized the Coase theorem, arguing that it 'is nothing but the first fundamental theorem of welfare economics in disguise...a truth confined to the logical fiction of a world without transactions costs' (p. 200). But Medema convincingly shows that the Coase theorem 'is better understood...as a useful fiction' (p. 187).

Medema's analysis of the role of self-interest in the economy gives the students of market failure and government failure much to ponder and provides them with the necessary theoretical tools to evaluate their assumptions and understanding of the two types of failure. But the book is not ideologically to the left or the right; rather, it is a scholarly and objective work that educates the readers without trying to persuade them to either camp. Finally, it is a work in the history of ideas which serves as a great example of scholarship and clarity.

Bibliography

Blaug, M. (2007) 'The fundamental theorems of modern welfare economics, historically contemplated,' *History of Political Economy* 39(2): 185–207.

Buckle, H.T. (1873) *History of Civilization in England*, vol. 1, 2nd London Edition, New York: D. Appleton and Company.

Medema, S.G. (2011) 'HES presidential address: the coase theorem, lessons from the study of the history of economic thought,' *Journal of the History of Economic Thought* 33(1): 1–18.

Myers, M. (1983) *The Soul of Modern Economic Man*, Chicago, IL: Chicago University Press.

Pope, A. (1734/1931) 'An essay on man,' in *The Complete Works of Alexander Pope*, Henry W. Boynton (ed.), Boston, MA: Houghton Mifflin Company.

James R. Otteson, *Adam Smith*

London: Continuum, 2011, 179pp.

ISBN: 978-0-8264-2983-4

Reviewed by Lauren Brubaker

James Otteson's second book on Adam Smith, titled simply *Adam Smith*, has most of the advantages, and a few of the drawbacks, of his first book, *Adam Smith's Marketplace of Life* (*Marketplace*), which I discussed as part of a roundtable for the second issue of ASR (Brubaker 2006a). Otteson reports that '(o)nly a short time ago I would not have imagined that I would write another book about Adam Smith' (p. xv). The change of mind is due to the need for a volume on Smith in the series 'Major Conservative and Libertarian Thinkers' edited by John Meadowcroft and published by Continuum. The series is designed to 'introduce these thinkers to a wider audience, providing an overview of their lives and works, as well as expert commentary on their enduring significance' (p. xii). Otteson's Smith accomplishes this goal and more.

There is some irony here, however, since my review of the first book was titled 'Why Adam Smith is neither a conservative nor a libertarian'. I argued there that Smith is best understood as a moderate liberal in the eighteenth century sense. Otteson now seems to agree: 'I would instead call Smith a classical liberal.' His justification of that label gives a good sense of the book's presentation of Smith:

> He was…an old-fashioned liberal: favoring individual liberty, endorsing state institutions to protect this liberty, and, where they conflicted, favoring the individual over the state as a default. But he was also a skeptical empiricist. He favored free trade, free markets, and a government robust but limited to the enforcement of a few central tasks not because they comported with a priori principles but because they seemed to work. He tended toward optimism about the future, and about what lay ahead for humanity if much of the apparatus of government meddling was dismantled; yet by the same token he was not optimistic that truly free trade – or, probably, truly free markets – would ever be fully realized, because doing so would make it too difficult for grasping politicians to extend their power and for corrupt businessmen to profit at others expense. Smith was also a champion of the poor. He was interested, as an empirical scientist should be, to discover how economies work and the way human psychology works; yet he was also interested, as a moral philosopher should be, to recommend political and economic strategies to minimize suffering and to maximize flourishing… He recognized that businessmen would often seek special privileges to increase their profits or decrease

competition, despite the fact that these privileges would invariably make the common man worse off. He thus strongly opposed partnerships between business and government. And he worried about the effects on workers of extreme division of labor.

(p. 165)

This is a concise and accurate, if fairly standard, summary. Otteson, however, goes beyond the commonplace, at least in his discussion of spontaneous order, or as he prefers, unintended order: 'Smith suggested that complex systems of human social order are typically not centrally planned or designed from the top but, rather, generated unintentionally by the behaviors and decisions of agents acting within them. Large-scale human social orders are thus systems of unintentional order' (p. 150). Drawing on his extensive discussion in *Marketplace*, he extends this idea from the more familiar economic marketplace to the development of both moral systems and language. He even suggests, after presenting a chart summarizing similarities of the market model in these three areas, that it applies to 'Smith's understanding of many other aspects of human life as well…I therefore propose the larger claim that Smith saw his market model as the key to understanding the creation, development, and maintenance of human social life generally' (p. 130–1). He adds that such coherence across language, morals and economics resolves any lingering doubts about whether Smith's moral philosophy and economics depend on the same principles, doubts often called the Adam Smith Problem: 'the central parts of Smith's corpus are, on a deep level, united' (p. 131). Otteson considers Smith's development of the idea of unintended order perhaps his most significant and enduring contribution. The details of his analysis are interesting and well worth considering in some detail, but that task will be left to the reader.

Otteson's sweeping claim that unintended systems 'tend to conduce to the benefit of everyone concerned…at least in the long run' raises an obvious and important question. If this accurately describes human societies, why has human history been such a rarely interrupted litany of oppression, injustice, poverty and violence? Otteson, to his credit, recognizes that the 'long run' is sometimes very long, but offers a superficial and even contradictory account of these problems:

There are numerous ways in which these systems of order can be derailed or corrupted, and hence not every system is actually or always beneficial. Smith seemed to think that only 'natural' systems of order would in fact be beneficial, and, conversely, that if a system was not beneficial it was because it had suffered corruption and was hence no longer 'natural'. Although he believed that some central aspects of human nature were fixed, he seemed to believe that moral philosophers could discern the fundamentals of nature and then base on them policies and institutions that would increase the chance of such creatures leading relatively happy and peaceful lives.

(p. 153)

The appeal to 'natural' systems merely exchanges one name for another without answering the question, although Smith did have a complex and nuanced view of nature that Otteson does not attempt to address (Brubaker (2006b,c). Nor does he offer much in the way of elaboration on 'corruption', a serious fault given that the history of human society suggests it is likely coextensive with unintended order. Further, by attributing a crucial role to moral philosophers, he would seem to be undercutting the 'natural' unintended beneficial order that is so crucial to his account of Smith's whole outlook. These seeming tensions, however, can be reconciled in a way I think is compatible with Otteson's view of Smith as a skeptical realist, although the reconciliation requires us to emphasize aspects that Otteson seems to want to downplay. Stated another way, Otteson's relative neglect of 'corruption' serves to beautify Smith in a way that, if left uncorrected, clashes with his claim that Smith is a 'skeptical, pragmatic, empirical libertarian' (p. 166). Smith does have a robust account of corruption, and its universal presence leads him to a limited and moderate defense of moral philosophy and statesmanship.

Otteson does briefly discuss one of the main and all too familiar sources of corruption: 'beneficial progress is often slowed and even reversed by vested interests, entrenched bureaucracies and government-business partnerships to plunder some for the sake of others'. He notes, but does not discuss (other than a footnote citing passages), that Smith recognizes that 'these problems and others impede society's progress' (p. 127). In one of the passages referred to, Smith lists two issues: the 'prejudices of the publick' and 'the private interests of many individuals'. Otteson's version seems mainly to refer to the second, although the first is arguably equally or more powerful, even if it is often encouraged by those very 'vested interests, entrenched bureaucracies'. These problems led Smith to conclude that to expect complete freedom of trade in Great Britain 'is as absurd as to expect that an Oceana or Utopia should ever be established' (*WN* IV.ii.43: 471). We would be hard pressed to claim that we have avoided those corrupting influences today. The actions of actors within a free market may represent unintended order, but the establishment of the conditions for the market is the result of pitched political battles, and their continuance always requires constant effort and vigilance. 'Natural liberty' is a historically rare political achievement, and until very recently tradition was always an obstacle.

If Otteson deserves partial credit for discussing one source of economic corruption, he barely deserves even that for moral corruption. In the one place I could find that he explicitly references a failure of mutual sympathy, he quotes Smith as attributing it to either 'different degrees of attention' or different 'degrees of natural acuteness' in imagining ourselves in the place of others (p. 48). Later, he merely notes that 'there are many ways that this process [development of moral judgments] can be corrupted, of course, as Smith is well aware'! Smith himself is tolerably explicit in *The Theory of Moral Sentiments* about moral corruption and his discussion bears directly on unintended order and the role of moral philosophy and statesmanship. 'The great and most universal cause of the corruption of our moral sentiments' is the ambition that arises from our desire of the praise of others and our 'disposition to admire, and almost to worship, the rich and powerful'

(I.iii.3.1: 61). Such ambition is a constant pull to 'abandon the paths of virtue' in the pursuit of vanity satisfying wealth and power (I.iii.3.8: 64). But note that this corruption is due to the natural desire for mutual sympathy and the natural desire to better our condition that, in other circumstances, are the motives to virtue and the driving force of the market. Smith's 'natural' system of morals yields decidedly mixed results. Further along in *TMS*, Smith discusses another source of moral corruption: 'Of all the corrupters of moral sentiments, therefore, faction and fanaticism have always been by far the greatest.' Such 'civil or ecclesiastical' faction can result in 'conduct towards one another' by 'the furious zealots of both parties' that can only be called 'atrocious' (III.3.43: 155–6). The impartial spectator is nowhere to be found within the hostile factions, while the all too partial fellow zealot is close at hand and dominates moral judgment. Once again our 'natural' moral sentiments work both sides of the street, generally resulting in conventional morality, but often acting to reinforce corruption.

The conclusion from this analysis is the same as in my review of Otteson's *Marketplace*. The desire for mutual sympathy and the standard of the impartial spectator are often insufficient to prevent the corruption of morals by economic interest, prejudice, faction and fanaticism. Otteson's unintended beneficial order in both economics and morals faces systematic obstacles grounded in Smithian human nature. Smith himself offers no guarantees, no magic solutions to these age old human problems. His analysis suggests political steps to improve the odds of a moderate and liberal politics. It makes a huge difference whether our tendency to put ourselves in the place of another and thus to develop an impartial standard of justice is reinforced or undermined by the dominant social and political dogmas and by the moral and political leaders of society. If society is arranged such that equality before the law and religious toleration are political dogma, the dangers of faction and fanaticism can be reduced, although never eliminated. If the administration of justice is both impartial and connected with economic opportunity and markets, society is more likely to reap the benefits of moderation and opulence. Otteson is correct that the expansion of markets on Smith's account leads, if not to friendship and familiarity, at least to the tendency to put oneself in the place of strangers sufficiently to understand what sorts of mutually beneficial commerce are possible. This, over time, breaks down other kinds of barriers that previously prevented sympathetic identification. Smith the moral philosopher advocated these opinions and institutions with the conscious intention to promote liberty and happiness. Otteson's discussion of unintended order and of the dangers of 'men of system' and the 'great mind fallacy' are helpful contributions to this same intention (p. 83ff, 97ff).

On the essential questions, Smith and Otteson are on the same side, the side of moderate and limited government and free markets, the side of classical liberalism. Otteson emphasizes that Smith advocated his system of natural liberty because he thought it would produce 'universal opulence' extending 'itself to the lowest ranks of the people'. He concludes that the evidence supporting Smith's prescience in this regard is 'voluminous'. 'Smithean political economy – including especially protections of private property, non-centrally planned market-based economies, and free trade – [has] been a greater benefit to humankind, including especially the poorest, than any other system of economic organization known' (p. 160). Smith is thus best understood as one of the 'world's great humanitarians' (p. 166). As to labels, Smith called himself a moral philosopher and Otteson agrees that it is the most fitting label.

Adam Smith is a fine introduction to Smith, but, as Otteson notes, it is no substitute to reading Smith himself. It is to be hoped that *Adam Smith* will encourage readers to pursue on their own Smith's anti-dogmatic and skeptical moral philosophy.

Bibliography

Brubaker, L. (2006a) 'Why Adam Smith is neither a conservative nor a libertarian' *Adam Smith Review*, 2: 197–202.

Brubaker, L. (2006b) 'Does the "wisdom of nature" need help?' L. Montes and E. Schliesser (eds), *New Voices on Adam Smith*, London: Routledge, pp. 168–92.

Brubaker, L. (2006c) 'Adam Smith on natural liberty and moral corruption: the wisdom of nature and the folly of legislators?' S. Minkov (ed.), *Enlightening Revolutions: Essays in Honor of Ralph Lerner*, Lanhan, MD: Lexington Books, pp. 191–217.

AUTHOR'S RESPONSE

James R. Otteson's response to review by Lauren Brubaker

I thank Lauren Brubaker for his review of my book *Adam Smith* and for the compliments that he pays to it.

Professor Brubaker's main criticism is that I underestimate, or do not sufficiently discuss, the sources of corruption that face the 'marketplace of life' interpretation I offer of Smith's moral theory and his political economy, an interpretation which, I argue, unites the project of both Smith's *Theory of Moral Sentiments* and his *Wealth of Nations*. Indeed, Professor Brubaker claims that this is 'a serious fault' in my book, 'given that the history of human society suggests it [i.e., corruption] is likely coextensive with unintended order'. Professor Brubaker believes this is such a fault, in fact, that in his brief review he uses the word 'corruption' or its cognates some sixteen times. It would seem that this is a central concern to Professor Brubaker.

I wonder, however, whether Professor Brubaker's focus on this single issue does not betray a misunderstanding of the purpose of my book. The task of the book, in keeping with the mission of the series of which it is a part, is to provide for educated lay readers a biography of Smith, an overview of all of his extant writings, an examination of what he got right and what he got wrong, a consideration of his contemporary relevance, and a bibliography, all within about 150 pages. That is surprisingly difficult to do. Judgments had to be made, therefore, about what to examine in detail, what to mention only sparingly, and what to leave out altogether. No doubt different people would make different judgments, but, in my estimation, the discussion of corruption fell into the second category: It required mentioning, but not examination in detail. This was not a book about 'Adam Smith on corruption' – as interesting as such a book might be. It was not even a book about

Smith's theory of spontaneous order or his moral philosophy. It was a book about his life and works. That means that much of the book's discussion would of course not satisfy the specialist scholar. Focusing on corruption to the extent that Professor Brubaker wanted would have meant sacrificing too many other issues of more central importance for a book meant to introduce non-specialists to the range and breadth of Smith's thought.

Thus, my response to, and criticism of, Professor Brubaker's review of my book is that he fails to mention, let alone examine, many of the main parts of my book. I wish, for example, that he had discussed, rather than only mentioning, my treatment of Smith's essay on 'Languages' and the link I argued it provided between Smith's two books. I wish he had discussed my treatment of Smith's essay on the *History of Astronomy* and the philosophy of science I claim it represents (including what I call Smith's Parsimony Principle), my discussion of whether Smith is a scientific realist, and my discussion of Smith's adaptation of a quasi-Newtonian methodology. I wish he had discussed the interpretation I give of the role the impartial spectator plays in Smith's account – an interpretation that differs in significant ways from other treatments, including D. D. Raphael's recent book-length treatment. I wish he had discussed my exploration of the extent to which Smith's developmental account of our moral sentiments is able to generate moral objectivity. I wish he had addressed my discussions of the role that self-interest, utility, and happiness play in Smith's account; of what I call Smith's 'Great Mind Fallacy', and how this alleged fallacy relates to Smith's discussion of the impartial spectator; of Smith's use of the term 'reasonable' and my claim that it grounds a Smithian theory of property; of the implications of Smith's political economy for contemporary discussions of deliberative democracy and the *Nudge*-style neo-behaviorism of Thaler and Sunstein; of my partial defense of Smith's much-maligned labor theory of value; and of my discussions of Smith's relation to other major figures in the history of philosophy and political economy, including Aristotle, Aquinas, Descartes, Locke, Hutcheson, Hume, Rousseau, Burke, Malthus, Marx, Schumpeter, and Hayek. Professor Brubaker writes that 'On the essential questions Smith and Otteson are on the same side.' While arguably true, Professor Brubaker omits to mention that I devoted an entire chapter to what Smith got wrong (ch. 8); perhaps he might have discussed, or mentioned, my evaluation of Smith's shortcomings.

Professor Brubaker concludes his review by suggesting that my book 'is a fine introduction to Smith.' I thank him for that. That was the book's main purpose. I join him in hoping that the book will 'encourage readers to pursue on their own Smith's anti-dogmatic and skeptical moral philosophy'.

Nicholas Phillipson, *Adam Smith: An enlightened life*

London: Penguin Books, 2011, 346pp.

ISBN: 978-0140287288

Reviewed by Gordon Graham

Nicholas Phillipson is widely regarded as – possibly – the leading historian of the Scottish Enlightenment. This biography of Adam Smith was published by Penguin Books in the same year as the (slightly) revised version of his biography of David Hume, originally published in 1989. Although the biography of Smith is newer and longer, the physical appearance of the two books – medallions of their profiles and reproductions of their signatures in the titles – invites comparison between them. Whether or not this was the intention, such comparison is in fact illuminating. The volume on Hume is subtitled 'The Philosopher as Historian'. The volume on Smith is subtitled 'An Enlightened Life'. As it seems to me, the parallel between the two books could have been more striking if the second had been subtitled 'The Economist as Philosopher'. This alternative subtitle, I think, would have given a better indication of what I judge to be the book's distinctive value.

The first problem for any biographer of Adam Smith is this: is it in fact possible to write an account of his life, as opposed to his thought? Smith published two very influential books that went into several editions in his lifetime. But he was a poor correspondent, did not keep a diary, and, before he died, oversaw the destruction of many papers, including unfinished manuscripts. If biography requires some insight into the psychological and emotional life of its subject, the prospects for a biography of Adam Smith are poor. There is almost no material to call on. Smith seems to have been sociable, and he certainly formed lasting friendships. Yet he preserved a nearly impenetrable personal privacy. Just what he felt, or believed, or hoped, loved or hated is virtually impossible to say with any degree of certainty. No sources have survived that would help us on these questions, probably because none ever existed.

That leaves only two sources out of which biography can be constructed – what he did and what he wrote. What he did – his career – is easily ascertained and well known but, in recounting his life and times, for the most part we have to be content with his times. On this score, Phillipson writes interestingly without the meticulous attention to detail that sometimes burdens Ian Ross's definitive biography. We learn a lot about Kirkcaldy at the time Smith was born, Glasgow, both city and university, when he was a student, Oxford during the period he spent there, Edinburgh and Glasgow during his years as a professor, continental Europe during his employment as a tutor to the young Duke of Buccleuch, and Edinburgh again in his latter years. Since everyone must, to some extent, be influenced by the social circumstances in which they live, we can say something about Smith by implication. But it is all highly conjectural. This is no criticism of Phillipson. There simply is nothing else to do, and his social histories of these places are full of interest. Still, the book is subtitled an enlightened *life*.

If we turn to what Smith thought, rather than his personal commitments, there is more promising material. Even here, though, a significant amount of conjecture is required. Smith's intellectual and academic career began with lectures on rhetoric and jurisprudence that he gave in Edinburgh between 1748 and 1751 under the patronage of Lord Kames. It is highly plausible to suppose that these lectures established his reputation as an effective lecturer and thinker of substance since at the end of this period he was appointed to the Chair of Logic at Glasgow, and soon thereafter translated to the Chair of Moral Philosophy, a position that his teacher Hutcheson had filled with such distinction. But what of the lectures that led to these professorial appointments? We have no text, or even notice of them, so that it is impossible to say where they were held, who attended them, or how they were received. Still less, obviously, is it possible to say what they contained. Phillipson fills this gap by saying that 'it is reasonable to suppose that the notes two students took of the course [he gave in Glasgow] in 1762–3 give a pretty fair guide to the essentials of a system of thought that had been developed in the 1740s' (p. 92). Perhaps, but this is rather slender ground upon which to entitle a twenty page chapter 'Smith's Edinburgh Lectures', and the subtitle's admission, 'a conjectural history', does nothing to offset this weakness.

The Glasgow lectures referred to here were never published. A carefully edited version of the students' very comprehensive notes form Volume IV of the Glasgow edition of Smith's Collected Works. This has given them a certain authority. One might nevertheless hesitate to accord them truly canonical status, because Smith was so particular about what he published, and so careful about whether he had successfully articulated the views he meant to advance. Smith did publish a paper in 1761 on the origins of language. This paper seems largely to replicate the third of these lectures, and it provides Phillipson with more grounds for speculation about the Edinburgh lectures. 'It was thinking which surely belongs in outline at least to the earliest stages of his philosophical career'. The words 'surely' and 'at least' have an element of special pleading to my ears.

We are on decidedly firmer ground when we turn to Smith's published works – the *Theory of Moral Sentiments* and the *Wealth of Nations*. Both made their mark in their day, and have continued to do so, and the revised editions, on which Smith himself worked, enable us to chart changes and developments in his thought, although the later editions of *WN* are not of any great consequence in this regard. Taken together, these works, from the time of their publication, have provided philosophers and others with a rich resource for scholarly debate and discussion, about both their relative merits and their relationship. The 'Adam Smith problem' famously formulated by German scholars, rested upon the idea that there was a fundamental disunity between the two – *TMS* taking mutual sympathy as its key concept, while *WN* was built around individual competition. If sympathy rules, then society rests upon natural sociability; if economic competition rules, then an 'invisible hand' is required to secure social coordination.

Almost all Smith scholars today hold that this 'problem' rests upon a superficial reading of the texts, but not all of them are as successful as Phillipson in uncovering the deep unity in Smith's work. *WN* is universally regarded as a foundational work in the emerging science of economics, while *TMS* is a work of moral philosophy, and for a long time this perception led to *WN* being heralded as Smith's real claim to fame. On this view of the matter, Smith moved from the study of philosophy to the study of economics, the latter being a highly innovative spin-off from the former. But Phillipson is excellent at showing just how the economics no less than the moral philosophy flows from the same underlying intellectual project – the 'science of man', a part philosophical, part empirical exploration of human nature that Smith engaged in alongside his contemporaries in the Scottish Enlightenment, especially David Hume. It is Phillipson's success in doing this that prompts my suggestion that a more informative subtitle for the book might be 'the economist as philosopher'.

For Phillipson, though, the science of human nature, of which both *TMS* and *WN* are such notable exercises, is importantly 'enlightened' because its major purpose is to counter the baneful effects of religion. '*The Theory of Moral Sentiments*, the *Wealth of Nations*, and indeed Smith's entire project for a modern science of man', he tells us, 'were built on the Enlightenment's quintessential assault on religion' (p. 190). What drives this 'assault' is a determination to displace 'superstition' by learning that is firmly grounded in empirical science. This desire to dispel superstition, Phillipson alleges, is as central to Smith's economic theory as to his moral philosophy.

> The belief that a nation's wealth and power depended on its foreign and not its domestic trade...had become the intellectual engine of national policies that were threatening the peace and prosperity of the modern world, a belief as dangerous to the progress of civilization as the religious superstitions that had fuelled the wars of religion...Smith devoted Book IV [of *WN*] to exploding this new superstition and attacking the merchants and theories who propagated it with the same vehemence that Voltaire and Hume had attacked priestcraft.
>
> (p. 224)

Here, it seems to me, Phillipson overstates his case. His evident deep admiration for Hume, and his own antipathy to religion perhaps, distorts his interpretation. The mercantilism that Smith was attacking is no doubt false, and harmful, but on these grounds alone it scarcely warrants the label 'superstition'. No doubt people in times past (and present) exhibit an irrationally reverential attitude to money, especially in the form of gold, but mercantilism is more than a mere fetish. It is a recurrently plausible belief about the relation between wealth accumulation and commercial prosperity, with important implications for attitudes to international competition. It was not superstition that led merchants to seek and rulers to grant monopolies. It was a narrow conception of self-interest and a mistaken belief about how to reckon national wellbeing.

The task of recounting Smith's biography as that of 'an enlightened life', combined with Phillipson's determination to identify 'enlightenment' as the rejection of all religion save the most minimal deism, leads to other distortions. He tells us that while 'a Christian might have argued' that the impartial spectator was 'the voice of conscience or the deity…Smith had made it perfectly clear that it was the voice of an entirely fictitious being…[S]trictly speaking the impartial spectator speaks of rules of morality which have roots in our own ethical lives and that of our nation and civilization, and cannot properly be regarded as the eternal, never-changing voice of a deity'. (p. 270). This contention does not sit very well with Smith's own assertion in *TMS* that the ideas of proper and improper conduct that are 'agreeable to our moral faculties', 'were plainly intended to be the governing principles of human nature [and] the rules which they prescribe are to be regarded as the commands and laws of the Deity, promulgated by those viceregents which he has thus set up within us' (*TMS* III. v. 6). On those occasions when, it seems, the world is so indifferent to right and wrong that people are likely to suffer for acting in accordance with the dictates of the impartial spectator '[r]eligion can alone afford them any effectual comfort. She alone can tell them, that it is of little importance what man [or nation and civilization?] may think of their conduct, while the all-seeing Judge of the world approves of it' (*TMS* III.ii. 12). It is not easy to dismiss these sentences as mere concessions to the piety of the times. They remained in place after a long process of review and revision by Smith himself, a process that resulted, notably, in other theological references being eliminated.

We know very little, if anything, about Smith's personal religious practice, although we do know that he took Panmure House in Edinburgh so that his aging mother, whom he revered, could get to church easily. Our ignorance in this respect is in large part due to Smith's own circumspection. On this score, Phillipson asserts that 'although he never shared Hume's notoriety as a public infidel, few Scots were in any doubt where his religious sympathies lay' (p. 281). This general claim does not seem very well supported by the handful of contemporary opinions he then goes on to cite. But, even if it is true, we are nonetheless left wondering whether the judgment of his contemporaries finally settles the matter. Given the previously noted paucity of personal material that might illuminate the question, and the extreme unlikelihood that new material will appear, all we have to go on are the two great works and a few other papers. On the strength of these, I am inclined to say, we can certainly agree with Phillipson that Smith the economist remained a philosopher. But if infidelity, or even thoroughgoing secularism, is the test of 'enlightenment', we cannot on the strength of these same works declare Smith to have led an 'enlightened' life.

Jeffrey T. Young (editor), *Elgar companion to Adam Smith*

Cheltenham: Edward Elgar 2009, 374pp.

ISBN: 978-1845420192

Reviewed by Eric Schliesser

The abundant strengths of this *Companion* are also the source of some of its weaknesses. First, at the time of publication, the nineteen substantial chapters collected in it are the best multi-author introduction to Adam Smith's thought easily supplanting the (2006) *Cambridge Companion*. Second, Young's *Companion* also gives a very good sense of the 'state-of-play' of research into Adam Smith among historians of economics within economics; the chapters make clear that research into Smith's thought has both decisively moved beyond *The Wealth of Nations* and has distanced itself from, say, the long influential Stigler (i.e., 'new Chicago School') interpretation of Smith – the construction of which (and contrast with the 'Good Old Chicago School' Smith associated with Viner, Knight, and Coase) is the topic of the very fine concluding chapter by Steven Medema.

Jeffrey Young is, moreover, to be congratulated for managing to get a nice mix of established scholars and some younger, important interpreters. It is also sobering to note that the late James Buchanan, Warren Samuels and Andrew Skinner contribute to this *Companion*.

Young's *Companion* is self-consciously not philosophical, but is 'oriented around the concerns of historians of economics' (p. xiii). Many of the best chapters are, in fact, straight contributions to the traditional history of economics, including chapters by Salim Rashid, Glenn Hueckel, Samuel Hollander, Medema and Samuels, and Levy and Peart. For example, while Hollander's (1973) book on Smith falls short of his best work on, say, Ricardo, here, Hollander is on great form with a brilliant analysis of Smith's treatment of usury and Bentham's famous critique. Hollander shows that Smith's treatment of usury is primarily motivated by two empirical claims: (1) that 'where "high" interest rates are available Smith attributed to lenders a bias favouring high-risk loans rather than a roughly equal distribution of preference across the spectrum of opportunities' (p. 280); and (2) 'banks were unable to calculate objectively the risk-worthiness of their clients and financed irresponsible projects' in addition to other forms of mismanagement (p. 287–8). Hollander is right to doubt that Smith (rightly) would not 'have been convinced by Bentham's objections' (p. 295). Even so, Hollander notes that much of the empirical basis of Smith's argument 'breaks down…after 1778', yet Smith does not change his position. This paper ought to be the start of more research in Smith's economics of finance.

Hueckel offers a very careful analysis of Smith's claims about the corn bounty, especially the paradoxical 'denial of the bounty's capacity to increase output' (p. 235), and the assertion that 'money price of corn regulates that of all other commodities'. Hueckel (correctly) reads these through the 'underlying polemical aim: Smith's 'very violent attack' on the Mercantile institutions' (p. 233). Hueckel very nicely integrates contextual empirical evidence to re-read Smith and his contemporary critics; the chapter is very good at conveying the interrelated intricacies of Smith's economics. One important insight is that Smith's analysis of the corn bounty differs greatly between LJ and *WN* (p. 254). Hueckel argues that any major inconsistencies in Smith's position disappear if we see the 'strictly static character' of Smith's argument (p. 243; see also p. 254). Appealing to Hollander (1973), Hueckel insists that 'the price of corn can be said to 'regulate' those of all other goods only within a particular 'period of improvement…the principle cannot be applied to a dynamical context' (p. 243). But this is, alas, not Smith's own view because, in the long 'Digression' at the end of Book I, Smith treats the price as corn as a stable measure on data covering more than 500 years (and – as Hueckel notes – in later editions, Smith also argued to the long-run harm of the bounty; p. 246).

Salim Rashid is his usual critical self on Adam Smith; he concludes, 'Adam Smith and his legacy has been a distinct brake on our understanding of economic development' (p. 226). Rashid's argument turns on contrasting Smith's views on development with Berkeley's *The Querist* (and Tucker). This is a clever choice because Smith admired Berkeley and both Berkeley and Smith were (among other things) interested in questions of development that would benefit the working poor. Rashid praises Berkeley for understanding that 'economic development was really but one aspect of human development' (p. 214). Rashid's main criticism of Smith turns on Smith's willingness, despite 'qualifications', to trust markets (p. 218); the more fundamental criticism is that Rashid believes that Smith 'failed to assert with equal force that every economy is embedded in a society and that the formation of individuals with market compatible beliefs is very much a task to be faced…society has to induce these' (p. 222).

There are two problems with Rashid's approach. First, Rashid seems to overlook Smith's treatment of (religious) education in Book V of *WN*. The presbytery of Scotland is praised not just for its relatively successful religious ('uniformity of faith, the fervour of devotion') effects, but especially for its socially useful moral-political consequences (viz. 'the spirit of order, regularity, and austere morals'; *WN* 5.1.g.41). It does so very cost effectively (the Swiss churches even more so). The good social effects are primarily felt by 'the common people' (*WN* 5.1.g.38). So, Smith's advocacy of religious disestablishment is, in part, designed to meet the aims that Rashid faults Smith for not even trying to secure.

Second, Rashid happily recycles an anecdote by Wilberforce about Smith's rejection of a scheme to 'provide fisheries for the Highlands poor' (p. 225). Now, Rashid does not consider the fact that in Wilberforce's narrative Smith's rejection of the scheme is clearly motivated by his expectation of corruption of the funds aimed at helping the poor; the problem concerns the (well-intentioned) means not the end. Moreover, Rashid does not stop to pause at the significance of Smith's regular meetings with Wilberforce; in addition to a fondness for free trade, they also both were opponents of slavery. As Caffentzis has emphasized, Rashid's favorite Berkeley had no such qualms. Moreover, Rashid overlooks the eugenics program (with a nod to Plato's Laws) that Berkeley advocates in the Querist (cf. Q 206–16, 512–14). I prefer Smith's approach to development over Berkeley's any day. So, I would echo about Rashid what Rashid says in a disarming footnote about Hont: 'my disagreement with' his claims 'does not diminish my admiration for his scholarship' (p. 227).

Despite the editor's and Jerry Evensky's assertions (p. 131) (unusually, Evensky's chapter, which is placed at the end of Part I, concludes with two paragraphs that sum up the three parts of the volume), the volume contains very little new on Smith's economics; the rather technical chapters by Witztum and Buchanan/Yoon are only very indirectly related to Smith's views. Paganelli does a nice job connecting Smith's views, especially in *TMS*, with recent work in experimental economics and notes that Smith is 'increasingly being read by experimental, behavior and neuro-economists' (p. 190). Unfortunately, Skinner (on Smith and mercantilism) and Groenewegen (on physiocracy) primarily recycle their earlier work. Skinner does a nice job connecting Smith's economics to his political projects, and does a very good job of setting up renewed study of the closing pages of *Wealth of Nations*. Groenewegen is mercifully brief, but he scandalously ignores all the scholarly work done in several decades. Medema and Samuels team up to offer a balanced analysis of Smith's views on the economic role of government.

Despite the editor's insistence that his *Companion* is contrasted the 'philosophical' outlook of the *Cambridge Companion*, at least eight chapters are devoted to issues in moral and political philosophy. David Levy and Sandy Peart do a very good job on focusing on Smith's concern over faction – highlighting the non-trivial fact that philosophical doctrines may well motivate behavior (343 with appeal to *TMS* 7.2.51). Leonidas Montes culminates a decade long concern with a very fine-grained analysis of Smith's views and their provenance (crucially and surprisingly in civic humanism) on the so-called 'standing army-debate.' McCloskey offers a useful précis of her views on Smith and virtue; Evensky offers an excellent introduction to the views of his (2005) book; Samuels' chapter on the invisible hand anticipates his posthumous book.

Unfortunately, Sheila Dow ignores much philosophic work on Smith's 'philosophy and economic methodology.' In addition to recycling outdated clichés about the Scottish Enlightenment, she exhibits carelessness in basic philosophical distinctions. For example, she writes 'if we take Smith's philosophy of science seriously, then we must take it that the principle of the division of labour is, like the principle of gravity, an appeal to the imagination rather than a 'real' phenomenon. For Newton, the principles on which the analysis is based were previously derived using the experimental method, and are this provisional (Montes 2006)' (p. 109).

First, in context (p. 108–9), Dow is commenting on a passage quoted from '*LRBL* 145–6,' where Smith is commenting on Newton's mode of presentation (contrasted with Aristotle's) not on Newton's methods of discovery, nor on Newton's epistemology, nor on Newton's metaphysics. (Oddly, even the very scholarly Vivenza [p. 30] misrepresents the passage from '*LRBL* ii.133'. Dow and Vivenza refer to the same passage with a different citation system. It is odd that, in a reference-style book on Adam Smith, the editor has not enforced a uniform way of citation; nor do all authors refer to the same editions of Adam Smith's writings.) Second, from the fact that the principles on which analysis is based are provisional nothing follows about the ontological status (real vs. imaginary) of one's explanations. Third, just because Smithian explanation appeals to the imagination it does not follow that Smith thinks that the explanandum is somehow not a 'real' phenomenon. (This is not to deny that Smith thinks that often, but not always, the explanans is fictitious.) Finally, even though she cites Montes as an authority here, she fails to note that according to Montes Smith is a modest realist about Newton's explanations (and his own).

Vivienne Brown's chapter is genuinely original and offers a fascinating treatment of Smith's views on agency. She treats *TMS* as offering a 'non-causal account of action' (p. 62, and different from Humean compatibilism, p. 58ff.); by contrast, according to Brown, not only is *Wealth of Nations* itself a deeply causal work, but it 'constructs the concept of economic agency that is required by these causal relations' (p. 66). Her treatment of *TMS* turns on a wonderful analysis of *TMS* 2.1.Intro.2. In particular, in that passage Smith is standardly taken to understand propriety as follows: (u) an exciting cause, which produces (v) a sentiment of heart, which leads to (w) an action and (x) its foreseeable effects, and, of course, (y) the actual effects produced by (w). Brown calls attention to (u) in order to deny that the step between (v) and (w) is causal. She does this because she wants to distinguish Smith's account of agency in *TMS* from Humean compatibilism.

In fact, if we were to take some of the evidence that Brown marshals for her position literally, then Smith is a member of a philosophical tradition that denies any causal power to finite beings other than God. For, as she argues, sometimes (*TMS* 1.1.3.5; 1.1.3.9; 2.3.Intro.1; 2.3.Intro.6) Smith embraces the locution 'gives occasion to,' when describing the transition from (v) to (w). (p. 60). Smith certainly is familiar with the writings of Malebranche and other so-called Occasionalists (e.g., *TMS* 3.4.3; Astronomy 3.1, EPS 48; the Letter to the Edinburgh Review 10, EPS 250, where Régis and Malebranche are presented as 'refinements upon the Meditations of Descartes'; and also Smith's long footnote in the History of Ancient Logics and Metaphysics, EPS 123). But such an Occassionalist reading of Smith simply cannot be sustained because in some of the very same passages from *TMS* that one would have to cite Smith happily embraces causal languages to describe the affairs of other finite beings without any hint of an explanation of such differential treatment. Moreover, in *WN*, Smith also uses 'occasions' (e.g., *WN* 1.1.4, 15; 1.1.10, 22), where, even by Brown's lights, Smith is constructing a 'system of causal relations' (p. 66). Moreover, Brown has to ignore that for Smith judgments of propriety and merit are (contextual) judgments of the proportionality of causal relata and that the upshot of Smith's treatment of moral bad luck (the so-called piacular) is an insistence that we embrace the fact that we can be even unwilling causes of harm of others. So, even in *TMS*, Smith embeds our agency in a rich causal nexus.

Brendan Long does Smith scholarship a useful service by collecting the many passages where Smith explicitly and implicitly appeals to biblical sources. Of course, from this fact little follows – Hobbes and Spinoza are both suffused with explicit and implicit biblical references, but nobody would argue that they 'held a moderate Christian theism' (p. 92). Smith, too, offers a hint of the treachery of Long's kind of interpretive strategy: 'Seneca, though a Stoic, the sect most opposite to that of Epicurus, yet quotes this philosopher more frequently than any other' (*TMS* 7.2.97)! Here, I cannot do justice to Long's arguments, but I want to register my surprise that Smith's supposed 'natural theology' (derived from a partial reading of *TMS*) is offered without any discussion of Smith's account of natural theology in the *Essays on Philosophical Subjects* (and its debts to Hume's Natural History, see Pack 1995).

Now, in the history of ancient physics, Smith argues that Christian theology got married to a conceptual framework that is not just inadequate, but unsuitable to it (Ancient Physics, 10, EPS 116). On Smith's view human worship becomes senseless if God has no interest in our affairs. This is why Aristotle's doctrine about the unmoved mover 'must have the same effects upon society as Atheism itself'. Smith leaves unclear if these effects are pernicious. Without any evidence Long interprets this remark as 'clearly pejorative' (p. 83). Yet, Long does not even pause at the significance of Smith's explicit criticism in the very same passage of Aristotle's commitment to divine intelligence in his natural theological explanation of heavenly motions (cf. Vivenza p. 30).

Either way, at *Astronomy*, 3.2–3, EPS 49–50 Smith offers what we would call 'an error theory' about the beliefs of 'savages;' they think that unusual events in the world are governed by passionate gods' actions, but, in reality, these are just anthropomorphic projections. The error theory diagnoses the savages' expectations, which are associated with necessity, and deviations from these are associated with godly interventions. By labeling all of this, 'vulgar superstition' Smith indicates he does not believe any of it.

Smith's treatment of heathen belief as imaginative projections springing from fear and ignorance has an Epicurean flavor reminiscent of Hume's *The Natural History of Religion* and Spinoza's Appendix to *Ethics* 1. To some of Smith's posthumous readers there may be a troubling consequence of this account: Smith explains how the heathen gods' actions appear as divine interventions in the ordinary course of nature (associated with necessity) as projections from the savages' imagination. For, a divine intervention in the course of necessity with the aim of some particular providence is ordinarily labeled a 'miracle' by even the most 'moderate' of Smith's Christian readers.

Bibliography

Berkeley, G. (1750) *The Querist*, London: W. Innys, C. Davis, C. Hitch & W. Bowyer.
Caffentzis, C.G. (2000) *Exciting the Industry of Mankind George Berkeley's Philosophy of Money* (Vol. 170), Dordrecht: Springer.

Evensky, J. (2005) *Adam Smith's Moral Philosophy*, Cambridge: Cambridge University Press.

Hollander, S. (1973) *The Economics of Adam Smith*, Toronto, ON: University of Toronto Press.

Pack, S.J. (1995) 'Theological (and hence economic) implications of Adam Smith's "principles which lead and direct philosophical enquiries,"' *History of Political Economy*, 27(2): 289–307.

Smith, A. ([1776] 1976) *An Inquiry into the Nature and Causes of the Wealth of Nations*, R.H. Campbell, A.S. Skinner and W.B. Todd (eds), Oxford: Oxford University Press.

Smith, A. ([1759] 1976b) *The Theory of Moral Sentiments*, D.D. Raphael and A.L. Macfie (eds), Oxford: Oxford University Press.

Smith, A. ([1795] 1980) *Essays on Philosophical Subjects*, W.P.D. Wightman (ed.), Oxford: Oxford University Press.

Smith, A. ([1762–63] 1983) *Lectures on Rhetoric and Belles Lettres*, Oxford: Oxford University Press.

AUTHOR'S RESPONSE

Salim Rashid's response to review by Eric Schliesser

I am delighted that Eric Schliesser has written a critique of my critical views of Adam Smith on economic development. As a frequent reader of his blog, I am happy at his readiness to provide different views of economics and have corresponded with him on several issues. I am even happier that he has not hesitated to apply the lash. This is as it should be. *Engage*.

Does Smith have any approach to development? Does he even recognize the problem of economic development in *WN*? I could have said 'no' and left it at that. But, since Smith would have profited from Berkeley on this question if he read the *Querist*, I thought it worthwhile to point out that Smith failed to recognize what has to be theorized upon. An economy dominated by a thoughtless landed class, determined to extract what wealth they could in order to spend it somewhere other than Ireland; a mass of poor who lacked both the will and the incentive to alter their condition; natural wealth that lay largely unexplored and undeveloped; a monetary system recognizable by its absence; a political elite indifferent to any claim other than that required by the English barracks. Archbishop William King characterised it pithily in 1715, well before Berkeley ever wrote: 'Our payments are like the fleecing of sheep, of which they have no benefit, but must prepare a new growth out of their bodies or remain naked'. Does Smith consider what life was like for such a people and did he even genuflect his theoretical system towards them? Prefer Smith to Berkeley on economic development: How does one prefer a non-existent body of thought?

In his magnificent introduction to the reprint of John Rae's *Life of Adam Smith*, Jacob Viner noted that the Highlands exemplified many of the aspects important to economic development and that, the contemporary literature dealing with the Highlands in Smith's day 'was rich in information and insights.' Viner's significant judgment on what Smith learned about the problem of underdevelopment in his own backyard and from his fellow Scots is as follows:

> Smith in *The Wealth of Nations* gave some attention to the special economic problems of the Highlands, but what attention to them he did there give was not focused on the plight of the Highlanders but was merely incidental to his search for illustrative material in connection with his general treatment of the problems of taxation, of bounties, of the economics of landlordism.
>
> (Viner)

The analysis of development is the central issue. I am loath to even mention the other points because it distracts us from that on which we should focus. But my continuous disagreements with Smith scholarship alone require some response. The observations about the impact of the presbytery are excellent in themselves; they would be valuable in the study of economic development if Smith had made them in the context of raising an improvident and leisure-loving poor into the discipline of market society (using means that can hardly win favor with liberals). It is Smith's responsibility to do his own theorizing. If one writes a thousand pages, it is hard not to write something of relevance on any given topic. But this is not theorizing.

As for Wilberforce, is there any suggestion that he was raising money for the Government? That should excite Smith's fervor. However, if both public and private charity are assumed to fail because of corruption, then of course there is no way left to help the poor. As to Berkeley's eugenics 'program' and his advocacy of slavery – I leave it to the reader to go to the originals, read what is said, compare it with what is known about Berkeley, and decide. We are not trying to find out who is lovable, but who thought clearly.

If Smith's ghost were to rise in his defence, he might say: 'I avoided talking about really poor economies. The Highlands were right by me; I knew of James Anderson, John Knox, George Dempster, Sir John Sinclair and all the others who were bent on "improving" the Highlands and outer islands. Jacob Viner noted the absence of any discussion by me on these areas in 1965 and charitably concluded that some newly discovered document would shed light on my silence. Why do people assume that I must have had something to say on every important economic question?'

Bibliography

Viner, J. (1965) *Guide to John Rae's Life of Adam Smith: Introduction.* New York: Augustus M. Kelley.

Notes for Contributors

Submissions to *The Adam Smith Review* are invited from any theoretical, disciplinary or interdisciplinary approach (max. 10,000 words, in English). Contributors are asked to make their arguments accessible to a wide multidisciplinary readership without sacrificing high standards of argument and scholarship. Please include an abstract not exceeding 100 words.

Please send all submissions, suggestions, and offers to edit symposia to the Editor, Fonna Forman, Department of Political Science, University of California, San Diego, 9500 Gilman Drive, La Jolla, California, USA; adamsmithreview @ucsd.edu. Email submissions are welcomed. Alternatively please send three hard copies in double-spaced type.

Please prepare your manuscript for anonymous refereeing and provide a separate title page with your name. Interdisciplinary submissions will be sent to referees will different disciplinary expertise. Submitted articles will be double-blind refereed and commissioned articles will be single-blind refereed. All contributions must be in English; it is the author's responsibility to ensure the quality of the English text. Where quotations in languages other than English are required, authors are asked to provide a translation into English.

Final versions of accepted papers will need to conform to the ASR Guidelines for Authors (Harvard reference system), but submitted papers are accepted in any format.

Submission to *The Adam Smith Review* will be taken to imply that the work is original and unpublished, and is not under consideration for publication elsewhere. By submitting a manuscript, authors agree that the exclusive rights to reproduce and distribute the article have been given to the Publishers, including reprints, photographic reproductions, microfilm, or any other reproductions of a similar nature, and translations.

Book reviews

Books relating to Adam Smith or of more general relevance for Adam Smith scholarship will be reviewed in *The Adam Smith Review*. It is editorial policy to invite authors to respond to reviews of their work. Offers to review works published in languages other than English are welcomed. Please send books for review to the Book Review Editor: Dr Craig Smith, Adam Smith Lecturer in the Scottish Enlightenment, School of Social and Political Sciences, The University of Glasgow, Adam Smith Building, 40 Bute Gardens, Glasgow, G12 8RT craig.smith@glasgow.ac.uk

The website of the Adam Smith Review is: www.adamsmithreview.org

For Product Safety Concerns and Information please contact our EU
representative GPSR@taylorandfrancis.com
Taylor & Francis Verlag GmbH, Kaufingerstraße 24, 80331 München, Germany

www.ingramcontent.com/pod-product-compliance
Ingram Content Group UK Ltd.
Pitfield, Milton Keynes, MK11 3LW, UK
UKHW021019180425
457613UK00020B/992